PROTESTANTISM
and the AMERICAN
FOUNDING

D1570498

LOYOLA TOPICS IN POLITICAL PHILOSOPHY

Thomas S. Engeman
Series Editor

This series originates in the Frank M. Covey, Jr., Lectures in Political Analysis. The books in the Loyola Topics in Political Philosophy series offer a number of responses of prominent scholars to issues addressed in the Covey Lectures. Each volume contains an introductory essay by the Covey lecturer and a concluding reflection on new issues raised by the contributors. The intention of the series is to offer the best available scholarship to teachers and students, as well as to general readers.

Thomas S. Engeman, editor
Thomas Jefferson and the Politics of Nature

Robert P. Kraynak and Glen Tinder, editors
In Defense of Human Dignity: Essays for Our Times

PROTESTANTISM
and the AMERICAN
FOUNDING

edited by
Thomas S. Engeman
and
Michael P. Zuckert

University of Notre Dame Press

Notre Dame, Indiana

Manufactured in the United States of America

The editors and the publisher are grateful for permission to publish:

Chapter 2, from "Religion and American Values," in Seymour Martin Lipset, *The First New Nation: The United States in Historical and Comparative Perspective* (New York: W. W. Norton, 1979). Copyright © Seymour Martin Lipset. Reprinted by permission of the author.

Chapter 3, selections from Alexis de Tocqueville, *Democracy in America,* translated, edited, and with an introduction by Harvey C. Mansfield and Delba Winthrop (Chicago: University of Chicago Press, 2000). Copyright © 2000 by The University of Chicago. Reprinted by permission of the University of Chicago Press.

Chapter 4, from "The Godless Constitution," in Isaac Kramnick and R. Laurence Moore, *The Godless Constitution: The Case against Religious Correctness.* Copyright © 1996 by Isaac Kramnick and R. Laurence Moore. Used by permission of W. W. Norton & Company, Inc.

Library of Congress Cataloging-in-Publication Data

Protestantism and the American founding / edited by Thomas S. Engeman and
Michael P. Zuckert.
    p. cm. — (Loyola topics in political philosophy)
    Includes index.
    ISBN 0-268-02768-4 (pbk. : alk. paper)
    1. Christianity and politics—United States—History.
2. Reformed Church—United States—Influence. 3. Christianity and politics—
Reformed Church—History. 4. United States—Politics and government.
I. Engeman, Thomas S. II. Zuckert, Michael P., 1942– III. Series.
BR517.P77 2004
322'.1'097309033—dc22

                          2004017231

Contents

Acknowledgments

Thomas Engeman thanks the contributors, Loyola University Chicago's Research Services, my graduate assistants, and last but not least my family, Susan and Morgan.

Michael Zuckert would like to acknowledge, as always, the assistance of Catherine.

PROTESTANTISM
and the AMERICAN
FOUNDING

Introduction

Thomas S. Engeman

Our inclusive and secular age finds the claim that Protestantism was central to the American founding peculiar, if not suspect. Certainly, Catholics, Jews, and Anglicans were present in the founding era. And J. Hector St. John de Crèvecoeur argues in his *Letters from an American Farmer* for the great variety of American religions.[1] But while there *were* many religions in 1787, overwhelmingly they were branches of the Reformed or Calvinist trunk. By one estimate, at least "three-fourths of the colonists at the time of the Revolution were identified with denominations that had arisen from the Reformed, Puritan wing of European Protestantism: Congregationalism, Presbyterianism, Baptists, German and Dutch Reformed."[2] Protestant thought and practice had even greater influence than the large number of Reformed Protestants suggests.

Proponents of the unique influence of Reformed Protestantism are known as exceptionalists. Alexis de Tocqueville initiated exceptionalism by arguing that America's social institutions had been formed by the Calvinist sects. "America is the only country where one has been able to witness the natural and tranquil developments of a society, and where it has been possible to specify the influence exerted by the point of departure on the future of states. . . . Puritanism was not only a religious doctrine; *it also blended at several points with the most absolute democratic and republican theories.*"[3]

Because the Reformed sects are the source of many of the institutions and principles we identify as distinctly American, before considering the theoretical questions raised by the essays in this volume we will first consider the characteristics of the Reformed sects which shaped our social and political institutions.

Educated, Middle Class. Compared with the hierarchical societies from which they emigrated, the Protestants were mainly well-educated, middle-class professionals. This middle class sought a more personal spirituality and more democratic institutions. But in the Old World aristocrats still controlled the offices of church and state, and opposed the spiritual as well as the social and political goals of the new middle class.

In America, the Puritans founded public schools and universities to guarantee for their children the education and religious training usually unobtainable by the middle class in Europe. Within a few years of the first major Puritan settlement in Boston (1630), township law provided for public education. Common taxes supported primary and secondary schools. The law decreed that "the municipal magistrates must see to it that parents send their children to schools; they have the right to levy fines on those who refuse to; and if the resistance continues, society, then putting itself in place of the family, takes possession of the child."[4]

Tocqueville, visiting almost two hundred years later (1831–32), commented on the nearly universal literacy of Americans at a time when less than 10 percent could read in post-revolutionary France. He argued that even among the seventeenth-century Puritans, "Proportionately, there was a greater mass of enlightenment spread among those men than within any European nation of our day. All, perhaps, without a single exception, had received a quite advanced education, and several among them had made themselves known in Europe by their talents and their science."[5] Public education encouraged the further development of the middle class, which dominated most of the states north of the Mason-Dixon Line.

Congregationalism. Unlike the European state churches, which ruled their members through the priesthood and civil law, the Protestant denominations usually governed themselves through a democratic congregationalism. As Allen Guelzo observes:

> The Puritans of Massachusetts Bay imported a fairly straitlaced predesti-narian Calvinism as their official theology, but they also imported a highly decentralized and well-nigh uncontrollable Congregational church order which licensed any individual congregation to revise Calvinist theology as it saw fit. And revise it they did."[6]

Local congregations were able to hire and fire their ministers, shape their liturgy, set budgets, open a new church and close an old one, and determine what charities to support. Tocqueville argues that Protestant congregationalism was the original teacher of American democracy. The organizational skills of the religious world had been transferred to the secular world, enabling the Puritans to conduct government, business, and educational institutions democratically.[7]

Like most Protestant immigrants, the Puritans had been oppressed in Europe. Therefore, unlike other immigrant groups who sought to preserve the familiar features of their homeland, the Puritans' fervent pursuit of a new perfect society—a "shining city on the Hill"—reflected their great antipathy to hierarchy and Anglicanism. Of the founders, Thomas Jefferson best articulated the hatred most Americans felt toward the aristocratic and religious hierarchies which had oppressed them. Jefferson condemned the inequality and tyranny of feudal land tenure and privilege, the established churches, and the industrial cities of Europe. Since he saw Alexander Hamilton and the Federalists as the functional equivalent of King George's aristocratic and ecclesiastical minions, his criticisms did double duty. Jefferson helped reform the laws of primogeniture and entail opening up land ownership, and with James Madison ended the Episcopal (Anglican) establishment in Virginia. Finally, Jefferson warned against the corruption of European industrial cities: "I view great cities as pestilential to the morals, the health, and the liberties of man. True they nourish some of the elegant arts, but the useful ones can thrive elsewhere, and less perfection in the others, with more health, virtue, and freedom, would be my choice."[8]

Hostility to the Old World made the Puritans ever more radical liberals, always ready to resist British "tyranny." America was the only British colony where Englishmen revolted against the mother country. Nothing like the American Revolution occurred in Canada, Australia, or New Zealand. Seymour Martin Lipset contrasts the still sharp differences between Anglican Canada and Protestant America:

> The United States is the country of the revolution, Canada of the counter-revolution. The former is the part of British North America that successfully seceded, while Canada is the area that remained British. . . . Conservatism in Canada is descended from Toryism and monarchical statism; in the United States, it is derived from Whiggism, classical anti-statist liberalism. After the revolution, about fifty thousand Tory Americans moved to Canada. Conversely, some Yankee residents of what was originally northern New England—Nova Scotia and New Brunswick—migrated to the new nation. The revolution produced an interesting transmutation of religion. Congregationalism had been strong in Nova Scotia and New Brunswick, as in the rest of New England before the

revolution. After the Treaty of Paris in 1783, many Congregational ministers moved south. Conversely, many Anglican priests went north. Hence a shift of populations in political and religious terms occurred within English-speaking North America.[9]

Congregationalism was a teacher of democracy. Local, self-governing, middle-class communities opposed the centralizing and hierarchal character of British rule, and taught democratic skills easily transferable to the other civil associations of American life.

Sectarianism. At the end of the eighteenth century every Christian nation—other than the United States—had a state church. Great Britain and her colonies were Anglican; Prussia and Scandinavia were Lutheran; most of Europe, and all of Central and South America, were Catholic; and on the eastern edges of Europe, Orthodoxy prevailed. Although American independence still left powerful state church establishments in the South and New England, these were already in retreat. State establishments were fighting what proved to be rearguard actions against powerful, rival religious sects, as well as the partisans of religious liberty, notably Thomas Jefferson and James Madison. By 1787, seven of the new states had abandoned religious establishments altogether. In the remaining six, the meaning of establishment had become remarkably liberal and sectarian. Leonard Levy observes about these liberal new "establishments":

> In every European precedent of an establishment, the religion established was that of a single church. Many different churches, or the religion held in common by all of them, that is, Christianity or Protestantism, were never simultaneously established by any European nation. Establishments in America, on the other hand, both in the colonial and the early state periods, were not limited in nature or in meaning to state support of one church. An establishment of religion in America at the time of the framing of the Bill of Rights meant government aid and sponsorship of religion, principally by impartial tax support of the institutions of religion, the churches.[10]

In most of these multiple church establishments, public taxes were distributed in proportion to the census determination of the membership of the state's religions.

This broad and competitive sectarianism encouraged the creation of many powerful religious sects which never posed any threat to political institutions.

In the famous Tenth Federalist, James Madison argues that sectarianism poses no threat to political liberty while it provides the remedy for religious "zeal." A large number of sects guarantees that no single sect can secure a political majority and take over the engine of government. Madison observes, "when a majority is included in a faction, the form of popular government . . . enables it to sacrifice to its ruling passion or interest, both the public good and the rights of other citizens." But where there are many competing sects to prevent a majority faction the situation is different. "If a faction consists of less than a majority, relief is supplied by the republican principle, which enables the majority to defeat its sinister views by a regular vote."[11] Therefore, "a religious sect, may degenerate into a political faction in a part of the Confederacy; but the variety of sects dispersed over the entire face of it, must secure the national Councils against any danger from that source."[12]

Free sectarian competition strengthens religious activity, creating a more religious society, and makes the religious better citizens. Religious freedom encourages loyalty to the democracy which protects it. Tocqueville observes:

> Americans associate to send priests into the new states of the West and to found schools and churches there; *they fear that religion will be lost in the midst of the woods, and that the people growing up may not be as free as the one from which it has issued.* I encountered wealthy inhabitants of New England who abandoned the land of their birth with the aim of going to lay the foundations of Christianity and freedom by the banks of the Mississippi.[13]

These evangelicals were following in the tradition of the first Protestant settlers who identified religious freedom and political democracy:

> The greatest part of English America has been peopled by men, who, after having escaped the authority of the pope, did not submit to any religious supremacy; they therefore brought to the New World a Christianity [Reformed Protestantism] that I cannot depict better than to call it democratic and republican: this singularly favors the establishment of a republic and of democracy in affairs. From the beginning, politics and religion were in accord, and they have not ceased to be so since.[14]

Similarly, Tocqueville argues, "Americans so confuse [Protestant] Christianity and freedom in their minds that it is impossible to have them conceive of one without the other. . . . Thus it is that in the United States religious zeal constantly warms itself at the hearth of patriotism."[15]

Moralistic Democracy.   In the Puritan communities, each member of society
was expected to enforce the civil law. In the early town meetings most decisions were made by consensus, without a taking of yeas and nays. Nathaniel
Hawthorne described the power of public opinion, and the rule of shame,
within Puritan communities, while Thomas West's essay reminds us that
shunning was a long-standing Puritan practice. For the first time since the
democracies of classical Greece citizen opinion ruled. Opinion determined
policies, which made everyone feel responsible for scrupulously enforcing
self-made law.

As a result, the Reformed sects believed faith and morality were the true
bases for social liberty and self-government. Only those capable of rigorous
self-governance should enjoy civil freedom. According to Tocqueville, "freedom sees in religion the companion of its struggles and its triumphs, the
cradle of its infancy, the divine source of its rights. It considers religion as the
safeguard of mores; and mores as the guarantee of laws and the pledge of its
own duration."[16]

By the time of the revolution, Protestant thought had come to accept a
more rational and less moralistic view of human nature. One scholar notes:
"Enlightenment rationalism persuaded New England's established leadership to
shuck off Calvinism for the more prestigious and "rational" religion of the deists
and unitarians."[17] Indeed, the utopian Calvinists had abandoned their hope that
small communities of believers could find perfection in a "shining city on the
Hill," and sought, according to Michael Zuckert, a "natural rights republic."

But within fifty years the new natural rights republic increasingly understood itself in religious terms—as the Redeemer Nation. Speaking at Peoria,
Abraham Lincoln compares the sanctity of the founders' republic to the purity
of Christ, warning that the once pure republic has fallen into sin:

> Our republican robe is soiled, and trailed in the dust. Let us repurify it.
> Let us turn and wash it white, in the spirit, if not the blood, of the Revo-
> lution. Let us turn slavery from its claims of "moral right," back upon its
> existing legal rights, and its arguments of "necessity." . . . If we do this, we
> shall not only have saved the Union; but we shall have so saved it, as to
> make, and to keep it, forever worthy of the saving. We shall have so saved
> it, that the succeeding millions of free happy people, the world over, shall
> rise up, and call us blessed, to the latest generations.[18]

Lincoln is following the rhetorical trope of the great nineteenth-century
reformers, who had, like the Puritans of an earlier day, identified the sins of
the new republic with sins against God. Lincoln, like the great New England

preachers, offers a powerful jeremiad. He warns freedom lovers everywhere that the American holy city of democracy faces collapse without a renewal of its "holy" spirit in a rebirth of faith in the principles of the Declaration of Independence.

Lincoln's rhetorical appeal to political sin and salvation was born out of the evangelical fires of the early nineteenth century. To flash forward a century, a recent Canadian observer is still astonished to find in America a nation with the soul of a church:

> My first encounter with American consensus was in the late sixties, when I crossed the border into the United States and found myself inside the myth of America. Not of North America, for the myth stopped short of the Canadian and Mexican borders, but of a country that despite its arbitrary frontiers, despite its bewildering mix of race and creed, could believe in something called the True America. . . . Here was the Jewish anarchist Paul Goodman berating the Midwest for abandoning the promise; here, the descendent of American slaves, Martin Luther King, denouncing injustice as a violation of the American way; here, an endless debate about national destiny . . . conservatives scavenging for un-Americans, New Left historians recalling the country to its sacred mission. . . . It was a hundred sects and factions, each apparently different from the others, yet all celebrating the same mission.[19]

As a result of the evangelicals' extraordinary success, "Puritan" utopianism found its final form in the Redeemer Nation's journey to political perfection. The evangelicals managed to combine the apparently irreconcilable goals of Christian rebirth with a modern, rational faith in democracy. The Christian kingdom (the City of God) and the progress of democracy (the City of Man) were joined in one visible political entity. The new American republic was the embodiment of God in this world. With the moral leadership of the faithful, American democracy would redeem mankind from millennia of oppression and ignorance. At the time of the Redeemer Republic's greatest trial in civil war, in "The Battle Hymn of the Republic" the abolitionist Julia Ward Howe placed the God of Wrath at the head of the Union battle columns:

> I have seen Him in the watch-fires of a hundred circling camps
> They have builded Him an altar in the evening dews and damps
> I can read His righteous sentence by the dim and flaring lamps
> His day is marching on
> Glory! Glory! Hallelujah!

Glory! Glory! Hallelujah!
Glory! Glory! Hallelujah!
His truth is marching on

I have read a fiery gospel writ in burnish'd rows of steel,
"As ye deal with my contemners, So with you my grace shall deal;"
Let the Hero, born of woman, crush the serpent with his heal
Since God is marching on
Glory! Glory! Hallelujah!
Glory! Glory! Hallelujah!
Glory! Glory! Hallelujah!
His truth is marching on

. . . .

As He died to make men holy
Let us die to make men free . . .

Howe makes the fallen Union soldiers into Christian martyrs, comparing the Confederate "serpents" to Satan in the Garden. The Union "Hero, born of woman" stops the fall of God's republic by crushing the Confederate "serpent with his heal."

In his second inaugural address, Abraham Lincoln invokes the New Testament to temper Howe's Old Testament fire. Lincoln defends his government's determination to prosecute the war to the total surrender of the Confederacy, and God's righteousness in demanding an "eye for an eye" by denying the Union a speedier and less bloody victory. Indeed, the Almighty is just even if he requires that:

all the wealth piled by the bond-man's two hundred and fifty years of unrequited toil shall be sunk, and until every drop of blood drawn with the lash, shall be paid by another drawn with the sword, as was said three thousand years ago, so shall it be said "the judgments of the Lord, are true and righteous altogether."

But Lincoln suggests that Reconstruction must be based on forgiveness, not retribution or revenge. The second inaugural concludes with Lincoln's great invocation of Christian compassion: "With malice toward none; with charity for all . . . let us . . . bind up the nation's wounds; to care for him who shall have borne the battle, and for his widow, and his orphan—to do all which may achieve and cherish a just, and a lasting peace. . . ." The veteran, widow, and orphan to whom Lincoln refers are the ailing and grieving Americans on both sides of the Mason-Dixon Line. While divine justice may demand that "every drop of blood drawn with the lash, shall be paid by another drawn with the sword," a true peace embraces the New Testament commandment to love one's neighbor as oneself.

During the great evangelical revivals and crusades that began in the 1790s, and continued until the Civil War, the voice of Protestant evangelicalism grew distinct and powerful. Howe's "Battle Hymn of the Republic," Lincoln's second inaugural address, and Harriet Beecher Stowe's *Uncle Tom's Cabin* all used Christianity to justify the Redeemer Nation's violent abolition of slavery, *and* the necessity of a compassionate peace.

PROTESTANTISM AND THE AMERICAN FOUNDING

Alexis de Tocqueville argues in *Democracy in America* that Michael Zuckert's cohabitation of religion and political liberty had been a settled fact at least since the Founding. While the First Amendment outlawed a national establishment of religion, and state establishments were voluntarily weakened and abolished, no great effort was made to further separate religion and government until the twentieth century. As we will see, the debate over the separation of church and state was framed in almost totally different terms at the beginning of the republic than it was in the twentieth century. First let us look at the original founding debate.

Thomas Jefferson feared that establishments of religion gave government power over key areas of policy, such as taxation and office holding, resulting in a tyranny over men's politics, purse, and conscience. Establishments also reduced the benevolent social influence of having numerous and powerful religious faiths. Although Jefferson and James Madison led the disestablishment forces in Virginia, both patronized and practiced Christianity while in the White House.[20] And disestablishment encouraged the proliferation of religious sects which initiated the Second Great Awakening.[21]

The belief in the necessity of an active religious society for a virtuous democracy went unchallenged until the Progressive era began at the turn of the twentieth century. The development of the new social sciences of economics, psychology, sociology, and politics promised a new egalitarian republic. The Progressive intellectuals passionately believed science must replace religion as the prime source of American manners and morals. Where the founders had looked to the religious, primarily to the liberty-loving Reformed Protestants, to support their regime, the Progressives believed religion opposed their new empirical truths about society and politics. Religion limited the teaching of the new sciences, a threat personified by the Scopes "Monkey Trial," and fostered social conservatism, including laws against divorce and liberated individualism. The Progressive-Liberals saw religion as an enemy of economic and political progress as well.

So the Progressive historians revisited the founders' view of establishment and religious liberty. Charles Beard argued that the leading founders, especially Thomas Jefferson, James Madison, and Benjamin Franklin, opposed the establishment of religion because they opposed religion altogether. These founders sought disestablishment to weaken religious influence and create a scientific, secular society.[22] The proto-Progressive founders already looked forward to ever new economic and political formations and relationships.

Despite the Progressives' claim, no major politician before the end of the nineteenth century advocated a secular society. Tocqueville observed that such a radical policy would have been political suicide in a tolerant, but still religious, America: "In the United States, when a political man attacks a sect, it is not a reason for the partisans even of that sect not to support him; but if he attacks all sects together, each flees him and he remains alone."[23] Nevertheless, the Progressive-Liberal belief that the intellectual founders favored disestablishment in order to create a scientific and secular society is still the accepted intellectual wisdom of our day. But major historians have begun to challenge the Progressive revisionism of the founders' overwhelming support of an active religious culture. For example, James H. Hutson has demonstrated Thomas Jefferson's support for the cohabitation between politics and religion.[24] Hutson chronicles the elaborate measures President Jefferson employed, including personal church attendance and opening federal buildings for religious services, to show himself a strong partisan of religion.[25]

Philip Hamburger and Daniel Dreisbach have also challenged the historical accuracy of the Supreme Court's interpretation of the establishment clause, based on Thomas Jefferson's famous "wall of separation" metaphor, beginning with *Everson v. Board of Education* (1947). Hamburger concludes that Justice Hugo Black's watershed majority opinion in *Everson*—"a proclamation of principle with which none of Black's brethren disagreed"—in fact radically distorted and rejected Jefferson's and the founders' view. In *Everson,* Black claimed that "'the establishment or religion' clause of the First Amendment means at least this: Neither a state nor the Federal Government can set up a church. Neither can pass laws which aid one religion, aid all religions, or prefer one religion over another. . . . No tax in any amount, large or small, can be levied to support any religious activities or institutions, whatever they may be called, or whatever form they may adopt to teach or practice religion."[26] If not quite officially noncognizance of religion, with Black's opinion, the Court assumed the "wall of separation" meant the abolition of direct relations between politics and religion, and neutrality, if not hostility, to any accommodation.

It seems Justice Black, and not Thomas Jefferson, was the true architect and mason of the high wall of separation. Hamburger and Dreisbach suggest Black's concern for the entanglement of religion and government stemmed from his long-standing animus toward the Catholic Church.[27] A nativist and staunch Klansman for most of his life, Black saw the Catholic Church as the greatest threat to Protestant America. Hamburger says:

> Black had long before sworn, under the light of flaming crosses, to preserve "the sacred constitutional rights" of "free public schools" and "separation of church and state." Subsequently, he had administered this oath to thousands of others in similar ceremonies and had spoken in churches and klaverns across Alabama on what his fellow Klan leader, Jim Esdale, euphemistically called "the history of the church."[28]

But of greater moment, Justice Black was a follower of the Progressive historian Charles Beard, one of the greatest of the intellectual popularizers of scientific modernism. Beard equated the development of American social democracy with the progress of science, and thought religion an enemy of both. To repeat, Beard argued that the intellectual founders, especially Thomas Jefferson, James Madison, and Benjamin Franklin, had sought a secular and scientific society. Hamburger notes that in writing for the majority in *Everson*, "Black drew upon Charles Beard's 1943 *The Republic*, which Black considered 'a great book' and the title of which he thought, 'might almost have been 'The Origin and Aim of the American Constitution.'"[29]

Philip Hamburger and Daniel Driesbach make a case that prior to the twentieth century no major religious or political group sought governmental neutrality, much less hostility, to religion. While they opposed establishment, the vast majority of the faithful, and of the population at large, believed religious practice should be encouraged for its own sake and as an essential support for democracy.

The essays collected here do not directly address the "separation of church and state," although they help make an understanding of it possible.[30] Among the central questions the essays raise are these: What was the proper balance between politics and religion for the founders? Is the Declaration's natural rights liberalism compatible with a religious society? Was the cohabitation between political liberty and religious faith as stable and long lasting as Tocqueville suggests, or was the secular component always the dominant partner?[31] Finally, is the scientific secularism of Progressive-Liberalism a further development of the founders' rationalism or a departure from it? Let us turn to the essays to see the many dimensions involved in the creation of the first government based on nature and natural right—founded without a state church—which nevertheless welcomes and encourages all religious faiths.

Unlike twentieth-century liberalism, which in the name of progress warred against religion, Michael Zuckert argues in the first essay that the founders sought an "amalgam" or cohabitation between liberty and faith. In America, political life would be based on the Lockean natural rights embodied in the Declaration of Independence. But the religious would be encouraged to practice their faith and express their views. Indeed, religious practice in America before 1787 had produced a consensus in favor of a close relationship between religion and politics. As a result, the founders thought the "cohabitation" of political liberty with powerful religious sects would produce a healthy debate between the free political realm and that of religious faith and duty. According to Zuckert, "the result has been remarkable—a society in which religion has been supportive of an essentially secular political orientation and in which private and public morality both have derived salutary aid from deep-flowing religious impulses."

Zuckert shows the founders' compromise was welcomed by all sides. Indeed, the Puritans had been moving toward a more rational theology and politics since the end of the seventeenth century. By 1787, a clear majority of divines accepted the rational teachings of the "great Mr. Locke." Locke and his followers, including Thomas Jefferson, argued that religion and religious ethics must supplement natural reason. Locke observed, since "the greatest part cannot *know* . . . they must believe." Thomas Jefferson repeated this thought in his *Notes on the State of Virginia:* "And can the liberties of a nation be thought secure when we have removed their only firm basis, a conviction in the minds of the people that these liberties are the gift of God? That they are not to be violated but with his wrath?" For Jefferson, the federal government had an interest in encouraging religious activity, even if the establishment clause limited in some ways the means it could use to do so.

Seymour Martin Lipset next shows the long-term influence of religious sectarianism on American life. Lipset, America's greatest political sociologist, demonstrates how sectarianism and congregationalism made Protestantism the perfect religion for the new democracy. His essay demonstrates how religion perfected individualism and provided the principles and institutional habits of American democracy.

Because Alexis de Tocqueville is widely regarded as the most seminal thinker on American religion, politics, and social habits we have included the major passages on religion from *Democracy in America* as a source and companion to the other essays. As we have discussed, Tocqueville initiated the view of American exceptionalism, arguing the unique, formative influence of Protestantism on American society.

In our next essay, Isaac Kramnick and R. Laurence Moore reiterate the importance of political liberty against the claims of contemporary evangelicals that America was founded as (and should remain) a Christian nation. The authors observe that the word "God" never appears in the Constitution, and that Article 6 explicitly excludes religious tests for holding public office. The Constitution is godless because the founders were Deists: "Deism was . . . a powerful force among the intellectuals of the founding generation, even among many of the delegates in Philadelphia. A nondoctrinaire religion, deism . . . posited a naturalistic religion with a God understood as a supreme intelligence who after creating the world destined it to operate forever after according to natural, rational, and scientific laws."

Kramnick and Moore believe "religious correctness" poses a great danger to political liberty. The radicalism of the new Christian zealots, when combined with their populist use of radio and television, makes religion even more potent today than in the nineteenth century. Groups like the Moral Majority are using electoral politics to overturn the Constitution's separation of church and state. Faced with this great danger, the two authors reject the non-preferential support for religion envisioned by most founders. Like the Progressive-Liberals, they believe religion poses an immediate threat to individual liberty. Therefore, government must constantly prevent religion from overstepping the limited place assigned to it by the rational, Deistic founders in the "Godless" Constitution.

Peter Lawler agrees with Kramnick and Moore's reading of Jefferson as a confirmed secularist. The hedonistic Epicureanism Jefferson defends in his letters, and perhaps practiced at Monticello, reflects the actual import of John Locke's selfish individualism. Moreover, Lawler accepts the premise of the "religiously correct" that Locke's rationalism destroys the foundations of faith. If the Calvinists were pious and virtuous, the founders, represented by Thomas Jefferson, sacrificed their piety and virtue on the "Godless" altar of modern freedom.

In Lawler's view, the founders' cohabitation between political liberty and an active religious society was a theoretical halfway house, an unstable compromise resulting in the triumph of the secular elements. Certainly, religious orthodoxy has declined in America in the face of sectarian competition and ever-increasing religious democracy. America inevitably became a more secular society.

Thomas G. West also indirectly supports Kramnick and Moore's argument that the founders were concerned above all with liberty and power, not faith and salvation. West argues that the new "natural rights republic" was correctly understood by the leading Puritan divines as the liberation of the Lockean natural man in the rational universe of God's creation. The religious supporters of the revolution had moved from *sola scriptura* and *sola fidei* to Deism: God created a wholly rational universe. But if, as West suggests, the central teachings of the New Testament governing God's plan for mankind are seen to be incredible in light of the reasoning of the Declaration of Independence, then it is ultimately impossible to equate the Declaration with Christianity. The fact that the founders' Deism found a friendly partner in the rationalistic "Old Light" Puritan divines doesn't mean that the Declaration of Independence, or Locke's rational theology, is Christian when understood in the light of Christianity's biblical source and transcendent end. Even if God made humans free, equal, and rational, liberty may still pose a threat to faith. However this may be, the American separation of church and state has strengthened religious practice as the founders desired.

Wilson Carey McWilliams takes up the danger to religion posed by the founders' synthesis of rationalism and Christianity in a slightly different way. Where Michael Zuckert and Thomas West emphasize the willingness of the majority of the leading Puritans to embrace Lockean human nature and liberal politics, McWilliams suggests the more conservative divines had serious reservations. These ministers recognized the need to separate from Anglican England and that the vast number of American sects required disestablishment. Bowing to these necessities, they did not voice their concerns in a manner harmful to the new liberal order. Instead, the influential Reverend Nathaniel Niles sought a subtle dialogue between the liberal founding and Christian piety. McWilliams observes,

> The "laudable" effort to secure civil liberty demands tactical accommodations to secular circumstance, and rhetoric tailored to the shape of political practice. But it is the quest for *spiritual* liberty that sets the measure, weighing tactical choices and defining principles which cannot be com-

promised and confrontations which cannot be avoided. And it reminds Christians that they speak a language—and seek a city—alien to even the best secular politics, seeing only idols where others see sacred laws. . . . And in such situations, if it needs saying, one guards one's tongue, partly in order to preserve the Word.

Willing to perfect the human kingdom through the founders' "new science of politics," Niles and his colleagues quietly subordinated the secular goals of the founding to the higher ends of faith.

And Christians have successfully elevated politics by carefully choosing their encounters. Religion has won important battles, especially against slavery and for civil rights, by providing "a critical voice, a vocabulary of protest, and, especially, an egalitarianism warmed into a conviction of fraternity." According to McWilliams, "Niles and his fellow Calvinists . . . had taught that, short of the end, fallen nature sets the general direction of history, only checked or deflected periodically by divine interventions, which themselves soon give way to resurgent nature."

Finally, Mark Noll makes an intriguing argument that the nineteenth-century evangelicals successfully tied Christian revivalism to traditional republicanism. The evangelicals argued that only religion, and not classical rationalism or the ideology of republicanism, could provide democracy with public virtue capable of producing true patriotism and self-sacrifice. For the evangelicals, the spirit of liberty and religion was joined in the vision of the Redeemer Republic, a free republic voluntarily pursuing Christian morality and salvation. Julia Ward Howe captured the spirit of this new evangelical amalgamation in "The Battle Hymn of the Republic": "as He died to make men holy, let us die to make men free." Thus the founders' secular "natural rights republic" was superseded by the more intense politics and religious moralism of these explicitly Christian Americans. It remains well attested that, as Zuckert puts it, "Both Locke and the ministers 'tended to treat natural and revealed law as two consistent, complementary, and interdependent expressions of a single divine will.'" Yet as Noll asserts, "it is also well attested that a secular language of republican virtue was also easily, swiftly, and massively infused with a language of Christian virtue [and republican patriotism]." Noll's essay reminds us of the strong support the Second Great Awakening offered for virtue, patriotism, and political reform throughout the nineteenth century. As we have seen, Christian conviction steeled Northern resolve to end slavery by washing our "republican robe" in the blood of new martyrs.

The remarkable historical development Noll details lends weight to the view that the founders, if Deists, thought disestablishment would serve the ends of political liberty *and* of strong religion. In Madison's language, the "multiplicity of [religious] sects" encourages the growth of new religious denominations while preventing the possibility of a majority faction created by the establishment of religion. The founders' compromise marked a significant advance of political liberty. Helping to abolish religious establishments, they created the legal framework for the Second Great Awakening, which reshaped nineteenth-century American society. Conversely, the intellectual and political ascendancy of Progressive-Liberalism in the twentieth century created a more secular American society than had ever previously existed.

As these essays attest, the debates over religion and the Constitution are still being fought between the advocates of science and reason and those of faith and morality. The fires first lit by the Reformation and Enlightenment still burn brightly in America; the culture war between the religious and rationally enlightened has no obvious end. The historical record—the actions and thoughts of Thomas Jefferson, James Madison, and the other founders—is appealed to by both sides.

But falling confidence in the social sciences, which had fueled Progressive-Liberal scientific secularism, has started another reappraisal of the contentious relationship between reason and faith. Signs of this reappraisal are hard to ignore. The Restoration of the Freedom of Religion Act (1983) works to restore the religious freedom envisioned by the founders. National Democratic leaders now routinely join Republicans in calling for private, faith-based social programs to replace the Progressive-Liberal model of bureaucratic social science. President George W. Bush, far more than his immediate predecessors, describes himself as a man of faith and sermonizes on the importance of prayer and of God's providence for the nation's well-being. Clearly, the Progressives' radical "separation of church and state" has been politically eclipsed for the foreseeable future by a more traditional and positive view of religion and politics.

Given America's nearly four-hundred-year social experience with religion and democracy—dating on these shores from the Puritans' landing in 1630—it is not surprising that through all the contention and controversy most Americans have always seen in the founders' amalgam of liberty and religion a reasonable compromise, and an intelligent constitutional construction. As these essays attest, the founders' friendly disestablishment continues to supply the foundation for a free, religious, and public-spirited democracy.[32]

Notes

1. J. Hector St. John de Crèvecoeur, *Letters from an American Farmer* (New York: Penguin Books, [1783] 1981), 74–76: "The Americans become as to religion what they are as to country, allied to all. In them the name of Englishman, Frenchman, and European is lost, and in like manner, the strict modes of Christianity as practiced in Europe are also lost. . . . Thus all sects are mixed, as well as all nations; thus religious indifference is imperceptibly disseminated from one end of the continent to the other, which is at present one of the strongest characteristics of the Americans."

2. Mark A. Noll, *Christians in the American Revolution* (Washington, D.C.: Christian College Consortium, 1977), 30.

3. Alexis de Tocqueville, *Democracy in America,* ed. and trans. Harvey C. Mansfield and Delba Winthrop (Chicago: University of Chicago Press, 2000), 28–32.

4. Tocqueville, *Democracy,* 41–42.

5. Ibid., 32.

6. Allen C. Guelzo, *Abraham Lincoln: Redeemer President* (Grand Rapids: William B. Eerdmans, 1999), 11.

7. Seymour Martin Lipset, *American Exceptionalism: A Double-Edged Sword* (New York: W. W. Norton, 1996), 39–46, 60–71.

8. Letter to Benjamin Rush, September 23, 1800. *Writings of Thomas Jefferson,* Merrill D. Peterson, ed. (New York: Viking Press, 1984), 1080.

9. Lipset, *American Exceptionalism,* 91.

10. Leonard W. Levy, *The Establishment Clause: Religion and the First Amendment* (New York: MacMillan, 1986), 61.

11. Alexander Hamilton, James Madison, and John Jay, *The Federalist* (Middletown, Conn.: Wesleyan University Press, 1961), 60.

12. Ibid., 64–65.

13. Tocqueville, *Democracy,* 281.

14. Ibid., 275.

15. Ibid., 280–81.

16. Ibid., 43–44.

17. Guelzo, *Abraham Lincoln,* 11.

18. Roy P. Basler, ed., *The Collected Works of Abraham Lincoln,* 8 vols. (New Brunswick, N.J.: Rutgers University Press, 1953), II:276. See Guelzo, *Abraham Lincoln,* 193.

19. Lipset, *American Exceptionalism,* 291.

20. James H. Hutson summarizes Jefferson's teaching on separation in this way: "Jefferson used the wall of separation metaphor in the sense of a wall of segmentation, as a partition demarcating the religious activities the government could and could not support. In his view, the government could not be a party to any attempt to impose upon the country a uniform religious exercise or observance; it could, on the other hand, support, as being in the public interest, voluntary, non-discriminatory religious activity, including church services, by putting at its disposal public property, public facilities, and

public personnel, including the president himself." *Religion and the Founding of the American Republic* (Washington, D.C.: Library of Congress, 1998), 93.

Hutson summarizes Jefferson's actual religious practice—including his regular church attendance, extensive contributions to different Christian churches, and encouragement of religious services in federal buildings during his presidency—with this descriptive quote: "Jefferson, according to [Reverend] Allen, was walking to church one Sunday 'with his red prayer book under his arm when a friend querying him after their mutual good morning said which way are you walking Mr. Jefferson. To which he replied to Church sir. You are going to Church Mr. J. You do not believe a word in it. Sir said Mr. J. No nation has ever existed or been governed without religion. Nor can be. The Christian religion is the best religion that has ever been given to man and I as chief Magistrate of this nation am bound to give it the sanction of my example. Good morning Sir.'" Ibid., 96.

21. Tocqueville, *Democracy*, 278–88.

22. Henry Steele Commager summarized the transforming influence of Darwin and the social sciences on the Progressives: "The impact of Darwin on truth was shattering; his impact on philosophy was revolutionary . . . it toppled Man from his exalted position as the end and purpose of creation, the crown of Nature, and the image of God, and classified him prosaically with the anthropoids. It repudiated the philosophical implications of the Newtonian system, substituted for the neat orderly universe governed by fixed laws a universe in constant flux whose beginnings were incomprehensible and whose ends were unimaginable, reduced man to a passive role, and by subjecting moral concepts to its implacable laws deprived them of that authority which had for so long furnished consolation and refuge to bewildered man. Every institution was required to yield to its sovereign claims, the church, the state, the family, property, law; every discipline was forced to adapt itself to its ineluctable pattern: history, economics, sociology, philology, art, literature, religion, ethics." *The American Mind: An Interpretation of American Thought and Character Since the 1880's.* (New Haven: Yale University Press, 1978 [1950]), 83. Of Benjamin Franklin, the Beards argue: "He was a member of all the important scientific associations of Europe and to him were sent opinions and criticisms touching the course of thought throughout the western world. . . . It is not too much to say that Benjamin Franklin, in the age of George II, almost divined the drift of the twentieth century." Charles A. Beard and Mary R. Beard, *The Rise of American Civilization* (New York: MacMillan, 1930), 159. Similarly, Vernon Louis Parrington praises Franklin's intellectual liberation from the prejudices of his age and open-minded orientation to change and progress: "No other man in America, and few in Europe, had so completely freed themselves from the prejudice of custom. The Calvinism in which he was bred left not the slightest trace upon him; and the middle-class world from which he emerged did not narrow his mind to its petty horizons. He was a free man who went his own way with imperturbable good will and unbiased intelligence." *Main Currents in American Thought: An Interpretation of American Literature from the Beginnings to 1920* (New York: Harcourt, Brace and Company, 1930), 165.

23. Tocqueville, *Democracy*, 280.

24. Garrett Ward Sheldon and Daniel L. Dreisbach, eds., *Religion and Political Culture in Jefferson's Virginia* (Lanham, Md.: Rowman and Littlefield, 2000); James H. Hutson, ed., *Religion and the New Republic* (Lanham, Md.: Rowman and Littlefield, 2000).

25. See 20 *supra*.

26. Philip Hamburger, *Separation of Church and State* (Cambridge, Mass.: Harvard University Press, 2002), 461.

27. Daniel L. Dreisbach, *Thomas Jefferson and the Wall of Separation between Church and State* (New York: New York University Press, 2002).

28. Hamburger, *Separation,* 461.

29. Ibid., n. 171.

30. The essays do address the same theme of religion and progress the Progressives would later turn into a political crusade.

31. The latter is the view of many partisan commentators on both the left and the right. The Progressive historians initiated the argument that the "best" or most intellectual founders desired a "godless constitution" and a "naked public square," and that their view should now become the view of the Supreme Court.

32. This is the position of Mark Noll and Michael Zuckert, as it was of Alexis de Tocqueville.

CHAPTER ONE

Natural Rights and Protestant Politics

Michael P. Zuckert

Surely the most familiar, as well as the most euphonic, assessment of the American political tradition yet proposed lies in the opening of Abraham Lincoln's Gettysburg Address. "Four score and seven years ago, our fathers brought forth upon this continent a new nation, conceived in liberty and dedicated to the proposition that all men are created equal." Within his near-biblical cadences Lincoln proffered at least two important claims about the American political order: first, that it was a new nation, new not only in time and place, but altogether new to mankind. America was a great experiment, an addition to the array of human political possibilities. In this judgment Lincoln echoes the founding generation itself when it, for example, adopted the motto *novus ordo seclorum*—a new order for the ages. Second, by Lincoln's reckoning, the new order dates from 1776, the year of independence, the year of the Declaration of Independence. It does not date, according to Lincoln, from 1620, the year the Pilgrims came to America and made their Mayflower Compact, nor from 1630, the year the Puritans joined them in Massachusetts Bay.

In seeing 1776 as the inauguration of the new order Lincoln implicitly took issue with another very well-known assessment of the American political order, Alexis de Tocqueville's *Democracy in America*. Tocqueville, to say the least, saw the Puritan experience as far more formative than Lincoln apparently did. Tocqueville puts much less weight on 1776, for, he seems to believe, the revolution did not so much cause as register an earlier disruption and discontinuity. Those who came to America were dissidents, people setting off to find a new heaven in the New World, or at least to build an unprecedented "city upon a hill" quite different from the corrupt and degenerating country they were leaving in the third and fourth decades of the seventeenth century.

The Puritans developed a distinctive set of institutions and a distinctive political culture, which, Tocqueville insisted, were the seed of later, postrevolutionary American politics. It is essential, even today, for political figures to invoke God, and America is said to be a nation marked beyond others by a "civil religion" articulating the divine origin and support for American politics.[1] America, according to this view, owes its specific political character to the religious and theological views and practices of its early settlers and the continuing religious character of its people.

Within Puritanism, the truly characteristic features of American politics were born. The concern with the individual that is reflected in the American commitment to individual rights, the democracy that flowered in America—these had their source among the Puritans. As Tocqueville put it, "Puritanism was not just a religious doctrine; in many respects it shared the most absolute democratic and republican theories." The Puritans, he concluded, were the source of that "spirit of freedom" that animates American democracy.[2]

The Tocqueville-Lincoln disagreement survives in the late twentieth-century debates about the character of America—secular or sacred, heirs of the Enlightenment or heirs of the Bible (of Puritanism? the Reformation? Christianity? Judeo-Christianity? as it is variously put). My argument (which I suspect is actually shared in one way or another by both Tocqueville and Lincoln) is that the stark set of alternatives puts matters far too simply. Lincoln is correct to see significant differences between the Protestant immigrants who settled America in the seventeenth century and the founding generation that "brought forth a new nation" in 1776. Yet, different as their antecedents have been, by the mid-eighteenth century there occurred a blending or amalgamation of Lockean Enlightenment political themes and American Protestantism. As Clinton Rossiter concluded:

> Had ministers been the only spokesman of the American cause, had Jefferson, the Adamses, and Otis never appeared in print, the political thought of the Revolution would have followed almost exactly the same line—with perhaps a little more mention of God, but certainly no less of John Locke. In the sermons of the patriot ministers, who were responsible for fully one-third of the total output of political thought in these years, we find expressed every possible refinement of the reigning secular faith.[3]

The convergence Rossiter notes between the preachers and the politicians was, perhaps, the dominant fact of the era of the revolution in America. In what follows I wish to explore the following topics: (1) the relationship between the political thought of the first generation of Pilgrim and Puritan settlers and the theory contained in the Declaration of Independence; (2) the amalgam of Protestant and Enlightenment political thought that developed by the mid-eighteenth century; and (3) the conditions for the possibility of the emergence of this amalgam and its significance, in itself and for America. This third task will require a brief excursion into the pristine form of Protestant political theology, the two kingdoms doctrine of Martin Luther.

THE FIRST GENERATION

Like much else about the earliest founding eras in America, the early story of Massachusetts had much to do with the accidents of English history. The story is a familiar one. Various groups of settlers came to New England seeking a more Protestantized church and state than was possible for them in England, at least up until the outbreak of the Civil War in 1642. They came both to escape from and to set an example for the Anglican church they wanted to change and at whose hands they often suffered, but also to realize the new possibilities—religious and political—that Reformation principles seemed to open up for them. In America the Puritans could construct for themselves and all humanity "a city upon a hill." As Edward Johnson, one of the early historians of New England, put it in the 1650s: "this is the place where the Lord will create a new Heaven, and a new Earth in, new Churches and a new Commonwealth together." They saw this city not only as their hope, but as the dread responsibility, a more than human responsibility, they bore: "if we shall deal falsely with our god in this work we have undertaken and so cause him to withdraw his present help from us, we shall be made a story and by-word throughout the world, [and] we shall open the mouth of enemies to speak evil of the ways of God and all professors for God's sake."[4]

New England was settled by two closely related but not identical groups, the Pilgrims and the Puritans, who over the course of a century in America easily blended together. Both started out among those Protestants in England who believed the reformation of the English church had not proceeded far enough. The theology of both groups was very similar—variations on Calvinist themes. The one difference between them concerned the church itself: the Puritans were committed to the further purification of the Church of

England while the Pilgrims had concluded that true religion required the establishment of different kinds of churches altogether, voluntary gatherings of believers. The very idea of a national church in which all residents, or at least all who had been baptized as infants, were automatically members was contrary to what the Pilgrims believed a church, a congregation of the faithful, truly was. Because of their belief in the need for a different kind of church they became known as Separatists, and it was this issue—whether to stay in the Church of England or to form separate voluntary or "gathered" churches—that distinguished them from the Puritans.[5]

Given the nature of the theological-political order in England, the Separatists were required to become Pilgrims in order to form the kinds of churches they sought. In an irony that may be taken to foreshadow the ultimate fate of their movement, they received a patent from the Virginia Company to form a colony in Virginia, but instead landed on the scrubby and rock-hard Massachusetts coast at Plymouth. That mistake bears in important ways on the Mayflower Compact. William Bradford, their governor, tells in his journal of the "combination" the settlers made "before they came ashore, being the first foundation of their govermente in this place; occasioned partly by the discontented and mutinous speeches that some of the strangers [those who were not church communicants] among them had let fall from them in the ship; That when they came ashore they would use their owne libertie; for none had power to command them, the patente they had being for Virginia, and not for New-england, which belonged to an other Government, with which the Virginia Company had nothing to doe."[6] This seminal political document was in some part the result of navigational errors and jurisdictional fissures. Such is the stuff of which great history is made.

As the "first foundation of their govermente" the Mayflower Compact stands to the Pilgrims much as the Declaration of Independence does to the new American order. The aptness of comparing the two documents has thus not gone unnoticed. The most common theme in the typical comparison derives from the observation that both documents affirm that government comes to be via a contract, or agreement, or covenant of those subject to it. Because of the agreement on contract, many scholars find the two documents identical or nearly identical as political theory.[7] The validity of that easy identification is thrown into question, however, by recent scholarship in the history of political thought. Contract theories can be quite different from each other, deriving their conclusions from different premises, and pointing toward different modes of conducting government.

More serious are scholars like Willmoore Kendall and George Carey, who rest their judgment of identity or continuity on more than the mere presence of contract or covenant in the two documents. "There was already . . . a very old tradition in America, when the Declaration [of Independence] was written; a tradition, moreover, that we must understand in order to understand the Declaration." That "very old tradition" begins with the Mayflower Compact and exists as a tradition because it consists of the regular "making and remaking [of] the Mayflower Compact."[8] The Declaration, they argue, is such a remaking. They thus would not read the Declaration through the lenses supplied by "Locke or the philosophers of the so-called age of enlightenment." They insist that to do so, as much of the "official literature" does, "cannot but help to lead to endless confusion and a basic misunderstanding . . . of the American political tradition." The real center of the Declaration lies in its being "the declaration of a religious people, of, more specifically, a *Christian* people, . . . a people who wish to make clear above all else their commitment to work the will of God.[9] Kendall and Carey's claims are important both for what they affirm—the Mayflower Compact and thus reform Christianity supplies the key to the American political tradition, including especially the Declaration—and for what they deny—modern political philosophy does not do so. It is this set of claims I wish to contest.

Adapting Kendall and Carey, we may discuss the Mayflower Compact under three heads: what, who, and why—that is, the announcement of what is being done here, the identification of the actors, and the purposes for which it is being done. These categories will allow us to compare it with comparable elements of the Declaration of Independence.

The Mayflower Compact, like the Declaration of Independence, is a performance, a speech-act. But the two do not perform the same act. The Pilgrims act to "covenant and combine [themselves] together into a civil Body Politick." It is not so much a description of a social compact, as the Declaration is, but is itself a compact. This compact begins its act of compacting with the words, "In the name of God, amen." As Kendall and Carey observe, these are "the first words of Western man's traditional Christian invocation." As they do not say, more specifically these are the typical opening words of Separatist church covenants, the agreements fellow believers made when they founded or joined a Separatist church.[10] The whole is an oath, "in the name of God," parallel to a church covenant. From this opening, Kendall and Carey conclude we have here a "nascent society that interprets itself . . . [as] in some sense a religious, more specifically a Christian, society, which calls God in as Witness to its act of founding—nay, even founds itself in His name." They find a close parallel in the Declaration of Independence, which, in its opening sentence, appeals to "the Laws of Nature and Nature's God." Or, as Donald Lutz has it, the reference to "'Nature's God' activates the religious grounding" invoked at the very opening of the Mayflower Compact.[11] Both documents thus appeal to the divine at or near their openings, and this is obviously a central ground for Kendall and Carey's assertions regarding the centrality of the religious or Christian element in the American political tradition.

The Mayflower Compact uses the form of appeal traditional in Christian churches and indeed that form used in the making of churches, themselves congregations of the faithful. The divinity invoked in the Mayflower Compact is beyond doubt the Christian God, the God of the Bible, the God of faith and of the faithful. The appeal to the divine in the Declaration is altogether different, however: here it is "Nature's God" and his "Laws," a God who speaks to humanity through reason and acts in and through nature. His laws are none other than the laws of nature, as understood by human reason. It is thus difficult to see what ground Lutz has for saying the Declaration "simultaneously appeals to reason and revelation." It appeals only to reason.[12] The Christian God is also the God of nature, of course, but *qua* Christian God, *qua* the God of the covenant of grace, he is the God of super-nature. The Christian events, the incarnation, the resurrection, the economy of salvation—these are miraculous, extraordinary events, not events in or of nature.

In accordance with its emphasis on the God of nature and the truths known in and through nature, the Declaration's crucial theoretical section begins, "We hold these truths to be self-evident." Thus, politics rests on "truths," not on blood, tradition, custom, or habit. It rests on "held truths," implying an element of reflection and thought. They are accessible to human beings as such, not to a charmed circle of true believers, graced with divine grace. The truths concern "all men," not the regenerate, or Protestants, or Christians. The truths are both accessible to and valid for all human beings; the principles of the Declaration are simply universal in character. They point toward a secular society open to the rational as such; they point toward a cosmopolitan, not a closed or sectarian, society. To be an American, therefore, is not to be of a certain descent or religious faith or original human type. To be an American is rather to accept these universal principles.[13]

Given the differences in the appeals made in our two documents, it is no wonder they tell or rest on different narratives of the nature and destiny of humanity, for the Declaration presents a short history of mankind parallel to the history of mankind presented in the Bible, but makes significant changes in it. According to the biblical account, human beings are placed by God in a garden, a place where their needs are spontaneously supplied. The beginning is good, even perfect. But what a good, powerful, and caring God provided for humanity, Adam through his own misdeed lost. In disobeying God, humanity brings upon itself death, labor, pain, crime, and ultimately kings, cities, and politics.

According to the Declaration's history, human beings are created free and equal, and endowed with rights. It would seem that according to the Declaration also humanity is well provided for by its creator. But, perhaps out of delicacy, Jefferson elided an important fact in his description of the pre-political situation: in that situation, rights are "insecure," for otherwise there would be no need to institute government "to secure these rights." The creator supplies human beings with rights, with claims, in the original situation, but not with the security of those rights, or the satisfaction of those claims. The security of these rights—the really valuable thing—is supplied not by God or nature, but by human beings themselves when they institute government. Human action is more nearly the foundation for human salvation than the basis for a fall. The Declaration's history reverses the Bible's history.

After the indication of what they are doing, taking an oath as part of making a covenant for their government, the covenanters (as Kendall and Carey put it) "identify themselves, say who they are." This is a necessary part of the Mayflower Compact, for the act of covenanting itself produces the ties that constitute the covenanted community—the church in the ordinary case, the political community in this extra-ordinary extension of the church covenant. The identification of the agents, who also sign the document in order to institute their membership, is thus part of the phenomenon of covenanting itself. The Constitution of 1787, with its opening "We the people of the United States," contains a more obvious parallel, but the Declaration also identifies those who are issuing the document: "We . . . the representatives of the United States of America, in general Congress, Assembled."[14] They speak for the "one people" who here "dissolve the political bands which have connected them with another" people.

This parallel between the two documents is much more significant for the differences it reveals than for any similarities, however. As Kendall and Carey notice, the Compact's signers identify themselves as "the legal subjects of our dread Sovereign Lord King James, by the grace of God . . . King, Defender of the Faith, *etc.*" They are covenanting or compacting to bring themselves under political authority, but there is no suggestion here that they are otherwise free of political allegiance. They are not, that is, moving from a state of nature to a civil society via their covenant; they are already subjects of James. There is, moreover, no hint that their subjection to James derived from some earlier act of covenanting like the one they are performing at that moment. James owes his authority not to their consent, but to "the grace of God." On the larger issues of political legitimacy and the origin of political authority, the *May-flower* compactors seem closer to the theorists of divine right than to the social contract theory.

If they are already subject, then what are they doing covenanting for future subjection? Here the story Bradford told of their navigational and juris-dictional mishaps takes on its relevance. They are subject, rightfully subject they insist, to James, who has delegated authority to the Virginia Company, which in turn has delegated authority to the Pilgrims to set up government in Virginia. Unfortunately, they never did arrive in Virginia, but landed in-stead in a place outside the jurisdiction of the Virginia Company and thus broke the chain of authorization linking them to James. Under these circum-stances, the Mayflower Compact represents not so much the embodiment of a general contractarian theory of political authority, but the first recorded instance of Yankee ingenuity.[15] They adapted the covenant form they knew from their ecclesiology in order to meet the emergency caused by the gap in the chain of authority. They claim nothing universal here, but only seek to reforge the broken link in order to reconnect themselves to their king, who rules "by grace of God."

The Declaration could hardly be more different. The 1776 document is more concerned to justify the dissolution of already existing political bonds than to forge bonds that do not exist, but it does so in terms of a universal theory of the source of political authority. All legitimate authority derives from covenant or compact, even the authority of King George, of whom it is cer-tainly not said that he rules "by the grace of God."[16]

As a universal theory of the source of all political power and not an expe-dient designed to meet an emergency, the Declaration commits to a set of doc-trines which either have no place in the Mayflower Compact or are simply contradicted there. There is no human authority prior to the human making of government, and so the Declaration contemplates a situation prior to gov-ernment, a situation prior to all authority, a state of nature, or in the language of the Declaration, an original "equality." Since the Mayflower Compact never contemplates human beings outside all authority, it has no room for the doc-trine of the state of nature or of equality as the Declaration understands that.[17]

The Declaration affirms equality as part of its mini-human history—from equality as no-authority to the creation of authority, to its abuse and refoun-dation through "altering or abolishing." This "history" is not meant as literal history, but as rationalist reconstruction of the human situation in nature. One way to see the constructivist character of the Declaration's narrative is to notice that it clearly intends the affirmation of equality in the Lockean sense rather than in the usage of the pre-Lockean Whig contractarian tradition, which looked to the pre-political situation as a pre-historical condition that human beings left behind at some distant date in the past when they made something called "the original compact." The Declaration insists, however, that *all men* are created equal and must constitute authority through their own consent, not just that of those at some past moment. The Mayflower Compact, by contrast, has nothing of the rationalist reconstruction about it. The consent contained here is quite literally that given by those who sign the document. They are much closer to the Whigs than to the Declaration, however, for they do not suggest that later members must consent in some way or other to political authority in order to be subject to it, just as they themselves did not have to consent to the authority of King James.[18]

Because the Mayflower Compact is an actual covenant, its operative element is the oath and consequent adherence to the political community so formed. The actual signers promise obedience; they sign up just as they would for a cable-TV subscription. The Declaration, more insistent on the consent of each and every human being, paradoxically has no such signing up. Even in the various state and national constitutions, there was nothing of this "sign up in order to be a member" quality we see in the Compact. Consent is necessary, but it is not expressed in the form of the Compact's membership oath.

A third element shared by both the Mayflower Compact and the Declaration of Independence is a statement of purposes. The Pilgrims "covenant and combine" themselves "into a civil Body Politick" for four purposes: (1) for their "better ordering and preservation," which in turn will allow them to accomplish the three chief ends of their undertaking, which were: (2) the glory of God, (3) the advancement of the Christian faith, and (4) the honor of king and country. It is difficult not to notice the prominence of their religious purposes. Although the Compact does not specify how these religious purposes are specifically to be accomplished, it does emphasize the instrumental or secondary character of their "ordering and preservation" as a purpose. In the Mayflower Compact the secular is for the sake of the sacred. This parallels the countermovement which we have already noted in the Compact: in order to institute their "civil Body Politick" they have adapted their church covenant to this secular service.

The Declaration of Independence also contains a statement of the ends for which human beings create civil orders: "in order to secure these rights governments are instituted among men." Government exists to secure rights, period.[19] Rights derive from the creator, it is true, but they neither come from some special relation to the divine nor are they necessarily instruments to further service of the divine. Of course, the secured rights to life, to liberty, and to the pursuit of happiness may be used to pursue one's eternal salvation or some other sacred purpose, but this is now entirely in the sphere of the private choice of the rights-holder. The Declaration, in other words, affirms a wholly this-worldly end for political life, and thus points ahead to the First Amendment's separation of church and state as its principled fulfillment.

Rights are a terrible stumbling block for those like Kendall and Carey who see a near identity between these two founding documents. Rights are prominent, nay central, in the Declaration and all the thinking and acting at the time of the 1776 founding, and have remained at or near the center of American political life ever since. Yet they are totally absent from the Mayflower Compact.

Kendall and Carey concede that the Declaration represents a "most difficult and most controversial" part of their account of the nature of the American tradition. They respond to this "difficult and controversial" passage in their journey by arguing, in part, that the Mayflower Compact, saying nothing explicit about rights, implicitly raises some important rights claims according to the following chain of reasoning. The covenanters promise "due obedience" to laws which are "just and equal," from which one can infer a duty in governors "to govern by just and equal laws deemed necessary for the public good." From this duty in governors, Kendall and Carey deduce that "each signer has henceforth an individual right to the performance of that duty by his fellow signers."[20]

Such might be a valid argument for the Compact, but it remains a far cry from the rights doctrine of the Declaration. The rights in the Declaration do not derive from some preexisting duty of rulers, but instead predate all rulers because they exist in the state of equality, that is, the state where there are no rulers. The rights are primary, and so far as rulers have duties these derive from the original human rights. The Declaration thus reverses the Kendall and Carey view of the Compact's rights theory. Moreover, in the Declaration the securing of these natural or pre-political rights is the sum and substance of the point of government. This surely is not true of the Compact, even in Kendall and Carey's abstruse chain of reasoning.

The Puritans apparently were better navigators than the Pilgrims, for they landed just where they aimed to, and came armed with their charter from the king. They suffered no gap in the chain of authority binding them back to the authority under which they were born. They had no need, therefore, to engage in the performance of constructing wholly new structures of authority—the basic structure with which they began was clearly outlined in their charter—nor of reforging broken links in old chains.[21] There is no "Arbella Compact" to match the Pilgrims' document, but that is not to say that the Puritans did not attempt to clarify for themselves the meaning and principles of what they were undertaking. In this case, the most striking Puritan statement that we have is a shipboard lay sermon titled "A Modell of Christian Charitie," written and probably delivered by the governor of the colony, John Winthrop.[22] Like the Pilgrims, the Puritans fell back on known religious forms in order to express what they needed to say regarding politics.[23]

Winthrop relies on a religious form, but much of the substance of his sermon reminds one of very traditional, quite secular statements. Those seeking evidence of continuity between Puritan political thinking and modern thought such as the Declaration of Independence are bound to be disappointed. The chief thesis of Winthrop's speech certainly stands in a different quadrant from the American Declaration's first "self-evident truth": "God Almightie in his most holy and wise providence hath soe disposed of the condicion of mankinde, as in all times some must be rich some poore, some highe and eminent in power and dignitie; others meane and in subjeccion."[24] Not "created equal" but ordained to be unequal—that is the first or axiomatic premise from which Winthrop's political thinking proceeds. It is impossible to overemphasize how much Winthrop's political teaching (and practice) turns on this beginning point, a beginning point he brought with him as part of his English inheritance.[25]

Yet Winthrop is not merely affirming traditional English theory. He Christianizes the inherited ideas so that they become something quite new, something more hopeful and far more grandiose than the traditional English theory. Winthrop looks to himself and his colleagues to establish a "city on a hill," that is to say, a new and exemplary kind of political community, going beyond any achievement of the Old World.[26]

For Winthrop the goodness of the English system of orders or estates does not rest simply on its antiquity, as the classical version of the theory of the English constitution had it. The goodness of the system of unequal orders rests instead on its connection to the divine order itself. Society, composed of different and unequal parts, reflects the character of the whole of God's creation, marked by "the variety and differrance of the Creatures." The composition of a whole out of very disparate parts shows forth the glory, power, and wisdom of God far more than a homogeneous universe could do. In the complementarity of different parts is also to be found the common good of human society: "that every man might have need of other." Winthrop seems to have partly in mind the social and economic division of labor, but also a moral challenge out of which can arise a deep bond between human beings, a bond going beyond mere mutual service and use: "That every man might have need of other, and from hence that they might be all knitt more nearly together in the Bond of brotherly affeccion." Equality is neither the beginning point nor the end point for politics as Winthrop conceives it. Rather his "modell" is one where the unequal orders of society are held together in harmony by "bonds of brotherly affection."[27] Neither Winthrop nor the other Puritans can be considered democrats, no matter how much in retrospect their institutions might be held to have contributed to the development of democracy. "There is no evidence," Stanley Gray concluded, "that Winthrop ever questioned monarchy as a valid form of government." Winthrop never spoke with any enthusiasm of democracy: "A Democracie is, among most civill nations, accounted the meanest and worst of all formes of government." Winthrop considered the Puritan polity a "mixt Aristocracie," and evidently considered that the best form, warranted both by English inheritance and scripture.[28]

Unlike the Declaration of Independence, Winthrop presents a political theology. His authorities are almost exclusively biblical, and, as one interpreter observed, "Winthrop never conceived of a political understanding which did not depend on religious teaching; he relied on scriptural and religious authority rather more, and secular classical writings rather less, than did his clerical contemporaries." This was apparently no mere affectation on his part, for he once blamed another speaker for his reliance on Greek and Roman authority:

> In his sermon he delivered many useful things, but in a moral and political discourse, grounding his propositions much upon the old Roman and Grecian governments, which sure is an error, for if religion makes men wiser than their neighbors, and these times have the advantage of all that have gone before us. . . . It is probable that by all these helps, we may better frame rules of government for ourselves than to receive others upon the bare authority of the wisdom, justice, etc., of those heathen commonwealths.

In place of the authority of "those heathens," Winthrop looks to the Bible.[29] One cannot understand or solve the political problem without the wisdom and help of biblical and specifically Christian materials. One needs to understand, for example, the role of love or charity in politics: the heathen believed politics was a matter of justice, or at best, friendship, but Winthrop insists on the necessity of love. The ground of love can be grasped only by those who understand the creation, the fall, and the new ground of love in the revelation of Christ.[30]

Winthrop's political thought thus differs from that in the Declaration of Independence in yet another way: not only does he begin with natural, or rather, divinely mandated inequality, including political inequality, but he also understands politics in the mode of political theology. Like the Pilgrims, he appeals to the biblical, the Christian God, and the central points of Christian theology. The Declaration, on the contrary, depends on an appeal to the God known by reason in and through nature. We see in the Declaration, therefore, a kind of appeal to creation, but none to the fall or the coming of Christ.

This is not a merely external dimension of difference, for everything peculiar to Winthrop follows from his appeal to these specifically Christian concepts. In the first place, his Christian understanding supplies him with both an analysis of why the ancient English mixed constitution has not succeeded in its own terms and points him towards a superior and novel solution. The way things were done in England will not suffice: "wee must not content ourselves with usuall ordinary meanes[;] whatsoever wee did or ought to have done when wee lived in England, the same must wee doe and more alsoe where we goe." He has one new or further "meanes" specially in mind: "That which most in theire Churches maineteine as a truthe in profession onely, wee must bring into familiar and constant practice, as in this duty of love[;] wee must love brotherly and without dissimulation, . . . wee must not look onely on our owne things, but alsoe on the things of our brethren."[31]

The Puritans must go beyond the practices of England because those practices have failed. The expedition to America occurred because life in England was fast decaying; in a widely quoted letter to his wife, Winthrop gave his first hint that he was considering emigration: "God will bring some heavye affliction upon this lande, [but] he will provide a shelter and a hidinge place for us and ours." Winthrop's foreboding sense of the evil fate awaiting England was not a bad forecast of developments that came to a head in the outbreak of civil war a decade or so after his emigration.

In the years just before his decision to embark for New England, Winthrop had been exposed to much of the disorder of the late 1620s, disorder that could only be taken as an indication of the imperfection of the ancient constitution. Winthrop's decision to emigrate and his hopes for a *novus ordo seclorum* no doubt grew out of his disillusion with the "old order of the ages" as he observed it during the 1620s. He came to see that the breakdown of the ancient mixed constitution reflected a fundamental defect in its very principle of construction. The task set for the ancient constitution, the knitting together of the disparate and unequal elements of the society into a community, was sound, but its typical means were quite incorrect. The only way to knit a society into "one body" is through its possession of the "proper ligamentes": "the ligamentes of this body which knitt together are love." A system of constitutional checks and balances, like the ancient mixed constitution, therefore takes the wrong tack; it is no surprise to Winthrop that the result was the supercharged contention of the 1620s.[32]

Although love is the required ligament, it is not at all easy to produce. Love is, indeed, natural to the human race in its original form: "Adam in his first estate was a perfect modell of mankinde in all their generacions, and in him this love was perfected." This happy original situation was disrupted, however, by the fall: "Adam rent in himselfe from his Creator, rent all his posterity allsoe one from another, whence it comes that every man is borne with this principle in him, to love and seek himselfe only."[33] The human situation thus has something of a tragic character to it; God has created and ordained a differentiated and unequal body of individuals and estates from which a whole akin to God's universe itself, or to an integral human body, must be made. But love, the ligament of this body, is lacking. Love of self monopolizes and drives human beings farther apart, rather than knits them together. The failure of the ancient constitution, and of pagan politics, follows inevitably.

Yet the tragedy is only temporary, and in Winthrop's moment, the moment of the revival of the true principles of Christianity, new or newly understood grounds for hope have appeared. "A man continueth" in the self-love to which he is condemned through Adam's fall, "till Christ comes and takes possession of the soule, and infuseth another principle[,] love to God and our brother." This love "cometh of God and every one that loveth is borne of God, soe that this love is the fruite of the new birth, and none can have it but the new Creature." The "new Creature," reborn in the love of Christ, is the only human being who can fulfill the requirements of successful political life. As Winthrop concludes: "This love is absolutely neccesary to the being of the body of Christ, as the sinewes and other ligaments of a natural body are to the being of that body."[34]

The Puritan political community must therefore be a "Company professing ourselves fellow members of Christ." Winthrop thus strongly defends the rights of the community to control its own membership; he supported laws limiting rights of immigration to those who bring "the true doctrine with them," and he generally supported (or led) efforts to expel the heterodox, like Roger Williams and Anne Hutchinson.[35] True doctrine is so important because a proper understanding of divine truth seems to be a necessary if not sufficient condition for Christ's "taking possession of the soul," and "infusing" it with the principle of love of God and of neighbor. Love of neighbor is difficult in the fallen state, for self-love dominates; when individuals look to others, they discover that "the great part of them are most unworthy if they be judged by their own merit" (as John Calvin put it). The pure Protestant faith teaches, however, that human beings do not receive the love of God or deserve the love of others for their merits: it is an act of grace alone, resting on the gracious love of God for humanity and promised through faith in Christ's redemptive act of love. So long as human beings focus on the merits of the other, the necessary love cannot be forthcoming. Love is for "the image of God" in others, "to which we owe all honor and love." Although all have the image of God, "it is among members of the house-hold of faith that this same image is more carefully to be noted, in so far as it has been renewed and restored through the spirit of Christ." The extreme demands of Christian love thus become possible:

> Assuredly there is but one way in which to achieve what is not merely difficult but utterly against human nature: to love those who hate us, to repay their evil deeds with benefits, to return blessings for reproaches. It is that we remember not to consider men's evil intention but to look upon the image of God in them, which cancels and effaces their transgressions, and with its beauty and dignity allures us to love and embrace them.[36]

Winthrop echoes these thoughts from Calvin quite precisely when he argues that:

> the ground of love is an apprehension of some resemblance in the things loved to that which affectes it, this is the cause why the Lord loves the Creature, soe farre as it hath any of his Image in it, he loves his elect because they are like himselfe, he beholds them in his beloved sonne. . . . Thus it is between the members of Christ, each discernes by the worke of the spirit his owne Image and resemblance in another, and therfore cannot but love him as he loves himselfe.[37]

Contrary to the image of the Puritans as dour pessimists, Winthrop projects a powerfully optimistic, "idealistic" image of new possibilities for political life, possibilities rooted firmly and exclusively in the Puritan-Protestant grasp of Christianity.[38] The hopes of New England, the original hopes of America as Winthrop voices them here, are simply remarkable, certainly more far-reaching than those of the men who issued the Declaration of Independence and then drafted the Constitution: their *novus ordo seclorum* continued to rest on the system of checks and balances Winthrop eschewed, and to aim at the securing of natural rights, themselves born and always rooted in primeval self-love, in "the selfish passions." Winthrop's statement on behalf of the Puritans thus shares as little, perhaps even less, with the Declaration as does the Mayflower Compact:

Where the Declaration appeals to "nature and nature's God," that is to say, is a form of natural theology, Winthrop appeals quite specifically to the Christian God and revealed Christian theology.

Where the Declaration affirms an original human equality or state of nature, Winthrop sees instead a divine ordination of inequality.

Where the Declaration affirms the ends of government to be the security of the universal and "unalienable rights" of human beings, Winthrop seems to know nothing of such rights, and sees the end of politics in serving God and seeking salvation. Where the Declaration mandates a universal and secular politics, Winthrop mandates a sectarian and religious politics, a good part of which will necessarily be devoted to the contentious and very difficult question of discerning just what God does require by way of service from us. The Declaration, by contrast, affirms the ends of politics in terms of rights—rights to life, liberty, and the pursuit of happiness. The understanding of the ends contained in the Declaration is just that expressed by Locke in his *Letter Concerning Toleration*:

> The commonwealth seems to me to be a society of men constituted only for the processing, preserving, and advancing of their own civil interests. Civil interests I call life, liberty, health, and indolence of body; and the possession of outward things, such as money, lands, houses, furniture, and the like.[39]

One task of statesmanship in a polity devoted to "civil interests" such as these is the encouragement of the increase of wealth "by established laws of liberty to secure protection and encouragement to the honest industry of mankind." Such a vision is alien to Winthrop: "if we . . . shall fall to embrace this present world and prosecute our carnall intencions, seekeing greate things for our selves and our posterity, the Lord will surely break out in wrathe against us and be revenged."[40]

About a decade and a half after the Arbella sermon, Winthrop discussed the topic of liberty, which helps bring out further the immense difference between the political thought animating the first American founding and that animating the second American founding. According to the natural rights philosophy, human beings possess an original and inherent liberty, which, as inalienable, is preserved even in the process of forming government. This liberty, as Jefferson explains, is a liberty for "innocent actions" only, that is, for actions that do not deprive others of their rights, or that do not interfere with the realization of the community welfare.

Winthrop is, by and large, an enemy of the liberty Jefferson affirms. "There is," he says, "a two-fold liberty, natural (I mean as our nature is now corrupt) and civil or federal." These two forms of liberty do not correspond precisely to Jefferson's discussion, for, according to Winthrop, natural liberty "is common to man with beasts and other creatures. By this, man, as he stands in relation to man singly, hath liberty to do what he lists; it is a liberty to evil as well as to good. This liberty is inconsistent with authority." The natural rights philosophy embodies quite a different understanding of natural liberty. The liberty right is not, in the first place, shared with beasts and other creatures. Human rights stand on special features of human nature, features that distinguish human beings from all other animals. Winthrop apparently has in mind liberty as a faculty *simpliciter,* a mere power, whereas within the natural rights philosophy liberty is a "moral faculty," that is to say, a right. As a right in the proper sense, it is not, and cannot be, a "liberty to evil as well as to good": it is not a liberty to evil or injustice, and it is not limited to being a liberty to good. This natural right to liberty is not "incompatible and inconsistent with authority," but its security is the point of authority.[41]

Winthrop recognizes a form of liberty that is compatible with authority and is moral in character. "It is a liberty to that only which is good, just and honest." This is not "natural liberty," but "civil" or "federal" or "moral," because it derives from or eventuates in the moral law and in "politic covenants and constitutions" between God and man or among men themselves. Winthrop elucidates the compatibility between this liberty and authority or even subjection in the example of marriage: "The woman's own choice makes such a man her husband; yet being so chosen, he is her lord, and she is subject to him." Liberty is the liberty to enter freely into one or another state of subjection. The one who so enters exercises his or her will only so far as to enter that state; the relationship so entered is not in any sense constituted by the wills of the parties, nor is the character of the relationship such as to seek to guarantee and preserve natural liberty. Thus Winthrop can say of magistrates that they are "called by" the people, but "have [their] authority from God, in way of an ordinance, such as hath the image of God eminently stamped upon it."[42]

Given his views of the origin and nature of political authority it is, perhaps, no great surprise that he resisted efforts by others in the community to control the discretionary powers of the magistrates. In a journal entry detailing the grounds for his opposition to a movement for determinate sentencing, this so-called forerunner of natural rights constitutionalism sounds far more like Sir Robert Filmer and the other partisans of divine right governance than like Locke or Jefferson.

> Judges are Gods upon earthe: therefore, in their Administrations, they are to holde forthe the wisdome and mercye of God (which are his Attributes) as well as his Justice: as occasion shall require, either in respecte of qualitye of the person, or for a more generall good.[43]

In accord with his conception of liberty, Winthrop presents a semicontractarian or covenantal doctrine that supplies the basis for many who accept the continuity thesis. In fact, however, Winthrop looks to a direct divine ordination as the origin of political (and other) authority, and as the source of the character and degree of authority within human relationships. Winthrop speaks of covenant in several different contexts and in several different ways. In the Arbella sermon, covenant is derivative and subordinate to divine commission: "When God gives a speciall commission he lookes to have it strictly observed in every Article." Winthrop gives the example of Saul, who failed to live up to "one of the least articles" of the commission God gave to him, with the penalty that he "lost . . . the kingdome, which should have beene his reward, if he had observed his Commission." The covenant Winthrop invokes is the acceptance by the people of the commission God lays upon them; it is a covenant because God binds himself to live up to his side—to prosper the people spiritually and otherwise—if they live up to their part.

> Wee are entered into a covenant with him for this worke, wee have taken out a commission. . . . Now if the Lord . . . bring us in peace to the place wee desire, then hath he ratified this covenant and sealed our commission [and] will expect a strickt performance of the Articles contained in it, but if we shall neglect the observacion of these Articles . . . the Lord will surely breake out in wrathe against us . . . and make us know the price of breache of such a covenant.

It should require no extended analysis to notice how far this notion of covenant is from the contractarianism of the Declaration. To mention just two points: Winthrop's covenant is between God and the people; the Declaration's is among the people themselves. Winthrop's covenant is to fulfill a special divine commission, set up for them as a new "chosen people"; the Declaration's is for "all men." The Declaration's compact is to establish rightful political power, dedicated to natural ends; Winthrop's is to dedicate the already established polity to a specific, nonnatural task.[44]

Winthrop also speaks of a covenant between the magistrates and the people in a 1645 speech defending himself publicly against accusations of arbitrary and extra-legal action.

> We account him a good servant, who breaks not his covenant. The covenant between you and us is the oath you have taken of us, which is to this purpose, that we shall govern you and judge your causes by the rules of God's laws and our own, according to our best skill.[45]

This notion of covenant is no closer to the contractarianism of the Declaration. It is an agreement between the magistrates and the people, not among the people in order to constitute political society. It sets bounds to the powers of rulers, but these bounds are much qualified by the commission Winthrop affirms to "rule" according to "God's laws"; it is in this very same speech that Winthrop insists, "So it is you yourselves who have called us to this office, and being called by you, we have our authority from God, in way of our ordinance, such as hath the image of God eminently stamped upon it."[46] Winthrop's contractarianism, such as it is, thus remains firmly within the context of a very different approach to the origin and purpose of political authority.[47] No matter how much he moves beyond anything in the Mayflower Compact by way of a general theory, nonetheless, his version of contractarianism remains quite distant from that within the natural rights philosophy, growing out of different soil and producing an entirely different politics.[48] The politics of the Declaration, beginning with the natural rights to liberty and the pursuit of happiness, contains a strong presumption favoring liberty; the politics of the Puritans, beginning with the distrust of natural liberty voiced by Winthrop, contains just as strong a presumption against liberty—thus all the legislation that has earned the censure of mankind as Puritanical. The tension helps to explain one abiding feature of American history and culture—the struggle between the liberal and the Puritan sides of the American inheritance, a struggle that does not make much sense if the continuity thesis is correct.

It is difficult, therefore, to agree with those scholars who see in the seventeenth-century Pilgrims and Puritans the originators of the fundamental American political doctrines of contract, consent, popular sovereignty, and the like. Winthrop and the Pilgrims do not, in a word, articulate "a new vision of political authority derived from agreements, covenants, and promises written into express compacts," at least not as these matters were understood in the second American founding.[49]

Lockean Puritans

Let us fast-forward almost one hundred and fifty years from Winthrop's sermon on the *Arbella* to Watertown, Massachusetts, at the end of May 1775. The battles at Lexington and Concord had recently occurred, and all the disorder had led the British to shut down the regular legal government of Massachusetts. An extralegal meeting of a "Congress" is assembled in Watertown, requiring, as tradition demanded, an election sermon from one of the colonies' ministerial luminaries. Samuel Langdon, president of Harvard College since 1774, is the eminence selected to address the political leaders of the colony at this moment of danger and decision. Representing a tradition from the fathers, he uses the occasion to berate his listeners for falling short of the fathers. The evil times on which they have fallen are due in part, he concedes, to "the present moral state of Great Britain. . . . *There is no truth, nor mercy, or knowledge of God in the land.*"[50] But, hitting all the chords of the classic Puritan jeremiad, Langdon blames his countrymen too:[51]

> But, alas! have not the sins of America and New England, in particular, had a hand in bringing down upon us the righteous judgments of heaven? . . . However unjustly and cruelly we have been treated by man, we certainly deserve, at the hand of God, all the calamities in which we are now involved. Have we not lost much of that spirit of genuine christianity, which so remarkably appeared in our ancestors? . . . Have we not departed from their virtues?[52]

Yet, plump in the midst of this appeal to the old Puritan fathers and the old Puritan ways is the natural rights philosophy of Locke and the Declaration of Independence. Although Langdon wishes to recall his audience of patriot leaders back to the "true religion" as present in "the purity and simplicity of the gospel," back to "the gospel of salvation," he nonetheless departs drastically from the example of Winthrop and other early Puritan political thinkers in failing to see in the Bible the indispensable and necessary ground for politics. "Thanks be to God," he says, "that he has given us, as men, natural rights independent on all human laws whatever, and that these rights are recognized by the grand Charter of British Liberties. By the law of nature any body of people, destitute of order and government, may form themselves into a civil society according to their best prudence, and so provide for their common safety and advantage."[53]

In the midst of his traditional appeal to tradition, Langdon imports the very untraditional form and substance of the Declaration's natural rights philosophy. The truths about politics are found in nature, via natural knowledge, the law of nature, and what concerns us "as men." This is no longer political theology, or if it is, it is political theology of the sort that Locke in his *Second Treatise* and Jefferson in his various writings patronized—natural political theology.

The deliverances of nature and nature's God according to Langdon are substantially identical to what Jefferson set down in the Declaration. Although Langdon develops the thought in even less detail than Jefferson's Declaration, nonetheless, the chief doctrinal points of the latter (and of Locke) are visible: natural rights prior to and independent of all human law, that is to say, natural rights as the endowment of human beings in a "state of nature"; the contractual or consent-based origin of government, the end of government as protection of these rights, and the "right to alter or abolish": "where one form is found by the majority, not to answer the grand purpose in any tolerable degree, they may by common consent put an end to it, and set up another." Just as Jefferson (following Locke) counsels prudence and restraint in the exercise of this formidable right, so does Langdon counsel his no doubt attentive audience to the same: "as all such great changes are attended with difficulty, and danger of confusion, they ought not to be attempted without urgent necessity."[54] Langdon agrees with Jefferson not only on the source and substance of the true political teaching, but on its (fortuitous?, providential?) embodiment in Anglo-American history: human laws are not the source of the rights of nature, but "these [natural] rights are recognized by the grand Charter of British Liberties."

Samuel Langdon, this heir of the Puritans, was by no means unique in combining Christian and Lockean argumentation. Indeed, the best and most thorough surveys of clerical writing and sermonizing of the second two quarters of the eighteenth century show how representative Langdon was, if not of the entire American mind, then at least of the mind of his fellow post-Puritan clerics. These surveys show both that the preachers spoke out regularly and vociferously on politics, and that they, like Langdon, spoke the language of Locke and the natural rights philosophy. Thomas Pangle conveniently summarizes the results of the researches of Alice Baldwin and Claude Newlin into the role of Locke in ministerial political thought:

> Baldwin's detailed study of the sermons and writings of the New England clergy leads her to conclude that Locke's influence, especially as regards

the political message of the preachers, was overwhelming: referring especially to Locke and Sidney, she writes, "all through the New England
colonies the ministers were helping to spread the theories of the philosophers and to give them religious sanctions." . . . Newlin shows in
some detail and with much fuller references how, in the course of the first
quarter of the eighteenth century, the "new philosophy" associated with
Bacon, Descartes, Boyle, Locke and Newton gradually came to predomi-
nate among the New England clergy.

Pangle tellingly restates Newlin's important conclusion: "The result was not
only a heightened regard for human reason, but a dramatic new openness to
'Natural Religion', which was founded on a philosophical, rather than on a
scriptural basis."[55]

The divines endorse Lockean political philosophy rather than the political theology of their fathers. How significant and deep-going a shift this is
becomes clear if we attend to the "theistic epistemology" that Locke and the
eighteenth-century preachers seem to accept in common. According to Steven
Dworetz, who has conducted the most thorough and up-to-date inquiry into
the connections between Locke and the American latter-day Protestants, Locke
and the ministers agree on the answer to the question of how "men know the
nature of God, or what God intends for or requires of them."[56] Both Locke
and the ministers "tended to treat natural and revealed law as two consistent,
complementary, and interdependent expressions of a single divine will."
Locke did indeed argue that reason and revelation, proceeding from the same
source and providing an account of the same world, must agree with one
another. According to Locke's official doctrine, however, the deliverances of
revelation may extend beyond, but never contradict, those of reason. Thus on
more than one occasion he says that reason may prove the existence of a god,
but not that of an afterlife. For knowledge of the latter, humanity must rely on
revelation.[57] In accord with this view, Locke often emphasizes the harmony
between the teachings of reason and revelation. For example, he says at
the opening of the important discussion of property in his *Second Treatise,*
"Whether we consider natural reason, which tells us that men, being once
born, have a right to their preservation, and consequently to meat and drink,
and such other things as nature affords for their subsistence; or revelation,
which gives an account of those grants God made of the world to Adam, and
to Noah, and his sons, it's very clear that God . . . 'has given the earth to the
children of men.'"[58]

Dworetz does not bring out so clearly, however, that Locke deploys this
doctrine to establish the self-sufficiency or even primacy of reason within the

sphere of moral and political philosophy. In the light of Protestant/Puritan political thought, it is jarring to see Locke develop his entire political philosophy in *Two Treatises* with no mention of Romans 13, the decisive text on politics for Luther, Calvin, and the early Puritans. So far as Locke appeals to theistic ideas in *Two Treatises,* he appeals to ideas he claims to be independent of scriptural revelation: the idea of a God, creation, and a natural law deriving therefrom.[59]

A Lockean journal entry, dated from 1681, shows how far Locke means to go: "Religion being that homage and obedience which man pays immediately to God, it supposes that man is capable of knowing that there is a God, and what is required and will be acceptable to him. . . . *That there is a God, and what that God is, nothing can discover to us, nor judge in us, but natural reason.*" From this principle, Locke draws the very strong conclusion: "Inspiration then . . . cannot be a ground to receive any doctrine not conformable to reason."[60] Reason must prove the possibility of revelation in general, the actuality of any revelation in particular, and, furthermore, must assent to the substance of any purported revelation.

In his political writings Locke applies this principle to supply him, at the very least, with a scriptural hermeneutic: biblical texts are to be construed, so far as possible, so as to agree with the teachings of reason, which, he decrees, is "our only star and compass."[61] So, when Locke does come to speak of Romans 13, in his *Paraphrase and Commentaries on St. Paul,* he construes it entirely differently from the way most Christian exegetes had. According to Locke, it validates only that conditional obligation to obey "the higher powers" that he found to be the truth according to reason in his *Second Treatise.*

Even more revealingly, Locke silently corrects the Bible when he cannot interpret it so as to cohere with his understanding of the rational truth. A good example is the passage quoted earlier from his discussion of property in the *Second Treatise.* Locke implies in this passage that reason and revelation agree in affirming "that men have a right to their preservation, and consequently to meat and drink." He cites the "grants God made . . . to Adam, and to Noah." But in his *First Treatise,* in the context of his polemic against the Protestant political theology of Sir Robert Filmer, Locke had emphasized the difference between the grants to Adam and Noah, and the absence of a right, according to the Bible, to eat meat in the entire period between Adam and Noah. That is to say, reason teaches that "once born" there is a right to meat; the Bible denies that there is such a natural right. So far as there is a right, it does not stem from nature, but from positive grant, and does not inhere in human beings "once born." Locke plays a complex game here and in related passages: he both calls attention to and blurs the differences between reason and revelation. In any case, Locke's ultimate position is clear: reason is *his* "only star and compass." His official doctrine on reason and revelation covers over how radical his position is. At the very least, Locke's view must be that much hitherto held to be revelation cannot really be so, for real revelations cannot contradict the teachings of reason.

Locke related reason and revelation at four levels, each progressively more challenging to received notions of orthodoxy; to recapitulate our discussion, these levels may be called, (1) the harmony of reason and revelation, (2) the self-sufficiency of reason, (3) the hermeneutical primacy of reason, and, finally, (4) the primacy of reason *simpliciter*. Dworetz establishes that many of the divines followed Locke at least to his third level. While the fourth level is obviously the most challenging to traditional doctrines, the other three also represent a significant transformation of Protestant thinking about reason and revelation, especially as applied to the sphere of politics and morality.

Even the first level, the mere claim of harmony, is challenging to many versions of Protestant thought, as is apparent in its opposition to the old formula: *sola scriptura,* i.e., the notion that the truths about religion, including one's religiously underwritten duties in the political sphere, must be garnered from scripture alone. Locke's official formula, on the other hand, echoes the understanding put forward by mainline Catholic thinkers from Thomas Aquinas to Francisco Suarez and Robert Bellarmine, and part of the initial Reformation impulse was to reject such accommodation—or dilution, as Luther would have it—of the word of God in favor of humanly construed truths. The elevated appreciation for the fall and the loss of human powers through the fall that characterized all forms of early Protestantism contributed to the Protestant distrust of reason and of the ability or rightfulness of raising reason to a level of authority equal to scripture.

John Calvin, the fountainhead of Puritan theology, shows how far the reformers were from Locke. Calvin concedes natural theological knowledge: "There is within the human mind, and indeed by natural instinct, an awareness of divinity." This natural knowledge or awareness has definite limits, however: "God has sown a seed of religion in all men, but scarcely one man in a hundred is met with who fosters it, once received, in his heart, and none in whom it ripens." God not only plants this "innate" awareness of divinity in the human bosom, but he has "revealed himself and daily discloses himself in the whole workmanship of the universe." Yet these evidences of God in his creation do not help: "although the Lord represents both himself and his everlasting Kingdom in the mirror of his works with very great clarity, such is our stupidity that we grow increasingly dull toward so manifest testimonies, and they flow away without profiting us. . . . It is therefore in vain that so many burning lamps shine for us in the workmanship of the universe to show forth the glory of its Author."[62]

Since the natural faculties fail us, another means of coming to knowledge is required: "in order that true religion may shine upon us, we ought to hold that it must take its beginning from heavenly doctrine and that no one can get even the slightest taste of right and sound doctrine unless he be a pupil of Scripture." Even more distinctly, Calvin concludes that "the human mind, because of its feebleness, can in no way attain to God unless it be aided and assisted by his Sacred Word." Calvin does not go so far as to deny all value to reason, but he certainly rejects the notion that reason operating on its own comes to an understanding of the world, of God, and of self parallel to or harmonious with what is taught in scripture. Calvin, in effect, calls for a hermeneutic the reverse of that of Locke and the eighteenth-century American theologians: not for reason to guide our interpretation of scripture, but for us to exercise our reason under the tutelage of scripture. The "revelation of God through faith" can serve as "spectacles" to sharpen up our woefully defective natural vision.[63] Calvin looks to scripture for the chief outlines of moral and political matters as much as for the truth about God or redemption through Christ.

The early Puritans for the most part followed Calvin's lead. The New England Puritans, according to Perry Miller, "insist . . . that the natural man, if left to himself, will not read the lessons of nature and reason correctly."[64] The rational faculties since the fall give but "little light." As Charles Norton put it, "The light of nature since the fall, compared with the light of the image of God, before the fall, hath not the proportion of star-light, to the bright sunlight at noon day. This indeed is but darkness."[65] To replenish the light, fallen humanity must have recourse to the Bible, which "must fill the place man made empty through his own folly," on account of which folly man "has thrown away his ability to profit from natural wisdom." Thus, according to Miller, the American Puritans arrived at just the same hermeneutic as did Calvin. "The Bible itself gives us the premises of reason. . . . We do not test the Bible by nature, but nature by the Bible. It is in this sense that the Puritan achieved, or thought he had achieved, the unity of faith and intellect, dogma and reason." In sum: "Reason does not discover fundamental principles in itself. The regenerate intellect does not fetch up truth from its own depths, like water from the well, but is filled with truth from the fountain of scripture."[66]

Early Puritan political thought, as we have seen, quite firmly embraces the position Miller attributes to it more generally; the fundaments of politics can be grasped only on the basis of knowledge supplied by scripture. Winthrop merely said in prosaic form what John Milton was to say several decades later in statelier rhythm. Referring to the wisdom of the heathen ancients, (Plato, Aristotle, and so on) in *Paradise Regained,* Christ asks:

> Alas what can they teach, and not mislead,
> Ignorant of themselves, of God much more,
> And how the world began, and how man fell
> Degraded by himself, on grace depending?[67]

So, when the divines of the eighteenth century endorsed the Lockean doctrine of the harmonious relationship between reason and revelation, the self-sufficiency of reason in the political sphere, and the primacy of a rational hermeneutic, they were enacting a substantial break with the reigning political theology of the previous century. Neither Locke nor the eighteenth-century ministers represented a straightforward continuation of traditional Protestant theism.

In order to understand the Lockeanization of Protestant politics, one must not only understand the political theology of the Puritans, but one must also see Puritan politics as a modification of the original Protestant understanding of politics. The inner meaning of the Puritan experiment lies precisely in this transformation of the original Protestant political teaching. The eighteenth-century Lockeanization in its turn can only be understood against the backdrop of the classic Protestant political theory. Thus we may identify three moments of Protestant (or quasi-Protestant) political thought relevant to our enterprise here: the original Protestant political theology, the seventeenth-century Puritan variant, and the eighteenth-century Lockean version.

The original doctrine was developed by Martin Luther in his doctrine of the Two Kingdoms, a doctrine confirmed in one way or another by nearly every major mainline Protestant thinker after Luther, including that all-important source for the Puritans, John Calvin.[68] Although Luther's central focus was surely not politics, nonetheless he directed much thinking to that subject and took some pride in his accomplishments there. "I might boast," he once boasted, "that not since the time of the apostles have the temporal sword and the temporal government been so clearly described or so highly praised as by me."[69] Luther's boast reveals several of the most striking features of his political thought: first, he praises the political very highly through establishing its specific dignity, and second, he sees himself in this, as in other matters, to be restoring a view held by the apostles, but since their time lost or corrupted.

Luther's central political conception can be readily stated in a few propositions:

1. There are two kingdoms, the Kingdom of God and the Kingdom of the World.

2. Both kingdoms are ordained by God. "God himself," Luther says, "is the founder, lord, master, protector, and rewarder of both [kingdoms]. . . . There is no human ordinance or authority in either, but each is a divine thing entirely."[70]

3. The Kingdom of God consists of those who are "true Christians." These are "all the true believers who are in Christ and under Christ."[71] The Kingdom of the World, on the other hand, consists, in the first instance, of those who are not true Christians, that is, most human beings.

4. The Kingdom of God is concerned with true or "saving righteousness," which comes only through faith. The Kingdom of the World, on the other hand, is concerned with "external righteousness." It is concerned with external deeds and external goodness, such as comes from conforming to rules or laws, and as derives from the imperfect or mixed motives which impel most men most of the time.

5. In the Kingdom of God there is no authority of a political sort, no human authority properly speaking at all. As Luther says: "Whatever belongs to heaven and the eternal kingdom, is exclusively under the Lord of Heaven."[72] While God retains an authority of a certain sort in the Kingdom of the World, here he also authorizes and ordains human authority. God gives this authority directly to the secular rulers and not indirectly through the church or spiritual authorities, or through the people. Luther is no kind of contractarian, and stands much closer to theorists of divine right, like Sir Robert Filmer, than to theorists like Locke or John Milton.

6. God has provided the Kingdom of the World as an "act of Mercy" for the unrighteous. Without it they would suffer from the wicked deeds they would commit. As Luther says, "[God] has subjected them to the sword so that . . . they are unable to practice their wickedness. . . . If this were not so, men would devour one another."[73]

7. The church is the earthly representative of the Kingdom of God; its only instruments are the divine word of scripture and the sacraments. Since it is concerned only with justification, and since justification is by faith alone, the church has no concern with "works"—external deeds—at all. It therefore has no power to regulate or control external deeds. Its concerns are purely spiritual. By the same token, since faith must be a "free" act, or is exclusively a gift of God's grace, the church can have no coercive authority in the realm of belief, either. Possessing control over neither deeds nor beliefs, the church has no proper claims to any coercive authority whatever. It certainly has no grounds to claim supremacy or supervisory jurisdiction over the temporal rulers.

8. The temporal rulers are the embodiment of the Kingdom of the World. Since that kingdom is ordained as a response to human unrighteousness and evil, it must use the sword to do its good work, for the wicked will be tamed only through the threat of the sword. Since temporal rule is concerned only with external righteousness, that is, deeds, life, property, etc., there is no incompatibility between its concerns and the exercise of coercive powers (as there is with the church and its work). Since temporal rule has no proper concern with saving righteousness or faith, it has no authority whatever over those matters. It cannot rightly use its coercive powers in this area to establish articles of faith, modes of worship, or similar matters.

9. While true Christians could, perhaps, live without temporal authorities, they are nonetheless obliged in the strictest terms to obey the secular authorities in all things within the sphere of their competence. Since the powers that be are ordained of God, Christians must obey them; since those powers are beneficial, and since Christians are obliged to do what is beneficial, Christians must support the temporal authorities. Indeed, since the temporal authorities are ordained by God, it is perfectly appropriate, indeed morally obligatory, for Christians to participate in political life.

10. The duty of submission is not unlimited, however. When the secular authorities command something outside their kingdom and its concerns, the Christian is obliged to disobey. If, for example, the emperor demanded that all Christians turn in their copies of the New Testament, all Christians would be justified in disobeying. Likewise, if the rulers command a clearly unjust act, e.g., to participate in an unjust war, the Christian may disobey. If the justice of the case is uncertain, the Christian is obliged to obey. Even where disobedience is permissible or required, resistance to rulers is not allowed. Use of force is never allowable against rulers, nor are attempts to supplant or depose rulers, no matter how tyrannical they may be.

One could summarize Luther's position on the two kingdoms with the now discredited phrase "separate but equal." The kingdoms are equal in the sense that both are ordained independently of each other by God. While the Kingdom of God has greater dignity, it does not stand in a hierarchical relationship to the Kingdom of the World. They are separate in the sense that they have separate concerns, that is, different kinds of righteousness; they have different means of operation (sword vs. word); they have separate jurisdictions over which the other must not step, that is, temporal vs. spiritual matters. Luther emphasizes the separate, even opposite, character very forcefully:

> God's kingdom is a kingdom of grace and mercy, not of wrath and punishment. In it there is only forgiveness, consideration for one another,

love, service, the doing of good, peace, joy, etc. But the kingdom of the world is a kingdom of wrath and severity. In it there is only punishment, repression, judgement and condemnation in order to restrain the wicked and protect the good.[74]

The separate character of the two kingdoms could be stated also in these terms: the Kingdom of God is the realm of freedom through Christ while the Kingdom of the World is the realm of subjection; the Kingdom of God is the realm of equality, (the equality of all believers) while the Kingdom of the World is the realm of inequality (through the distinction of rulers and ruled, and the class differences resulting from private property).

Like everything important in his thinking, Luther claimed to derive his doctrine of the Two Kingdoms from the Bible. The decisive text was Romans 13: "Let every person be subject to the governing authorities. For there is no authority except from God, and those that exist have been instituted by God. Therefore he who resists the authorities resists what God has appointed. . . . Therefore one must be subject, not only to avoid God's wrath, but for the sake of conscience also."

But Romans 13, with its clear endorsement of the temporal power, is not the only text relevant to politics in the New Testament and some of the others seem much less supportive of the political. For example, in Romans 12, Paul says, "Repay no one evil for evil . . . never avenge yourselves, but leave it to the wrath of God, for it is written, 'Vengeance is mine, I will repay, says the Lord.' . . . Do not be overcome by evil, but overcome evil with good." Temporal power is constituted above all by the execution of the very retributive justice which seems here to be forbidden. It would thus seem that the New Testament both underwrites and undercuts the temporal authority at once. Luther's doctrine of the Two Kingdoms emerges from the attempt to reconcile these two thrusts of the biblical teaching. The prohibition of all retribution applies to the subjects of the Kingdom of God. For themselves, they are forbidden to take vengeance, or to oppose evil with evil. So obliged, they would seem unable to participate in political life.

But the faith that justifies a Christian also produces "good works" as its fruit. These good works are not strictly speaking part of the economy of salvation—they do not earn salvation, but they follow from the right kind of faith. Luther describes these good works as "works of love," which means the Christian is impelled and therefore obligated to "love his neighbor" and to do that towards his neighbor that expresses that love. Given the wickedness of the world, love for the neighbor requires that the Christian support the secular authority for the sake of the neighbor. It requires not a grudging and unwilling subjection to the authorities, but an enthusiastic and loving submission. It requires not only submission but positive cooperation and aid. It is not only permissible but even obligatory for a Christian to be an obedient and enthusiastic citizen, or even ruler, of his polity.

The Christian is thus both obliged to the higher authorities, as in Luther's interpretation of Romans 13, and obliged not to seek retribution, as in Romans 12. That means that Christians are to be active and enthusiastic citizens— veritable scourges of justice—on behalf of everyone but themselves. So far is Luther from the point of view of modern politics, which sees the assertion and protection of one's own rights, liberties, and interests as the foundation of politics, that he even forbids the Christian from going to law for his own sake. A Christian may, on the other hand, do an act of love and become a soldier and kill with a good conscience on behalf of his ruler.

Luther adumbrates his doctrine of the Two Kingdoms in the first instance for the sake of the church and of faith. The temporal authorities are the beneficiaries of Luther's analysis of the causes for the deep and vicious corruption in the Roman Church. Luther differs from many of the other critics of abuses in the church of his time in that he links these abuses to a full-scale theologico-political analysis, an analysis which relates the abuses to the entire structure of the medieval church, including its theology. According to Luther, the church has gone wrong in confusing the two kingdoms. It is no accident that the first abuse Luther lists in his great list of abuses in his *Open Letter to the Christian Nobility* is that the pope, "who claims the title of 'most holy' and 'most spiritual', is more worldly than the world itself."[75] The church forgets its own office and intrudes into the Kingdom of the World to the detriment of both. This intrusion in turn is made possible by the church's having forgotten, or having failed to hold sufficiently tightly, to the chief doctrinal claim of Christianity— justification by faith alone—for only through trapping men in the belief in works has the church come to mix itself so perniciously in the Kingdom of the World.

Luther sees a very substantial reordering of the ecclesiastical-political structure following from his doctrine of the Two Kingdoms. The church must give up all claims to temporal authority in its own right, and it must also give up all claims to supremacy over the secular authorities. It must give up its claimed right to legislate rules and prohibitions on external deeds as required for salvation. The separation of the two kingdoms both follows from and enforces the doctrine of justification by faith alone, and thus is the precondition for the church's playing its part in the all-important and highest human task of seeking God.

Luther's separation of the two kingdoms is not intended to benefit and purify only the church, but to improve the condition of the Kingdom of the

World as well. This kingdom suffers as much from the confusion of the two kingdoms as does the church. Many, if not all, of the major political disputes of Luther's time and before stemmed from the conflicts and tensions between the church and the secular authorities, and derived, Luther believes, either from the efforts of the church to assert its supremacy over secular authorities, or to claim immunities for its persons and property, or to extract various resources from the secular authorities. Medieval history was punctuated by a series of dramatic conflicts between the ecclesiastical and secular authorities. In addition, Luther sees the church's claims as contributing to the difficulties the secular rulers have in governing their kingdoms well. The separate canon law and ecclesiastical immunity from ordinary civil law mean there is a "state within a state" in every Christian polity, that there are large areas where the secular rulers are unable to extend the rule of their law. Luther is especially distressed over the amount of wealth the church extracts from Germany in the form of indulgences and other devices that amount to taxation. This leaves the people poor and siphons off a source of revenue from the secular rulers. So Luther sees his doctrine of separation redounding to the benefit of the secular authorities as well, by curbing those and other practices which harm civil peace and derogate from civil authority.

Despite his confidence in it, Luther's political doctrine did not prove an unmitigated success, even within Protestantism. Because it failed to establish itself as particularly authoritative, we find later and other versions of Protestant political theology, like Winthrop's. Luther's own doctrine was itself unstable. He preached almost unlimited submission until 1530, when he changed his position somewhat in the light of threats to his followers from the emperor. He preached the illegitimacy of intrusion by the Kingdom of the World in the Kingdom of God, as in, for example, matters of heresy, but he shortly authorized a most brutal suppression of various "left-wing" Protestant groups that arose in the wake of his reformation. Luther, moreover, was unable to establish authoritatively the content of his political doctrine from the principles on which he based it. For example, Paul says, "Be subject to the higher powers"— but who are the higher powers? Are all who claim political power equally ordained of God? What does it take to become so? In one direction, this question led to the adumbration of doctrines of divine right of kings, extreme doctrines indeed in the hands of men like Robert Filmer, who implied that kings were so absolute that they might eat their subjects if they so desired. In the other direction, this question led to the doctrines of a John Milton, in whose hands the Reformation principles became warrant for regicide.[76]

These difficulties and others did not remain merely theoretical; they produced the tremendous fragmentation not only of Protestant sects, but of

Protestant politics. The liberal solution probably arose in England before it arose elsewhere, because in England the failure of the Reformation to find an authoritative or definitive political embodiment produced not only the mass migration to America of the Puritans, but also a civil war of major magnitude between two Protestant parties, a war which was only the most violent event in a century-long intramural struggle within Protestantism. Luther believed he had arrived at the true and in principle final political teaching. That belief proved false, and the political thought of the American Puritans, although showing many of the marks of Luther's stamp, was one of the versions of Protestant political thought that strayed significantly from Luther's formulations.

The remarkable character of the Puritan experiment shows up extraordinarily well when compared to Luther's doctrine of the Two Kingdoms. Although Winthrop and the Puritans pay more than lip service to the central Lutheran thesis of the separation of the two kingdoms, they modify the Lutheran position in several places, the overall effect of which is to consistently threaten to overcome the separation that was its hallmark. In Winthrop's sermon we can see this tendency in two particularly prominent places—with regard to the end of politics, and with regard to the necessary means of politics. The "work" he and his fellows have in hand, he asserts, is "to seeke out a place of habitation and consorteshipp under a due form of goverrnment both civile and ecclesiasticall"; that is to say, to establish Luther's two kingdoms in America. But unlike Luther, he does not attribute different ends to the two kingdoms; both have one comprehensive set of ends: "The end is to improve our lives to doe more service to the Lord[,] the comforte and encrease of the body of Christe wherof wee are members that our selves and posterity may be the better preserved from the Common corrupcions of this evil world to serve the Lord and worke out our Salvacion under the power and purity of his holy Ordinances." As Susan Power concludes, Winthrop "thought the major purpose of a government was to protect, aid, and advance religion and the church. The sword was under the control of the state, but . . . government existed to serve religious ends and purposes, as these ends and purposes were defined by the Church."[77] Exactly like the Pilgrims, and quite differently from Luther, the Puritans conceive their end nondualistically, "to serve the Lord and worke out our Salvacion." This is not merely the end of the Kingdom of God, but of the Kingdom of the World as well. "Serving the Lord" apparently does not mean only "working out salvation"; it includes, at a minimum, achieving that communal harmony and integrity in the human social world that imitates the divinely ordained harmony in the universe as a whole. The Puritans have a strong political and social dimension to their sense of religious mission. Unlike many other Protestant sects, they are not politically quietist because oriented solely toward individual salvation.

The means by which Winthrop envisions his flock achieving this "extraordinary" end is that equally extraordinary practice of love, grounded in genuine Christian spirit, that we have already noticed.[78] The Kingdom of the World in both its end and its means must draw very near to the Kingdom of God. Luther's Kingdom of the World thus loses its autonomy, self-sufficiency, and specific difference from the Kingdom of God. Although the Puritans retain a commitment to the formal separation of the institutions of church and state, there nonetheless exist right in the heart of Puritan aspiration and conception forces drawing the two kingdoms together.

The Pilgrims and the Puritans reveal the same underlying tendency of thought and practice. More striking, perhaps, because done so briefly and unself-consciously, the Pilgrims in their Mayflower Compact display that quality that will return to plague the entire Puritan experiment in America. In the Mayflower Compact the form of covenant migrates—in a very limited context and with a narrow meaning, to be sure—from the sphere of the sacred to the sphere of the secular. At the same time, the ends or purposes of the secular are relatively straightforwardly and unproblematically set as means to sacred purposes. In these movements are presaged the ironic fate of the Puritan polity—theocracy. Protestantism began with the rejection of what were taken to be the theocratic aspirations of Roman Christianity and then ended up reinstating a version of that very order. This happened, of course, not only in America, but also in Calvin's Geneva, and the battle for the soul of the Puritan revolution in England was in part a battle over whether the victory of Parliament in the Civil War would mean the institution of a theocracy there.[79]

But it could certainly be argued that theocracy was nowhere more firmly established than in seventeenth-century New England, for it was there that the connection between political power and the church was most tightly drawn via two crucial practices. On the one hand, political rights were limited to those who were full members of the churches—a relatively democratic standard according to the practices of the time, but nonetheless one that premised one's status in the secular society on one's status in the ecclesiastical society.[80] On the other hand, church membership was limited to those who could give persuasive testimony to the experience of saving grace, a criterion that both tended to limit the number of those who could become members and to put the judgment over who would be admitted to membership in the hands of the powers in the church, the ministers and the church elders. This was not, to be sure, a normal or formal theocracy in which the priests ruled; the Puritans maintained formal separation of the instruments of church and state by forbidding, for example, the holding of formal office in both institutions by the same person at the same time. Nonetheless, at a more informal level, the principle of the separateness of the two spheres was constantly overcome. This was reinforced when a law was passed in the 1640s requiring approval by the authorities for the formation of any new church congregations. That is, "rogue churches" would not be allowed to create new members and thus new citizens.[81]

As we have seen, eligibility for membership in the political community, to say nothing of citizenship, was defined in terms of the spiritual purposes of the community. Although the Puritans found it difficult to live up to the standards of Christian love Winthrop so hopefully outlined in his sermon, the process of governance also reflected a consistent tendency to break down the border between the spheres. Winthrop's *Journals* reveal how frequently "informal" conclaves of the ministers were called on to resolve difficult issues facing the community. Formal institutions do not always express the totality of political reality. Finally, the interpenetration of the secular kingdom with spiritual purpose guaranteed that the secular sphere would be constantly pressed into service for spiritual ends—establishments of religion, requirements of church attendance, adumbration of moral rules and regulations inspired by religious conceptions.[82] Even so great an admirer of the Puritans as Tocqueville commented on the character of their legislation:

> The framers of these penal codes were especially concerned with the maintenance of good behavior and sound mores in society, so they constantly invaded the sphere of conscience, and there was hardly a sin not subject to the magistrate's censure. . . . Such deviations undoubtedly bring shame on the spirit of man; they attest the inferiority of our nature. . . .[83]

Tocqueville's judgment is probably just, but he fails to recognize how much this legislation flows not from mere flaws of human nature, but from the specific character of Puritan principles and aspirations.

Just as the American Puritans represented a modification of the original Protestant political theology, so the eighteenth-century theorists represent a further modification, a modification involving the Lockeanization of the earlier Puritan politics. Ironically, perhaps, this Lockeanization was made possible by a partial reversion to the older doctrine of the Two Kingdoms.

The Lockean provenance of the transformation of Puritan thought appears particularly clearly in an election sermon by Abraham Williams, a pastor at the outlying church at Sandwich. According to Edmund Morgan, Williams was not one of the real luminaries of the era; he is memorable chiefly because of his "illustrativeness," which is to say, his representation of "the transformation that had taken place in Puritan ideas."[84]

Despite his lack of distinction, Williams preached the election sermon before the General Court of Massachusetts in 1762, and gave the assembled legislators a remarkably nuanced version of Lockean political philosophy. All the Lockean theses familiar from the Declaration of Independence are there.

Most significantly, Williams roots his political theory in the divine order exactly as Jefferson does. "The Law of Nature (or those Rules of Behavior, which the Nature God had given Men . . .) is the Law and Will of the *God of Nature,* which all then are obliged to obey."[85] Williams is emphatic that the core of politics derives from the "Nature God," not the God of Abraham, much less the God who so loved the world that he gave his only begotten son. The obligations inherent in political life derive from nature, not from positive divine command, not, for example, from Romans 13. Williams not only agrees in substance with Locke and Jefferson, but his entire style of argument is theirs. Gone is the scriptural politics of Luther and Calvin, Winthrop and Cotton.

Recognition of the Lockeanization of Puritan politics is necessary, for it is only on that basis that the truly interesting questions emerge. These are two: (1) Was the convergence of Lockean political philosophy and Puritan political thought all in one direction, or did Protestantism contribute something of its own, so that Lockeanism was also transformed in the process of constructing the amalgam? (2) What made possible this remarkable assimilation of Puritan thought by Locke?

Dependent as the ministers are on Locke, their political statements do often add elements to Locke of a loosely Christian character. In his momentous election sermon, for example, Samuel Langdon combined Lockean doctrine with the more traditional Puritan jeremiad. He was not atypical in giving firmer religious overtones to Lockean political philosophy than did more secular Lockeans such as Trenchard and Gordon, writing as Cato in England earlier in the eighteenth century. The ministers gave greater weight to three themes in particular than did Locke himself or Cato: (1) they attended much more to scriptural passages and argumentation; (2) they gave greater emphasis to divine providence and divine judgment; and (3) they dwelt far more on the practical requirements of sound religious practice in producing healthy politics. What is most remarkable, however, about the clerical modifications is how shallow they are, how little they really change or add. It would not be correct to say they are merely rhetorical, but it would be incorrect to say that Lockean doctrine is substantially christianized by their patronage of it.

The clerical appeal to scripture is most revealing. All the clerics use scripture far more than Locke had done, and probably all of them appeal to and discuss at greater or lesser length the crucial text, Romans 13, a text which Locke had mentioned not even once in his presentation of his political philosophy. As Christians and men of faith, as Protestants devoted to *scriptura,* if not *sola scriptura,* they needed to give some account to themselves and their congregations of how the political and moral principles they were taking over from Locke cohered with the touchstone of their faith. But what they say about biblical texts reveals how much has changed with their adherence to Locke. In a text which Luther had seen as the unanswerable basis for a duty of passive obedience and the divine ordination of "the powers that be," American preachers like Jonathan Mayhew found a right, or even a duty, to resist rulers.[86]   •

Samuel West of Dartmouth, close friend to many Massachusetts revolutionary leaders, and later selected to attend the constitutional convention, delivered an election sermon in 1776 in which he illustrates very clearly the Lockeanized version of Romans. He opens with a statement of "the nature and design of civil government" in order to "discover the foundation of the magistrate's authority to command, and the duty of subjects to obey"; to do that, he insists, "we must consider what 'state all men are naturally in,' and that is (as Mr. Locke observes) a state of perfect freedom." After outlining, mostly in Lockean language, the Lockean doctrines of equality, liberty, state of nature, natural rights, right to enforce the law of nature, the breakdown of the state of nature, the creation of government through consent, the limitations on the rightful power of rulers, and the resulting limitations on the duty of obedience in subjects, he observes, "This account of the nature and design of civil government, which is so clearly suggested to us by the plain principles of common sense and reason, is abundantly confirmed by the sacred scriptures." Notice, it is the commonsensical and reasonable (i.e., Lockean) explanation that comes first and guides the interpretation of biblical texts, "which have often been brought by men of slavish principles to establish the absurd doctrine of unlimited passive obedience and non-resistance." Romans 13, of course, is the chief of these texts, and West's thoroughly Lockean version of it reverses the old "slavish" reading.

> If the apostle, then, asserts that rulers are ordained of God only because they are a terror to evil works and a praise to them that do well; . . . it follows, by undeniable consequence [even though Paul himself says no such thing] that when they become pests of human society . . . they then

cease being the ordinance of God; . . . and in many cases it may be highly criminal to refuse resisting and opposing them to the utmost of our power.[87]

Scriptural materials not only receive a very different substantive interpretation in the sermons of the post-Lockean divines from their earlier readings by Luther, Calvin, and the others, but they also serve a very different function in the argument. Not the primary source of insight, they are discussed in order to confirm the teachings of (Lockean) reason and to clear any imputation of inconsistency between Lockean theory and biblical teaching. Once this has been accomplished, the biblical texts are then free to fulfill yet another, and politically very significant, function: the higher or more intense authority of religion now stands behind the cool rationalism of Locke. There can be little doubt that the enlistment of St. Paul in Locke's army had much to do with the fervor Americans of the revolutionary era brought to the political conflicts of the day.

Many explanations have been offered over the years for the remarkable affinity the New England clergy showed for Locke, most of which do not seem very plausible. The suggestion that the descendants of the Puritans found Locke so congenial because he and they were all theists fails to convince, not only because Locke's theism, such as it is, is far different from Puritan theism, but also because theism as such coheres with many different kinds of political commitments.

The suggestion that the ministers had a special openness to Locke because their traditional covenantal theology resonated with Locke's contractarianism is only slightly more plausible than the argument about theism. The Puritans were not, it turns out, so "covenantal" in their political theory as often claimed, and so far as covenant or contract did play a role in their political understanding, it was really quite different from the natural rights/social contract position of Locke and the Declaration of Independence, of the Massachusetts constitution and the writings of Jonathan Mayhew or Abraham Williams or Samuel West. This is not to say that contractarian motifs in earlier Puritan thought were entirely irrelevant. At the very least there was a familiar sound to the idea of contract, even if the natural rights philosophy appealed to a very different sort of contract.

It is often speculated, further, that the historical experiences of the American settlers made them particularly open to Lockean motifs—the idea of a state of nature, of an identifiable and deliberate beginning to political life resonating with their experience of the wilderness and the founding of new communities in a way it never could in stable, well-established, long-settled communities which seemed to "grow" and not to have been founded. On the whole this suggestion also fails to persuade. After all, the Puritans were closest to their "state of nature" experience in the seventeenth century, when their system of thought was most distant from the natural rights philosophy. Only as their communities came to be more settled and historical did the natural rights position come to be established.

As an alternative to these explanations I want to suggest that it is precisely the way Locke's political philosophy relates to the traditions of Protestant political thought that accounts for his remarkable triumph among the Americans. The most revealing text is an extraordinary pamphlet by Massachusetts-turned-Connecticut clergyman-turned-politician Elisha Williams. Williams was great-grandson of the leading Puritan minister of the founding generation, John Cotton, and, judging by his "The Essential Rights and Liberties of Protestants," a formidable thinker in his own right. He published his pamphlet in 1744 in direct response to a 1742 Connecticut statute aiming to curb the itinerant preaching of revivalist preachers during the Great Awakening. The law set limitations on who could lawfully preach where, and thus in effect maintained the monopolies of ministers in their own parishes. Williams wrote against this law in the strongest terms, deploying arguments for the most part from two quite different sources: Locke and Luther. The power of his argument derives from the way he fits those two sources together and produces a viable synthesis of them.

The question posed for him by the Connecticut law concerns "the extent of the civil magistrate's power respecting religion." Many strategies are open to one seeking to answer such a question, but Williams thinks it "needful to look back to the end, and therefore to the original" of the magistrate's power. For the treatment of "the origin and end of civil government," for an understanding of what these things "be in their own nature," and of "what reason teaches concerning them," Williams admits that he has but "given a short sketch of what the celebrated Mr. Lock in his *Treatise of Government* has largely demonstrated." Locke is a great authority, it appears, for Williams thinks "it is justly to be presumed all are agreed [in Locke's philosophy] who understand the natural rights of mankind." Locke is thus for Williams "the great Mr. Lock."[88] Williams implies that Locke's political philosophy already stands high in the minds of his countrymen. After Williams's pamphlet we begin to see the real dominance of Lockean theory.

Williams counters the Connecticut law with a two-pronged argument, the first clearly deriving from the *Two Treatises*, the second to some degree from the *Letter Concerning Toleration*, but also drawing on Luther's doctrine of the Two Kingdoms. The first prong approaches the question of the magistrate's authority in religious matters via a straightforward Lockean argument beginning with the natural equality of the state of nature and proceeding via the social contract to the issue of what powers rational actors would or could rightly give the political authorities they establish. Control over religious beliefs or practices being no part of the purpose for which human beings can be conceived to construct government, they would not empower the civil authorities to control religion. "So much of liberty and no more is departed from, as is necessary to secure . . . the ends for which men enter into a state of government." Williams correctly follows Locke in noting that the so-called executive power of the law of nature must be wholly given up, and "the power that every one has in a state of nature *to do whatever he judgeth fit,* for the preservation of his power and property . . . he gives up to be regulated by laws made by the society, so far forth as the preservation of himself (his person and property) and the rest of that society shall require." In sum, he concludes, "*no more natural liberty or power is given up than is necessary to the preservation of person and property.*"[89]

The rights of conscience are among those that human beings have no reason to surrender when they form government. "The members of a civil state *do retain their natural liberty or right of judging for themselves in matters of religion.*" The surrender of this right cannot be justified by the supposed need "to have unity of faith and uniformity of practice in religion" in order to have "peace and good order in the state." The latter is certainly a (or the) valid end of the entire process of governmental authorization, but enforced unity of religion is not a means to its achievement. Uniformity in religion cannot "be effected . . . by any such legal establishment of religion." Human beings differ too much "with respect to their understandings" for there to be genuine "uniformity of opinion and practice of religion." The best that can occur is "artificial conformity," and this can be won only at potentially great cost in oppression.[90]

Rational actors in the state of nature will notice the cost of this artificial, imposed conformity and will recognize further that "such unity, or uniformity in religion is not necessary to the peace of a civil state." Rational actors will accept as "natural and unavoidable" differences in matters of religion and will conclude from this fact that "the civil authority's protecting all in their just rights, and particularly this inestimable and unalienable one, *the right of private judgment* in matters of religion" is the best way to civil peace.[91] The uniform platform of rights can supply a sufficient basis for civil unity and peace, and the mutual acceptance and toleration of difference can further, not hinder, that peace. Indeed, the attempt to impose uniformity threatens civil peace far more than it ever contributes to its achievement. "Civil punishments have no tendency to convince the conscience, but only to inflame the passions against the advisers and inflicters of them."[92]

Rational actors in the state of nature not only would be entirely unwilling to authorize civil control over religion, but they would be morally incapable of doing so even if they did want to. The "natural liberty or right of judging" for oneself "in matters of religion . . . is an original right of the humane nature, and so far from being given up by the individuals of a community that it cannot be given up by them." It is, he says, "an unalienable right."

> This *right of judging everyone for himself in matters of religion* results from the nature of man, and is so inseparably connected therewith, that a man can no more part with it than he can with his power of thinking. . . . A man . . . cannot transfer the rights of conscience, unless he could destroy his rational and moral powers.[93]

In short compass we thus have the main outlines of the first prong, the Lockean prong, of Williams's argument. It is clear in his presentation that this argument is meant to be purely rationalist in character and perfectly universalist in scope. It makes no appeal to specifically Christian or Protestant doctrines, nor is it limited in application to Christians or Protestants. The "unalienable rights of conscience" belong to all human beings, of whatever religious profession.

Williams's second prong supplements the first with an argument of a quite different character. It is based on the principles of Protestant Christianity; it appeals to the Bible, and it establishes religious freedom in the first instance for Protestants, although by extension for others as well. It proceeds in the opposite direction from the first argument, establishing not the limits of the civil authority, but the necessity that the true Christian religion be entirely free from civil control.

That he has two prongs, and that these are the two prongs, represents another respect in which Williams parallels Locke's discussion in the *Letter Concerning Toleration.* In that text Locke had first explicated the "jurisdiction of the civil magistrate," showing that it does not extend to religious matters, and then "what a church is," showing both its immunities from civil authorities and the limits of its powers.[94] Despite this parallel, Williams's development has a rather different tone and spirit about it, deriving from the much heavier and more explicit reliance on particular themes of Protestant theology for the development of the second prong of the argument. He begins his examination of religion by affirming a traditional Reformation principle, harking back to Luther: "the sacred scriptures are the alone rule of faith and practice to every individual christian."[95] This contrasts strongly with the sway of rational principles in the political sphere.[96]

Williams draws this Protestant principle in an extremely individualistic and libertarian direction. "Now inasmuch as the scriptures are the only rule of faith and practice to a Christian; hence every one has an unalienable right to read, enquire into, and impartially judge of the sense and meaning of it for himself." From this follows for Williams a strongly separationist conclusion: "the civil authority hath no power to make or ordain articles of faith, creeds, forms of worship or church government." Nor do "the civil authorities have [any] authority to determine for Christians the *form of church government,* and that for the reasons before given, viz. Because this would be going beside the end of civil government, and because this is already done by Christ." By the same token, churches exercise no authority approaching the coercive powers characteristic of the civil rulers. Church structure, articles of faith, and forms of worship thus remain voluntarist and pluralistic. There is no power in civil or ecclesiastical authorities to definitively "determine this or the other ceremony or mode of attending them." Each "worshipping assembly" is to decide for itself how it interprets Christ's word with respect to worship.[97]

Williams, far more than the Puritans, and even more than Locke, moves toward a reinstatement of Luther's doctrine of the Two Kingdoms, separate, autonomous, and moved by entirely different principles of action. Williams calls attention to this side of his thought when he reminds that "Christ is the head of his church, a king in his owne kingdom." More than most other American Puritan writers, Williams makes explicit reference to Luther as well.[98]

As much as Williams reminds of Locke, Luther, and his Puritan forbears, his achievement can only be appreciated by comparing his position more systematically with each of the other three. This reveals the nature of the transformation that occurred in American Puritan thought when it assimilated or was assimilated by Lockean thought. The comparison with Locke can be quickly restated: Williams makes a clearer and stronger appeal to specifically Protestant principles to articulate the character of the religious sphere. Locke's *Toleration* is not entirely lacking such appeals, but the whole has a more secular and universalistic tone. Locke does not endorse Williams's claim that the only rule in faith and religious practice is scripture; in his *Reasonableness of Christianity,* he argues, in effect, that reason is as good (or perhaps a better) "rule" whereby to understand the principles of Christianity. He does say that scripture, properly understood, will harmonize with the teaching of reason, but given the ambiguities of scripture, reason turns out to be at least as authoritative as scripture.

Williams thus seems even closer to Luther than to Locke. That is not quite correct, however, for he makes three important changes in the Lutheran doctrine of the Two Kingdoms. Williams derives the principles of the secular or political sphere from reason (as delivered by that oracle, "the great Mr. Lock"); Luther derives the principles for the understanding and governance of the secular sphere, the Kingdom of the World, from scripture. Luther and Williams (and Locke) agree in the principle of the separateness of the spheres, but Luther derives the principles for both spheres from the Bible. Thus his political thought is a form of political theology, whereas Williams's is a form of political philosophy. Luther's depends decisively on texts like Romans 13, from which he derives a conscientious duty of nearly absolute obedience. Williams subordinates Romans 13 and other biblical texts on politics to the Lockean rationalist account. Williams, no more than Locke, relies on Romans (or any biblical text) to develop the main outlines of the civil sphere.

Williams departs from Luther not only in finding the principles of the secular sphere in wholly secular reasoning, but also in his description of the ruling principles governing the Kingdom of Christ. He endorses Luther's notion of *sola scriptura,* but he notably holds back from accepting Luther's even more central claim—*sola fide*—salvation by faith alone. Luther had derived the principles to govern the religious sphere from this very principle; and in Luther, this emphasis on faith alone had two rather important results for the fate of the separateness of the two kingdoms. On the one hand, Luther's Kingdom of God was much more monistic than Williams's—for Luther there is but one true Christianity. Each believer must have his or her own faith, but what each believer must do is have faith. And Luther knows perfectly well what faith that is. Because the one saving faith is all that is necessary, many other matters become more or less indifferent from the point of view of salvation and absolute religious duty—the whole sphere of works, to say nothing of matters of ecclesiology and ceremony. The complete immunity and freedom required in the Kingdom of God does not, it turns out, require complete immunity of the entire institutional sphere of religion from the civil authorities. Luther's doctrine of the separateness of the two kingdoms thus culminates, paradoxically, in an established church, largely under the civil authorities.

Williams's version of the doctrine of the Two Kingdoms resists this breakdown of the separateness and autonomy of the two spheres. Each Christian must judge for him- or herself what scripture requires of a Christian, but Williams leaves it perfectly open what that may be, either as to belief or practice. Nothing can be rightly mandated, except the freedom for each to judge for him- or herself and to act on the basis of that judgment. Nobody can decree what must be believed, and nobody can decree that all matters like church organization or ceremonial practices are essentially indifferent. The institutions and practices of Christianity must have complete autonomy from all authority, civil or ecclesiastical.

Williams's third modification of Luther seems to derive mainly from Locke. He affirms confidently that "the rule" for religion must be scripture, but that each Christian must be free to determine what that rule requires. Williams is far less confident than Luther that the one true scriptural teaching can be identified with any certainty. "Since God has formed the understandings of men so different, with respect to clearness, strength, and compass, and placed them in such very different circumstances; a difference of sentiments in some things in religion, seems natural and unavoidable." Nobody has a sufficiently privileged position to justify imposing a uniformity to overcome this diversity, especially since the one perfectly clear principle is that each person is personally required to take scripture as a rule. Locke had also emphasized this inevitable disagreement and the toleration for the opinions of others that ought to follow.[99] Since disagreement about religion is both inevitable and highly charged when it occurs, the only solution for both Williams and Locke is to leave religious opinion and practice per se entirely in the sphere of the private and voluntary, and to base public coerced life on rational principles presumably more open to agreement, or at least less explosive.

Williams's differences from his orthodox Puritan ancestors are at least as significant as his differences from Luther. The Calvinists accepted the doctrine of the Two Kingdoms in principle, but in practice they were even more emphatic in overcoming the institutional separateness of the two spheres. Their regime constantly faced the threat of falling into theocracy; the secular sphere was with little ado made subordinate to the sacred both with regard to ends and means. Rather than the purely autonomous missions Luther and Williams identified for the authorities in the Kingdom of the World, the Puritans saw the purpose of this world in terms of its service to the needs and goods of the next world.[100]

A particularly helpful source for understanding the way in which the Puritans moved toward bridging the chasm between the two kingdoms is the major work of Protestant theology called *The Decades*, published by Henry Bullinger of Zurich in the 1570s. Bullinger was a Calvinist who had much contact with the Marian exiles who became the inspiration of the English Puritan movement in the seventeenth century. There is, thus, a known chain of transmission from Bullinger to the American Puritans.

Bullinger considers the regime that Luther appears to, and Williams actually does, opt for: "many are of opinion, that the care and ordering of religion doth belong to bishops [or churches] alone, and that kings, princes, and senators ought not to meddle therewith." He quite decisively rejects this separationist position, however: "the care of religion doth especially belong to the magistrate; and that it is not in his power only, but his office and duty also, to dispose and advance religion." This involves, at the least, what Williams would consider an establishment of religion. The secular ruler must "provide to have the word of God preached to his people, and cause them to be taught the true worship of God, by that means making himself, as it were, the minister of true religion." More than that, the ruler is not to respect liberty of religion, either. "The magistrate [is] to make trial of doctrines, and to kill those that do stubbornly teach against the scriptures, and draw the people from the true God."

For Bullinger, the magistrate's duties with regard to religion ultimately root in the scripturally imposed prohibition of idolatry and the consequent "command to advance true religion." As he concludes in the most general terms, "the care of religion belongeth to the magistrate."[101] Bullinger has in turn merely echoed the views of Calvin, who asserts unambiguously that the duty of magistrates "extends to both Tables of the Law," that is, to religious as well as moral duties. "No government," Calvin insists, "can be happily established unless piety is the first concern; . . . those laws are preposterous which neglect God's right and provide only for men."

If anything, the American Puritans take the religious duties of the civil rulers even more seriously than Calvin and Bullinger. The Cambridge Platform of 1648, a document epitomizing first-generation American Puritan views, not only presented the doctrines but in many cases spoke the very language of Calvin and Bullinger. "It is the duty of the Magistrate," pronounced the sixth article of the Platform, "to take care of matters of religion and to impose his civil authority for the observing of the duties commanded in the first, as well as for observing of the duties commanded in the second table." The Puritans retain the form of the distinction between the inner and the outer, but the magistrate's authority extends to religious matters the moment they have an external manifestation. "The objects of the powr of the magistrate, are not things merely inward, and so not subject to his cognizance and view, as in unbeliefe, hardness of heart, erroneous opinions not vented; but only such things as are acted by the outward man." The magistrate's brief includes a broad array of evils afflicting the religious sphere. "Idolatry, Blasphemy, Heresy, venting corrupt and pernicious opinions, that destroy the foundation, open contempt of the word preached, prophanation of the Lords day, disturbing the peaceable administration and exercise of the worship and holy things of God, and the like, are to be restrayned, and punished by civil authority."[102]

Elisha Williams makes an extremely strong case for the incorrectness of the Calvinist-Puritan version of the relation between the two spheres, and along with that for the insertion of Locke as the most adequate account of the principles governing the secular sphere. That is to say, Williams makes a case for the convergence of Locke and a certain version of Protestantism; or, to use the language of John Rawls, he shows how Lockean political philosophy can be a "module" within a version of Luther's doctrine of the Two Kingdoms, or, perhaps more accurately, how Luther can be a module within the Lockean argument.[103] Williams especially reminds of Luther in his dissociation from the Puritan affirmation of the sacred as the end of the secular.

Williams helps to engineer a convergence between Locke and Protestantism; Lockean principles are no mere continuation of Protestant principles, either in their Lutheran or their Calvinist variant. Nonetheless, Williams does bring out a deep-lying contribution that Protestantism made to the ultimate emergence of liberal modernity of the Lockean sort. In the context of discussing the biblical text (Hebrews 13:17) regarding the duty of officials to "watch for the souls" of their subjects, Williams insists that this must relate to ecclesiastical officers, and not civil officers, for "care of the soul" is not within the ambit of the latter. It is not part of the authority of secular rulers, because within Protestantism the true "good of the soul" is understood entirely in terms of the soul's ultimate fate in the eyes of God. The "good of the soul" is salvation, and salvation cannot be effected by civil authorities. Some versions of Protestantism may assign religious duties to magistrates, but no version of Protestantism claims that the magistrate can serve "the good of the soul." Protestantism has effected a more or less complete disassociation of the "good of the soul" from political life. This is, of course, a major shift from the perspective of ancient political philosophy, or of the Christian Aristotelianism that dominated Christendom on the eve of the Reformation. Although the Protestant doctrines remain quite different, they may be said to prepare the way for the liberal focus on rights as the central category of politics; a rights emphasis effects the same dissociation of the fundamental norms governing political life from the good of the soul. Protestantism was perhaps a necessary prerequisite for the emergence of liberal modernity.

By any measure, the success of Lockean doctrine in conquering Puritan political theology was quite remarkable and suggests the presence of historical conditions that made eighteenth-century Americans in New England ripe for assimilating Locke. While a good deal more research than has yet been done is required to speak with anything approaching certainty on such a complex and elusive matter, several trends in the long-term sweep of developments within American Puritanism are certainly suggestive. The Puritan project began in a combination of confidence and hope—confidence that the one true ecclesiastical-political order was readily visible in the holy documents of the Christian revelation if only those documents were read in the right spirit and without the wrong presuppositions or by-interests; hope that churches and states founded on these principles, inhabited by godly men and women, could accomplish unheard of things, could build a "city upon a hill."

The confidence was soon challenged by the rapid emergence within the community of disagreements over theology and the principles of social, political, and ecclesiastical ordering. Roger Williams did not accept the community's way of constituting churches, nor its conception of the relation between political power and religious life. Anne Hutchinson and her many supporters questioned the entire delicate adjustment the Calvinist community had achieved among its various theological and moral commitments, frighteningly holding open to momentary view the possibility that the Puritan ordering was internally incoherent, the worldly and heavenly spheres hopelessly out of harmony with one another. They and other dissenters and heretics were banished, expelled, or denied admission. Others voluntarily departed to found new settlements revolving around other readings of the "plain meaning" of these plain doctrines, Connecticut and New Haven joining Massachusetts Bay and Rhode Island as independent centers of settlement.

So long as the hope remained strong, these challenges to confidence did not, apparently, lead to widespread loss of confidence. Hope in the form of enthusiasm led to redoubled assertion of the orthodox way: the Cambridge Platform of 1648, a product of the closing moments of the founding generation of New England, confirmed in strong and uncompromising terms all the important features of the ordering and norms worked out by the first generation. Part of that confirmation was a reaffirmation of the founding confidence: the magistrate's duties to foster the true religion extend to "such acts, as are commanded and forbidden in the word; yea, such as the word doth clearly determine, though not always clearly the judgement of the Magistrate or others, yet clearly in it selfe."[104] Those acts "clearly determined" extend, it will be recalled, to the full gamut of issues the civil authorities are to apply coercion to deal with: idolatry, heresy, blasphemy, corrupt and pernicious opinion, and so on. Yet, perhaps most remarkable about this provision of the Platform is the oddly tense notion that although neither the magistrates nor others may recognize these matters as the plain meaning of "the word," they are "yet clearly in it selfe." This represents, on the one hand, continuing institutional ascendancy of the clergy—the operational meaning of "clearly in it selfe" must be, "found to be so by the experts"; it represents, on the other hand, the community's efforts to hold on to its confidence in the wake of the confidence-challenging events of the decade and a half before. Even though not everyone sees the clarity of what is "clear in it selfe," it is clear nonetheless. So long as the hope remained strong, the confidence could withstand challenge.

Over time, however, enthusiasm and hope for extraordinary things waned. The most universal and cosmic forces combined to undermine Puritan hope and Puritan enthusiasm. Perry Miller has emphasized the irony of the Puritan experience in space: these settlers came to America as an offshoot of international Calvinism; they saw themselves as a model for the Christian church and state at home; they were not initially a provincial backwater, but a vanguard. With the coming of the Civil War and the triumph of Puritan forces in England, their hopes seemed to be nearing fulfillment: the way was open or opening to the installation of the models of church and state they had pioneered in England itself. Yet developments at home went in quite another direction: Cromwell instituted a regime of toleration and backed away from the hopes for a Calvinist commonwealth that inspired the Americans.[105] The American Puritans were convinced their English peers had taken a wrong turn, but it had to become apparent to them that the fracturing of their own order, which they had resolved through sending dissidents out into the wilderness, was a yet more severe problem in England, where the variety of sects and alternatives was much greater, and where the wilderness solution was not so readily available. The godly commonwealth proved unattainable in England, and since the hopes of the Americans were never merely for themselves as an isolated people, the possibilities they had been pursuing appeared to recede from grasp just when they seemed closest to realization. The complete and utter failure of the Puritan Commonwealth achieved official and public recognition in the restoration of the old order in England in 1660, the restoration of the Stuart monarchy, and the Church of England as it had been, complete with bishops. With the Restoration, the American Puritans were more isolated than before—if not physically, then in terms of aspiration. No set of hopes or enthusiasms could withstand the disappointments the parallel history of England inflicted in those years.

Simultaneously, time buffeted the New Englanders as well. Many historians have detailed the generational changing of the guard in New England. The original settlers were certainly classic cases of an "intentional community"— men and women with a mission, with a belief in, a hope for, an enthusiasm about, and a commitment to a task for which they would and did suffer nearly any hardship, tolerate nearly any deprivation. That commitment made their settlements successful beyond any European settlements yet planted in the New World. The hopes and commitments of the first generation were born of the enthusiasms of the early seventeenth century in Europe—the international Calvinist movement, the unleashing of reform zeal in England in those years, the strength added by opposition, conflict, the arousal of spirited resistance.

The younger generation lacked these formative experiences and, the evidence shows, cooled in their enthusiasm. A striking instance is the so-called "Half-Way Covenant" of 1662, a facing up by the community to the fact that the children of the original settlers were not demonstrating the same intense religious enthusiasm, the same testimonials of personal faith and conversion that had been the basis at first for church membership. Church membership, and along with that, eligibility for political privileges, became a far more external matter—descendants of members became eligible for membership in a compromised or lesser, yet real, way.[106] With the waning of enthusiasm went the waning of the extraordinary hopes of the first generation. With the waning of hope went the resistance to challenges to confidence. The Puritan mission was no longer so clear cut, and the biblical warrant no longer so visible for all—or perhaps any—to see.

In the later years of the seventeenth century Puritan thinkers, if they can still be rightly called such, turned increasingly toward natural religion as a supplement, if not a replacement, for the older scriptural theology. With that came a turn away from some of the more stringent doctrines of the old Puritanism—predestination, the strict line between faith and works, the stringency of politically enforced discipline.[107] According to Claude Newlin and to Perry Miller, it was apparently in this context that Locke first began to make inroads on "the New England Mind," as the philosopher who knew the map of the human mind and outlined both the limitations and possibilities of human knowledge, and as the purveyor of a "rational christianity" related to the Bible, yet deploying reason all along the way to guide the interpretation of that ambiguous book.[108] That Locke had become the most celebrated philosopher in Europe surely did not hurt; it also did not hurt that Locke had been allied with the Whigs and had defended the Glorious Revolution against the Stuarts, traditional enemies to the Puritans in England, and new enemies now because of James II's efforts to reorganize and thus reduce the autonomy of the New England colonies.[109]

It would be misleading to draw the history of New England as a one-directional ebbing of religious enthusiasm. That was not so, as the very occasion for Elisha Williams's treatise serves to remind. In the 1740s, the largest of a series of religious revivals, the Great Awakening, occurred. New England was swept with a renewed enthusiasm for "New Light" preaching, an enthusiasm seen as a threat and, perhaps, an embarrassment by mainline churchmen, who attempted to control the new preaching via the law Williams was protesting. The revivalism of the 1740s, like latter-day revivalism in general, was not the community-oriented, even political thing, the old Puritanism was, however. It concerned the individual and his or her faith and relationship to God. The revived religious enthusiasm of the eighteenth century, in other words, was concerned exclusively with Luther's Kingdom of God. It did not renew Puritan social and political commitment to remake the public sphere in the image of Calvinism.

Williams's version of Christian Lockeanism was an ideal response to this situation. The secular sphere was affirmed to have its own autonomous principles, rooted in reason, and consistent with the Kingdom of Christ largely through keeping a strict line of separation from it. Room had been made for each to be a module in the other. Thus Americans were able to bring their still lively religious sensibilities to the sphere of politics, but in the service of a substantive politics very different from the traditional political teachings of Christianity. The natural rights philosophy, while not itself a Christian philosophy or even particularly descended from Christian positions, was able to win the support of American Christians and Christianity. Thus began that potent alliance Tocqueville noticed and all American politics has attested to for two centuries in what Robert Bellah and others have spoken of as the American civil religion. The result has been remarkable—a society in which religion has been supportive of an essentially secular political orientation and in which private and public morality both have derived salutary aid from deep-flowing religious impulses. Religion has been supportive of the secular sphere, and the secular sphere respectful and mildly supportive of the sacred, all within a context of a real separation of church and state and a very wide protection for freedom of religion.

Although the history of political religion in America is more complex than can reasonably be surveyed here, nevertheless Tocqueville's general view seems largely correct—America has worked best when the convergence between liberal modern (Lockean) politics and religion has held most tensionlessly. American politics seems beset by its gravest moments of self-doubt and sense of crisis when the two fall into disharmony and tension, as is the case in the late twentieth century. However, this is surely not the first time such tensions have existed, and American culture has in the past shown the capacity to reforge the ties between religion and liberal politics, and such may be possible once again.

The alliance between religion and liberal philosophy in America was not at all an unwelcome development to the main sponsors of the modern liberal orientation. Both Locke and Jefferson, to take two particularly important examples, insisted that modernist liberal politics required the support of religion. As Locke put it, since "the greatest part cannot *know*, . . . they must believe." They cannot know the full ground of morality and rights. Most human beings lack the time and, perhaps, the ability to follow demonstrations such as might supply the philosophic ground for rights. "You may as soon hope to have all the day-labourers and tradesmen, the spinsters and dairy maids, perfect mathematicians, as to have them perfect in ethics this way." The only effective form of popular ethics is an authoritative, i.e., religious ethics.[110] Jefferson made the point in his *Notes on Virginia*: "And can the liberties of a nation be thought secure when we have removed their only firm basis, a conviction in the minds of the people that these liberties are the gift of God? That they are not to be violated but with his wrath?"[111]

NOTES

This essay is based on material in *The Natural Rights Republic: Studies in the Foundation of the American Political Tradition*, by Michael P. Zuckert (Notre Dame, Ind.: University of Notre Dame Press, 1996).

1. Cf. Jeffrey Poelvoorde, "American Civil Religion," in *How Does the Constitution Protect Religious Freedom?* ed. Robert A. Goldwin and Arthur Kaufman (Washington, D.C., 1979).

2. Alexis de Tocqueville, *Democracy in America* I, ed. J. P. Mayer (Garden City, N.Y., 1969), 1.2.

3. Clinton Rossiter, *The Political Thought of the American Revolution* (New York, 1963), 8.

4. Quoted in Perry Miller and Edward Johnson, *The Puritans* I (New York, 1938), 199; John Winthrop, "A Modell of Christian Charitie," in *Puritan Political Ideas,* ed. Edmund S. Morgan (Indianapolis, 1965), 93.

5. Charles McLaughlin, *The Foundations of American Constitutionalism* (New York, 1961), 17–19; Edmund S. Morgan, *Visible Saints: The History of a Puritan Idea* (Ithaca, N.Y., 1965), 26, 64, 77.

6. William Bradford, *History of Plimoth Plantation*, in Miller and Johnson, *Puritans* I, 101–2.

7. Morgan speaks of the Reformation-generated impulse to contract in both church and state. *Visible Saints,* 29; see also McLaughlin, *Foundations,* 20.

8. Willmoore Kendall and George Carey, *The Basic Symbols of the American Political Tradition* (Baton Rouge, La., 1970), 8, 151.

9. Kendall and Carey, *Basic Symbols*, 12, 83, 84.

10. For an example of a church covenant, see Donald Lutz, *The Origins of American Constitutionalism* (Baton Rouge, La., 1988), 25.

11. Lutz (*Origins*, 25–26) gives a detailed and helpful account of the parallels between the standard church covenant and the Mayflower Compact. He sees in the Declaration of Independence many of the same elements (*Origins*, 115–16).

12. Kendall and Carey, *Basic Symbols*, 31, 36, 77; cf. Lutz, *Origins*, 118. Lutz concedes that the invocatory language in the Declaration "stops short" of what would be expected of a theistic covenant (*Origins*, 124).

13. See Gordon Wood, "The Trials and Tribulations of Thomas Jefferson," in *Jeffersonian Legacies*, ed. Peter Onuf (Charlottesville, Va., 1993), 403. For Jefferson, "as long as Americans believed certain things [the Declaration's truths], they remained Americans."

14. Kendall and Carey, *Basic Symbols*, 32; Lutz, *Origins*, 31.

15. On the parallel situation for the Pisquataqua combination, see Lutz, *Origins*, 30–31.

16. See Lutz, *Origins*, 121: the Declaration "created a new model as well as a universally valid justification for building political societies."

17. See Kendall and Carey, *Basic Symbols*, 39: "Equality in any meaning of the term that would be acceptable to the custodians of our official literature, is wholly absent from the vocabulary of the authors of the compact."

18. Thus Kendall and Carey overstate the parallels when they assert that the Declaration's doctrine of consent is "implicitly" affirmed in the Mayflower Compact (*Basic Symbols*, 42).

19. See Paul Rahe, *Republics Ancient and Modern* (Chapel Hill, N.C., 1992), 357, for a similar comparison of the ends of government as revealed in the two documents.

20. Kendall and Carey, *Basic Symbols*, 38.

21. The charter can be found in Henry Steele Commager, *Documents in American History* I (New York, 1963), 16–18.

22. There is no documentary evidence that Winthrop delivered the sermon, but given its character—and his penchant for sermonizing—it is more than likely that he did deliver it aboard ship. See Lee Schwenninger, *John Winthrop* (Boston, 1990), 42, for conjectures on the circumstances of the sermon. There is general agreement that this sermon is the most important of Winthrop's statements and perhaps the most important American Puritan political statement.

23. Schwenninger, *Winthrop*, 42–44, shows how Winthrop's speech conforms to standard formal patterns of Puritan sermons.

24. Winthrop, "Modell," 76; see Miller and Johnson, *Puritans*, 193: "There was no idea of the equality of all men."

25. Consider the discussion between Lord Say and Seal and John Cotton for an indication of how widespread this beginning point was, but also of its limits in the American context. See Morgan, *Puritan Political Ideas*, 161–73.

26. Winthrop, "Modell," 93; Wilson Carey McWilliams, *The Idea of Fraternity in America* (Berkeley, Calif., 1973), 136.

27. McWilliams, *Fraternity,* 76–77.

28. Stanley Gray, "The Political Thought of John Winthrop," *New England Quarterly* 3 (1930): 685.

29. McWilliams, *Fraternity,* 133; Schwenninger, *Winthrop,* 42; Rossiter, *Political Thought,* 8.

30. Winthrop, "Modell," 87–89; see Susan M. Power, *Before the Convention: Religion and the Founding* (Lanham, Md., 1984), 10: Winthrop "placed his primary trust in the presence of charity and love in men's hearts."

31. Winthrop, "Modell," 91.

32. McWilliams, *Fraternity,* 136.

33. Winthrop, "Modell," 86; McWilliams, *Fraternity,* 133–34.

34. McWilliams, *Fraternity,* 86, 89; on the role of love, see Loren Baritz, *City on a Hill* (New York, 1961), 15–17, 23.

35. McWilliams, *Fraternity,* 90; Winthrop, "A Declaration in Defense of an Order of Court Made in May, 1637," in Morgan, ed., 146.

36. John Calvin, *Institutes of the Christian Religion,* ed. John T. McNeill (Philadelphia, 1960), III, 7.6.

37. Winthrop, "Modell," 87.

38. See Schwenninger, *Winthrop,* 44: Winthrop's is an "idealistic" attempt to create a "perfect church-state."

39. John Locke, *Letter Concerning Toleration,* in *Political Writing of John Locke,* ed. David Wootton (New York, 1993), 393.

40. Locke, *Two Treatises of Government,* ed. Peter Laslett (Cambridge, 1960), 42; Winthrop, "Modell," 92.

41. Winthrop, "Journal," in Morgan, ed., 138.

42. Ibid., 137.

43. Winthrop, "On Arbitrary Government," in Morgan, ed., 152.

44. Winthrop, "Modell," 91–92.

45. Winthrop, "Journal," 138.

46. Ibid., 137, 138.

47. Winthrop made one other statement of a contractarian sort that appears to be much closer to the natural rights position; he says that "no common weale can be founded but by free consent," and affirms that "no man hath lawfull power over another, but by birth or consent" ("Journal," 144, 145). These claims could be taken to point toward something more like the philosophy of the Declaration, as Gray, for example, does, but several considerations speak against reading them this way: (1) these assertions are also consistent with the many different contractarianisms discussed in the text; (2) they are not joined here with any other of the key elements of the natural rights philosophy, particularly natural rights themselves; (3) the context of Winthrop's statement is a speech defending the exclusion of such immigrants as the magistrates conclude will not fit well into the community, "such as come and bring not the true doctrine with

them." As we have seen, this is related for Winthrop to the special tasks and possibilities of the Puritan commonwealth, notions entirely foreign to the natural rights philosophy.

48. John Cotton, the important Boston minister of the first Puritan generation in Massachusetts, is often held to have purveyed a fuller-bodied contractarianism than that to be found in Winthrop. (See McLaughlin, *Foundations,* 68.) In a sermon on politics, Cotton stated, for example: "It is fit . . . for the people, in whom fundamentally all power lyes, to give as much power as God in his word gives to men." This is not in fact very different from Winthrop's position, and certainly not the same as the doctrine in the Declaration. The similarity to Winthrop is visible in Cotton's appeal to the same analogy Winthrop had used. "It is good for the Wife to acknowledge all power and authority to the Husband, and for the Husband to acknowledge honour to the Wife, but still give them that which God hath given them, and no more nor lesse." Human beings in their liberty enter into authority relations that God has already ordained and drawn the outlines of. Humans have a secondary power (and task) of ratifying or recognizing the divinely ordained outlines. The source of human knowledge of the divine pattern in these authority relations is "God's word." On all these counts, Cotton essentially agrees with Winthrop and differs from the Declaration.

49. Power, *Before the Convention,* 19; cf. 79.

50. Samuel Langdon, "Government Corrupted by Vice, and Recovered by Righteousness," in Morgan, ed., 361. Emphasis in original.

51. On the jeremiad, see Perry Miller, *From Colony to Province* (Cambridge, Mass., 1953), 27–39; Sacvan Bercovitch, *The American Jeremiad* (Madison, Wis., 1978), 23–26; Edmund Morgan, "The Puritan Ethic and the American Revolution," *William and Mary Quarterly* 64 (January 1969): 6.

52. Langdon, "Government Corrupted by Vice," 364–65.

53. Ibid., 365, 367.

54. Ibid., 367–68.

55. Thomas Pangle, *The Spirit of Modern Republicanism* (Chicago, 1988), 22–23.

56. Steven Dworetz, *The Unvarnished Doctrine: Locke, Liberalism, and the American Revolution* (Durham, N.C., 1990), 138.

57. For Locke's official theory, see *An Essay concerning Human Understanding,* ed. Peter H. Nidditch (Oxford, 1990), IV xviii–xix; *The Reasonableness of Christianity,* ed. George Erwing (Chicago, 1965); for discussion, see Zuckert, "Locke and the Problem of Civil Religion," in *The Moral Foundations of the American Republic,* ed. Robert Horwitz (Charlottesville, Va., 1986).

58. *Two Treatises* II, 25.

59. See Zuckert, *Natural Rights and the New Republicanism* (Princeton, 1994), chapters 7–9 for a discussion of the workmanship argument and its tentative role in Locke's larger argument.

60. Locke, "Inspiration," in Wootton, *Political Writings,* 238, 239. Emphasis added.

61. *Two Treatises* I, 58.

62. Calvin, *Institutes,* I, 3.1; I, 4.1; I, 5.1, 11, 14.

63. Ibid., I, 5.14; I, 6.2, 4; II, 8; III, 19; IV, 20.

64. Miller, *The New England Mind,* vol. 2: *From Colony to Province,* 52.

65. Ibid., 52.

66. Ibid., 52, 54–55.

67. John Milton, *Paradise Regained,* in *Complete Poems and Major Prose,* ed. Merritt Y. Hughes (New York, 1957), 309–13; for further discussion, see Zuckert, *Natural Rights and the New Republicanism,* 83–84.

68. See Calvin, *Institutes,* III, 19.15.

69. Martin Luther, *Whether Soldiers, Too, Can Be Saved,* in *Works of Martin Luther* V, trans. C. M. Jacobs (Philadelphia, 1931), 46:95.

70. Ibid., 46:100.

71. Martin Luther, *Secular Authority: To What Extent It Should Be Obeyed,* in *Works of Martin Luther* III, trans. J. J. Schindel (Philadelphia, 1931), 45:88.

72. Ibid., 45:111.

73. Ibid., 45:90–91; Martin Luther, *Open Letter on a Hard Book Against the Peasants,* in *Works of Martin Luther* IV, trans. C. M. Jacobs (Philadelphia, 1931), 46:71–73.

74. Luther, *Open Letter on a Hard Book,* 46:69–70.

75. Luther, *An Open Letter to the Nobility of the German Nation,* in *Three Treatises,* ed. and trans. C. M. Jacobs, A. T. H. Steinhaeuser, and H. A. Lambert (Philadelphia, 1947), 27.

76. See Zuckert, *Natural Rights and the New Republicanism,* 29–94.

77. Power, *Before the Convention,* 7.

78. Ibid., 71.

79. On the tendency to theocracy within Calvinist politics, see J. W. Gough, *The Social Contract* (Oxford, 1957), 85; Duncan Forrester, "Luther and Calvin," in *A History of Political Philosophy,* eds. Leo Strauss and Joseph Cropsey (Chicago, 1982), 328–29; Morgan, *Puritan Political Ideas,* xxix, xxxi; Baritz, *City,* 23, 24; Gray, "Political Thought," 698–702; for an important caveat, see Edmund S. Morgan, *The Puritan Dilemma: The Story of John Winthrop* (Boston, 1958), 95–96, 163; on indirect influence of clergy, 163–64.

80. See Miller and Johnson, *Puritans* I, 128–29, 135, 191–92; Edward Johnson, *Wonder-Working Providence,* in Miller and Johnson I, 151.

81. Morgan, *Visible Saints,* 101–5; Morgan, *Puritan Dilemma,* 84–100.

82. See Morgan, *Inventing the People* (New York, 1988), 141; Perry Miller, *Errand into the Wilderness* (Cambridge, Mass., 1956), 32–35.

83. Tocqueville, *Democracy* I, 1, 2 (42–43). Also see Massachusetts Body of Liberties, Art. 94. For an account of theocratic tendencies as late as 1773, see Isaac Backus, "An Appeal to the Public for Religious Liberty," in *Political Sermons of the Founding Era,* ed. Ellis Sandoz (Indianapolis, 1991), 339–62; a crusty account is in Albert Jay Nock, *Our Enemy, the State* (Delavan, Wis., 1963), 62 and 62n.

84. Morgan, *Puritan Political Ideas,* 331.

85. Abraham Williams, "An Election Sermon," in *American Political Writing during the Founding Era,* eds. Charles S. Hyneman and Donald S. Lutz (Indianapolis, 1983), 337 (emphasis in the original). See also "The *Law of Nature,* which is the Constitution of the God of Nature, is universally obliging." Ibid., 348).

86. See Dworetz, *Unvarnished Doctrine,* 155–72.

87. Samuel West, "On the Right to Rebel Against Governors," in Hyneman and Lutz, eds., 427.

88. Elisha Williams, "Essential Rights and Liberties," in Sandoz, ed., 55, 56, 59, 83.

89. Ibid., 59, 60. Emphasis in the original.

90. Ibid., 61, 91, 92. Emphasis in the original.

91. Ibid., 92, 93, 94. Emphasis in the original.

92. Ibid., 94, 95, 96. Emphasis in the original.

93. Ibid., 61–62. Emphasis in the original.

94. Locke, *Letter Concerning Toleration,* 17, 23.

95. Williams, "Essential Rights and Liberties," 67, 68, 69, 70, 71.

96. Ibid., 62.

97. Ibid., 67, 68, 69, 70, 71.

98. Ibid., 72, 82, 83.

99. Ibid., 92–93, cf. 77, 91; Locke, *Essay Concerning Human Understanding* IV, 16.3–4.

100. McWilliams, *Fraternity,* 142.

101. Heinrich Bullinger, *The Decades,* in Morgan, ed., 23.

102. Cambridge Platform, Arts. 6, 8, 9, in Commager, *Documents* I, 30–31.

103. John Rawls, *Political Liberalism* (New York, 1991), I, 2.2.

104. Cambridge Platform, Art. 6, in Commager, *Documents* I, 30.

105. Miller, *The New England Mind,* esp. 3–15.

106. Ibid., 82–104; Morgan, *Visible Saints.*

107. Miller, *From Colony to Province,* 395–481.

108. Claude M. Newlin, *Philosophy and Religion in Colonial America* (New York, 1962).

109. See McWilliams, *Fraternity,* 156.

110. Locke, *The Reasonableness of Christianity,* paras. 242–43.

111. Thomas Jefferson, *Notes on Virginia,* in Merrill D. Peterson, ed., *Thomas Jefferson: Writings* (New York, 1984), Query XVIII, 289.

CHAPTER TWO

RELIGION AND
AMERICAN VALUES

Seymour Martin Lipset

It is widely assumed that structural changes inherent in industrialization and urbanization, with consequent bureaucratization and an increase in "other directedness," have resulted in two major changes in American religious practice and belief. First it is argued that many more people outwardly adhere to formal religion and attend church than ever before; and second, that this increase in formal practice does not reflect greater religiosity—on the contrary, it is suggested that American religion itself is now secularized, that it has increasingly adjusted to the sentiments of the general society.

> It is variously noted that much of religion has become a matter of private ethical convictions; that the churches are active in secular affairs; that religious observances have been losing their supernatural or other-worldly character. It is said that religion in America tends to be religion at a very low temperature. . . .[1]

These trends in American religion have been related to the urbanization and suburbanization of American society that have taken place in the twentieth century. When the different sects were geographically isolated from each other, and when immigrant Catholics and Jews were segregated in urban slums, the differences in their fundamental beliefs were relatively unimportant. Those who professed one set of beliefs were insulated against encountering beliefs that contradicted them. Now that no group is really isolated, the different professions of faith in America exhibit "other-directed" traits by emphasizing what is common in their beliefs.[2] Will Herberg points out that the interfaith movement, which has been reasonably successful on a national level, consists of pruning the transcendental beliefs of all three religions to bring about greater harmony among them.[3]

Recent changes in American society may have accentuated these aspects of American religion much as they have reinforced "other-directed" traits in the American character. However, I would suggest that . . . much of the historical record indicates that these aspects have always distinguished American religion from religion in other nations. American religion, like all other institutions, has made major adjustments in response to changes in the size and scope of the nation, but as the institution most intimately linked with values it has shown the tenacity exhibited by the value system itself.[4]

ALL-PERVASIVENESS, A CONSISTENT CHARACTERISTIC OF AMERICAN RELIGION

Widespread interest in religion is not a new aspect of American society. For almost a century, prominent European visitors who wrote on American life have been unanimous in remarking on the exceptional religiosity of the society. After his visit to America in 1830, Tocqueville commented: ". . . there is no country in the world where the Christian religion retains a greater influence over the souls of men than in America."[5] Martineau in 1834, Trollope in 1860, Bryce in 1883, and Weber in 1904, all arrived at similar conclusions.[6] Their accounts agree substantially with that of a historian's summary of the impressions of pre-Civil War English travelers who

> pointed to the fact that America, though still largely a primitive country, had as many churches as the British Isles, that religious assemblages were being held at one place or another practically all the time; that large donations were constantly being made for religious purposes. America, they concluded, was basically a very religious country. . . . Church services were always crowded on Sundays. . . . Church-going, reported Maxwell, was all the rage in New York. . . . The high percentage of males in the audience was in sharp contrast to their paucity at English services.[7]

Religious practitioners reached similar conclusions. Thus Robert Baird, an American Presbyterian minister who spent eight years in Europe between 1835 and 1843, wrote on his return home:

> In no other part of the world, perhaps, do the inhabitants attend church in a larger proportion than in the United States; certainly no part of the

Continent of Europe can compare with them in that respect. The contrast between the two must strike anyone who, after having travelled much in the one, comes to see any of the cities of the other.[8]

Philip Schaff, a Swiss theologian who eventually emigrated to America, reported in similar terms to German Lutheran bodies. He witnessed much greater church attendance in New York and Brooklyn than in Berlin. He stated unequivocally: "There are in America probably more awakened souls, and more individual effort and self-sacrifice for religious purposes, proportionately, than in any other country, Scotland alone perhaps excepted."[9]

And a German liberal foe of religion, who found the prevalence of religious practice in America distasteful to his agnostic sentiments, testified to the same set of facts which he, like others, linked in a very materialistic fashion to the effects of the separation of church and state:

> Clergymen in America must . . . defend themselves to the last, like other businessmen; they must meet competition and build up a trade, and it's their own fault if their income is not large enough. Now is it clear why heaven and hell are moved to drive the people to the churches, and why attendance is more common here than anywhere else in the world?[10]

The statistical data which bear on the question also suggest that the increase in church affiliation in recent times is not as significant as has been claimed. The earliest quantitative estimates of religious adherence in America that I have been able to locate are those reported in *The American Almanac and Repository of Useful Knowledge* which was published regularly for some years beginning about 1830. These volumes reported detailed statistics for members *and adherents* of the various denominations. The membership data were taken from statements by the different church groups while the estimates of the number of adherents were derived from various unmentioned publications. In 1831 the total number of adherents listed was 12,136,953, in 1832 the total was 12,496,953, and in 1837 it had risen to 14,585,000. Since in 1831 the total national population was 13,321,000 and in 1837 it was 15,843,000,[11] these data testify to an almost universal religious adherence by Americans in the 1830's, comparable to the results obtained by public opinion surveys in the past few decades which report that almost every American identifies with a given denomination.

In 1856 Robert Baird published statistical data which also differentiated between members and "those under the influence of the evangelical denominations." The total identified with these groups was 17,763,000. (The total population of the country at the time was 26,500,000.) These figures do not include Catholics, Unitarians, Universalists, Mormons, Jews, and various other small, non-evangelical groups. Without describing how he obtained his estimate of over 17 million supporters of the evangelical groups, Baird states: "Accuracy in such a calculation is hardly to be expected, but I have taken the best data I could find, and doubt that the estimate I have made is much wide of the truth. Including all the evangelical 'Friends,' this estimate would fall but little short of eighteen million."[12]

While the obvious problems of reliability and validity involved in the use of American church membership statistics make it difficult to reach any conclusions, the available evidence does suggest that, from some time early in American history down to the present, the United States has experienced a continuous "boom" in religious adherence and belief.

These data and observations pose the problem of how to reconcile the estimates concerning the general commitment to religion in the first half of the nineteenth century with the various estimates reported in the *Year Book of American Churches* which indicate a steep rise in membership in religious groups, particularly in the twentieth century.[13] There are many methodological problems concerning the reliability of any historical estimates of church membership, since all of them are presumably based on voluntary replies of church officers to questionnaires, and it is difficult to find out how the reports for much of the nineteenth century were compiled.[14] To some considerable degree, however, the rapid growth in reported membership after 1890 is a result of the considerable increase in the non-Protestant denominations, whose concept of a church member differed greatly from those of the Protestants. These groups, largely Catholic and Orthodox, reported as a member every person born in the faith, regardless of age or religious status, while most Protestant denominations all through the nineteenth century only considered as members those who had joined the church as adults, often after fulfilling a rigorous set of requirements.

The discrepancy between the travelers' reports that most Americans attended church regularly and the relatively small proportion of the population who actually belonged to a church may be accounted for by the fact that *during this period most of those who attended churches did not belong to a given denomination.* Baird, for example, described the situation as of the 1840's in the following terms:

Not only do persons who have not yet become members, by formal admission as such, attend our churches; they form a very large part of our congregations. In many cases they constitute two thirds, three fourths, or even more; this depending much on the length of the period during which the congregation has been organized, and hardly ever less than a half, even in the most highly-favoured churches. Nor do they attend only; they are cheerful supporters of the public worship, and are often found as liberal in contributing of their substance for the promotion of good objects, as the members of the church themselves, with whom they are intimately connected by the ordinary business of life, and by family ties. . . . The non-professing hearers of the Word, then, are to be considered as simply what we call them, members of the congregation, not of the church. . . .[15]

The reasons why men might attend church and support a given denomination without becoming a member are not difficult to understand, given the conditions for membership which existed for most of the nineteenth century:

Certainly by modern standards, church membership was a strenuous affair. All evangelical sects required of communicants a personal experience of conversion and a consistent life. Two worship services and Sunday School on the Sabbath were customary. The Methodists invariably kept new converts on "probation" for many months. Wesley's followers also attended a weekly class meeting. . . . Laymen of most denominations were responsible for a large amount of missionary and benevolent work. . . .[16]

Perhaps the most comprehensive attempt to specify the number of "adherents" as distinct from "communicants" of the different Protestant denominations is the study by H. K. Carroll, who was in charge of the Division of Churches for the 1890 U.S. Census.[17] His efforts led him to conclude that in 1890 with a population of 62,622,250, only 5 million people were *not* communicants or adherents. In percentage terms, he estimated that 92 per cent of the population in 1890 and 91 per cent in 1910 were linked to a denomination. These estimates are comparable to those suggested by Ouseley for the 1830's and by Baird for the 1840's and 1850's, and are similar to the results of public opinion surveys since the mid-1930's and to the 1957 U.S. Census Sample Survey of Religious Affiliation. And these statistical conclusions, of course, reiterate the almost unanimous comments made for close to a century and a half by various foreign travelers, who have never ceased to indicate their amazement at the rarity of atheists or anti-religious people in America.[18]

More precise historical data which belie the claim of drastic changes in religious practice are provided by the Census reports for the second half of the nineteenth century, which present the number of seats available in all American churches. These data indicate an increase in the ratio of church seats to population of from 62 to 69 per cent,[19] although the *Year Book of American Churches,* the most frequently quoted source on church affiliation in the United States, estimates a growth in membership between 1850 and 1900 of from 15 to 36 per cent of the total population. Since the 1850 population included two million slaves (almost one-seventh of the population), a group which on the whole lacked substantial church accommodations, it seems probable that the relatively small increase in available church facilities was added by the Negroes. All during the second half of the nineteenth century, the churches kept up with the tremendous population expansion in providing accommodations for almost the entire adult population.

Figures on number of clergymen in America from 1850 to 1950 also reveal a striking constancy. In each census year there has been approximately one clergyman for every 1,000 persons. In 1850 there were 1.16 clergymen per 1,000 population; by 1960, the figure had changed to 1.13. Actually, there has been *no effective change* in the ratio of clergy to total population during the past century, although the proportions of others in professional occupations increased sharply, a difference which is shown in Table I.

Table I. Number of Clergymen and Professionals Per 1,000 Population for Census Years 1900–1960

	Clergymen	Professionals
1900	1.22	14.2
1910	1.28	18.6
1920	1.20	20.6
1930	1.21	26.5
1940	1.09	26.2
1950	1.12	32.8
1960	1.13	40.3

Sources: Data for clergy in G. Stigler, *Trends in Employment in the Service Industries* (Princeton, N.J.: Princeton University Press, 1956), p. 108; data for professionals calculated from Alba M. Edwards, *Comparative Occupational Statistics for the United States, 1870 to 1940,* Bureau of the Census, 1943, and *Statistical Abstracts,* 1952.

This lack of an increase in the proportion of ministers adds further support to the idea that there has been little change in the strength of institutionalized religion, although in itself it is not conclusive evidence. Certainly the ratio of parishioners to clergy may have changed, so that modern clergymen may serve more members than those of the past. However, arguing against this possibility is the fact that the proportion of ministers has failed to rise with the long-term increasing wealth of the American people. That a congregation's ability to pay for religion would be a factor is suggested by the sharp drop in the depression decade revealed in the table.

Some of those who contend that religious adherence in American society has reached an all time high in recent times point to evidence derived from public opinion surveys and the 1957 U.S. Sample Survey of Religious Affiliation conducted by the Census Bureau, which indicate that over 95 per cent of the population state a belief in God and declare an identification with some specific religious group. There are, of course, no comparable interview data for the nineteenth century except for the nearly unanimous reports by foreign travelers that almost everyone they spoke to expressed religious beliefs and commitments. It is possible, however, to contrast the answers given by undergraduates in American colleges before World War I and in 1952 to questionnaires concerning their religious beliefs.

In a study made in 1913, 927 students in nine colleges of "high rank" replied to questions concerning their belief in God. Eighty-seven per cent of the men and 93 per cent of the women reported belief.[20] The same author received replies from 90 per cent of the students in "one college of high rank," of whom 70 per cent believed in immortality and after-life.[21] Four decades later, in 1952, a group of Cornell sociologists administered questionnaires to 4,585 students selected through statistical sampling procedures to be representative of *male* undergraduates at eleven colleges and universities. Twenty-four per cent of the men were atheists or agnostics.[22] Comparing the findings of these two studies suggests that at least for college students the supposed religious "revival" of the 1950's still has considerable distance to go before belief reaches a point comparable to that of 1913.[23]

Such statistical data as we have examined all argue against the thesis that religious practice in America in the mid-twentieth century is at its high point. Rather, one concludes from these data that, although there have been ebbs and flows in enthusiasm, basic long-term changes in formal religious affiliation and practice have not occurred, and the current high level of religious belief and observance existed in the past as well. As the foreign travelers noted in their books, Americans have been and continue to be a highly religious people. In fact, the one empirical generalization which does seem justified about American religion is that from the early nineteenth century down to the present, the United States has been among the most religious countries in the Christian world. Considerably lower proportions of religious responses (belief in God) are reported by pollsters for European countries than for the United States.[24] With respect to attendance, it is misleading to compare national rates because of the varying proportions of Catholics and Protestants (who manifest divergent church-going patterns) within populations. But American Protestants attend church more frequently than Protestants in Sweden, Denmark, Czechoslovakia (before the Communist coup); and Great Britain.[25]

SECULARITY, A PERSISTENT TRAIT OF AMERICAN RELIGION

From the available evidence it is difficult to discern actual trends with respect to the secularization of religion. There does appear to have been a historic trend toward secularization but it does not seem to be as great as many have argued. The supporters of the thesis of increased secularization would seem to minimize two somewhat contradictory but co-existent tendencies. First, they ignore the possibility that the supposedly modern, secularized religion may have characterized much of American behavior in previous periods. Second, they are inattentive to the fact that, now as in the past, a considerable number of Americans have a propensity to follow evangelical religions— and middle-class intellectuals tend to compare nineteenth century evangelical movements which they know from historical records with contemporary middle- and upper-class liberal religion, the form they are personally acquainted with. They forget that the religion of the better educated and more privileged has always tended to be more secularly oriented than that of the lower strata.

In the past three decades, as in the early nineteenth century, the more orthodox and fundamentalist denominations, e.g., the Southern Baptists, the Missouri Synod of the Lutheran Church, the Catholic Church, and the numerous small Pentecostal and fundamentalist sects, have had more success in recruiting members than the "established" denominations which belong to the National Council of Churches—much as in the nineteenth century the then revivalist Methodists and Baptists had much greater success than the older higher status and more secularized denominations such as the Episcopalians, Congregationalists, and Unitarians.[26]

There is no question that various denominations have become more secularized and less evangelical over time. But this change within specific denominations such as the Presbyterians and the Methodists in large part reflects the fact that their constituency has changed, from "out" groups to "in" groups. Concentrating on the history of a given Protestant denomination necessarily results in the misleading conclusion that there has been a sharp change from ascetic fervor to a more secularized religious liberalism.

American religious denominations, like ethnic groups, have experienced collective upward mobility. In the early years of the Republic, the Presbyterians were among the more depressed strata economically and socially, and their religious and political behavior reflected this fact.[27] They, however, soon became identified with the Congregationalists, the Quakers, the Unitarians, and the Episcopalians, as the churches of the more well-to-do and the urban middle classes. The Methodists and Baptists became the predominant religions of the constantly expanding frontier population and the urban working classes. With economic and population growth, the Methodists, too, gained proportionally in middle-class members, and the ministry, which had been largely uneducated, gradually became a seminary or university trained one, a phenomenon which tended to reduce their evangelical fervor and their appeal to the "displaced" strata. New sects arose to satisfy the need for religious enthusiasm. The upward mobility of the members of the older Protestant denominations was also facilitated by immigration from Europe, largely of Catholic and Lutheran background, followed by increasing numbers of Jews and adherents of the Greek Orthodox creed. Most recently, southern Negroes have moved into the cities. Since most of these immigrants and Negroes have occupied the lowest positions in the class structure, many white Protestant groups, particularly the Methodists who had been the predominant evangelical sect for much of the nineteenth century, necessarily improved their location on the status ladder. Thus, while the denominational affiliations of urban middle-class Americans may have changed from a statistical point of view, the pattern of American religion has remained fairly constant. Negro religious behavior resembles that of the nineteenth century lower status migrant white population. The Catholics have taken on the coloration of a fundamentalist orthodox religion comparable in tone and style, if not in theology, to the nineteenth-century evangelical Protestant sects. Recently, a leading French Dominican student of the American Church has complained that American Catholics resemble American Baptists more than they do Mexican or French Catholics. He comments that "one often has the impression that American Catholics are more Puritan than anybody else and that they are close to setting themselves up as the champions of Puritanism."[28]

The historic American pattern of a more secularized higher status religion has been well described by Baltzell, who points out that, from the beginning of the nineteenth century, men often turned to the Episcopal Church as they became well-to-do. This was true for Presbyterian cotton planters in the South, for the upper-class Quakers of Philadelphia, and even for many old-family New England Unitarians and Congregationalists.[29] The secular motivations underlying such conversions were not a secret to their contemporaries. Foreign travelers also were well aware of the relationship between status-seeking and church membership.[30]

Many of the foreign observers also confessed their surprise to find that the system of competing denominations in the United States did not mean that the different groups rejected each other for adhering to "false creeds." An Italian Jesuit, Giovanni Grassi, who served for five years, 1812 to 1817, as President of Georgetown College before returning to Rome, commented in disturbed tones on these "other-directed" religious phenomena:

> Every sect there is held as good, every road as correct, and every error as the insignificant weakness of poor mortals. . . .
>
> Although how can one speak of sects? Those who describe themselves as members of one or another of the sects do not thereby profess an abiding adherence to the doctrines of the founders of the sect. . . . Thus the Anglicans of today no longer take much account of their thirty-nine articles, nor the Lutherans of the Confession of Augsburg, nor the Presbyterians of the teachings of Calvin or of Knox. . . .
>
> Among the peculiarities of America, not the most extreme is that of finding persons who live together for several years without knowing each other's religion. And many, when asked, do not answer, "I believe," but simply, "I was brought up in such a persuasion."[31]

Timothy Smith concludes from his detailed examination of the writings of many nineteenth-century ministerial foreign travelers that visiting "Evangelicals were especially heartened to discover that the elimination of legal privilege [separation of church and state in America] seemed to lessen sectarian rivalry."[32] He cites one English visitor in the 1830's who "noted with pleasure *the numerous exchanges of pulpits, union prayer meetings and joint efforts in Bible Society, Sunday school, and mission Work.* She decided that the sectarian spirit of Europe's churches arise not so much from 'conscientious scruples and differences of opinion on government or doctrine' as from the fact that some had endowments and some did not."[33] A leading French Calvinist pastor who visited the United States two decades later confessed his surprise at this phenomenon of mutual esteem among competing sects:

We thought, until our visit to the United States, that the multiplicity of sects there, must, of necessity, present an obstacle to the progress of the spirit of brotherly love. We do not yet think that a diversity of communions is an efficacious means of developing among Christians the principle of charity; but we are glad to acknowledge that our American brethren have combatted very effectually the attendant dangers. So far as we have been able to judge, there exists much harmony and good feeling, between all the evangelical denominations. The pastors and members of the various religious communities even among those most widely differing in church polity speak mutually of each other with much kindness and esteem.[34]

Tocqueville's companion on his visit to America, Gustave de Beaumont, was also struck by this behavior and confessed his puzzlement as to how Americans could be fervent in their particular belief yet approve of exchange of pulpits among ministers of different Protestant denominations:

As a matter of fact, nothing is commoner in the United States than this indifference toward the nature of religions, which doesn't, however eliminate the religious fervour of each for the cult he has chosen. Actually, this extreme tolerance on the one hand towards religions in general—on the other this considerable zeal of each individual for his own religion, is a phenomenon I can't yet explain to myself. I would gladly know how a lively and sincere faith can get on with such a perfect toleration; how one can have equal respect for religions whose dogmas differ. . . .[35]

And Beaumont asked the same question about American religion in the 1830's that many have raised in recent years: "Would it not be from their outward show of religion that *there is more breadth than depth in it?*"[36]

Tocqueville himself commented that in no other country is Christianity "clothed with fewer forms, figures, and observances than in the United States, or where it presents more distinct, simple and general notions to the mind. Although the Christians of America are divided into a multitude of sects, they look upon their religion in the same light."[37] And in his private notes Tocqueville reported:

Go into the churches (I mean the Protestant ones), you will hear morality preached, of dogma not a word. Nothing which can at all shock the neighbour; nothing which can arouse the idea of dissent. . . . [Ministers

preach to other denominations.] But, said I, how do these men and children, who are communicants of one sect, like hearing the minister of
another? The infallible response is this: The different preachers, treating
only the common ground of morality, cannot do each other any harm.[38]

His English contemporary, Harriet Martineau, who stated that almost
everyone professed some form of Christian belief, perceptively added that
people are not supposed to feel intensely about a particular religion:

One circumstance struck me throughout the country. Almost as often as
the conversation between myself and any other person on religious subjects became intimate and earnest, I was met by the supposition that I
was a convert. It was the same in other instances: wherever there was a
strong interest in the Christian religion, conversion to a particular profession of it was confidentially supposed. This fact speaks volumes.[39]

In 1860 Anthony Trollope was struck by the fact that "the question of a
man's religion is regarded in a free and easy way." He notes that fathers believe
"that a young lad should go somewhere on a Sunday; but a sermon is a sermon. . . . Everybody is bound to have a religion, but it does not much matter what it is."[40] And in 1900, the German sociologist Max Weber was also
impressed, during his visit, with the seeming secularization of religion and
acceptance of religious diversity. He reported: "In the main, the congregations
refused entirely to listen to the preaching of 'dogma' and to confessional distinctions. 'Ethics' alone could be offered. . . . Today the kind of denomination [to which one belongs] is rather irrelevant. It does not matter whether
one be a Freemason, Christian Scientist, Adventist, Quaker, or what not."[41]
    The foremost modern British scholar of America concludes his discussion
of late nineteenth-century religious life:

Religion became a matter of conduct, of good deeds, of works with only
a vague background of faith. It became highly functional, highly pragmatic; it became a guarantee of success, moral and material. . . . Theological schools turned from theology to a form of anthropology—a moralistic
and optimistic form, but anthropology all the same. That 'the proper
study of mankind is man' was the evasion by which many American
divines escaped the necessity for thought about God.[42]

Reports that American religion is much more secular than that found in
other nations have been just as consistent as reports that it has relatively more

adherents. Secularity has long been cited as a persistent trait of American religion and cannot simply be attributed to an increase in socially motivated church-going in the past few decades.

However, secularity is not the only notable characteristic of American religion throughout its history. New sects have developed more readily here than anywhere else in the world.[43] For the most part, these are drawn from economically and socially depressed strata, and their theology reflects this fact, such as in the belief that wealth or ostentation is sinful or corrupting.[44] During the last Great Depression, when efforts to form significant protest political parties failed totally, the religious sectarians grew, while other religions declined or showed no change.[45]

Since all of these characteristics have made American religion unique throughout its history, they must be attributed to those features of American society that have consistently distinguished it from other cultures, rather than to recent changes. In each age, men have seen in the almost total allegiance to religion by Americans a further evidence of the conformist propensity of democratic man. Analysts, in the past as well as the present,[46] have also attributed the secular quality of American religion to its relationship with democracy. Tocqueville felt that the emphasis upon morality, rather than transcendental beliefs, in American religion, was a result of the numerous sects and religions being given equal status before the law and in the eyes of men. He observed:

> [The sects] all differ in respect to the worship which is due to the Creator, but they all agree in respect to the duties which are due from man to man. Each sect adores the Deity in its own peculiar manner, but all sects preach the same moral law in the name of God. . . . Society has no future life to hope for or to fear; and provided the citizens profess a religion, the peculiar tenets of that religion are of little importance to its interests.[47]

In this respect, he does not differ too greatly from Herberg, who says:

> Just as the three great religions are the basic subdivisions of the American people, so are the three great communions felt to be recognized expressions of the spiritual aspect of the American Way of Life. This underlying unity not only supplies limits within which their conflicts and tensions may operate and beyond which they cannot go—it also supplies the common content of the three communities.[48]

Each of these analyses implies that both the secular and the all-pervasive character of American religion is a result of its being viewed as part of the

"American Way of Life." Tocqueville found that "the whole nation," "every rank of society," felt that religion was indispensable to the maintenance of republican institutions. And he believed that this was why, on the one hand, even those who did not "profess the doctrines of Christianity from sincere belief in them" did so hypocritically "because they fear[ed] to be suspected of unbelief"; and why, on the other hand, Christian morality rather than transcendental beliefs stood out in American religious attitudes.[49]

American Protestantism has concentrated on the moral rather than the contemplative, mystical, or communal and traditional elements of religion partially because of its Puritan roots. The contemplative and the mystical have not played a significant role in Protestantism in general, and in addition "the intellectual, theological element, though prominent in Puritan Christianity came with the growth of the churches of the common man and the triumph of pietism to be neglected in American religion":

> In the main drift of religion in America the theological and liturgical and mystical and contemplative move into the background; the hierarchical and communal give place to the individualistic, the traditional to the immediate, the authoritative to the freely decided, the appeal to the mind and the aesthetic sense to the appeal to the will, the awareness of the ultimate to the concern with the practical life. The penumbra of beyondness, absoluteness, and mystery fades away, and leaves—as the core of what Americans think religion to be—the moral.[50]

VOLUNTARISM, THE SOURCE OF RELIGIOUS STRENGTH

In seeking to explain the special character of American religion many of the foreign visitors singled out the effect of the separation of church and state, which resulted in American churches being voluntary organizations in which congregational self-government was the predominant form of church government. More specifically, the special quality of American religion has been linked to three elements in the American past: first, New England Puritanism infused certain ascetic values into the very concept of Protestantism—the Puritans' "Protestant ethic" lay close to the heart of most denominations, regardless of doctrinal differences; second, ideological emphases and institutional changes which flowed from the American Revolution led to forms of church organization analogous to popularly based institutions; and third, the fact that all sections of the United States were formed out of an unsettled frontier without any traditional class structure or significant aid or control from a central government meant that religious institutions had to be created almost completely from the resources of the local population, and hence closely reflected their specific religious needs and their secular values.

It is difficult to separate out the contributions of each of these, and of other factors. As in all complex structures, the various elements tend to interact continually. Thus, Puritanism has been credited with supplying much of the motivation behind the Revolution.[51] Congregationalist pastors overwhelmingly backed the Revolution, while the hierarchically organized Episcopalians tended to be Tories. Congregationalism, with its stress on self-government within the church, contributed to secular self-government in the form of the New England town meeting. Comparative studies of frontier settlement in Canada, Latin America, and Australia have suggested that part of the democratic aspects of American frontier settlement reflected the American ethos and political system, not simply the needs of any new frontier society. In Canada . . . central authorities played a much greater role in settling and governing the frontier than was true in the United States. And in examining developments in American religion, it seems obvious that the ideology which flowed from the Revolution and the subsequent political triumph of the "left" in the early decades of the Republic led to the decisive decision in favor of "disestablishment." The withdrawal of government support from religion made American Protestantism unique in the Christian world. The United States became the first nation in which religious groups were viewed as purely voluntary associations. To exist, American churches had to compete in the marketplace for support. And conversely, membership in a given religious denomination was a voluntary act.

This emphasis on voluntary associations which struck Tocqueville and other foreign travelers as one of the distinctive American traits, and which was also supportive of political democracy, has been traced by some as essentially derivative from "voluntary religion." Sidney Mead points out that even the Episcopalians became consciously aware of the fact that with the end of the Revolution they could now exist only as "voluntary associations" (a term explicitly used in such an analysis by an Episcopalian minister). This meant they had to involve the laity in church government, and that a priest would have only as much influence as there was good opinion of his ability. As Mead says, "the acceptance of religious freedom and separation" came to mean that ministers had only "persuasive or political power."[52]

The end of religious Establishment and the growth of the sects meant that a new structure of moral authority had to be created to replace the once dominant link between Church and State. In New England, many Congregationalist ministers and laymen consciously recognized that they had to establish voluntary organizations to safeguard morality in a democratic society that deemphasized the links between Church and Government.[53] The early organization of local and national associations for domestic missionary work, for the distribution of Bibles, for temperance, for opposition to slavery, and for peace, was invariably undertaken by well-to-do religious people, and by ministers adhering to the historic New England denominations, who felt these were the only ways they could preserve and extend a moral society. Eventually a host of voluntary groups developed around the voluntary churches.

> The separation of Church and State, and other causes, have given rise to a new species of social organization, before unknown in history. . . . Then opened on the American world the new era of the Religious and Benevolent Society system, and summoned into the field an immense body of superior and highly-cultivated talent. . . .
>
> As to the right or wrong of these institutions, or as to whether they are good or bad, is not, in this place, a subject of inquiry; but simply the fact of their social importance, and their power. . . . And it happens, that these voluntary associations are so numerous, so great, so active and influential, that, as a whole, they now constitute the great school of public education, in the formation of those practical opinions, religious, social, and political, which lead the public mind and govern the country. . . .[54]

American Protestantism, although Calvinist in origin, fairly early in its history became Arminian. A large majority of the Calvinist denominations, as well as most of the non-Calvinist ones, came to accept the Arminian "doctrines of free will, free grace, and unlimited hope for the conversion of all men."[55] To maintain themselves after disestablishment, practically all the Protestant groups had become proselytizing churches. And the Calvinist belief in predestination "could hardly survive amidst the evangelists' earnest entreaties to 'come to Jesus.'"[56] American Protestantism, with its emphasis on the personal achievement of grace, reinforced the stress on personal achievement which was dominant in the secular value system. Both sets of values stressed individual responsibility, both rejected hereditary status. The two dominant denominations, the Methodists and the Baptists, which contained most Protestants, stressed religious doctrines that reinforced "anti-aristocratic tendencies."[57] Here again it is possible to suggest an interacting complex. An early nineteenth-century analyst of American religion argued that the reason that these denominations outgrew others was that the "disciplinary habits, the political opinions, and ideological tenets, both of the Baptists and Wesleyans, are more congenial to American democracy, than those of the better educated and more accomplished religious sects. . . . Hence—the political opinions of America having been before determined—those forms of religion best adapted to harmonize with them, were likely to prevail most. . . ."[58] To understand the character and strength of religion in America, it is therefore important to see its fundamental links with the prevalent secular values.

The fact of disestablishment, that is, the absence of a state church, served also to enhance the application of religious morality to politics. The existence of a state Church in Europe meant that "even 'sin,' in European culture had been institutionalized."

> There, an actual place had been made for it in life's crucial experience. It had been classified from time out of mind and given specific names; the reality of "lust," "avarice," and "oppression" had given rise to the most intricate of social arrangements, not for eliminating them, but for softening their impact and limiting their scope—for protecting the weak and defining the responsibilities of the strong. . . . All this may well have been in [Henry] James's mind when he exclaimed of America: "no church."
>
> What, then, might be expected to happen if sin should suddenly become apparent, in a nation whose every individual was, at least symbolically, expected to stand on his own two feet? The reaction was altogether destructive. The sense of outrage was personal, the sense of personal guilt was crushing. The gentle American of mild vices was transformed into the bloody avenger.[59]

The need to assuage the sense of personal responsibility has meant that Americans have been particularly wont to support movements for the elimination of evil by violent means if necessary. The movements for temperance and prohibition, for the abolition of slavery, for resistance to the growth of Catholicism, and most recently for the elimination of Communists, have all drawn their vigor from the stress developed within American society on personal responsibility for the struggle against evil.[60]

Certainly there has been an interplay between religious and democratic values from the beginning of the nation's history. The gradual identification of Enlightenment ideals with national identity in turn affected the content of our religious values. J. Franklin Jameson explains the amazingly rapid decline of Calvinist doctrine in America after the Revolution, and its replacement by Arminian religious beliefs, not only as a reflection of the doctrinal need of evangelical revivalistic religion, but also by the assumption that, "in a period when the special privileges of individuals were being called into question or being destroyed, there would naturally be less favor for that form of theology which was dominated by the doctrine of the especial election of a part of mankind, a growing favor for forms which seemed more distinctly to be based upon the idea of the natural equality of all men."[61]

The Arminian emphasis on the personal attainment of grace, perhaps even more than the Calvinist stress on the existence of an "elect," served as a religious parallel to the secular emphasis on equality of opportunity and achievement. This parallelism, and even mutual reinforcement, was noted by many nineteenth-century foreign visitors. Unlike the situation in many European countries, in which economic materialism was viewed by the social and religious establishments—that is, the traditional aristocracy and the church—as conducive to uncouth behavior and immorality, in the United States hard work and economic ambition have been perceived as the proper activity of a devout man. Schaff commented that the "acquisition of riches is to them [the Americans] only a help toward higher spiritual and moral ends."[62] The considerable sums, as well as time, contributed to philanthropic works, which reached heights undreamed of in Europe, have also been perceived as part of the interrelationship between religious and secular activities. The emphasis on "voluntarism" in both areas has clearly been mutually reinforcing. For much of the nineteenth century many voluntary activities, such as those dealing with charity, education, and moral and social reform were closely linked to religious concerns. Men were expected to be righteous, hardworking, and ambitious. Righteousness was to be rewarded both in the present and the hereafter, and the successful had an obligation to engage in good works and to share the bounty they had attained.

It is important to stress also that the strong commitment to a voluntaristic denominational Protestantism reinforced the support for minority rights even in the religious sphere itself. Although Sunday Blue Laws continued for many decades after the Revolution, the rights of the irreligious found considerable backing, as reflected in the insistence—already noted—by the Democrats that the mails be delivered on Sundays. In 1830—twenty years after the passage of the Sunday mails bill—a Senate committee report, authored by a future Vice-President and endorsed by a majority of that House, stated explicitly that in the United States religion and irreligion had equal rights, and that laws proclaiming that the government should not provide services on Sunday would work an injustice to irreligious people or non-Christians, and would constitute a special favor for Christians as a group. The report, written by a deeply religious active Baptist, stated these principles in unequivocal terms:

The Constitution regards the conscience of the Jew as sacred as that of the Christian, and gives no more authority to adopt a measure affecting the conscience of a solitary individual than that of a whole community. . . . If Congress shall declare the first day of the week holy, it will not satisfy the Jew nor the Sabbatarian. It will dissatisfy both and, consequently convert neither. . . . It must be recollected that, in the earliest settlement of this country, the spirit of persecution, which drove the pilgrims from their native homes, was brought with them to their new habitations; and that some Christians were scourged and others put to death for no other crime than dissenting from the dogmas of their rulers.

. . . If a solemn act of legislation shall in *one* point define the God or point out to the citizen one religious duty, it may with equal propriety define *every* part of divine revelation and enforce *every* religious obligation, even to the forms and ceremonies of worship, the endowment of the church, and the support of the clergy.

. . . It is the duty of this government to affirm to *all*—to the Jew or Gentile, Pagan, or Christian—the protection and advantages of our benignant institutions on *Sunday,* as well as every day of the week.[63]

Before the Civil War, successful struggles, often led by deeply believing Protestants, were waged in many areas to eliminate any relationship between state supported education and religion. By so doing, these Protestants acknowledged the rights of all, even of the completely irreligious. In 1853, in defending a ruling that prayers "could not be required as a part of the school exercises" in New York state, a devout State Superintendent of Schools wrote as follows:

[T]he position was early, distinctly, and almost universally taken by our statesmen, legislators, and prominent friends of education—men of the warmest religious zeal and belonging to every sect—that *religious education must be banished from the common school and consigned to the family and church.* . . . Accordingly, the instruction in our schools has been limited to that ordinarily included under the head of intellectual culture, and to the propagation of those principles of morality in which all sects, and *good men belonging to no sect,* can equally agree. . . .

Not only have the Episcopalian, the Presbyterian, the Baptist and the Methodist met on *common* and *neutral* ground in the schoolroom, but with them the Unitarian, the Universalist, the Quaker and even *the denier of all creeds.*[64]

The fact that public officials could openly advocate that the federal and state governments must consider the rights of non-believers indicates the extent to which many believing Protestants of the first half century of the United States were able to tolerate religious variety. Only Catholicism, viewed by many American Protestants not as a different set of religious beliefs but as an alien conspiracy seeking to undermine the American Way of Life, was outside the pale.

Thus we may say, once again, that Tocqueville and other early foreign travelers "foresaw" trends in American religious institutions, just as they "foresaw" trends in the American character. These trends have become accentuated as the nation's values have adjusted to the vast changes that have taken place in the fabric of American society. The identification which Tocqueville observed between democratic ideals and an affirmation of religion seems even greater today.[65]

While the secular and all-pervasive character of American religion may stem from the intertwining of democratic and religious values, it is easier to show how the propensity to form sects is a product of the way democracy affected the structural position of religion in America. Perhaps this can best be seen by comparing the growth of religion in Canada and the United States. Religious sects have tended to develop, in both Canada and the United States, where rapid social change, the heavy shift of population to the frontier or the growing cities, and the consequent social mobility, have torn individuals from their traditional ties. However, the fact that religion is less explicitly separated from the "national community" in Canada has meant that sects have been less able to survive there than in the United States. In Canada:

> Political pressures have forced the community to come to the support of organized religion and such support has placed a definite limitation upon sectarian activity. With the collective weight of the community brought to bear upon them, the sects have been forced either to retreat behind a wall of isolation or build themselves into an integral part of the community, or else to seek denominational supports by aligning themselves with the state and with the traditional institutions of the community.[66]

Once the sects aligned themselves with the traditional institutions in the community, their differences became less important and they found it easier to unite. As a result the union of churches proceeded more rapidly in Canada than in the United States.

The "religious fecundity" of American Protestantism seems to be an outgrowth of the intertwining of the democratic value of free expression of all political ideas with the Protestant stress on the obligation to follow individual conscience.[67] The norms of political tolerance and religious tolerance have been mutually reinforcing. The special pressure on churches to proselytize *and* to tolerate each other, brought about by "voluntarism," is reinforced by another particular trait of American society—its geographic, occupational, and class mobility. "This means that people have to be won over and over again as they move geographically and as they change their class orientations and find different aspirations for themselves."[68] With the massive shifting of populations that has characterized American history, neither individual churches or national denominations could remain satisfied with holding their own. Those denominations which did little proselytizing fell far behind in the competition for members and adherents. In the past as in the present, those who changed their circumstances have often been potential converts to another denomination. And the wide-spreading religious mobility from one sect to another, which has been stimulated by other forms of mobility, has meant that in all periods of American history a large proportion of the population has adhered to a denomination other than the one in which they were reared. It has been suggested that at least one consequence of this heterogeneity of the religious backgrounds of church members is the "ecumenical movement in which major groups recognize the legitimacy of each other."[69]

The fact that American religion is denominational has facilitated the development of religious groups which tend to serve only those parishioners who are roughly on the same social level in society. And the absence of multi-class religions (such as exist in countries where the church is established or represents the sole religion of the country) has meant that each "class" or ethnic religion could adapt its practices and specific beliefs to suit the needs of the group which it serves.[70] This has also meant that in this country religion could be either conservative or radical in its view of the class structure. No major social group has long been excluded from, or caused to be disaffected from, the "normal" religious life of the nation. Thus, denominationalism may have served to stabilize the polity.

By virtue of their need to survive, denominational religions have historically resisted state control over different aspects of cultural life and in so doing have supported democracy. Tocqueville pointed out that, because of the survival need, even American Catholics, laymen and clergy alike, adopted democratic and republican principles. And he says: "They constitute a minority, and all rights must be respected in order to insure to them the free exercise of their own privileges. These . . . causes induce them, even unconsciously, to adopt political doctrines which they would perhaps support with less zeal if they were preponderant."[71] This explanation of Catholic support for democratic values could easily be extended to all the denominations in the society, since none of them is large enough to constitute a majority. Such religious support for democracy constitutes the background for *religious affiliation* being considered a part of the "American Way of Life."

The separation of the church and state has increasingly given religion *per se* a specific rather than a diffuse role in American society. The minister, the priest, and the rabbi, all deal in generalizations that extend beyond the confines of the church itself; but the members of the congregation do not necessarily carry these with them to their other activities, because they judge the religious leader in his specific role. Democracy's giving religion a specific role in American society—as Sunday Religion—may have, oddly enough, contributed to its all-pervasive and secular qualities. The only mention of religion on "weekdays" must be in terms of generally agreed upon morality which cannot be identified with the teachings of any given denomination. In so far as the secular and all-pervasive characteristics of American religion are a result of the emphasis on role specificity in American society, they have become accentuated with urbanization and industrialization. However, the consistency over time of foreign observers' remarks to the effect that American religion is unique in these characteristics shows that neither of them has grown simply as a result of these modern trends.

The emphasis upon equality, between religions as among men, which intensified after the American Revolution, gave the subsequent development of religious institutions in America its special character. Democratic and religious values have grown together. The results have been that, on the one hand, Americans see religion as essential to the support of the democratic institutions they cherish, and therefore feel that all Americans should profess some sort of religious faith; on the other hand, American denominations stress the ethical side of religion which they all have in common (and which is closely associated with other democratic values) rather than stressing transcendental beliefs wherein they differ. At the same time, democracy, by giving religious institutions a specific role in American society, has allowed them to proliferate, to adjust to peculiar needs, and to have a limited influence on their members' lives.

Thus the consistency with which both secularization and widespread adherence have distinguished American religion throughout its history is a result of the fact that democratic values have continued to influence the growth of religious institutions as the society has changed. In this respect, the persistent traits in American religion resemble the constant traits in the American character. They have continued to distinguish America from other countries, precisely because they have stemmed from the basic American values that have remained relatively stable as the economy, population, and society of the country have changed.

NOTES

1. Robin Williams, *American Society* (New York: Alfred A. Knopf, 1957), p. 344.

2. Ibid., pp. 344–345.

3. Will Herberg, *Protestant-Catholic-Jew: An Essay in American Religious Sociology* (Garden City, N.Y.: Doubleday, 1955), chapter 10.

4. Talcott Parsons presents essentially the same thesis: "Looked at by comparison with earlier forms, religion seems to have lost much. But . . . the losses are mainly the consequence of processes of structural differentiation in the society, which correspond to changes in the character of the religious values themselves." Talcott Parsons, *Structure and Process in Modern Societies* (Glencoe, Ill.: The Free Press, 1960), p. 320.

5. Alexis de Tocqueville, *Democracy in America* (New York: Vintage Books, 1954), Vol. I, p. 314.

6. Harriet Martineau, *Society in America* (New York: Saunders and Otlay, 1837), II, p. 317; Anthony Trollope, *North America* (New York: Alfred A. Knopf, 1951), p. 277; James Bryce, *The American Commonwealth* (New York: Macmillan, 1912), Vol. II, pp. 770, 778; H. H. Gerth and C. Wright Mills, ed., *From Max Weber: Essays in Sociology* (New York: Oxford University Press, 1946), pp. 302–303.

7. Max Berger, *The British Traveller in America, 1836–1860* (New York: Columbia University Press, 1943), pp. 133–134.

8. Robert Baird, *Religion in America* (New York: Harper & Bros., 1844), p. 188.

9. Philip Schaff, *America: A Sketch of the Political, Social, and Religious Character of the United States of North America* (New York: C. Scribner, 1855), pp. 94, 118.

10. Karl T. Griesinger, "Lebende Bilder aus Amerika" (1858), a section of which is translated in Oscar Handlin, ed., *This Was America* (Cambridge, Mass.: Harvard University Press, 1949), p. 261.

11. For estimates of religious adherence see William G. Ouseley, *Remarks on the Statistics and Political Institutions of the United States* (Philadelphia: Carey and Lea, 1832), p. 207; *The American Almanac and Repository of Useful Knowledge for the Year 1833* (Boston: Gray and Bowen, 1832), p. 156; *The American Almanac and Repository of Useful Knowledge for the Year 1838* (Boston: Charles Bowen, 1837), p. 172. For population statistics see U.S. Bureau of the Census, *Historical Statistics of the United States, Colonial Times to 1957* (Washington, D.C.: U.S. Government Printing Office, 1960), p. 7.

12. Baird, *Religion in America* (1856 edition), pp. 530–532.

13. Benson Y. Landis, ed., *Year Book of American Churches* (New York: National Council of the Churches of Christ in the U.S.A., 1961), p. 247.

14. The lack of reliability of church membership data, even in recent times, has been pointed out in a critique of the statistics assembled by the *Year Book of American Churches,* which indicates considerable growth in church membership since 1940. Winthrop Hudson concludes that the supposed boom is "largely an illusion." Among the many problems with the statistics is the fact that increases often reflect reports from denominations which had never reported before, as well as peculiar and suspicious increases, the validity of which are never questioned. For example "when the Christ Unity Church was listed for the first time in the 1952 *Year Book* with 682,172 members, it alone accounted for more than one-third of the 1,842,515 gain reported that year. The following year, the American Carpatho-Russian Orthodox Greek Catholic Church and the Ukrainian Orthodox Church, each with 75,000 members, were listed for the first time. The year after that, five bodies listed for the first time contributed 195,804 to the total increase in church membership." Winthrop S. Hudson, "Are Churches Really Booming?" *The Christian Century,* 72 (1955), p. 1494. A critique of the reliability of data indicating Catholic growth may be found in B. G. Mulvaney, "Catholic Population Revealed in Catholic Baptisms," *American Ecclesiastical Review,* 133 (1955), pp. 183–193. A number of large denominations simply report their membership in round figures, such as one million for the Greek Orthodox. Others have reported amazing differences from year to year such as "the Romanian Orthodox Church, which reported an increase in the 1952 *Year Book* from 390 to 50,000. What these figures mean can best be seen in terms of a single year's report. The greatest gain in church membership that has been reported was in 1952—3,604,124. For this year, nine bodies with a total membership of 335,528 were listed for the first time. The Russian Orthodox Church reported an increase of membership from 400,000 to 750,000; the Churches of Christ, an increase from 209,615 to 1,500,000; Christ Unity Science Church, from 682,172 to 1,112,123. (The following year the Christ Unity Science Church reported a further 469,163 increase, making a total gain of 1,581,286 for the three year period.) These items alone account for 2,405,864 of the 3,604,124 gain in church membership for the year. If one subtracts the reported gain in Roman Catholic membership [which is also very dubious], all other religious bodies are left with no increase in membership, to say nothing of keeping up with the increase in population." A further difficulty rests in the extensive geographical mobility in the United States which "may have resulted in . . . duplications of church membership, with many people joining a new church without removing their names from the roll of the old church. Some spot checks of membership have tended to confirm this conjecture." Hudson, op. cit., p. 1495.

A detailed look at the data provided by the twelve largest affiliates of the National Council of Churches, who together account for 30 million of the 35 million affiliated to the Council, indicates that their membership, relative to total population, actually "declined" between 1940 and 1954, the period dealt with by Hudson. He concludes that far "from offering 'proof' of a boom in church membership, the statistics . . . show that the boom is largely a fiction." Ibid., p. 1496.

15. Baird, *Religion in America*, p. 188.

16. Timothy L. Smith, *Revivalism and Social Reform in Mid-Nineteenth Century America* (New York: Abingdon Press, 1957), p. 18; Baird, *Religion in America*, pp. 185–187.

17. He secured an estimate of the ratio of communicants to adherents by "a comparison between the census returns of the religious populations of various communions in Canada [where the Census asks each person his religious affiliation] with those which the denominations give themselves of communicants." H. K. Carroll, *The Religious Forces in the United States* (New York: The Christian Literature Co., 1893), p. xxxv. The average of Canadian Protestant adherents to communicants was 3.2. To be on the safe side, Carroll suggested, however, that this ratio was probably higher than in the United States since there were many smaller and obscure denominations here, and he concluded that he would be safe in assuming "that there are at least 2.5 adherents in the United States to each Protestant communicant." Relating reports on Protestant membership to this estimate, he derived a total estimate of 49,630,000 for the aggregate of Protestant communicants and adherents. He also determined the adherents and communicants for Catholic, Jewish, and other religious groups. Some similar procedures were employed by Dr. Carroll two decades later using 1910 materials. Carroll, op. cit. (1912 edition), pp. lxxi–lxxii. The ratio of communicants to adherents, however, had to be reduced from 2.5 to 2 in view of the large gain in actual church membership reported. In seeking to interpret the great gain in church memberships in the 1910 report, we must note that little, if any resulted from any significant growth in Protestant religious enthusiasm. Rather, as Dr. Carroll pointed out, the churches had changed their definition of a member. "All Churches receive children into that relation much earlier in life than formerly and there are other factors tending to reduce the ratio of adherents to communicants, particularly the relaxation of discipline. . . ." Ibid., p. lxxxii.

18. It is undoubtedly significant that the major change in the requirements for church membership among the traditionally evangelical denominations occurred within two or three years after the 1906 Census of Religion. This Census (gathered like previous ones through reports by church bodies of their membership) followed two decades of massive, largely non-Protestant, immigration. The difference between the Protestant and the Catholic-Greek Orthodox-Jewish concept of member resulted in a gross underestimate of the actual numerical strength of the Protestant groups. While the reasons advanced for the changes made by the various denominations in their membership standards did not allude to such competitive considerations, there can be little doubt that these played a role. The decision to admit children to membership simply added numbers. Other modifications in the requirements, however, made it much easier for adults to join, as may be seen in the example of the Methodists. The 1908 Conference of the Methodist Episcopal Church dropped the requirement that a new member must have "met for at least six months in class," and the further condition that he be "on trial" for six months "under the care of the leaders" for the simple obligation that he be "properly recommended." Franklin Hamlin Littell, *From State Church to Pluralism* (Garden City, N.Y.: Doubleday Anchor, 1962), p. 81.

19. Unfortunately, the Census stopped reporting this datum so that we have no comparable figures for this century.

20. James H. Leuba, *The Belief in God and Immortality* (Chicago: Open Court Publishing Co., 1921), pp. 184–202.

21. Ibid., pp. 213–216.

22. Philip E. Jacob, *Changing Values in College* (New York: Harper & Bros., 1957), p. 108. Universities differed: Almost one-third (32 per cent) of the Harvard College students do not believe in God as compared with 13 per cent of those at the University of Texas.

23. Actually, such a conclusion—that there is less belief today than four decades ago—would not be warranted since the sampling methods and questions asked differed greatly.

24. Leo Rosten, *A Guide to the Religions of America* (New York: Simon & Schuster, 1955), p. 247.

25. Hadley Cantril, *Public Opinion 1935–1946* (Princeton, N. J.: Princeton University Press, 1951), p. 699.

26. Hudson, "Are Churches Really Booming?" op. cit., pp. 1495–1496.

27. Manning Dauer, *The Adams Federalists* (Baltimore: Johns Hopkins Press, 1953), pp. 28–29.

28. R. L. Bruckberger, "The American Catholics as a Minority," in Thomas T. McAvoy, ed., *Roman Catholicism and the American Way of Life* (Notre Dame, Ind.: University of Notre Dame Press, 1960), pp. 45–47.

29. E. Digby Baltzell, *Philadelphia Gentlemen: The Making of a National Upper Class* (Glencoe, Ill.: The Free Press, 1958), pp. 225–233. See also Dixon Wecter, *The Saga of American Society* (New York: Scribner's, 1937), pp. 480–481.

30. Schaff, *America*, pp. 154–155. See also Thomas C. Grattan, *Civilized America* (London: Bradbury and Evans, 1895), Vol. I, pp. 60–61.

31. Giovanni Grassi, *Notizie varie sullo stato presente della republica degli Stati Uniti dell' America* (1819), section translated in Oscar Handlin, ed., *This Was America* (Cambridge, Mass.: Harvard University Press, 1949), pp. 147–148.

32. Smith, *Revivalism and Social Reform in Mid-Nineteenth Century America*, p. 37.

33. Ibid., p. 19. (Emphasis mine.)

34. J. H. Grand Pierre, *A Parisian Pastor's Glance at America* (Boston: Gould and Lincoln, 1854), pp. 63–64.

35. Quoted in George W. Pierson, *Tocqueville in America* (Garden City, N.Y.: Doubleday Anchor, 1959), p. 70.

36. Loc. cit. (Emphasis mine.)

37. Tocqueville, *Democracy in America*, Vol. II, p. 28.

38. Pierson, *Tocqueville in America*, p. 100.

39. Martineau, *Society in America*, Vol. II, p. 336.

40. Trollope, *North America*, p. 278.

41. Gerth and Mills, eds., *From Max Weber*, p. 307.

42. Denis W. Brogan, *The American Character* (New York: Alfred A. Knopf, 1944), p. 102. Stow Persons states that "by the middle of the nineteenth century . . . the denominational pattern that had matured . . . conformed closely to the contours of American social life. Under no other ecclesiastical system could the expressions of the religious spirit have been expected to reflect so immediately the character and outlook of the parishioners. . . . The middle classes generally preferred a more sedate and formal worship in which traditional dogmas were wedded to the individualistic ethic of the Gospel of Wealth. Urban professionals and intellectuals who were sensitive to currents of opinion in the secular world were frequently drawn into that new phenomenon, the big city parish, centered on the resonant personality of a pulpit orator who blended the elements of an innocuous theology with discussion of current interests to produce a romantic individualism." "Religion and Modernity, 1865–1914," in J. W. Smith and L. Jamison, eds., *The Shaping of American Religion* (Princeton, N. J.: Princeton University Press, 1961), pp. 370–372.

43. There are more than 200 Protestant denominations in the United States. "Democracy has not only permitted the continuance of all the divisions of Protestantism; it has also allowed, if not encouraged, the growth of new groups." H. Richard Niebuhr, "The Protestant Movement and Democracy in the United States," in J. W. Smith and L. Jamison, eds., *The Shaping of American Religion,* pp. 52–53. See pp. 25–26 for a classification of Protestant denominations in the United States based on the times of their origins.

44. E. T. Clark, *The Small Sects in America* (New York: Abingdon-Cokesbury, 1949), p. 17. Stow Persons, in discussing Clark's account of the Millerite movement and its reaction to the anticipated day of the Second Coming, interestingly concludes that millenialism "cannot be explained as a product of poverty or persecution [but rather] represented a stubborn refusal to accept a modernist version of the historical process in which divine immanence was reconciled with events naturalistically conceived." He finds evidence of diffuse anxiety, rather than misery or tragedy, in Adventist literature. Stow Persons, "Religion and Modernity, 1865–1914," op. cit., pp. 399–400.

45. William W. Sweet, *The American Churches* (New York: Abingdon-Cokesbury, 1947), p. 73; A. T. Boisen, *Religion in Crisis and Custom* (New York: Harper & Bros., 1955), pp. 71–75; also Michael Argyle, *Religious Behavior* (Glencoe, Ill.: The Free Press, 1958), pp. 138–140.

46. H. Richard Niebuhr, indulging in a kind of animistic thinking, attributes "other-directedness" to Protestant groups themselves. "Seeking to survive, thrown into competition for attention, membership, and economic support, not only with each other but with secular enterprises claiming the same resources, they appear to have adjusted themselves all too well to the wishes of the people. . . . If Protestantism in America has . . . accepted . . . the dogmas of democratic faith, then indeed it has lost its independence, then it no longer challenges the social faith but is a passive representative of the culture." "The Protestant Movement and Democracy . . . ," op. cit., pp. 57, 67.

47. Tocqueville, *Democracy in America,* Vol. I, p. 314.

48. Herberg, *Protestant—Catholic—Jew,* p. 247.

49. Tocqueville, *Democracy in America,* Vol. I, pp. 315–316.

50. William Lee Miller, "American Religion and American Political Attitudes," in J. W. Smith and L. Jamison, eds., *The Shaping of American Religion* (Princeton, N.J.: Princeton University Press, 1961), p. 94.

51. The best treatment of the relationship of religion to the background of the Revolution is Carl Bridenbaugh, *Mitre and Sceptre* (New York: Oxford University Press, 1962).

52. Sidney E. Mead, "The Rise of the Evangelical Conception of the Ministry in America (1607–1850)," in H. Richard Niebuhr and Daniel D. Williams, eds., *The Ministry in Historical Perspectives* (New York: Harper & Bros., 1956), pp. 214–215. An excellent, detailed analysis of the interrelationship between voluntary organizations and religious practice in the early United States may be found in Baird, *Religion in America.*

53. See Clifford S. Griffin, *Their Brothers' Keepers* (New Brunswick, N.J.: Rutgers University Press, 1960), pp. 23–43, for a description of the organization of these societies.

54. An American Gentleman (Calvin Colton), *A Voice from America to England* (London: Henry Colburn, 1839), pp. 87–88, 97.

55. Smith, *Revivalism and Social Reform in Mid-Nineteenth Century America,* pp. 88–89.

56. Ibid., p. 89.

57. Ibid., pp. 24–25.

58. Calvin Colton, *A Voice from America to England,* pp. 69–70. Colton himself was an Episcopalian conservative and disliked these tendencies.

59. Stanley Elkins, *Slavery* (Chicago: University of Chicago Press, 1959), p. 35.

60. I have discussed these aspects of American political life in another publication dealing with "Religion and Politics in America," in Robert Lee, ed., *Religion and Social Conflict* (New York: Oxford University Press, 1964).

61. J. Franklin Jameson, *The American Revolution Considered as a Social Movement* (Princeton, N.J.: Princeton University Press, 1926), p. 157.

62. Schaff, *America,* p. 259.

63. Richard Mentor Johnson, "Sunday Observance and the Mail," reprinted in George E. Probst, ed., *The Happy Republic* (New York: Harper Torchbooks, 1962), pp. 250–254. (Emphasis in original.)

64. Cited in R. Freeman Butts, *The American Tradition in Religion and Education* (Boston: The Beacon Press, 1950), pp. 136–137. (Emphases are Butts's.)

65. Evarts B. Greene, *Religion and the State* (Ithaca, N.Y.: Great Seal Books, 1959), p. 101.

66. S. D. Clark, *The Developing Canadian Community* (Toronto: University of Toronto Press, 1962), p. 178.

67. See A. T. Mollegen, "Ethics of Protestantism," in F. Ernest Johnson, ed., *Patterns of Ethics in America Today* (New York: [Institute for Religious and Social Studies], Harper & Bros., 1960), p. 53. "Christians and non-Christians . . . have a claim to our consid-

eration both of their criticism of our own position and of their positive programs which differ from ours. This is the Protestant support of the democratic forum of public opinions. . . . They do it . . . in order that Christians may know the shock of sincere Christians differing deeply and thus be humbled in their own positions even when they cannot in conscience change them." Ibid., p. 59.

68. Albert T. Rasmussen, "Contemporary Religious Appeals and Who Responds," in Jane C. Zahn, ed., *Religion and the Face of America* (Berkeley: University Extension, 1958), p. 4.

69. Loc. cit.

70. See Niebuhr, "The Protestant Movement and Democracy . . . ," op. cit., pp. 57–59; and Persons, "Religion and Modernity . . . , op. cit., pp. 371–372.

71. Tocqueville, *Democracy in America,* Vol. II, p. 312.

Protestantism in *Democracy in America*

Selections

Alexis de Tocqueville

On the Point of Departure and Its Importance for the Future of the Anglo-Americans

. . . The emigrants who came at different periods to occupy the territory that today covers the American Union differed from one another in many points; their goal was not the same, and they governed themselves according to diverse principles.

Nevertheless, these men had some common features among themselves, and they all found themselves in an analogous situation.

The bond of language is perhaps the strongest and most lasting that can unite men. All the emigrants spoke the same tongue; they were all children of one and the same people. Born in a country that the struggle of parties had agitated for centuries, and where factions had been obliged in their turn to place themselves under the protection of the laws, their political education had taken place in that rough school, and one saw more notions of rights, more principles of true freedom spread among them than in most of the peoples of Europe. In the period of the first emigrations, township government, that fertile seed of free institutions, had already entered profoundly into English habits, and with it the dogma of the sovereignty of the people was introduced into the very heart of the Tudor monarchy.

They were then in the midst of the religious quarrels that agitated the Christian world. England had thrown itself with a sort of fury onto this new course. The character of the inhabitants, which had always been grave and reflective, had become austere and argumentative. Education had been much increased in these intellectual struggles; the mind had received a more profound cultivation. While they had been absorbed in speaking of religion, mores had become purer. All these general features of the nation were found more or less in the physiognomy of those of its sons who had come to seek a new future on the opposite shores of the ocean.

One remark, moreover, which we shall have occasion to come back to later,[1] is applicable not only to the English, but also to the French, the Spanish, and all the Europeans who came successively to settle on the shores of the New World. All the new European colonies contained, if not the development, at least the seed of a complete democracy. Two causes led to this result: one can say that in general, on their departure from the mother country, the emigrants had no idea of any superiority whatsoever of some over others. It is hardly the happy and the powerful who go into exile, and poverty as well as misfortune are the best guarantees of equality known among men. It nevertheless happened that on several occasions great lords came to America as a consequence of political or religious quarrels. Laws were made to establish a hierarchy of ranks, but they soon perceived that the American soil absolutely repelled territorial aristocracy. They saw that to clear that rebellious land, nothing less than the constant and interested efforts of the property owner himself were necessary. When the ground was prepared, it was found that its profits were not great enough to enrich a master and a tenant farmer at once. The territory was therefore naturally cut up into small estates that the property owner alone cultivated. Now, aristocracy takes to the land; it attaches to the soil and leans on it; it is not established by privileges alone, nor constituted by birth; it is landed property transmitted by heredity. A nation can offer immense fortunes and great miseries; but if these fortunes are not territorial, one sees poor and rich within it; there is, to tell the truth, no aristocracy.

All the English colonies therefore had among them, at the period of their birth, a great family resemblance. All, from their beginning,[2] seemed destined to offer the development of freedom, not the aristocratic freedom of their mother country, but the bourgeois and democratic freedom of which the history of the world had still not offered a complete model.

In this general complexion, however, were very strong nuances that are necessary to show.

In the great Anglo-American family one can distinguish two principal off-shoots that, up to the present, have grown without being entirely confused, one in the South, the other in the North.

Virginia received the first English colony. The emigrants arrived there in 1607. Europe at that period was still singularly preoccupied with the idea that gold and silver mines made the wealth of peoples: a fatal idea that has more impoverished the European nations that gave themselves to it, and destroyed more men in America, than have war and all bad laws together. It was thus gold seekers who were sent to Virginia,[3] people without resources or without [good] conduct, whose restive and turbulent spirits troubled the infancy of the colony [4] and rendered its progress uncertain. Afterwards, the industrialists and farmers arrived, a more moral and tranquil race, but one that was elevated in almost no points above the level of the lower classes of England.[5] No noble thought, no immaterial scheme presided at the foundation of the new settlements. Hardly had the colony been created when they introduced slavery;[6] that was the capital fact that was bound to exert an immense influence on the character, the laws, and the whole future of the South.

Slavery, as we shall explain later,[7] dishonors work; it introduces idleness into society, and with it, ignorance and haughtiness, poverty and luxury. It enervates the forces of the intellect and puts human activity to sleep. The influence of slavery, combined with the English character, explains the mores and social state of the South.

In the North, altogether contrary nuances were woven into this same English background. Here I shall be permitted some details.

In the English colonies of the North, better known under the name of the New England states,[8] the two or three principal ideas that today form the bases of the social theory of the United States were combined.

New England's principles spread at first to the neighboring states; later, they gradually won out in the most distant, and in the end, if I can express myself so, they *penetrated* the entire confederation. They now exert their influence beyond its limits, over the whole American world. The civilization of New England has been like those fires lit in the hills that, after having spread heat around them, still tinge the furthest reaches of the horizon with their light.

The founding of New England offered a new spectacle; everything there was singular and original.

Almost all colonies have had for their first inhabitants men without education and without resources, whom misery and misconduct drove out of the country that gave birth to them, or greedy speculators and industrial entrepreneurs. There are colonies that cannot even claim this origin: Santo Domingo was founded by pirates, and in our day the English courts of justice have taken charge of peopling Australia.

The emigrants who came to settle on the shores of New England all belonged to the well-to-do classes of the mother country. Their gathering on American soil presented, from the origin, the singular phenomenon of a society in which there were neither great lords nor a people, and, so to speak, neither poor nor rich. Proportionately, there was a greater mass of enlightenment spread among those men than within any European nation of our day. All, perhaps without a single exception, had received a quite advanced education, and several among them had made themselves known in Europe by their talents and their science. The other colonies had been founded by adventurers without family; the emigrants of New England brought with them admirable elements of order and morality; they went to the wilderness accompanied by their wives and children. But what distinguished them above all from all the others was the very goal of their undertaking. It was not necessity that forced them to abandon their country; they left a social position they might regret and secure means of living; nor did they come to the New World in order to improve their situation or to increase their wealth; they tore themselves away from the sweetness of their native country to obey a purely intellectual need; in exposing themselves to the inevitable miseries of exile, they wanted to make *an idea* triumph.

The emigrants or, as they so well called themselves, the *pilgrims,* belonged to that sect in England whose austere principles had brought the name Puritan to be given to it. Puritanism was not only a religious doctrine; it also blended at several points with the most absolute democratic and republican theories. Hence came its most dangerous adversaries. Persecuted by the government of the mother country, the rigor of their principles offended by the daily workings of the society in which they lived, the Puritans sought a land so barbarous and so abandoned by the world that they might yet be permitted to live there in their manner and pray to God in freedom. . . .

In New England, the township was completely and definitively constituted from 1650 on. Interests, passions, duties, and rights came to be grouped around the township's individuality and strongly attached to it. In the heart of the township one sees a real, active, altogether democratic and republican political life reigning. The colonies still recognize the supremacy of the metropolis; monarchy is the law of the state, but a republic is already very much alive in the township.

The township names its magistrates[9] of every kind; it taxes itself; it apportions and levies the impost on itself.[10] In the New England township the law of representation is not followed. Affairs that touch the interest of all are treated in the public square and within the general assembly of citizens, as in Athens.

When one studies attentively the laws that were promulgated during this first age of the American republics, one is struck by the intelligence about government and advanced theories of the legislator.

It is evident that he has a more elevated and more complete idea of the duties of society toward its members than European legislators at that time, and that he imposes on it obligations that it still avoided elsewhere. In the New England states, from the origin, the lot of the poor was made secure;[11] severe measures were taken for the upkeep of highways, they named officials to oversee them;[12] townships had public registers in which the result of general deliberations, deaths, marriages, the birth of citizens were inscribed;[13] court clerks were assigned for the keeping of these registers;[14] some officers were charged with administering vacant estates, others with overseeing the boundaries of inheritances; several had as their principal function to maintain public tranquillity in the township.[15]

The law enters into a thousand diverse details to anticipate and satisfy a host of social needs, about which in our day there are still only confused sentiments in France.

But it is by the prescriptions relative to public education that, from the beginning,[16] one sees revealed in the full light of day the original character of American civilization.

"It being one chief project," says the law, "of that old deluder, Satan, to keep men from the knowledge of the scriptures, as in former times, keeping them in an unknown tongue, so in these latter times, by persuading them from the use of tongues, so that at least, the true sense and meaning of the original might be clouded with false glosses of saint seeming deceivers; and that learning may not be buried in the grave of our forefathers, in church and commonwealth, the Lord assisting our endeavors . . ."[17] There follow the provisions that create schools in all townships and oblige the inhabitants, under penalty of heavy fines, to tax themselves to support them. In the most populous districts, high schools are founded in the same manner. Municipal magistrates must see to it that parents send their children to schools; they have the right to levy fines on those who refuse to; and if the resistance continues, society, then putting itself in place of the family, takes possession of the child and takes away from the parents the rights that nature gave them, but which they so poorly knew how to use.[18] The reader will doubtless have remarked the preamble of these ordinances: in America, it is religion that leads to enlightenment; it is the observance of divine laws that guides man to freedom. . . .

The founders of New England were at once ardent sectarians and exalted innovators. While held within the tightest bonds of certain religious beliefs, they were free of all political prejudices.

Hence there are two tendencies, diverse but not contrary, traces of which it is easy to find everywhere in mores as in laws.

Men sacrifice their friends, their family, and their native country to a religious opinion; one can believe them to be absorbed in the pursuit of the intellectual good that they have come to buy at such a high price. One nevertheless sees them seeking with an almost equal ardor material wealth and moral satisfactions, Heaven in the other world and well-being and freedom in this one.

In their hands, political principles, laws, and human institutions seem malleable things that can be turned and combined at will.

Before them fall the barriers that imprisoned the society in whose bosom they were born; old opinions that have been directing the world for centuries vanish; an almost boundless course, a field without a horizon, are discovered: the human mind rushes toward them; it traverses them in all directions; but, when it arrives at the limits of the political world, it halts; trembling, it leaves off the use of its most formidable faculties; it abjures doubt; it renounces the need to innovate; it even abstains from sweeping away the veil of the sanctuary; it bows with respect before truths that it accepts without discussion.

Thus in the moral world, everything is classified, coordinated, foreseen, decided in advance. In the political world, everything is agitated, contested, uncertain; in the one, there is passive though voluntary obedience; in the other, there are independence, contempt for experience, and jealousy of every authority.

Far from harming each other, these two tendencies, apparently so opposed, advance in accord and seem to lend each other a mutual support.

Religion sees in civil freedom a noble exercise of the faculties of man; in the political world, a field left by the Creator to the efforts of intelligence. Free and powerful in its sphere, satisfied with the place that is reserved for it, it knows that its empire is all the better established when it reigns by its own strength alone and dominates over hearts without support.

Freedom sees in religion the companion of its struggles and its triumphs, the cradle of its infancy, the divine source of its rights. It considers religion as the safeguard of mores; and mores as the guarantee of laws and the pledge of its own duration.

INDIRECT INFLUENCE THAT RELIGIOUS BELIEFS EXERT ON POLITICAL SOCIETY IN THE UNITED STATES

I have just shown what the direct action of religion on politics is in the United States. Its indirect action seems to me more powerful still, and it is when it does not speak of freedom that it best teaches Americans the art of being free.

There is an innumerable multitude of sects in the United States. All differ in the worship one must render to the Creator, but all agree on the duties of men toward one another. Each sect therefore adores God in its manner, but all sects preach the same morality in the name of God. If it serves man very much as an individual that his religion be true, this is not so for society. Society has nothing to fear nor to hope from the other life; and what is most important to it is not so much that all citizens profess the true religion but that they profess a religion. Besides, all the sects in the United States are within the great Christian unity, and the morality of Christianity is everywhere the same.

It is permissible to think that a certain number of Americans follow their habits more than their convictions in the worship they render to God. In the United States, moreover, the sovereign is religious, and consequently hypocrisy ought to be common; America is, however, still the place in the world where the Christian religion has most preserved genuine powers over souls; and nothing shows better how useful and natural to man it is in our day, since the country in which it exercises the greatest empire is at the same time the most enlightened and most free.

I have said that American priests pronounce themselves in a general manner to be in favor of civil freedom without excepting even those who do not accept religious freedom; however, one does not see them lend their support to any political system in particular. They take care to keep themselves outside affairs and do not mix in the schemes of the parties. Therefore one cannot say that in the United States religion exerts an influence on the laws or on the details of political opinions, but it directs mores, and it is in regulating the family that it works to regulate the state.

I do not doubt for an instant that the great severity of mores that one remarks in the United States has its primary source in beliefs. Religion there is often powerless to restrain man in the midst of the innumerable temptations that fortune presents to him. It cannot moderate the ardor in him for enriching himself, which everything comes to excite, but it reigns as a sovereign over the soul of woman, and it is woman who makes mores. Of the world's countries, America is surely the one where the bond of marriage is most respected and where they have conceived the highest and most just idea of conjugal happiness.

In Europe, almost all the disorders of society are born around the domestic hearth, not far from the nuptial bed. It is there that men conceive their scorn for natural bonds and permitted pleasures, their taste for disorder, their restiveness of heart, their instability of desires. Agitated by the tumultuous passions that have often troubled his own dwelling, the European submits only with difficulty to the legislative powers of the state. When, on leaving the agitations of the political world, the American returns to the bosom of his family, he immediately meets the image of order and peace. There, all his pleasures are simple and natural, his joys innocent and tranquil; and as he arrives at happiness through regularity of life, he becomes habituated to regulating his opinions as well as his tastes without difficulty.

While the European seeks to escape his domestic sorrows by troubling society, the American draws from his home the love of order, which he afterwards brings into affairs of state.

In the United States religion not only regulates mores, but extends its empire over intelligence.

Among the Anglo-Americans, some profess Christian dogmas because they believe them, others because they are afraid of not looking like they believe them. Christianity therefore reigns without obstacles, on the administration of all; the result, as I have already said elsewhere,[19] is that everything is certain and fixed in the moral world, although the political world seems to be abandoned to the discussion and attempts of men. So the human spirit never perceives an unlimited field before itself: however bold it may be, from time to time it feels that it ought to halt before insurmountable barriers. Before innovating, it is forced to accept certain primary givens and to submit its boldest conceptions to certain forms that delay and halt it.

The imagination of Americans in its greatest leaps has therefore only a circumspect and uncertain step; its pace is hindered and its works are incomplete. These habits of restraint are to be found in political society and singularly favor the tranquillity of the people as well as the longevity of the institutions it has given itself. Nature and circumstances have made the inhabitant of the United States an audacious man; it is easy to judge of this when one sees the manner in which he pursues his fortune. If the spirit of the Americans were free of all impediments, one would soon encounter among them the boldest innovators and the most implacable logicians in the world. But revolutionaries in America are obliged to profess openly a certain respect for the morality and equity of Christianity, which does not permit them to violate its laws easily when they are opposed to the execution of their designs; and if they could raise themselves above their own scruples, they would still feel they were stopped by those of their partisans. Up to now, no one has been encountered in the United States who dared to advance the maxim that everything is permitted in the interest of society. An impious maxim—one that seems to have been invented in a century of freedom to legitimate all the tyrants to come.

So, therefore, at the same time that the law permits the American people to do everything, religion prevents them from conceiving everything and forbids them to dare everything.

Religion, which, among Americans, never mixes directly in the government of society, should therefore be considered as the first of their political institutions; for if it does not give them the taste for freedom, it singularly facilitates their use of it.

It is also from this point of view that the inhabitants of the United States themselves consider religious beliefs. I do not know if all Americans have faith in their religion—for who can read to the bottom of hearts?—but I am sure that they believe it necessary to the maintenance of republican institutions. This opinion does not belong only to one class of citizens or to one party, but to the entire nation; one finds it in all ranks.

In the United States, when a political man attacks a sect, it is not a reason for the partisans even of that sect not to support him; but if he attacks all sects together, each flees him and he remains alone.

While I was in America, a witness presented himself to the assizes of the county of Chester (state of New York) and declared that he did not believe in the existence of God and the immortality of the soul. The presiding officer refused to accept his oath, given, he said, that the witness had destroyed in advance all the faith that could have been put in his words.[20] The newspapers reported the fact without commentary.

Americans so completely confuse Christianity and freedom in their minds that it is almost impossible to have them conceive of the one without the other; and among them, this is not one of those sterile beliefs that the past wills to the present and which seems less to live than to stagnate in the bottom of the soul.

I saw Americans associating to send priests into the new states of the West and to found schools and churches there; they fear that religion will be lost in the midst of the woods, and that the people growing up may not be as free as the one from which it has issued. I encountered wealthy inhabitants of New England who abandoned the land of their birth with the aim of going to lay the foundations of Christianity and freedom by the banks of the Mississippi or on the prairies of Illinois. Thus it is that in the United States religious zeal constantly warms itself at the hearth of patriotism. You think that these men act solely in consideration of the other life, but you are mistaken: eternity is

only one of their cares. If you interrogate these missionaries of Christian civilization, you will be altogether surprised to hear them speak so often of the goods
of this world, and to find the political where you believe you will see only the
religious. "All American republics are in solidarity with one another," they will
say to you; "if the republics of the West fell into anarchy or came under the
yoke of despotism, the republican institutions that flourish on the edges of
the Atlantic Ocean would be in great peril; we therefore have an interest in the
new states' being religious so that they permit us to remain free."

Such are the opinions of Americans; but their error is clear: for, it is
proven to me daily in a very learned manner that all is well in America except
precisely the religious spirit that I admire; and I learn that on the other side of
the ocean the freedom and happiness of the human species lack nothing
except to believe with Spinoza in the eternity of the world and to assert with
Cabanis that the brain secretes thought.[21] To that I have truly nothing to respond if not that those who hold to this language have not been in America,
and have no more seen religious peoples than free peoples. I therefore await
them on their return [from America].

There are people in France who consider republican institutions to be the
temporary instrument of their greatness. They measure with their eyes the
immense space that separates their vices and their miseries from power and
wealth, and they would like to pile ruins into this abyss to try to fill it. Those
people are to freedom what the condottieri of the Middle Ages were to the
kings; they make war for their own account even as they bear his colors: the
republic will at least live long enough to lift them out of their present degra-
dation. It is not to them that I am speaking; but there are others who see in
the republic a permanent and tranquil state, a necessary goal toward which
ideas and mores carry modern societies each day, and who sincerely wish to
prepare men to be free. When these attack religious beliefs, they follow their
passions and not their interests. Despotism can do without faith, but freedom
cannot. Religion is much more necessary in the republic they extol than in the
monarchy they attack, and in democratic republics more than all others. How
could society fail to perish if, while the political bond is relaxed, the moral
bond were not tightened? And what makes a people master of itself if it has
not submitted to God?

ON THE PRINCIPAL CAUSES THAT MAKE RELIGION POWERFUL IN AMERICA

The philosophers of the eighteenth century explained the gradual weakening of beliefs in an altogether simple fashion. Religious zeal, they said, will

be extinguished as freedom and enlightenment increase. It is unfortunate that the facts do not accord with this theory.

There is a certain European population whose disbelief is equaled only by their brutishness and ignorance, whereas in America one sees one of the freest and most enlightened peoples in the world eagerly fulfill all the external duties of religion.

On my arrival in the United States it was the religious aspect of the country that first struck my eye. As I prolonged my stay, I perceived the great political consequences that flowed from these new facts.

Among us, I had seen the spirit of religion and the spirit of freedom almost always move in contrary directions. Here I found them united intimately with one another: they reigned together on the same soil.

I felt my desire to know the cause of this phenomenon growing daily.

To learn it, I interrogated the faithful of all communions; above all, I sought the society of priests, who keep the depositories of the different beliefs and who have a personal interest in their duration. The religion that I profess brought me together particularly with the Catholic clergy, and I was not slow to bond in a sort of intimacy with several of its members. To each of them I expressed my astonishment and exposed my doubts: I found that all these men differed among themselves only on details; but all attributed the peaceful dominion that religion exercises in their country principally to the complete separation of church and state. I do not fear to affirm that during my stay in America I did not encounter a single man, priest or layman, who did not come to accord on this point.

This led me to examine more attentively than I had until then the position that American priests occupy in political society. I learned with surprise that they did not fill any public post.[22] I did not see a single one in the administration, and I discovered that they were not even represented within the assemblies.

The law in several states had closed any political career to them;[23] opinion did so in all the others.

When I finally came to inquire what the mind of the clergy itself was, I perceived that most of its members seemed to distance themselves from power voluntarily and take a sort of professional pride in remaining strangers to it.

I heard them anathematize ambition and bad faith, whatever might be the political opinions with which these took care to cover themselves. But I learned in listening to them that men cannot be condemnable in the eyes of God because of these same opinions when they are sincere, and that there is no more sin in erring in matters of government than in being mistaken about the manner in which one must build a dwelling or plow a furrow.

I saw them separate themselves carefully from all parties, and avoid contact with them with all the ardor of personal interest.

These facts served to prove to me that I had been told the truth. Then I wanted to bring the facts back to the causes: I wondered how it could happen that in diminishing the apparent force of a religion one came to increase its real power, and I believed that it was not impossible to discover this.

The short space of sixty years will never confine the whole imagination of man; the incomplete joys of this world will never suffice for his heart. Alone among all the beings, man shows a natural disgust for existence and an immense desire to exist: he scorns life and fears nothingness. These different instincts constantly drive his soul toward contemplation of another world, and it is religion that guides it there. Religion is therefore only a particular form of hope, and it is as natural to the human heart as hope itself. Only by a kind of aberration of the intellect and with the aid of a sort of moral violence exercised on their own nature do men stray from religious beliefs; an invincible inclination leads them back to them. Disbelief is an accident; faith alone is the permanent state of humanity.

In considering religions from a purely human point of view, one can therefore say that all religions draw from man himself an element of strength that can never fail them, because it depends on one of the constituent principles of human nature.

I know that there are times when religion can add to the influence that is proper to it the artificial power of the laws and the support of the material powers that direct society. One has seen religions intimately united with earthly governments, dominating souls by terror and by faith at the same time; but when a religion contracts an alliance like this, I do not fear to say that it acts as a man would: it sacrifices the future with a view to the present, and in obtaining a power that is not due to it, it risks its legitimate power.

When a religion seeks to found its empire only on the desire for immortality that torments the hearts of all men equally, it can aim at universality; but when it comes to be united with a government, it must adopt maxims that are applicable only to certain peoples. So, therefore, in allying itself with a political power, religion increases its power over some and loses the hope of reigning over all.

As long as a religion is supported only by sentiments that are the consolation of all miseries, it can attract the hearts of the human race to it. Mixed with the bitter passions of this world, it is sometimes constrained to defend allies given it by interest rather than love; and it must repel as adversaries men who often still love it, while they are combating those with whom it has united.

Religion, therefore, cannot share the material force of those who govern without being burdened with a part of the hatreds to which they give rise. . . .

Insofar as a nation takes on a democratic social state, and societies are seen to incline toward republics, it becomes more and more dangerous for religion to unite with authority; for the time approaches when power is going to pass from hand to hand, when political theories will succeed one another, when men, laws, and constitutions themselves will disappear or be modified daily—and this lasting not only for a time, but constantly. Agitation and instability are due to the nature of democratic republics, just as immobility and sleep form the law of absolute monarchies.

If the Americans, who change their head of state every four years, who every two years make choice of new legislators and replace provincial administrators each year; if the Americans, who have delivered the political world to the attempts of innovators, had not placed their religion somewhere outside of that, what could it hold onto in the ebb and flow of human opinions? In the midst of the parties' struggle, where would the respect be that is due it? What would become of its immortality when everything around it was perishing?

American priests have perceived this truth before all others, and they conform their behavior to it. They saw that they had to renounce religious influence if they wanted to acquire a political power, and they preferred to lose the support of power rather than share in its vicissitudes.

In America, religion is perhaps less powerful than it has been in certain times and among certain peoples, but its influence is more lasting. It is reduced to its own strength, which no one can take away from it; it acts in one sphere only, but it covers the whole of it and dominates it without effort.

How, in the United States, Religion Knows How to Make Use of Democratic Instincts

I established in one of the preceding chapters[24] that men cannot do without dogmatic beliefs and that it was even very much to be wished that they have them. I add here that among all dogmatic beliefs the most desirable seem to me to be dogmatic beliefs in the matter of religion; that may be deduced very clearly even if one wants to pay attention only to the interests of this world.

There is almost no human action, however particular one supposes it, that does not arise from a very general idea that men have conceived of God, of his relations with the human race, of the nature of their souls, and of their duties toward those like them. One cannot keep these ideas from being the common source from which all the rest flow.

Men therefore have an immense interest in making very fixed ideas for themselves about God, their souls, their general duties toward their Creator and those like them; for doubt about these first points would deliver all their actions to chance and condemn them to a sort of disorder and impotence.

That, therefore, is the matter about which it is most important that each of us have fixed ideas; and unfortunately it is also the one in which it is most difficult for each person, left to himself, to come to fix his ideas solely by the effort of his reason.

Only minds very free of the ordinary preoccupations of life, very penetrating, very agile, very practiced, can, with the aid of much time and care, break through to these so necessary truths.

Still we see that these philosophers themselves are almost always surrounded by uncertainties; that at each step the natural light that enlightens them is obscured and threatens to be extinguished, and that despite all their efforts, they still have been able to discover only a few contradictory notions, in the midst of which the human mind has constantly floated for thousands of years without being able to seize the truth firmly or even to find new errors. Such studies are much above the average capacity of men, and even if most men should be capable of engaging in them, it is evident that they would not have the leisure for it.

Some fixed ideas about God and human nature are indispensable to the daily practice of their lives, and that practice keeps them from being able to acquire them.

That appears to me to be unique. Among the sciences there are some that are useful to the crowd and are within its reach; others are accessible only to a few persons and are not cultivated by the majority, who need only their most remote applications; but the daily use of this [science] is indispensable to all, though its study is inaccessible to most.

General ideas relative to God and human nature are therefore, among all ideas, the ones it is most fitting to shield from the habitual action of individual reason and for which there is most to gain and least to lose in recognizing an authority.

The first object and one of the principal advantages of religions is to furnish a solution for each of these primordial questions that is clear, precise, intelligible to the crowd, and very lasting.

There are religions that are very false and very absurd; nevertheless one can say that every religion that remains within the circle I have just indicated and that does not claim to leave it, as several have attempted to do, in order to stop the free ascent of the human mind in all directions, imposes a salutary yoke on the intellect; and one must recognize that if it does not save men in the other world, it is at least very useful to their happiness and their greatness in this one.

That is above all true of men who live in free countries.

When religion is destroyed in a people, doubt takes hold of the highest portions of the intellect and half paralyzes all the others. Each becomes accustomed to having only confused and changing notions about matters that most interest those like him and himself; one defends one's opinions badly or abandons them, and as one despairs of being able to resolve by oneself the greatest problems that human destiny presents, one is reduced, like a coward, to not thinking about them at all.

Such a state cannot fail to enervate souls; it slackens the springs of the will and prepares citizens for servitude.

Not only does it then happen that they allow their freedom to be taken away, but often they give it over.

When authority in the matter of religion no longer exists, nor in the matter of politics, men are soon frightened at the aspect of this limitless independence. This perpetual agitation of all things makes them restive and fatigues them. As everything is moving in the world of the intellect, they want at least that all be firm and stable in the material order; and as they are no longer able to recapture their former beliefs, they give themselves a master.

As for me, I doubt that man can ever support a complete religious independence and an entire political freedom at once; and I am brought to think that if he has no faith, he must serve, and if he is free, he must believe.

I do not know, however, whether this great utility of religions is not still more visible among peoples where conditions are equal than among all others.

One must recognize that equality, which introduces great goods into the world, nevertheless suggests to men very dangerous instincts, as will be shown hereafter;[25] it tends to isolate them from one another and to bring each of them to be occupied with himself alone.

It opens their souls excessively to the love of material enjoyments.

The greatest advantage of religions is to inspire wholly contrary instincts. There is no religion that does not place man's desires beyond and above earthly goods and that does not naturally raise his soul toward regions much superior to those of the senses. Nor is there any that does not impose on each some duties toward the human species or in common with it, and that does not thus draw him, from time to time, away from contemplation of himself. This one meets even in the most false and dangerous religions.

Religious peoples are therefore naturally strong in precisely the spot where democratic peoples are weak; this makes very visible how important it is that men keep to their religion when becoming equal.

I have neither the right nor the will to examine the supernatural means God uses to make a religious belief reach the heart of man. For the moment I view religions only from a purely human point of view; I seek the manner in which they can most easily preserve their empire in the democratic centuries that we are entering.

I have brought out how, in times of enlightenment and equality, the human mind consents to receive dogmatic beliefs only with difficulty and feels the need of them keenly only in the case of religion. This indicates first that in those centuries more than in all others religions ought to keep themselves discreetly within the bounds that are proper to them and not seek to leave them; for in wishing to extend their power further than religious matters, they risk no longer being believed in any matter. They ought therefore to trace carefully the sphere within which they claim to fix the human mind, and beyond that to leave it entirely free to be abandoned to itself.

Mohammed had not only religious doctrines descend from Heaven and placed in the Koran, but political maxims, civil and criminal laws, and scientific theories. The Gospels, in contrast, speak only of the general relations of men to God and among themselves. Outside of that they teach nothing and oblige nothing to be believed. That alone, among a thousand other reasons, is enough to show that the first of these two religions cannot dominate for long in enlightened and democratic times, whereas the second is destined to reign in these centuries as in all the others.

If I continue this same inquiry further, I find that for religions to be able, humanly speaking, to maintain themselves in democratic centuries, they must not only confine themselves carefully to the sphere of religious matters; their power depends even more on the nature of the beliefs they profess, the external forms they adopt, and the obligations they impose.

What I said previously, that equality brings men to very general and vast ideas, ought to be understood principally in the matter of religion.[26] Men who are alike and equal readily conceive the notion of a single God imposing the same rules on each of them and granting them future happiness at the same price. The idea of the unity of the human race constantly leads them back to the idea of the unity of the Creator, whereas on the contrary, men very separate from one another and very unalike willingly come to make as many divinities as there are peoples, castes, classes and families, and to trace a thousand particular paths for going to Heaven.

One cannot deny that Christianity itself has in some fashion come under the influence exerted over religious beliefs by the social and political state.

At the moment when the Christian religion appeared on earth, Providence, which was undoubtedly preparing the world for its coming, had united a great part of the human species, like an immense flock, under the scepter of the Caesars. The men who composed that multitude differed much from one another, but they nevertheless had this common point: they all obeyed the same laws; and each of them was so weak and small in relation to the greatness of the prince that they all appeared equal when one came to compare them to him.

One must recognize that this new and particular state of humanity ought to have disposed men to receive the general truths taught by Christianity, and serves to explain the easy and rapid manner with which it then penetrated the human mind.

The corresponding proof came after the destruction of the Empire.

As the Roman world was then shattering, so to speak, into a thousand shards, each nation returned to its former individuality. Inside those nations, ranks were soon graduated to infinity; races were marked out, castes partitioned each nation into several peoples. In the midst of this common effort that seemed to bring human societies to subdivide themselves into as many fragments as it was possible to conceive, Christianity did not lose sight of the principal general ideas it had brought to light. But it nonetheless appeared to lend itself, as much as it could, to the new tendencies arising from the fragmentation of the human species. Men continued to adore one God alone as creator and preserver of all things; but each people, each city, and so to speak each man, believed himself able to obtain some separate privilege and to create for himself particular protectors before the sovereign master. Unable to divide the Divinity, they at least multiplied it and magnified its agents beyond measure; the homage due to angels and saints became an almost idolatrous worship for most Christians, and one could fear a moment might come when the Christian religion would regress to the religions it had defeated.

It appears evident to me that the more the barriers that separate nations within humanity and citizens within the interior of each people tend to disappear, the more the human mind is directed, as if by itself, toward the idea of a single omnipotent being, dispensing the same laws to each man equally and in the same manner. It is therefore particularly in centuries of democracy that it is important not to allow the homage rendered to secondary agents to be confused with the worship that is due only the Creator.

Another truth appears very clear to me: that religions should be less bur-dened with external practices in democratic times than in all others.

I have brought out, concerning the philosophic method of the Ameri-cans, that nothing revolts the human mind more in times of equality than the idea of submitting to forms.[27] Men who live in these times suffer [represen-tational] figures with impatience; symbols appear to them to be puerile arti-fices that are used to veil or adorn for their eyes truths it would be more natural to show to them altogether naked and in broad daylight; the sight of ceremonies leaves them cold, and they are naturally brought to attach only a secondary importance to the details of worship.

Those charged with regulating the external form of religions in demo-cratic centuries ought indeed to pay attention to these natural instincts of human intelligence in order not to struggle unnecessarily against them.

I believe firmly in the necessity of forms; I know that they fix the human mind in the contemplation of abstract truths, and by aiding it to grasp them forcefully, they make it embrace them ardently. I do not imagine that it is pos-sible to maintain a religion without external practices; but on the other hand, I think that in the centuries we are entering, it would be particularly danger-ous to multiply them beyond measure; that one must rather restrict them, and that one ought to retain only what is absolutely necessary for the perpetuation of the dogma itself, which is the substance of religions,[28] whereas worship is only the form. A religion that would become more minute, inflexible, and burdened with small observances at the same time that men were becoming more equal would soon see itself reduced to a flock of impassioned zealots in the midst of an incredulous multitude.

I know that one will not fail to object that since all religions have gen-eral and eternal truths for their object, they cannot so yield to the inconstant instincts of each century without losing the character of certainty in the eyes of men: I shall still respond here that one must distinguish very carefully the principal opinions that constitute a belief and that form what theologians call articles of faith, from the accessory notions that are linked to them. Religions are obliged always to hold firm in the first, whatever the particular spirit of the times may be; but they would do well to keep from binding themselves in the same manner to the second in centuries in which everything constantly changes place and in which the mind, habituated to the moving spectacle of human things, suffers itself to be held fixed only with regret. Immobility in external and secondary things appears to me to have a chance of lasting only when civil society itself is immobile; everywhere else, I am brought to believe that it is a peril.

We shall see[29] that among all the passions that equality gives birth to or favors, there is one that it renders particularly keen and that it sets in the hearts of all men at the same time: the love of well-being. The taste for well-being forms the salient and indelible feature of democratic ages.

One may believe that a religion that undertook to destroy this mother passion would in the end be destroyed by it; if it wanted to tear men entirely from contemplation of the goods of this world to deliver them solely to the thought of those of the other world, one can foresee that their souls would finally escape from its hands to go plunge themselves, far away from it, only in material and present enjoyments.

The principal business of religions is to purify, regulate, and restrain the too ardent and too exclusive taste for well-being that men in times of equality feel; but I believe that they would be wrong to try to subdue it entirely and to destroy it. They will not succeed in turning men away from love of wealth; but they can still persuade them to enrich themselves only by honest means.

This leads me to a final consideration that in some fashion comprises all the others. As men become more alike and equal, it is more important that religions, while carefully putting themselves out of the way of the daily movement of affairs, not collide unnecessarily with the generally accepted ideas and permanent interests that reign among the mass; for common opinion appears more and more as the first and most irresistible of powers; there is no support outside of it strong enough to permit long resistance to its blows. That is no less true in a democratic people subject to a despot than in a republic. In centuries of equality, kings often make one obey, but it is always the majority that makes one believe; it is therefore the majority that one must please in all that is not contrary to the faith.

I showed in my first work how American priests keep their distance from public affairs.[30] This is the most striking, but not the only, example of their restraint. In America religion is a world apart, where the priest reigns, but which he is careful never to leave; within its limits he guides intelligence; outside of it, he leaves men to themselves and abandons them to the independence and instability that are proper to their nature and to the times. I have not seen a country where Christianity wraps itself less in forms, practices, and [representational] figures than the United States, and presents ideas more clearly, simply, and generally to the human mind. Although Christians of America are divided into a multitude of sects, they all perceive their religion in the same light. This applies to Catholicism as well as to other beliefs. There are no Catholic priests who show less taste for small, individual observances, for extraordinary and particular methods of gaining salvation, or who cling more to the spirit of the law and less to its letter, than the Catholic priests of the United States; nowhere does one teach more clearly or follow better the doctrine of the Church that forbids rendering to saints the worship that is reserved only for God. Nevertheless, Catholics of America are very submissive and very sincere.

Another remark is applicable to the clergy of all communions: American priests do not try to attract and fix all the attentions of man on the future life; they willingly abandon a part of his heart to present cares; they seem to consider the goods of the world as important although secondary objects; if they do not associate themselves with industry, they are at least interested in its progress and applaud it, and while constantly showing to the faithful the other world as the great object of their hopes and fears, they do not forbid them from honestly searching for well-being in this one. Far from bringing out how these two things are divided and contrary, they rather apply themselves to finding the spot at which they touch and are bound to each other.

All American priests know the intellectual empire the majority exercises and respect it. They never support any but necessary struggles against it. They do not mix in the quarrels of the parties, but they willingly adopt the general opinions of their country and time, and they let themselves go without resistance in the current of sentiments and ideas that carries away all things around them. They strive to correct their contemporaries, but they do not separate themselves from them. Public opinion is never, therefore, their enemy; rather it supports and protects them, and their beliefs reign both by the forces that are proper to them and by those of the majority that they borrow.

Thus it is in respecting all the democratic instincts that are not contrary to it and in taking aid from several of them that religion succeeds in struggling to its advantage against the spirit of individual independence that is the most dangerous of all to it.

Notes

1. *Democracy in America* [DA] I 2.9.
2. Or, "from their principle."
3. The charter granted by the English Crown in 1609 had among other clauses that the colonists should pay the Crown a fifth of the profit of gold and silver mines. See *Life of Washington*, by Marshall, vol. 1, 18–66. [John Marshall, *Vie de George Washington*, 5 vols. (Paris: Dentu, 1807). English edition: *The Life of George Washington* (Lon-

don, 1804). John Marshall (1755–1835) was Chief Justice of the United States Supreme Court from 1801 until his death.]

4. A great part of the new colonists, says [William] Stith (*History of Virginia*), were young people of disordered families whose parents had sent them to spare them from an ignominious fate; former domestics, fraudulent bankrupts, debauched persons and other people of this kind, more suited to pillage and destroy than to consolidate the settlement, formed the rest. Seditious heads easily carried this troop along into all sorts of extravagances and excesses. See, relative to the history of Virginia, the following works:

History of Virginia from the First Settlements to the Year 1624, by Smith [John Smith, *The Generall Historie of Virginia, New England, and the Summer Isles: With the Names of the Adventurers, Planters, and Governours from Their First Beginning, Ano. 1584, to This Present 1624* (London: Michael Sparkes, 1624)].

History of Virginia, by William Stith [William Stith, *The History of the First Discovery and Settlement of Virginia: Being an Essay towards a General History of This Colony*, 8 vols. (Williamsburg, Va.: William Parks, 1747)].

History of Virginia from the Earliest Period, by Beverley, translated into French in 1807 [Robert Beverley, *The History and Present State of Virginia* (London: R. Parker, 1705). French edition: *Histoire de la Virginie* (Amsterdam: T. Lombrail, 1707)].

5. Only later did a certain number of rich English property owners come to settle in the colony.

6. Slavery was introduced around the year 1620 by a Dutch vessel that unloaded twenty Negroes on the shores of the James River. See Chalmers [George Chalmers, *An Introduction to the History of the Revolt of the American Colonies*, vol. 1, 13 (London, 1782)].

7. *DA* I 2.10.

8. The states of New England are those situated to the east of the Hudson: today they are six in number: (1) Connecticut; (2) Rhode Island; (3) Massachusetts; (4) Vermont; (5) New Hampshire; (6) Maine.

9. As AT will make clear in *DA* I 2.5, he uses the term "magistrate" to mean "all those who are charged with having the laws executed."

10. *Code of 1650*, 80[f.].

11. *Code of 1650*, 78.

12. *Code of 1650*, 49[-50].

13. See [Thomas] Hutchinson's *History*, vol. 1, 455.

14. *Code of 1650*, 86[f.].

15. *Code of 1650*, 40[-41].

16. Or, "from principle."

17. *Code of 1650*, 90[-91]. [AT's version of the quotation is: "Whereas," says the law, "Satan, enemy of the human race, finds in the ignorance of men his most powerful arms, and whereas it is important that the enlightenment our fathers brought not remain buried in their tombs;—whereas the education of children is one of the first interests of the state, with the assistance of the Lord . . ."]

18. *Code of 1650*, 83 [38–39, 91].

19. *DA* I 1.2.

20. Here are the words in which the *New York Spectator* of August 23, 1831, reports the fact: "The court of common pleas of Chester county (New York) a few days since rejected a witness who declared his disbelief in the existence of God. The presiding judge remarked that he had not before been aware that there was a man living who did not believe in the existence of God; that this belief constituted the sanction of all testimony in a court of justice and that he knew of no case in a Christian country where a witness had been permitted to testify without such a belief." [Cited in English.]

21. The philosopher Benedict Spinoza (1632–1677) and the medical doctor Pierre-Jean Georges Cabanis (1757–1808), who authored several philosophic works.

22. Unless one gives this name to the offices that many of them occupy in schools. The greater part of education is entrusted to the clergy.

23. See the Constitution of New York [1821], art. 7, sec. 4; Constitution of North Carolina [1776], art. 31; Constitution of Virginia; Constitution of South Carolina [1790], art. 1, sec. 23; Constitution of Kentucky [1799], art. 2, sec. 26; Constitution of Tennessee [1796], art. 8, sec. 1; Constitution of Louisiana, art. 2, sec. 22. The article of the Constitution of New York is conceived thus:

> Ministers of the Gospel, being by their profession consecrated to the service of God and given to the care of directing souls, ought not to be troubled in the exercise of these important duties; consequently no minister of the Gospel or priest, to whatever sect he may belong, shall be able to be vested with any public offices, civil or military.

24. *DA* II 1.2.

25. See especially *DA* II 2.2.

26. *DA* II 1.3.

27. *DA* II 1.1.

28. In all religions there are ceremonies that are inherent in the very substance of belief and in which one must indeed guard against changing anything. That is seen particularly in Catholicism, in which the form and the foundation are often so tightly united that they are one.

29. *DA* II 2.10.

30. *DA* I 2.9.

CHAPTER FOUR

The Godless Constitution

Isaac Kramnick & R. Laurence Moore

Americans revere the Constitution. Drafted in Philadelphia in the summer of 1787, the Constitution stands with the flag as a symbol of national unity. America has no royal family, no heritage of timeless and integrative state institutions and symbols, no national church. Add to that America's history of being peopled by diverse religious, national, and racial stocks, many of whom came, or were brought here, long after the founding, and one can see how the Constitution could become such a focus of national identity and loyalty. There is precious little else to compete with it as a unifying and symbolic evocation of America. To this day, in fact, to become an American citizen it is traditional for immigrants to have to pass a test on the Constitution. Unlike the American flag, however, which has changed dramatically over the years, with the ever expanding number of states, the Constitution has endured virtually unchanged over two hundred years. This is, surely, another important source of its status as the focus of American identity—its stability and unchanging quality.

The U.S. Constitution is a strikingly spare document with but seven articles. Its very leanness suggested to contemporaries that they had produced a unique and metahistoric achievement. John Adams described it as "if not the greatest exertion of human understanding, [then] the greatest single effort of national deliberation that the world has ever seen." Foreigners have echoed this sentiment. On the Constitution's centennial in 1887 the English statesman William Gladstone contended that it "was the most wonderful work ever struck off at a given time by the brain and purpose of man."

Not only is that same Constitution (with its later amendments) still revered in America; it still functions repeatedly as a touchstone in debates about contemporary legislation and public policy—as it should. The views of the framers as codified in their Olympian document are constantly invoked and given respect in discussions of matters as diverse as gun control, budgets, and welfare reform. In no area of public debate is this more evident than in the issues of religion and politics. Americans are continually told that the framers were deeply religious, God-fearing Christians who, as Newt Gingrich likes to note, would, as Jefferson did, often integrate into their political prose pious phrases like "'upon the altar of God' I proclaim this or that." It follows that such religious men drafted a Christian Constitution in which God presides over and inspires a Christian political system. "The Constitution was designed to perpetuate a Christian order," the Christian right's Focus on the Family informs us.

That's not what happened in 1787. God and Christianity are nowhere to be found in the American Constitution, a reality that infuriated many at the time. The U.S. Constitution, drafted in 1787 and ratified in 1788, is a godless document. Its utter neglect of religion was no oversight; it was apparent to all. Self-consciously designed to be an instrument with which to structure the secular politics of individual interest and happiness, the Constitution was bitterly attacked for its failure to mention God or Christianity. Our history books usually describe in great detail the major arguments made against the federal Constitution by its Anti-Federalist opponents: it meant death to the states and introduced an elitist Senate and a monarchical presidency. They seldom mention, however, the concerted campaign to discredit the Constitution as irreligious, which for many of its opponents was its principal flaw. It is as if recognizing the dimension of this criticism would draw too much attention to what was being attacked—the secularism of the Constitution. In fact, this underdocumented and underremembered controversy of 1787–88 over the godless Constitution was one of the most important public debates ever held in America over the place of religion in politics. The advocates of a secular state won, and it is their Constitution we revere today.

Their advocacy overturned a host of precedents. Jefferson's Declaration of Independence has famously invoked the "Creator" in laying out the human rights that propelled the colonists into revolt against England. The Articles of Confederation of 1776, America's first framework of government, gave credit to "the Great Governor of the World," and most of the earliest state constitutions contained an explicit acknowledgment of God and of the relationship of Christianity to civil order. The Massachusetts state constitution of 1780, for example, contains in Article 2 the injunction "It is the duty of all men in society publicly and at stated seasons to worship the Supreme Being, the great Creator and Preserver of the universe." The U.S. Constitution of 1787, however, contains no mention of "God," the "Great Governor," "Creator and Preserver," or "Supreme Being" whatsoever. God is nowhere to be found in the Constitution, which also has nothing to say about the social value of Christian belief or about the importance of religion for a moral public life. Alongside its utter silence with respect to God and to the United States as a Christian nation, the Constitution's sole reference to religion made matters worse, only adding insult to injury. Article 6 declares that "no religious test shall ever be required as a qualification to any office or public trust under the United States." It was this provision that served as the textual focus for the great debate on religion and the Constitution at the founding.

While passionately debated in the new nation, the "no religious test" clause elicited surprisingly little discussion at the Philadelphia Constitutional Convention itself. It was introduced by Charles Pinckney, the governor of South Carolina, on August 20, whereupon it was referred immediately to the Committee on Detail without any debate among the delegates. The committee presented its general report on August 30 and made no reference to Pinckney's proposal. Not to be ignored, Pinckney moved it again from the convention floor. Roger Sherman of Connecticut, the committee chairman, held that the prohibition was "unnecessary," the prevailing "liberality" being a sufficient security against such tests. Gouverneur Morris and General Charles Cotesworth Pinckney seconded Governor Pinckney's motion, however. It was then voted on and, according to the Maryland delegate Luther Martin, "adopted by a very great majority of the convention, and without much debate." No records exist of the exact vote, but Madison's personal notes of the convention report that North Carolina voted no and that Maryland was divided. According to Luther Martin, "there were some members *so unfashionable* [his italics] as to think that *a belief in the existence of a Deity* and of a *state of future rewards and punishments* would be some security for the good conduct of our rulers, and that in a Christian country it would be at *least decent* to hold out some distinction between the professors of Christianity and downright infidelity or paganism."

Well might these "unfashionable" members be surprised at the position taken so easily by the majority at the Constitutional Convention, for eleven of the thirteen states had religious tests for public offices in their constitutions in 1787. Even in Rhode Island, once the most religiously pluralistic and liberal state, where small numbers of Catholics and Jews freely worshiped, only Protestants could vote or hold office. New Hampshire, New Jersey, both Carolinas, Vermont, and Georgia also required officials to be Protestants. Massachusetts and Maryland insisted on belief in the Christian religion as a qualification for office. Pennsylvania required its officials to be Protestants who believed in God and the divine inspiration of the Old and New Testaments; in Delaware all elected and appointed public officials were required to profess "faith in

God the Father, and in Jesus Christ His only son, and in the Holy Ghost, one God blessed forevermore." Several state constitutions also required officeholders to acknowledge that God was a "rewarder of the good and punisher of the wicked."

Not that there weren't voices in the states opposing religious tests. The Catholic John Carroll of Maryland noted acerbically in 1787 that even as many state constitutions had been drafted in 1776 reserving public office to Protestants, "the American army swarmed with Roman Catholic soldiers." People of all faiths fought in the Revolution, he noted, assuming that they would not be "shackled by religious tests" and would be "entitled to a participation in the common blessings which crowned their efforts" once they returned to their states. Jews in Pennsylvania petitioned the state government in 1783 and 1787 to remove the requirement that officeholders be Protestants and believers in the New Testament, since it "deprives the Jews of the most eminent right of freemen." In Gorham, Massachusetts (now Maine), the inhabitants instructed their delegates to the Massachusetts constitutional convention of 1779 "that no restriction be required of any officer or ruler but merit, viz. a sufficient knowledge and understanding in matters relative to the office, and fidelity and firmness in the cause of Liberty." The Gorham delegates were unsuccessful in Boston.

The two exceptions among the state constitutions were those of Virginia and New York. In the former, Madison's and Jefferson's "Statute for Religious Freedom," passed in 1786, specified that no religious test could be applied to the holding of public office. Even more interesting was New York's constitution, which in 1777 self-consciously repudiated tests that sought to maintain "any particular denomination of Christians." The absence of religious tests would, the New York constitution claimed, "guard against that spiritual oppression and intolerance wherewith the bigotry and ambition of weak and wicked priests and princes have scourged mankind."

In Philadelphia the principles of Virginia and New York were written into the new federal Constitution "without much debate," reflecting perhaps the towering influence Madison and Hamilton had at the Constitutional Convention. New York's Hamilton had, in fact, earlier given Virginia's Madison his draft for a constitution, which included the clause "nor shall any religious test for any office or place, be ever established by law." As for Madison's views in 1787 on religion and politics, we have the evidence of his contributions to the Federalist papers, written by him, Hamilton, and John Jay in 1787 and 1788 to persuade New York state delegates to ratify the Constitution at their convention. These essays fail to mention God anywhere. (Newt Gingrich, so convinced that the Federalist papers are the final word on American politics that he urged all the members of the House of Representatives to read them when he became Speaker, must realize that nowhere do they discuss America as a Christian people with a Christian government.) Indeed, the one extended reference in the Federalist papers to religion, written by Madison, totally undercuts its value as a governmental means to promote civic virtue. In the famous Federalist No. 10 Madison argues that zealous pursuit of religious opinions, far from leading men to "cooperate for their common good," causes them to hate each other and disposes them "to vex and oppress each other."

If there was little debate in Philadelphia over the "no religious test" clause, a veritable firestorm broke out in the country at large during the ratification conventions in each of the states. Outraged Protestants attacked what they saw, correctly, as a godless Constitution. The "no religious test" clause was perceived by many to be the gravest defect of the Constitution. Colonel Jones, a Massachusetts delegate, told the state's ratifying convention that American political leaders had to believe in God and Jesus Christ. Amos Singletary, another delegate to the Massachusetts ratification convention, was upset at the Constitution's not requiring men in power to be religious "and though he hoped to see Christians [in office], yet by the Constitution, a papist, or an infidel was as eligible as they." In New Hampshire the fear was of "a papist, a Mohomatan [sic], a deist, yea an atheist at the helm of government." Henry Abbot, a delegate to the North Carolina convention, warned that "the exclusion of religious tests" was "dangerous and impolitic" and that "pagans, deists, and Mahometans [sic] might obtain offices among us." If there is no religious test, he asked, "to whom Will they [officeholders] swear support—the ancient pagan gods of Jupiter, Juno, Minerva, or Pluto?"

More specific fears were clearly at work here. The absence of religious tests, it was feared, would open up the national government to control by Jews, Catholics, and Quakers. The Reverend David Caldwell, a Presbyterian minister and delegate in North Carolina, worried that the Constitution now offered an invitation to "Jews and pagans of every kind" to govern us. Major Thomas Lusk, a delegate in Massachusetts, denounced Article 6 of the Constitution and shuddered "at the idea that Roman Catholics, Papists, and Pagans might be introduced into office, and that Popery and the Inquisition may be established in America." A delegate in North Carolina waved a pamphlet that depicted the possibility that the pope of Rome might be elected president. Calming himself down, he warned the delegates that in "the course of four or five hundred years" it was most certain that "Papists may occupy that [presidential] chair." More realistically, it was fear of Quakers, and of their pacifism and antislavery views, that helped fuel the debate. In Charleston, South Carolina, a writer in the *City Gazette* warned on January 3, 1788, that "as there will be no religious test," the Quakers "will have weight, in proportion to their numbers, in the great scale of continental government." An anti-constitutional article written for the *New York Daily Advertiser* that same January and widely reprinted within days in Connecticut, New Hampshire, and Massachusetts papers pulled no punches about the social repercussions of Article 6. No religious tests admitted to national lawmaking: "1st. Quakers, who will make the blacks saucy, and at the same time deprive us of the means of defence—2dly. Mahometans, who ridicule the doctrine of the Trinity—3dly. Deists, abominable wretches—4thly. Negroes, the seed of Cain—5thly. Beggars, who when set on horseback will ride to the devil—6thly. Jews etc. etc." Not quite finished with the last, the newspaper writer feared that since the Constitution stupidly gave command of the whole militia to the president, "should he hereafter be a Jew, our dear posterity may be ordered to rebuild Jerusalem."

The prohibition of religious tests was seen by many opponents as the operative sign of the Constitution's more basic flaw—its general godless quality, its seeming indifference to religion. Disputants around America complained, as the writer "Philadelphiensis" did in November 1787, of the framers' "silence" and "indifference about religion." An anonymous writer in the *Virginia Independent Chronicle* cautioned in October 1787 about "the pernicious effects" of the Constitution's "general disregard of religion," its "cold indifference towards religion." Thomas Wilson, also of Virginia, insisted that the "Constitution is de[i]stical in principle, and in all probability the composers had no thought of God in all their consultations." There is some truth in Mr. Wilson's observation. When Benjamin Franklin, who presided over the Constitutional Convention, urged the delegates to open their sessions with prayers, a request cited often today by the religious right, the delegates, more worried about worldly matters like Shays's Rebellion and America's financial instability under the Articles of Confederation, voted to adjourn for the day rather than discuss Franklin's suggestion. The matter was never brought up again.

Deism was, as we shall see, a powerful force among the intellectuals of the founding generation, even among many of the delegates in Philadelphia. A nondoctrinaire religion, deism rejected a supernatural faith built around an anthropomorphic God who intervened in human affairs, either in answer to prayer or for other, inscrutable reasons. Instead, it posited a naturalistic religion with a God understood as a supreme intelligence who after creating the world destined it to operate forever after according to natural, rational, and scientific laws. No surprise, then, that a frequent claim heard in 1787 and

1788 was that the Constitution represented a deistic conspiracy to overthrow the Christian commonwealth. This view was most powerfully put by the Carlisle, Pennsylvania, pamphleteer "Aristocrotis" in a piece aptly titled "The Government of Nature Delineated or An Exact Picture of the New Federal Constitution."

Aristocrotis contends that the delegates in Philadelphia have created a government that for the first time in world history removes religion from public life. Until 1787 "there was never a nation in the world whose government was not circumscribed by religion." But this was no problem for the Constitutional Convention intent on creating "a government founded upon nature." What, he asks, "is the world to the federal convention but as the drop of a bucket, or the small dust in the balance! What the world could not accomplish from the commencement of time till now, they easily performed in a few moments by declaring that 'no religious test shall ever be required as a qualification to any office, or public trust, under the United States.'" This, Aristocrotis suggests, "is laying the ax to the root of the tree; whereas other nations only lopped off a few noxious branches." He argues that the "new Constitution, disdains . . . belief of a deity, the immortality of the soul, or the resurrection of the body, a day of judgement, or a future state of rewards and punishments," because its authors are committed to a natural religion that is deistic nonreligion. He concludes with irony: "If some religion must be had the religion of nature will certainly be preferred by a government founded upon the law of nature. One great argument in favor of this religion is, that most of the members of the grand convention are great admirers of it; and they certainly are the best models to form our religious as well as our civil belief on."

Other critics of the Constitution shared Aristocrotis' demand for the retention of a Christian commonwealth, with a similar desire to see religion be an integral part of public life. In New Hampshire, "A Friend to the Rights of the People," writing against "the discarding of all religious tests," asked in an interesting shift, "Will this be good policy to discard all religion?" The answer was, of course, no, for despite the Constitution "it is acknowledged by all that civil government can't well be supported without the assistance of religion." No man, he concluded, "is fit to be a ruler of protestants, without he can honestly profess to be of the protestant religion." During this same New Hampshire ratification debate, a delegate argued that to ratify the Constitution would be to overturn all religion and introduce a godless America, suggesting even that if the Constitution were adopted "congress might deprive the people of the use of the holy scriptures." An Anti-Federalist writer warned in a

Boston newspaper on January 10, 1788, that since God was absent from the Constitution, Americans would suffer the fate that the prophet Samuel foretold to Saul: "because thou hast rejected the word of the Lord, he hath also rejected thee." In short, if Americans in their new fundamental law forgot God and His Christian commonwealth, God would soon forget them, and they would perish. The same apocalyptic theme was picked up by the Massachusetts Anti-Federalist Charles Turner, who feared that "without the presence of Christian piety and morals the best Republican Constitution can never save us from slavery and ruin."

One of the most moving rejections of the godless Constitution in favor of an overtly Christian government came from one "David" in the *Massachusetts Gazette* on March 7, 1788. His message was clear. Public virtue and civic peace required governmental encouragement of and involvement with Christian religion. He defended Massachusetts' "religious test, which requires all public officers to be of some Christian, protestant persuasion," and criticized the federal Constitution's "public inattention" to religion and the framers' "leaving religion to shift wholly for itself." The new nation was embarking on a futile course, for "it is more difficult to build an elegant house without tools to work with, than it is to establish a durable government without the publick protection of religion."

A letter to the delegates at the Virginia ratifying convention in June 1788 urged them to insist on adding to the first or second article of the Constitution a clause requiring the creation "at every proper place through the United States" of academies regulated by Congress where young people would learn "the principles of the Christian religion without regard to any sect, but pure and unadulterated as left by its divine author and his apostle." The social benefits expected to flow from these obligatory Christian academies sound very much like a 1788 version of the projected fruits of compulsory school prayer as urged by today's Christian right. Were compulsory Christian education established, the Virginian affirms, "we would have fewer law suits, less backbiting, slander, and mean observations, more industry, justice and real happiness than at present."

Like this Virginian, those opposed to the godless Constitution did not just complain; their advocacy of a Christian commonwealth led them to propose specific changes in the Constitution at various state ratifying conventions, all of which were rejected. In Connecticut, William Williams, a delegate, formally moved that the Constitution's one-sentence preamble be enlarged to include a Christian conception of politics. He proposed that it be changed to read, "We the people of the United States in a firm belief of the being and perfection of the one living and true God, the creator and supreme Governor of the World, in His universal providence and the authority of His laws: that He will require of all moral agents an account of their conduct, that all rightful powers among men are ordained of, and mediately derived from God, therefore in a dependence on His blessing and acknowledgment of His efficient protection in establishing our Independence, whereby it is become necessary to agree upon and settle a Constitution of federal government for ourselves, and in order to form a more perfect union, etc., as it is expressed in the present introduction, do ordain, etc." Williams also moved that a religious test along these lines be required for all federal officials. One hundred and sixty years later the Pledge of Allegiance might be changed by Congress to include the brief "under God." But in 1788 the delegates in Connecticut chose not to introduce God, via Williams's wordy resolution, into the U.S. Constitution.

Equally unsuccessful was the Virginia initiative in April and May 1788 to change the wording of Article 6 itself. "No religious test shall ever be required as a qualification to any office of public trust under the United States" became "no other religious test shall ever be required than a belief in the one only true God, who is the rewarder of the good, and the punisher of the evil." This change was rejected.

The defenders of Article 6 were, of course, equally outspoken. Twice in February 1788, in the *Federalist* Nos. 51 and 56, James Madison cited the "no religious test" clause as one of the glories of the new Constitution. "The door," Madison wrote, "of the Federal Government, is open to merit of every description, whether native or adoptive, whether young or old, and without regard to poverty or wealth, or to any particular profession of religious faith."

Tenche Coxe, a wealthy merchant and former member of the Continental Congress from Philadelphia, thrilled to America's unique and bold departure from the heavy hand of religious meddling in politics. A foremost recommendation of the new Constitution, he wrote in October 1787, is that "no religious test is ever to be required" for the servants of the American people. In Italy, Spain, and Portugal public office was denied to Protestants and "in England, every Presbyterian, and other person not of their established church, is incapable of holding an office." The convention in Philadelphia had then "the honor of proposing the first public act, by which any nation" declared that public service is for "any wise or good citizen." "Danger from ecclesiastical tyranny, that long standing and still remaining curse of the people," Coxe wrote, "can be feared by no man in the United States." He envisioned great economic potential for America as a result of its novel path. The "no religious test" clause constituted, he suggested, a declaration of freedom to all the world, and he predicted that, like Holland, America would become "an asylum of religious liberty," which would produce the same economic vitality and success that graced tolerant Holland.

In North Carolina the critics of the absence of religious tests were pointedly answered by James Iredell, future associate justice of the U.S. Supreme Court. Test laws, he argued, were a vile form of "discrimination." Their ban was a guarantee in the Constitution of the "principle of religious freedom." He had no problem with the possibility that Americans may choose "representatives who have no religion at all, and that pagans and Mahometans" may be elected. How, he asks, "is it possible to exclude any set of men" without thus laying "the foundation on which persecution has been raised in every part of the world." For a New York writer the absence of religious tests signified the Constitution's "relief of the mind from religious thraldom, which has been productive of so many evils in other countries."

The "no religious test" clause also had clerical supporters. The Virginia Baptist leader John Leland lauded Article 6 for its consistency with his conviction that the integrity of religious faith required governmental noninvolvement in religion. Samuel Spencer in North Carolina insisted that religion stand on its own "without any connection with temporal authority." Making a similar argument, indeed calling the absence of religious tests "one of the great ornaments of the Constitution," was the Reverend Samuel Langdon of New Hampshire. He told the New Hampshire ratifying convention that he "took a general view of religion as unconnected with and detached from the civil power—that [as] it was an obligation between God and his creatures, the civil authority could not interfere without infringing upon the rights of conscience."

At the Massachusetts convention a Congregational minister, the Reverend Daniel Shute, argued that religious tests for office deprived citizens of their civil rights. "Who should be excluded from national trusts?" he asked. "Whatever bigotry may suggest, the dictates of candor and equity, I conceive, will be, none," even, he added, "those who have no other guide, in the way to virtue and heaven, than the dictates of natural religion." At the same convention a distinguished Baptist minister, the Reverend Isaac Backus, supported the absence of a religious test. "Nothing is more evident," he commented, "both in reason and The Holy Scriptures, than that religion is ever a matter between God and individuals; and, therefore, no man or men can impose any religious test without invading the essential prerogatives of our Lord Jesus Christ. . . . And let the history of all nations be searched . . . and it will appear that the imposing of religious tests had been the greatest engine of tyranny in the world." So much for religious correctness for the Reverend Backus.

In a wonderfully American coalition, there stood alongside these clerical defenders of Article 6 a number of unabashed advocates of secularism who gloried in the very godlessness of the Constitution. Such was one "Elihu," whose self-proclaimed deistic defense of the Constitution was printed in Connecticut and Massachusetts newspapers in February 1788. The Constitution, he wrote, is a rational document for a wise people in an enlightened age. The time has passed "when nations could be kept in awe with stories of God's sitting with legislators and dictating laws." The exclusion of religious tests was a glorious step, for no longer would politicians and clerics use religion "to establish their own power on the credulity of the people, shackling their uninformed minds with incredible tales." Sounding much like the French Enlightenment writers who . . . so influenced Jefferson, Elihu claimed that the Constitution created a political order appropriate for the new age when "the light of philosophy has arisen . . . miracles have ceased, oracles are silenced, monkish darkness is dissipated. . . . Mankind are no longer to be deluded with fable." The most brilliant achievement of the Constitution's framers, Elihu noted, is that they have refused "to dazzle even the superstitious, by a hint about grace or ghostly knowledge. They come to us in the plain language of common sense, and propose to our understanding a system of government, as the invention of mere human wisdom; no deity comes down to dictate it, not even a god appears in a dream to propose any part of it."

Yet another thinker holding nondogmatic religious beliefs, William Van Murray, Esq., applauded the absence of religious tests in a 1787 essay in the *American Museum*. America, he wrote, "will be the great philosophical theater of the world," since its Constitution recognizes that "Christians are not the only people there." Religious tests are "A VIOLATION OF THE LAW OF NATURE." Governments are created, he held, according to the "laws of nature. These are unacquainted with the distinctions of religious opinion; and of the terms Christian, Mohamentan, Jew or Gentile."

Lest Elihu's and Van Murray's enlightened and secular readings of the Constitution appear to be the eccentric rantings of men hostile to religion, we should note the similarity of their arguments to that offered by the more sober, moderate, and famous John Adams. Writing in 1786, just before the federal Constitution was written, he took it as given that political constitutions were wholly secular enterprises free of godly involvement or inspiration. "The United States of America," he wrote, marks "the first example of governments erected on the simple principles of nature." The architects of American governments never "had interviews with the gods or were in any degree under the inspiration of Heaven." Government, Adams insisted, is "contrived merely by the use of reason and the senses." Adams's view of constitution making is also caught up in the secular ideals of the Age of Reason. "Neither the people nor their conventions, committees, or subcommittees," he wrote, "considered legislation in any other light than as ordinary arts and sciences, only more important. . . . The people were universally too enlightened to be imposed on by artifice. . . . [G]overnments thus founded on the natural authority of the people alone, without a pretense of miracle or mystery, and which are destined to spread over the northern part of that whole quarter of the globe, are a great point gained in favour of the rights of mankind."

In the fierce debate over the "no religious test" clause itself, Adams's secular view of politics is best found in the lengthy defense of Article 6 published under the name "A Landholder" on December 17, 1787, for the *Connecticut Courant* and widely reprinted in nearby states. The author was no ordinary Connecticut farmer, however; he was Oliver Ellsworth, recently a delegate to the federal Constitutional Convention in Philadelphia, who would soon be a member of the first U.S. Congress and eventually, for a brief time, chief justice of the U.S. Supreme Court. Seeking to persuade the Connecticut ratifying convention to approve the Constitution, Ellsworth provides a veritable lecture on the relationship of religion and politics, especially of "systems of religious error adopted in times of ignorance." He excoriates the English Test Acts . . . for seeking to exclude first Catholics and then Protestant dissenters from the political realm. From his detailed account of these acts, he suggests, "there arises an unfavorable presumption against them." Even more significant, "they are useless, tyrannical, and peculiarly unfit for the people of this country."

A religious test would be absurd in America, Ellsworth argues; there are too many denominations. To favor one religious sect with public office would incapacitate the many others "and thus degrade them from the rank of freemen." What, then, of a general test, reserving public office to those who proclaim the simple belief in God and the divine authority of the Scriptures? Ellsworth rejects this as well, for an unprincipled man could easily dissemble and proclaim such beliefs simply to qualify for public office. At this point, Ellsworth moves from his practical arguments against religious tests to his main theoretical concern:

> To come to the true principle. . . . The business of civil government is to protect the citizen in his rights. . . . civil government has no business to meddle with the private opinions of the people. . . . I am accountable not to man, but to God, for the religious opinions which I embrace. . . . A test

law is . . . the offspring of error and the spirit of persecution. Legislatures have no right to set up an inquisition and examine into the private opinions of men.

Arguments like Ellsworth's proved successful in keeping the U.S. Constitution godless in the state ratification votes of 1787 and 1789, as they would be in the nineteenth century . . . in rebuffing the periodic efforts to rewrite the Constitution's preamble to include a definitive commitment to the Christian religion. But what about those states' own constitutions, many of which required officeholders to be Protestants or believers in a Christian God? The reactions varied, with some states preserving the older view that good rulers had to believe in God. The Pennsylvania constitution dropped its religious test in 1790, insisting only that officeholders be supporters of the Constitution. In 1792 Delaware added to its constitution a "no religious test" clause. Georgia and South Carolina followed quickly. But Vermont and New Jersey retained their religious tests for officeholders until 1844, and New Hampshire its until 1877. New states entering the Union in the nineteenth century occasionally did include in their constitutions the requirement that officeholders believe in the Christian God. Not until 1961, in fact, did all state constitutional religious tests fall, with the Supreme Court's ruling in *Torasco v. Watkins* that the Maryland constitution could not require, as it did (though no longer enforced), that state officers be Christians.

Among those who shared this secular ideal of excluding religion from politics were some, it should be noted, who worried that the existence of the "no religious test" clause might actually imply that politics would, in turn, not be excluded from religion. A wall of separation, after all, prevents trespassing in both directions. Paradoxically, then, some opposed Article 6 because it suggested to them that the Constitution did not go far enough in creating a state utterly uninterested in religion. An opponent of the Constitution, for example, wrote in the *New York Journal* in November 1787 that it left the liberty of conscience unprotected. The prohibition of religious tests, he argued, implies that the new American state could in general regulate religion and matters of private conscience, but specifically denies itself this one power to impose religious tests. Similarly, Governor Edmund Randolph, a supporter of the Constitution, wrote to Madison in February 1788 that he heard some ask, "Does not the exception as to a religious test imply, that the Congress by the general words had power over religion?"

Such critics of Article 6 were, of course, offering friendly amendments to the godless Constitution, literally so. They were part of the larger chorus that during the ratification process insisted that a truly secular state required even more, a specific provision in the document that protects the private rights of conscience. The laissez-faire liberal American state leaving individuals alone with their own religious beliefs evolves next and almost immediately with the First Amendment, championed by those outspoken theorists of the secular state—Madison and Jefferson. We must, however, acknowledge here, as the writer in the *Virginia Independent Chronicle* did in October 1787, that the U.S. Constitution is "coldly indifferent towards religion," and a good thing too.

There remains a crucial final reminder. The political convictions of the men who struggled to ratify a godless Constitution were not products of personal godlessness. Far from it. Almost everyone who participated in the debates about the Constitution shared a concern about the health of religion. The success of democracy depended upon a moral citizenry; and for most American thinkers of the eighteenth century, morality rested on some sort of religious convictions. So did a theory of human rights. Many of the men who championed the godless Constitution stayed aloof from dogmatic forms of Christian faith, but most of them believed in a God who rewarded good and punished evil in an afterlife. They respected the moral teachings of Christ and hoped that they would prosper among Americans and in the churches that Americans attended. So why did they refuse to assign government, whose very existence depended upon morality, any responsibility for promoting religion?

The answer to that question pushes us back in time to English thinkers of the seventeenth century and to the experience of the American colonists with the mother country and with their own colonial governments. While the idea of a godless Constitution clearly incorporated certain secular ideals, important and forceful justifications for such a secular document lay in religious thought. No one in American experience has cared more about religion than Roger Williams. And virtually no one in American experience has fashioned a stronger argument for a godless politics.

CHAPTER FIVE

PROTESTANT PRUDENCE
AND THE NATURAL
RIGHTS REPUBLIC

Wilson Carey McWilliams

As usual, Alexis de Tocqueville got it right: from the beginning of the republic, American political culture has been incoherent, an unresolved argument—ordinarily implicit and more or less civil—between the "spirit of liberty" and the "spirit of religion."[1]

Over the years, just as Tocqueville expected, the "spirit of liberty," entrenched in the laws, has gained ground at the expense of its rival, so that today the languages of individualism dominate moral discourse.[2] In contemporary society, the prevailing norms seem to be an almost universal tolerance and a respect for private liberty, while the biblical voice in American culture is increasingly marginalized or inarticulate.[3] Nevertheless, that the old quarrel persists is clear from the headlines: devoted to material well-being, Americans are also prone to militant and bizarre faiths, unquestioning in their belief in equality yet apparently inclined to accept inequalities greater than those in any other industrial country. And it is only a little less evident that the old contest is still being waged in and for American souls.

Michael Zuckert is right, on the whole, in emphasizing the Lockean secularity of the American founding, the framers' devotion to natural right. I will be arguing, however, that he understates the peculiar harmonics of the American tradition. G. K. Chesterton argued that America is a "nation with the soul of a church," its creed stated in the Declaration of Independence, and up to that point, his view of America's civil theology parallels Zuckert's.[4] But in Chesterton's reading, *equality,* not natural rights, is the foundation of the

American tradition, a teaching that follows Lincoln in seeing a nation "conceived in liberty" but "dedicated to the proposition that all men are created equal."

Linked with Gettysburg in our memory, the battle hymn of our "natural rights republic" is a distinctly Protestant counterpoint, and even in these later days, one can hear that sound, as I suspect Lincoln did, in the silences even more than the tumults of national life.

In the founding era, Americans were already a "people of paradox," easily convinced of their rights and attracted by Lockean teaching, yet in their various ways attached to Christianity.[5] In practice, consequently, political speech was necessarily a kind of compromise, its idiom shaped by the ambivalences of publics—and speakers, for that matter—and by the demands of coalition-building (especially, of course, if one hoped to address thirteen colonies, diverse in faith and politics). This ambiguity was partly a rhetorical stratagem, adopted to beguile or persuade, but it was also a defining characteristic, even a fundamental principle, of the American founding itself: an agreement not to agree or to insist on intellectual rigor, a decision to leave disagreements on ultimate issues to a later time and to the subsequent politics of the republic.[6]

In any case, Americans shared considerable common ground, especially where politics was concerned. Virtually all of them were the products of British experience, more or less accustomed to English institutions and law. They were, almost without exception, devoted to the freedom of conscience (although a great many held that liberty to be compatible with religious establishments). And with some exceptions—Quakers, for example, or High Tory Anglicans—they held at least similar views on the propriety of resistance to oppressive governments.

Zuckert regards this commonality as the result of Lockean influences on Protestant thinking, pointing to the gap between Martin Luther's interpretation of Romans 13 as a demand for passive submission to civil authority and Samuel West's reading of the same text as justifying resistance to unjust government. Certainly, West (and similar thinkers, like Jonathan Mayhew) reflected Locke's influence, especially in his enthusiasm for the right to rebel. But Zuckert slights the extent to which West's treatment of Romans 13 is truer to the text and has its own thoroughly Protestant provenance.

If rulers, as Paul declares, are "not a terror to good works, but to the evil," divinely appointed "to execute wrath on him that doeth evil," then a ruler who commands or even condones evil has violated the terms of his commission—what Calvin called the "true and natural duty of the magistrate"—and is essentially no ruler at all: "dictatorships and unjust authorities," Calvin wrote, "are not ordained governments."[7] The power of magistrates, in these terms, is not unbridled: they are "responsible to God *and to men* in the exercise of their rule" (my italics).[8] While Calvin held that even tyranny protects human society, and hence has some claim on us, his argument also indicated that human beings have some title to hold government accountable. Luther, as Zuckert indicates, followed much of the Christian tradition in prescribing nonviolent resistance to illegitimate authority; Calvin famously opened the door, on secular grounds, to resistance of a more active sort.[9]

Still, Zuckert's distinction is pointed: even when they supported armed resistance to Great Britain, the orthodox Protestant clergy ordinarily spoke of reconciliation as *desirable,* if it could be had without violation of the rights of the colonies. Seeing human beings as naturally social and so many parts of a created whole, they tended to see just dependence as the proper human standard. That view, obviously, is one of the targets of Tom Paine's case for independence in *Common Sense,* an argument which proceeds from a thoroughgoing understanding of the proposition that human beings are naturally free.[10]

The leading spirits of the founding generation were rarely as extreme—and even less frequently, as indiscreet—as Paine. Nevertheless, they spoke a decisively secular political language, deriving civil government from natural rights and essentially private purposes, and most were at least skeptical about revealed religion.[11] Yet even those not given to piety had at least three reasons to conciliate and speak respectfully of religion.

In the first place, they were bound to acknowledge the power of religion, its hold on the allegiance of the broader American public: in *Common Sense,* even Paine appealed, albeit deviously, to biblical authority. Second, they saw religion, properly limited, as an invaluable support for secular, civil morality.

In their theorizing, for example, contract was the foundation of civil society, and it was easy to lay out a compelling argument for making the promises necessary to bring society and government into being. But while society and government are clearly useful, the case for keeping promises *in* civil society is less certain, since for a self-regarding person, the truly desirable state would be the freedom to break one's promises while others keep theirs. The response that it is in my interest to keep my promises (including obedience to the laws) because violators are likely to be detected and punished, is too unreliable for civil comfort. The possible gains may easily seem to outweigh the risks where desires are strong, where the prize is very great, or where those who are tempted to break the rules are like the poor, or slaves, or women—people on the margins of society who have little or nothing to lose. The more insecure the society, moreover, the more impossible it is to limit the role of government: a free society, consequently, must treat the obligation of contracts as holy, beyond question or calculation. Hence Locke, defending toleration, excluded atheists: "The taking away of God, but even in thought, dissolves all."[12] The American framers did not go so far, but they treated religion in the private sphere as a crucial ally of the laws.

Third, religion made sovereign claims, if only subtly, on the moral reasoning of the founders. Reason, Locke had argued, indicates that human beings have some responsibility to and for what they have begotten. But reason is *not* enough, Locke observed in *The Reasonableness of Christianity,* to forbid parents to kill their children by exposing them, as the undeniably civilized ancients had done.[13] That prohibition, Locke conceded, depends on revelation.

The moral rule protecting infants is one Americans still accept, even in these days when "reproductive rights" receive the support of considerable majorities. In fact, both Locke's argument and American civil morals go beyond negative rights and the obligations of contract: they assert that we owe a *duty* to nurture children once born, that children have a positive right to be cared for which is clearly not "contractual," since children, as they often remind us, did not ask to be born.

In the founding era and since, many Americans have linked such moral propositions to an evolving moral "sense" or "instinct," giving a secular turn to the argument.[14] Even such thinkers, however, are obliged to concede that American culture—and with it, American ideas of what is rational or self-evident—incorporates teachings historically, if not necessarily, rooted in revelation.[15]

Zuckert's analysis, while shrewd, underrates the multivocality of the Declaration of Independence. He is right, of course, to reject Kendall and Carey's reading of the Declaration as an effort "to make clear above all else" the founders' "commitment to the will of God."[16] But the Declaration's artful ambiguities were designed to *allow* such interpretations, even if the Declaration's authors were thinking, inwardly, in very different terms. Moreover, Zuckert's claim that the duties of rulers, as envisioned by the Declaration, solely "derive from the original rights" is not entirely accurate—or not unambiguously accurate. Those rights, an endowment or trust, are explicitly unalienable, an entail *on* natural rights that must derive from the Creator's dowering, since it is not evident from the rights themselves.[17]

Similarly, Zuckert to the contrary, the Declaration does not say that there is no authority prior to government; it does not refer to a "state of nature" or even to a "social contract." Rather, Jefferson used a term with grand, Calvinist associations, saying that "to secure these rights, governments are *instituted . . .*" (my italics).

This usage was at least open to the theory on which the Puritans (and most Calvinists) relied, that while it is unnatural for human beings to be without government, God leaves it to them to "institute" it, allowing a certain latitude for human framing and naming. Hence, as Zuckert indicates, John Winthrop held that while magistrates are "called" to office by the people, their authority and duty derives from God.[18] In the same way, while Samuel Langdon's 1775 sermon, "Government Corrupted by Vice," adopts the language of natural rights, as Zuckert observes, and is broadly agnostic about the forms of government, Langdon also refers to the human condition without government as "the vilest of slavery and worse than death." Notably, Langdon does not call this "dreadful" situation a state of nature, since he thinks of it as profoundly unnatural, just as he does not think of it as a state of unlimited liberty, but of slavery. For Langdon, in fact, the crucial natural right is that of forming "order and government." The rights that matter to Langdon are collective; he does not speak of individual rights at all, and unlike Jefferson, he is tolerably specific about the forms and ways—principally majority rule—by which a "people" can be said to act.[19] Yet Langdon's political doctrine, with some squeezing here and there, can be fitted into the frame of the Declaration, as Jefferson and his committee almost certainly intended.

Most important, beyond bare assertion, the Declaration is silent about the meaning of its first principle of human rights, the proposition that human beings are "created equal." It is hard to imagine that this vagueness is not designed, since on its face, the doctrine of equality is contrary to common sense, a mystery calling for explanation.[20]

Up to a point, the "spirit of liberty" and the "spirit of religion" agree about equality. Both John Winthrop and John Locke—and the Declaration, for that matter—treat equality as compatible with differences of wealth and rank, a moral principle not everywhere applied in practice. But at a fundamental level, the two views are at odds.

Locke begins with an equality of *rights,* the "equal right that every man hath to his natural freedom" that effectively gives first place to liberty.[21] Government may rest on equality before the law, but its purpose is to allow inequalities to emerge from the indistinction of the state of nature: the "first object of government," Madison declares, is to protect the "diversity in the faculties of men."[22] Following that view, Zuckert uncharacteristically departs from the text of the Declaration to argue that the Declaration's implicit view of history begins with human beings who are "free and equal," hence naturally independent. Yet while Jefferson's drafts assert this view, the Declaration's text makes liberty a separate endowment, and one that yields precedence to equality.

In so doing, the Declaration conciliates the "spirit of religion." John Winthrop argued, in his "Model of Christian Charity," that God made human beings different in ability so that they would be forced by need to recognize communality and prodded toward equality. Human beings vary only as parts of a whole: "noe man is made more honourable than another, or more wealthy etc., out of any particuler and singuler respect to himselfe but for the glory of his Creator and the Common Good of the Creature, Man."[23] Where Locke treats equal rights as a means to differentiation, Winthrop makes difference a means to equality.

Moreover, like his text in I Corinthians, Winthrop goes on to maintain that human beings need charity in order to warm mere interdependence into cherished and hallowed community.[24] The echoes carry to Gettysburg and beyond: a political society can be *dedicated* to equality, Winthrop holds, only to the extent that its members are linked in civic fraternity.

As Zuckert indicates, the Declaration and the Constitution accept a lower standard, a more diffuse and diverse communion, its union relying on cooler sentiments and calculations of interest. Yet even in that diminished sense, it is still true that any political community affords benefits that are undeserved, most obviously through birthright, but also through the civil rights indiscriminately granted to all citizens—a kind of grace, Winthrop would remind us, the mirror of the love God feels for humankind.[25] Democratic citizenship requires that we love our fellows enough to sacrifice for them, when necessary abridging our natural rights to liberty, life, and property out of a sense of civic obligation.[26]

Nevertheless, for all their silences and ambiguities, the Declaration and the Constitution do change the terms of the debate between two visions of equality and political community, giving the "spirit of liberty" a comfort in the laws that is denied to the "spirit of religion." Even so, in the founding era and since, the "spirit of religion" has offered its own rebuttal, sometimes in tumults, but more often—and perhaps most tellingly—in a voice that is soft or still.

Itself beset by disagreements and resentments, and necessarily multivocal, eighteenth-century American religion had its own motives for civic accommodation, and hence the emollients of its varieties of politic discourse.[27]

Protestantism included many ministers and believers who, for all the reasons Zuckert indicates, had come to adopt Locke's teaching, at least in politics and often in religion.[28] The leading congregations in Massachusetts were already sliding toward Unitarianism, and Natural Religion was intellectually voguish almost everywhere.

Even among the more or less orthodox, as Zuckert points out, a growing number of Protestants, like Elisha Williams, had taken an important step in the direction of the "natural rights republic." Older Calvinist doctrine treated salvation as highest *among* the goods of the soul, a list which also included political community and life according to "rules of holiness, integrity and sobriety," a schooling in the "duties of humanity and civility."[29] By contrast, Williams *identified* the "good of the soul" with salvation, separating the soul from politics in a way that is compatible with secular liberalism.[30] And in the long term, just as Zuckert suggests, teachings like Williams's have tended to become stronger in American religion.[31] In the eighteenth century, however, such thinking was at best radically controversial: Williams's doctrine was so offensive to his fellow Protestants, "Old Light" and "New Light" alike, that he was denied reelection to the Connecticut Supreme Court.[32]

Protestant orthodoxy was still American religion's dominant voice, though hearing its subtleties requires a trained ear. In the first place, its teaching was profoundly rationalistic—despite the "New Light" emphasis on an appeal to the affections—although it held that faith is necessary to reason's full realization. In principle, reason can discern the created whole and can even catch a hint of its Creator: the universe is full of "lamps."[33] But the Fall distorts reason: self-centered human beings resent and resist the truth, that witness to our finitude and mortality. Revelation, by contrast, can liberate us to follow reason, acting in a way analogous to the effect of "spectacles" on natural vision, helping to mediate our quarrel with our own nature.[34] And even though unaided reason falls short of reason informed by revelation, the two overlap: reason marks out a common ground, a public space in which the logic of discourse leads us beyond simple self-preoccupation and in which, up to a point, political deliberation is possible.

Partly as a necessary concession to the speech of that public sphere, the spokesmen of orthodox religion often felt compelled to adapt their teaching to the new intellectual climate, recognizing that "the language of modern heresy would not adequately be refuted by old-fashioned dogmatism."[35] It was common, consequently, for champions of the older understanding to adopt the terms of the newer theorizing as starting points, aiming to turn modern teaching right-side up by a combination of dialectic and guile. As Perry Miller wrote of John Wise, who drew on Pufendorf and referred to Locke, "he would use what he had found, but his tongue was in his cheek," and his rhetoric, shaped to the demands of practice, was full of "tricks to catch the unwary."[36]

This tendency to make concessions to prevailing public language, moreover, was more than a design for persuasion. In the political sphere, Protestant doctrine supported a special prudence and restraint in speech as a matter of *duty*. Christians, Luther argues, are inwardly free, raised by their link to Jesus above all earthly conventions, able to discern the essential equality of human beings. Consequently, they are bound to disdain—in spirit—the distinctions of nation, class, and gender which are indispensable to secular life, including the law, which for a Christian should be needless.[37]

However, Luther goes on to contend that in practice, in a world that includes unbelievers as well as believers—where in fact, believers come in all degrees of faith, and no faith is *perfect*—"we cannot live our lives without ceremonies and works." The ordering of secular life demands forms, distinctions, and laws, their boundaries marked by natural reason as opposed to faith.[38]

A Christian's freedom makes him inwardly aware of the inadequacy of such forms, but a believer feels no need for that liberty to be "witnessed by men."[39] Free thought does not entail free expression. Quite the contrary, exercising liberty in the highest sense, a Christian freely limits his speech and conduct in a way suited to the moral and spiritual upbuilding of his fellows, observing and respecting laws made for the sake of the weaker and less edified: as a Christian, Luther wrote, I am to "give myself as a Christ to my neighbor."[40] And for eighteenth-century Calvinists, Alan Heimert observed, it was almost axiomatic that one should not "neglect the spiritual needs of the many in order to titillate the few."[41]

It must be emphasized that this concession to secular practice is not simply a matter of going along with established authorities or prevailing opinions.[42] It is intended to be artful, speaking such truth as circumstance can bear, an educational stratagem in a grand struggle fought for spiritual and moral stakes.[43] "I am made all things to all men," Paul had declared, "that I might by all means save some."[44] This Christian prudence, in its own way, can rival Machiavelli's; Jesus told his disciples that, sent "as sheep among wolves," they should not only be "as harmless as doves" but also "as wise as serpents," the subtlest of the beasts.[45]

Consider only one example, the first of Nathaniel Niles's remarkable *Two Discourses on Liberty,* originally delivered at Newburyport in 1774.[46] Beyond the inherent force of his argument, Niles spoke with formidable Protestant credentials, in the pulpit or in practical politics: his sermon, as Heimert wrote, affords "an entrance to the mind of Revolutionary Calvinism," and not the least, to its rhetoric.[47]

Certainly, Niles ranks among the sharpest critics of liberal theorizing, in politics or religion.[48] He upheld the traditional view that community is magisterial, concerned with the education of the soul—if only because civil liberty depends on liberty in spirit—so that religion and politics are inextricably linked. And as will become clear, Niles was no champion of natural rights, at least in the ordinary sense of that term.

At the same time, however, Niles's proximate political aim in 1774 was to support the colonies in their quarrel with Great Britain. That purpose, obviously, ranged Niles on the side of thinkers who departed from or flatly rejected Christian orthodoxy, especially in its political claims. Pragmatically interested in the working unity of that coalition, Niles—on other occasions, a grand controversialist—hoped to avoid giving needless offense to his allies.[49]

Yet Niles also wanted to remind his shrewdest readers of the fundamental antagonism that divided them from secular liberals and partisans of natural religion.[50] Any cooperation was necessarily tentative and transient; those who stood with Niles had to be kept on their guard, alert for the signs of that fundamental conflict. His discourse is accordingly artful, furnished with clues and hints, silently affirming what politic speech seemed to forbid.[51]

Niles made this tolerably clear in the "Advertisement" that preceded the printed version of his *Two Discourses*.[52] He cannot provide an "exact copy" of the sermon, Niles claims, because he spoke extemporaneously, for the most part. But he has "carefully preserved" those things of which a copy might be desired, retaining the "ideas" and adding "several new thoughts" to replace some now-forgotten "expressions." This indicates a design, a teaching which preserves its essentials but has also been changed, adapted to a new and presumably broader audience. Yet Niles claims to be hurried, calling attention to "imperfections" in "stile and manner" which, he says, doubtless will be observed. Still, he goes on, "every means, however imperfect" is needed to advance the spirit of "true liberty."[53] Lacking complete knowledge of the various "branches of civil liberty," Niles says that he attends only to the "main ideas"—an apparent humility which also asserts his command of liberty's first principles. And he concludes with the observation that "the inquisitive mind will be able to draw a number of important consequences." Niles's "inquisitive readers," in other words, are invited to look beyond the text and to see through its "imperfections" to the purpose that inspired them.

Niles's aim, he says, is to "awaken" proper sentiments regarding spiritual and religious liberty, and specifically, to argue that civil liberty without spiritual liberty is like "a body without a soul." (In Niles's sense, of course, liberty of spirit does not refer to freedom of conscience from external control, but to a spirit that is free inwardly, unensnared by the world's temptations and undaunted by its powers.) This purpose assumes that some of Niles's countrymen *deny* this, and that others have been lulled by them: Niles, in other words, is contending against an insinuating secularism, all too successful in his America.

His text is 1 Corinthians 7:21, a classic statement of the doctrine of Christian liberty: "Art thou called, being a servant? Care not for it. But if thou mayest be free, use it rather." Paul assures believers, in other words, that their spirits can be free despite this-worldly necessities and restraints, but also—Niles points out—that it is preferable to be at liberty.[54] And if freedom is a good when enjoyed by one, Niles argues, it must be a greater good when enjoyed by many: hence, he concludes emphatically, "CIVIL LIBERTY IS A GREAT GOOD."[55]

Like Paul, Niles teaches that human beings, though ordinarily blind to the truth, are already emancipated, "bought for a price" by Jesus' sacrifice of himself—of his life, of course, but also of his very divinity.[56] To the discerning, the incarnation shows that the highest sort of freedom, beyond fears and ambitions, beyond the control of "principalities and powers," is the limitation or sacrifice of self out of love for others.[57] Our freedom, consequently, is measured by our capacity to love, and our civil liberty, by our dedication to the common good. If we are to "perfect freedom," Niles contends, "Everyone must be required to do all that he can that tends to the highest good of the state."[58]

"Originally," Niles declares, "there were no private interests," and one presumes, no private rights.[59] Even Niles's first audience was probably a little startled, and it would take some considerable agility to make his assertion even minimally compatible with natural rights doctrine.[60] Niles's argument is implicitly Aristotelian: our individuality is developed in and through the polis.[61] Our private rights and interests are "constructed," as we might say nowadays, by the public, "distributed among . . . individuals according as they appear in the eyes of the body politic, to be qualified to use them for the good of the whole."[62] In that sense, what we conventionally call the "particular properties of each individual member" are actually "the public interest deposited in the hands of individuals."[63]

For Niles, as for his Puritan ancestors, political society is a moral and educational enterprise, of which liberty is a part. "Good government is essential to the very being of liberty. . . . Their rise and fall is exactly uniform." Civil liberty demands a regime of laws—for the inclinations and opinions of sinful humanity are no adequate foundation—but law itself aims at edification. It should see that bad citizens are punished, but also that good ones are rewarded, hoping to turn even low passions to decent behavior: rightly ordered liberty, Niles comments, "renders political virtue fashionable" and, promoting industry, frugality, and "decent conversation and courteous behaviour," prompts "even pride and avarice to mimic humanity, and every generous sentiment."[64]

The goal of civic education is the free spirit, "a spirit that is consonant to a free constitution—a spirit that seeks the highest good of the community, in its proper place," capable of self-government and linked to its fellows by fraternal affection, the old Puritan utopia.[65]

Niles concedes that "there never has been, nor ever will be, such a general state of mind" (even contending, in his second discourse, that given the necessary imperfections of politics, the "degree of liberty that can reasonably be expected of earthly states is very low" and tainted with bitterness and blood), but he rejects the implied Machiavellian critique.[66] In fact, Niles argues, the seen points to the unseen: we infer the nature of liberty from "the small degree of liberty, with which we are acquainted." And, implicit in practice, the ideal is the standard by which we properly judge and measure the excellence of the politically possible, just as truly free spirits, though rare, are like "spices" scattered through a society, capable of giving it flavor.[67]

Every good regime, Niles observes, needs an element of free-spiritedness. Even very secular thinkers, as noted earlier, recognized that self-interest is an inadequate support for contracts: breaking one's faith is detestable precisely because contracts are "sacred things." (And if sacred, Niles goes on, addressing his immediate political concern, then binding on kings: anyone who teaches otherwise "dethrones the King, and subverts the constitution of nature itself.")[68]

Moreover, liberty requires watchfulness, the vigilance that comes from seeing freedom as a "sacred loan" from God, to be guarded not only so far as it agrees with our interest or comfort but as a duty.[69] Even government by majority—the safest form of rule, Niles emphasizes, and also the best— may become inattentive or tyrannical, and to oppose or unsettle it is likely to prove at least unpopular and perhaps mortally perilous.[70] Democratic self-government requires an element of nobility, the recognition that "It is great, it is glorious, to espouse a good cause, and it is still more great and glorious to stand alone."[71]

Finally, the free spirit—aware of liberty as a gift from God—discerns that freedom for some is incompatible spiritually with the slavery of others. To enslave another is to pander to the slavishness in ourselves, our desire to avoid labor, our dependence on what gratifies, our itch for dominion. Americans, Niles observes, have been guilty of "a tyrannical spirit in a free country," and as such, have no consistent moral case against would-be oppressors: "let us either cease to enslave our fellow-men, or else let us cease to complain of those that would enslave us. Let us either wash our hands from blood, or never hope to escape the avenger."[72]

And for the end immediately in view, Niles urges his hearers to return to "the plain manner of our fore-fathers" and unite, with "piety and oeconomy," in advancing the case of the colonies against Great Britain. In that controversy, Niles argues for defending colonial rights while upholding the authority of the king, the nominally constitutional "personal union" favored by many of those, especially in the clergy, who hoped for some sort of reconciliation. But he also leaves no doubt that Americans should treat the right as "inexpressibly dear."

In the body of his sermon, in other words, Niles presents a communitarian Protestant's political polemic, including the obligatory invocation of the danger of "popery" as well as military despotism, directed largely to practice and conduct, with only incidental reference to the intellectual combats of the day.[73]

Niles's footnotes are a different matter. His first—a very long one—extends his rejection of the idea of natural private rights, beginning with a theological reflection on God's ownership of all things. Locke had argued that God, as maker of heaven and earth, has "given the world to men in common" for "the best advantage of life and convenience," although even in this original state of commonality, "every man has a property in his person, thence natural rights."[74] Niles contends that God gave the world to Adam and his posterity only "in certain respects" and "to be managed for the grand company" (i.e., God, angels, and humans). Thus in Niles's telling, the original gift is limited— in some ways, angels have management of the world—and for the *common* good, not simply for self-preservation. And against Locke, Niles argues that in a state of nature, human beings "have nothing that they can call their own" to the exclusion of God, angels, or their fellow men. Even our *persons,* in other words, naturally belong to the whole.[75]

Earthly states, Niles argues, turning to politics, were formed either (1) by the predominance of one individual who acquired despotic power to rule, preempting the claims of the public in the service of his own interests or passions, or (2) by the compact of the few or the many to secure their own private interests. But *both* of these regimes, Niles contends, are based on usurpation, the subordination of what is common to the service of private claims. A greater number of private interests checking each other may moderate the worst effects of despotism; it does not change the thing itself. "It matters not whether men who build their notions of government on self-interest, call themselves whigs or tories, friends to prerogative, or to the liberties of the people." And when Niles goes on that "They cannot blame their neighbour for commencing tory when it will be most conducive to his private interest," he makes it reasonably clear that his real animus is directed against Whigs.[76]

Niles is both more pointed and more cryptic at the end of his second footnote, which speaks of that sanctity of contracts which binds both subjects and kings. He refers "truce breakers and traitors" to 2 Timothy 3:1–4, "if they know where to find it," so that they may see "with whom they are ranked by their Maker."[77] The slighting aside, "if they know where to find it" evidently indicates Niles is speaking of people who, if religious at all, are not inclined to dote on scripture. Just as clearly, it is an invitation to consult the passage Niles has cited, in which Paul speaks of covetous "self-lovers" who pursue pleasure without "natural affection." In other words, self-seeking individualism, even when allied with a deist's faith in a "Maker" (though not the revealed word), inherently works to undermine the contracts which are the basis of individualistic social theory.[78]

Even more striking, however, is the subtext that underlies Niles's plea for unity—and the willingness to endure austerity—in the colonial quarrel with Britain. If salvation has not come from King George, Niles comments, "we cannot expect it from the hills. We must look still higher."[79] This is an obvious reference to the 121st Psalm—"I will lift up mine eyes unto the hills, from whence cometh my help"—but Niles's comment is odd, apparently contrary to the psalmist's, since Niles argues that Americans *cannot* expect help from the hills. Looking "still higher" might refer to the Lord, but the Lord, according to the psalmist, is the source of the help he expects from the hills.[80] Since it is unlikely that Niles is disdaining the divine aid to which he repeatedly appeals, it seems plausible that Niles's "higher" involves a double entendre, "above" as in a text, referring to Psalm 120.

In that psalm, the singer says that he has lived "with him, that hateth peace," and asks to be delivered "from lying lips and a false tongue." The psalm concludes, "I am for peace [or, I am a man of peace], but when I speak, they are for war."[81] The psalmist indicates that conflict is concealed beneath fair words and the appearance of unity, a combat that will become evident if the psalmist speaks openly. But that, it immediately becomes clear, Niles has no intention of doing.

He advises Americans not to rail against man, preferring the example of Michael, "who railed not against the Devil himself."[82] Niles refers to the ninth chapter of Jude, in which Michael is said not to have *dared* to rail against Satan, leaving it to the Lord to rebuke him: some criticism is, in the order of things, best left to God. Yet the appeal to Jude is apposite in another way: Jude denounces men who "crept in unawares," corrupting faith and conduct: "These speak evil of those things which they know not, but what they know naturally, as the brute beasts" and who "separate themselves sensual, having not the spirit."[83] This sounds rather like Lockeans, or at least like advocates of natural religion, so apt to reject spiritual knowledge along with revelation in favor of the instinctive, passional knowledge shared with the beasts, or that knowledge derived from the senses. A number of these had surely "crept" into pulpits or positions of influence, if not entirely "unawares": even so, Niles hints, it is not the time to attack them directly.

"David said of Shimei," Niles goes on, "let him curse, for the Lord hath bidden him." In Niles's account, David accepted Shimei's cursing as a punishment from God, "while he was not insensible to the wickedness of Shimei."[84] In this great story in 2 Samuel, David says pretty much what Niles attributes to him, noting sadly that his son Absalom is also in rebellion against him. But he does so from calculation: seeing him bear this affliction, David says, God "will requite me good for his cursing."[85]

Moreover, the story does not end there. When Absalom is defeated, Shimei comes seeking pardon. The "sons of Zeruiah," presumably including the formidable Joab, again urge David to have him killed. David, however, rejects this counsel in the interests of reconciliation, promising to spare Shimei's life.[86] Finally, however, in 1 Kings, a dying David advises Solomon to have Shimei (and Joab, for that matter) put to death.[87] For Solomon to execute Shimei—like Don Corleone's posthumous retaliation through his son, Michael—does not violate *David's* promise.[88] And as David recognizes, Shimei is too treacherous and too dangerous to be left alive, given the uncertain hand and authority of a new king.

Directing his attentive readers to that story, Niles was teaching that there are times when forbearance is prudent, especially in the interest of avoiding civil conflict. But there are also times, at moments of crisis, and particularly in founding a new regime, when fundamental animosities must be confronted and ultimate loyalties addressed.

Muting denunciations of those enemies in theory who are, for the moment, allies in practice—"there's no evil in the city which the Lord hath not done"—Niles suggests that, like Daniel, he and his fellows should "pour out our hearts before God."[89] This presumably refers to the ninth chapter of Daniel, where the prophet prays for forgiveness and for Jerusalem and receives assurance that the messianic kingdom will eventually arrive, but is warned that "unto the end of the war, desolations are determined."[90] Daniel himself is rendered dumb, having seen the glory of the coming of the Lord: in relation to theoretical disagreements—especially in relation to the city upon the hill—silence or civil debate should be the political rule, at least until the end of the struggle, and possibly until the last days.

Niles designed his two discourses as the mirrors of Protestantism's two modes of speech. In the first place, the "laudable" effort to secure civil liberty demands tactical accommodations to secular circumstance, and rhetoric tailored to the shape of political practice.[91] But it is the quest for *spiritual* liberty that sets the measure, weighing tactical choices and defining principles which cannot be compromised and confrontations which cannot be avoided.[92] And it reminds Christians that they speak a language—and seek a city—alien to even the best secular politics, seeing only idols where others see sacred laws. In this world, Niles reminded his hearers, Christians are like Israel, a formerly "enslaved people" passing through "barbarous nations" on their way to liberty: servitude in Egypt yields only to a politics in which all are at least moderately slavish. Consequently, Christians must always be spiritually armed and on guard. They live in a state of "steady warfare, a constant skirmish."[93] Conflict is never overcome, only suppressed; any "cessation of arms," whether from "fear of one another," or from love and hope, leaves Christians in the "precincts of battle."[94] And in such situations, if it needs saying, one guards one's tongue, partly in order to preserve the Word.

And yet, there are times and seasons when the moral stakes in secular politics call for religion to speak in something more like its own voice, discarding old alliances and institutions in favor of renovation or renewal.[95]

At "the end of the war," as Daniel had been counseled, the founding of a new regime brought the differences between Americans into the political foreground, divisions that—like with Solomon and Shimei—often seemed matters of life and death.[96] And religion has won its victories, sometimes great ones, in those early battles and in the republic's succeeding moments of decision—slavery and the "crisis of the house divided," for example, or the grand combats of the Age of Reform, or in the Civil Rights Movement—providing a critical voice, a vocabulary of protest, and, especially, an egalitarianism warmed into a conviction of fraternity.[97]

That, nevertheless, individualism has gained the upper hand in American life and thought, or that acquisitiveness and increasing inequality are defining characteristics in contemporary American society, would not have surprised Niles and his fellow Calvinists. Jonathan Edwards had taught that, short of the end, fallen nature sets the general direction of history, only checked or deflected periodically by divine interventions, which themselves soon give way to resurgent nature.[98]

Believers persist despite these chronic disappointments, Niles and his school argued, because they are confident in final victory. The frustrating delay of that triumph is a test of faith and perseverance: waiting for the end is also an opportunity for witness. It is also a reflection of divine artistry: God chose to give scope to wickedness, Joseph Bellamy contended, because against the background of its apparent success, God's glory would seem even more luminous and beautiful.[99] The sanctified, Niles wrote, expect to see the universe "rising in perfection forever and ever."[100]

Even a smaller degree of that assurance, lightening despair, moderates any felt need for desperate measures. It encourages a willingness to accept, for this time, the second-rate decencies of civil liberty, to endure the flawed coalitions and abide by the armed truce of republican life.

For that matter, a secular faith in progress can make liberals more willing to conciliate religion, making a place for it at the table of public life, readier to trust democratic politics without insisting as a precondition on a distinctively liberal code of rights and neutralities.

If contemporary America is racked by "culture wars," it may be because *both* sides of the combat have less faith in the end, and are hence more eager for signs and proximate victories.[101] A "spirit of liberty" confident that it speaks for nature and a "spirit of religion" that reaches beyond tragedy might find their way back to civility, to serious and reasoned discourse about what is human. And that, if it needs saying, is something we urgently need.[102]

NOTES

1. Alexis de Tocqueville, *Democracy in America* (New York: Knopf, 1980), i:43.

2. Robert Bellah, et al., *Habits of the Heart* (Berkeley and Los Angeles: University of California Press, 1985).

3. Alan Wolfe, *One Nation After All* (New York: Viking, 1998).

4. G. K. Chesterton, *What I Saw in America* (New York: Dodd Mead, 1922).

5. Michael Kammen, *People of Paradox* (New York: Knopf, 1972).

6. This has been, of course, a very persistent pattern in American history. See John Murray Cuddihy, *No Offense: Civil Religion and Protestant Taste* (New York: Seabury, 1978).

7. Romans 13:3–4; John Calvin, *Commentaries on the Epistles of Paul to the Romans and to the Thessalonians,* trans. Ross Mackenzie, in *Calvin's New Testament Commentaries,* ed. David and Thomas Torrance (Grand Rapids: Eerdmans, 1980), 8:281–82.

8. Calvin, *Commentaries,* 8:282.

9. John Calvin, *Institutes of the Christian Religion,* IV:xx:32; Sheldon S. Wolin, *Politics and Vision* (Boston: Little Brown, 1960), 188–89; Luther would have agreed with Calvin that those who would "bear rule over men's consciences" will find no support for their "blasphemous tyranny" in Romans 13. Calvin, *Commentaries,* 8:283.

10. See my essay, "The Bible in the American Political Tradition," in *Religion and Politics,* ed. Myron Aronoff (New Brunswick, N.J.: Transaction, 1984), 24.

11. Locke's teaching treated human beings as social animals in fact; it regarded them as separate, rights-bearing individuals *normatively* and before the law. See Ruth Grant, "Locke's Political Anthropology and Lockean Individualism," *Journal of Politics* 50 (1988): 42–63. Notably, Locke rejects Christian virtue as a standard for public policy. *Letter Concerning Toleration* (Indianapolis: Bobbs Merrill, 1955), 42.

12. Locke, *Letter Concerning Toleration,* 52.

13. Locke, *The Reasonableness of Christianity,* ed. I. T. Ramsey (Stanford, Calif.: Stanford University Press, 1958), 64.

14. For example, William Graham Sumner accepted a duty to children despite his general rejection of claims on "other people's labor and self-denial," but he asserted that this sense of duty is "spontaneous," and in fact, the only such case known to nature (*What Social Classes Owe to Each Other* [Caldwell: Caxton, 1978], 8, 64). Sumner's argument, obviously, can answer Locke's objection only by holding that the ancients were perverse.

15. There are "signs of divine origin," Hannah Arendt wrote, in what the American founders took to be self-evident truth, just as, in the "enlightened conscience" they often heard "an inner voice which was still the voice of God." Arendt, *On Revolution* (New York: Viking, 1963), 194–95. The principle of inclusiveness our contemporaries discern in liberalism has the same quality: liberal ideas of natural and equal rights imply the right to make contracts and to apply for admission to existing ones, but on their own terms do not suggest a right to be included. See my essay, "On Rogers Smith's *Civic Ideals,*" *Studies in American Political Development* 13 (1999): 221.

16. Willmoore Kendall and George Carey, *The Basic Symbols of the American Political Tradition* (Baton Rouge: Louisiana State University Press, 1979), 84.

17. In the same way, since natural rights are unalienable, there are limits to proper consent; the "consent of the governed" can convey only "just powers" to government.

18. "The Journal of John Winthrop," in *Puritan Political Ideas,* ed. Edmund Morgan (Indianapolis: Bobbs Merrill, 1965), 138.

19. Morgan, ed., *Puritan Political Ideas,* 358, 367–68. Langdon does suggest that the "civil polity of Israel" has special claims as a regime.

20. Chesterton, *What I Saw in America,* 17; John H. Schaar, "Some Ways of Thinking about Equality," *Journal of Politics* 26 (1964): 881.

21. Locke, *Second Treatise on Civil Government,* section 54.

22. James Madison, *The Federalist,* #10; see Robert Ginsberg, "Equality and Justice in the Declaration of Independence," *Journal of Social Philosophy* 6 (1975): 8.

23. John Winthrop, "A Model of Christian Charity," in *Puritan Political Ideas,* 77.

24. 1 Corinthians 12:12–31.

25. Winthrop "A Model of Christian Charity," 87.

26. Sheldon S. Wolin, "Contract and Birthright," in *The Presence of the Past* (Baltimore: Johns Hopkins University Press, 1989), 137–50.

27. On the divisions of method and doctrine within American Protestantism, see Jerald C. Brauer, "Puritanism, Revivalism and the Revolution," in *Religion and the American Revolution,* ed. Jerald C. Brauer (Philadelphia: Fortress, 1976), 25.

28. Steven M. Dworetz, *The Unvarnished Doctrine* (Durham, N.C.: Duke University Press, 1990).

29. Calvin, *Institutes of the Christian Religion,* III:xix:15.

30. Sidney Mead, "Christendom, Enlightenment and the Revolution," in *Religion and the American Revolution,* ed. Jerald Brauer, 40–41.

31. Joseph Haroutunian, "Theology and the American Experience," *Criterion* (Winter 1964): 7–9.

32. *Political Sermons of the American Founding Era,* ed. Ellis Sandoz (Indianapolis: Liberty Fund, 1990), 53.

33. Romans 1:19–20, 2:14–15.

34. Calvin, *Institutes of the Christian Religion,* I:v:1,11,14; I:vi:2,4; see also St. Augustine, "The Predestination of the Saints," in *The Essential Augustine,* ed. Vernon Bourke (Indianapolis: Hackett, 1985), 22.

35. Perry Miller, *The New England Mind: From Colony to Province* (Boston: Beacon, 1961), 426–27.

36. Ibid., 300.

37. Martin Luther, "The Freedom of a Christian," in *Martin Luther: Three Treatises,* trans. W. A. Lambert (Philadelphia: Fortress, 1960), 284; compare Galatians 3:28; Romans 8:38–39.

38. Luther, "The Freedom of a Christian," 313, 315; Ephesians 6:1–9.

39. Calvin, *Institutes of the Christian Religion,* III:xix:10.

40. Luther, "The Freedom of a Christian," 304, 312–15; 1 Corinthians 8:9; following the Divine example, Calvin argues, we should encourage our fellows to improve in spite of their imperfections, not crush them by insisting on their defects: our rule, consequently, should be to restrict the expression of our liberty in accordance with the demands of charity and moral education (*studendum charitati et spectanda proximi aedificatio*). *Institutes of the Christian Religion,* III:xix:12; see also III:xix:5.

41. Alan Heimert, *Religion and the American Mind* (Cambridge, Mass.: Harvard University Press, 1966), 174.

42. The "love of our neighbor," Calvin wrote, must not be carried so far as to "offend God." *Institutes of the Christian Religion,* III:xix:13.

43. "All things are lawful for me," Paul taught, "but not everything is expedient and not everything edifies." 1 Corinthians 10:23–24; see also Ephesians 6:10–17.

44. 1 Corinthians 9:19–22.

45. Matthew 10:16; Genesis 3:1.

46. Nathaniel Niles, *Two Discourses on Liberty* (Newburyport, Mass.: Thomas and Tinges, 1774). I will refer here and there to Niles's second discourse, but that work, less concerned with civil liberty, is also less to the purpose here.

47. Heimert, *Religion and the American Mind,* 454. Niles (1741–1828) was never ordained, but was much in demand as a preacher, and the printing and reprinting of several of his sermons indicates, on Nathan Hatch's argument, that he spoke for a significant body of religious opinion. (Hatch, *The Sacred Cause of Liberty* [New Haven: Yale University Press, 1977], 181). His family eminently reflected the Puritan tradition: his grandfather, the redoubtable Samuel Niles (1674–1762), occupied the pulpit at Braintree, Massachusetts, for more than fifty years and was the author of such works as *Tristitiae Ecclesiarum: or a Brief and Sorrowful Account of the Present State of Churches in New England* (Boston: Draper, 1745); Niles's father was a judge and a friend of John Adams. Niles himself graduated from Princeton (then the College of New Jersey) and later studied with Joseph Bellamy, thus coming to stand in the direct line of intellectual descent from Jonathan Edwards (Heimert, 455). Niles tried his hand at various trades, but the consistent themes of his career were religious and political, like the tradition in which he stood: in the founding era, Niles served three terms in the Connecticut legislature (1779–1781), eight in the Vermont lower house, where he was Speaker in 1784, three years (1784–1787) on the Vermont Supreme Court, and—after participating in Vermont's ratifying convention (1791)—in the U.S. House of Representatives (1791–1795). An anti-Federalist and a Jeffersonian, he was also anti-slavery and anti-bank.

48. In this, like his sometime teacher, Joseph Bellamy: see Heimert, *Religion and the American Mind,* 167.

49. This was especially true because, in Connecticut, Joseph Bellamy's denunciation of upper-class Arminians had inspired disorders which came close to "civil war." Bellamy and his school, appalled, were delighted that a new "common enemy," the British, afforded both the basis for civic unity and for the effort to develop a new politics. Heimert, *Religion and the American Mind,* 347–49.

50. Heimert, *Religion and the American Mind,* 301.

51. Craft of this sort was familiar in Niles's intellectual circle. As Heimert notes, Bellamy's writings, almost anathema to John Witherspoon, circulated furtively among Princeton students, and those attracted by Bellamy's teaching, facing or fearing persecution from more established clergy, developed a "private, highly metaphorical language" for communicating their views. *Religion and the American Mind,* 168n.

52. Niles, *Two Discourses on Liberty,* 5.

53. A proposition, it will be noted, which assumes that the end justifies the means.

54. At the beginning of his second discourse, while emphasizing that spiritual liberty is to be preferred, Niles points out that Jesus (in John 8:32, 36) uses the same word, *lĕuthĕria,* to refer to both civil and spiritual freedom. Niles, *Two Discourses,* 40, 41.

55. Niles, *Two Discourses,* 5, 6.

56. Philippians 2:5–8.

57. Romans 8:38–39; Niles, *Two Discourses*, 47. As in the argument discussed earlier, this evidently calls for restraint on self-expression. Love, one might say, frees us even from the sway of liberty.

58. Niles, *Two Discourses*, 9.

59. Ibid.

60. For example, the anti-Federalist who wrote under the name William Penn identified natural rights with liberty, defined as the "unlimited power of doing good," hence dependent on moral education. Essay in the *Philadelphia Independent Gazetteer*, January 2, 1788, in *The Complete Anti-Federalist*, ed. Herbert J. Storing (Chicago: University of Chicago Press, 1981), 3:169–70.

61. Aristotle, *Politics*, 1253a19–29.

62. Niles, *Two Discourses*, 14–15.

63. Ibid., 16.

64. Ibid., 23–24, 28. Niles was contemptuous of teachings that rely on sympathy and the benefactions of private individuals, finding them wanting in respect for reason, justice, and manliness, all of which speak of a duty to the common good which calls for public authority and the sanction of law. *The Perfection of God, The Fountain of Good, Two Sermons Delivered at Torringford, Connecticut, December 21, 1777* (Norwich, Conn.: Green and Spooner, 1778).

65. Niles, *Two Discourses*, 26. See Joseph Bellamy's 1762 "Election Sermon," in *The Works of Joseph Bellamy, D.D.* (Boston: Doctrinal Tract and Book Society, 1850), I:590.

66. Niles, *Two Discourses*, 28, 45; perfect justice and liberty would require perfect knowledge, not only of general rules, but of circumstances and occasions, down to the most minute. More important, human beings cannot know the hearts and souls of their fellows: political society must judge by external expressions. And all human judgment, of course, is at least tinged with self-interest. *Two Discourses*, 42–44.

67. Niles, *Two Discourses*, 26, 28, 45.

68. Ibid., 23–24n.

69. Ibid., 31–32. Our forefathers, Niles writes, "however they might greatly err in some particular instances," were inspired to risk their lives by this "generous scheme of liberty," and it is to be hoped that we will not allow ourselves "to be enslaved by an India herb, or English manufactures." *Two Discourses*, 15n. That advice might be repeated, with less confidence, to contemporary Americans.

70. Niles, *Two Discourses*, 19–20. Part of the virtue of majority rule, Niles holds, is that most of those disposed to a genuine concern for the public good—partly because they are less tempted by the delusion of independence—are in the lower classes; only a "very small proportion" are found in the higher orders. *Two Discourses*, 45–46 (see also Bellamy's "Election Sermon," *Works* I:590–96). The potential danger of majority rule is accentuated because so many take up the cause of liberty out of a desire for popularity, as opposed to real conviction (*Two Discourses*, 58).

71. Niles, *Two Discourses*, 36. Confronting McCarthyism, Elmer Davis found himself reminded of the hymn, "Dare to be a Daniel. Dare to stand alone." *But We Were Born Free* (New York: Bobbs Merrill, 1953).

72. Niles, *Two Discourses*, 37–38.

73. Ibid., 38.

74. Locke, *Second Treatise on Civil Government*, sections 26, 27; notably, Locke begins his discussion of property by referring to natural reason, and hence self-preservation, turning only afterward to revelation. Section 25.

75. Niles, *Two Discourses*, 10n.

76. Ibid., 11–12n. Niles's typology parallels Harrington's distinction between ancient and modern prudence, the latter devoted to the pursuit of private benefit; Niles's emphasis on a "system of laws" also at least resembles Harrington's appeal to contrivance against either form of prudence, although Niles, of course, also depends on free-spiritedness. James Harrington, *Oceana*, in *The Political Works of James Harrington*, ed. J. G. A. Pocock (Cambridge: Cambridge University Press, 1977), 161, 205.

77. Niles, *Two Discourses*, 24n.

78. See Niles's argument in *The Substance of Two Sermons Delivered To The Second Society of Norwich, July 12, 1778* (Norwich, Conn.: John Trumbull, 1779).

79. Niles, *Two Discourses*, 34.

80. Psalms 121:1–2.

81. Psalms 120:2, 6–7.

82. Niles, *Two Discourses*, 34.

83. Jude: 9, 11, 19.

84. Niles, *Two Discourses*, 34.

85. 2 Samuel 16:5–13.

86. 2 Samuel 19:16–23.

87. 1 Kings 2:8–9.

88. The allusion, needless to say, is to Mario Puzo's *The Godfather* (New York: Putnam's, 1969).

89. Niles, *Two Discourses*, 34.

90. Daniel 9:26.

91. Niles, *Two Discourses*, 39, 55.

92. Ibid., 57–58.

93. Ibid., 48.

94. The phrases, of course, are taken from Hobbes's *Leviathan* chapter 18.

95. Joseph Bellamy, "The Nature and Glory of the Gospel," in *Works*, II:344, as well as his "Election Sermon," *Works*, I:590–96.

96. Joyce Appleby, *Inheriting the Revolution: The First Generation of Americans* (Cambridge, Mass.: Harvard University Press, 2000); compare Madison's *The Federalist*, #49. Timothy Dwight, whose political inclinations were at poles with Niles's, also advised postponing confrontations until the end of the war. Heimert, *Religion and the American Mind*, 348.

97. John G. West, *The Politics of Revelation and Reason* (Lawrence: University Press of Kansas, 1996); the "crisis of the house divided," of course, refers both to Lincoln's grand scriptural metaphor and to Harry V. Jaffa, *Crisis of the House Divided* (Chicago: University of Chicago Press, 1959).

98. Jonathan Edwards, *The Great Christian Doctrine of Original Sin Defended,* in *The Works of Jonathan Edwards,* ed. Edward Hickman (Carlisle, Pa.: Banner of Truth Trust, 1987), I:170.

99. Joseph Bellamy, *The Millennium,* in *Works,* I:445, 452, 460.

100. Niles, *Two Discourses,* 53.

101. Mark 8:12; Matthew 12:39, 16:4; James Davison Hunter, *Culture War* (New York: Basic Books, 1991).

102. Bill Joy, "Why the Future Doesn't Need Us," *Wired,* April 2000, 238–62.

CHAPTER SIX

Religion, Philosophy, and the American Founding

Peter Augustine Lawler

I want to consider the adequacy of Michael Zuckert's interpretation of the American founding and religion.[1] I do not mean to question this interpretation's historical accuracy, because Zuckert claims that what counts as historical evidence depends on the perspective brought to the evidence; his perspective is philosophy, not history.[2] Americans should take their bearings from the most rational or philosophic of the founders. From his perspective, the founders are those most open to philosophic rationalism, and the most philosophic of those philosophic men should be regarded as *the* founder. For Zuckert, Thomas Jefferson, author of the Declaration of Independence and *Notes on Virginia,* is America's founder. This view of the founding did not, of course, originate with Zuckert. But I think he presents it in the most radical, penetrating, and honest way so far.

In truth, this rational or philosophic interpretation of America stands in sharp contrast to most American opinion during the founding generation (and in our time). It has been criticized most ably by Barry Shain, who has shown that most of the Americans of the founding generation were Calvinist Christians.[3] But I do not view that criticism of Zuckert as decisive. My aim is to present a philosophical criticism of Zuckert's philosophical interpretation of America. I want to open the way for a philosophic defense of what Zuckert calls the continuity thesis: The American founding, at its best, should be regarded as a modification, not a rejection, of the nation's Christian natural-law inheritance. While other writers emphasize the *historical* continuity between American, Christian, and premodern forms of thought, I highlight the *philosophic* necessity for taking the continuity seriously. Zuckert argues, on the contrary, that because a choice must be made between historical traditionalism and philosophical rationalism (which I deny), it makes sense to celebrate American history as the progressive victory of reason over tradition. Following Zuckert's lead, I will focus my attention on Jefferson, beginning with his presentation of Jefferson's thought. My analysis of the limitations of Jefferson's thought is not meant to detract from his greatness, or from his deserved reputation as in some ways the most admirable and the most philosophic of the founders, but to demonstrate the founders' theoretical failure.

AMERICA AND NATURAL RIGHTS

Zuckert defends "the centrality of the natural rights orientation" in understanding America.[4] So he argues against classical republicanism, contemporary communitarianism, and Protestant communalism. Beginning with Jefferson's Declaration of Independence, Americans view government as concerned with "abstract individuals and their natural rights," with individuals freed from their political, social, and religious ties. This abstracted or not fully real "picture of the freely choosing individual" is opposed to the classical republican's picture of political animals or engaged citizens, and to the communitarian and Christian picture of social or communally engaged beings.[5]

The necessity of radical liberation from communal and political life leads directly to the conclusion that our political principles are not particularly American at all. They are "accessible to and valid for all human beings," because they "are simply universal in character." A society based on these principles is necessarily both "secular" and "open to the rational as such." That society is "cosmopolitan, not closed or sectarian." "To be an American" is not a matter of race, blood, culture, or faith, but "to accept those universal principles."[6] To be an American is to be open to philosophical truth by becoming uprooted from the social, political, and religious impediments to its acceptance. In Jefferson's view, to be an American is almost to be transpolitical, to be a member of the cosmopolis of philosophers, not the closed "cave" of citizens.

The Americans were the first to act on the modern philosopher John Locke's rational view that government comes neither from nature or God. Government is a human, rational construction to serve human purposes.[7] According to Jefferson, author of *Notes on the State of Virginia*, the most philosophic book of the founding generation, human beings are different from other animals because they "consciously understand their mortality and their vulnerability, and thus consciously shape the world so as to guarantee their survival."[8] While other animals are merely concerned with immediate survival, human beings pursue "security." Government is made by human beings to make themselves more secure as individuals, and it exists to suit their convenience as individuals.

In Jefferson's mind, the American founders, freed from "monkish ignorance and superstition," came "to understand better than ever before how and why to make government." The result was a "great improvement in their political life," and the expectation of more improvements to come. According to Zuckert, the idea that government is a human construct is one source "of the frequently noted progressive attitude to politics and society in America." And Jefferson finds that progress most reasonable.[9]

Zuckert, following Jefferson, contrasts the premodern and modern or American views of political life. The former is that "political life is understood as derived from God or nature," which "suggests a limit to what can be done with it." But the authentically American view is that government, as a human construct, is "open to indefinite improvement."[10] So America is based on a philosophy of unlimited human freedom. Zuckert acknowledges that the God of the Declaration is "Nature's God," but only to dismiss the idea that Jefferson relied at all on supernatural guidance. For Jefferson the only guidance nature provides human beings is negative: the drive for security points them away from nature. But there is no natural limit to the extent to which human beings might overcome nature through inventions, such as government. The movement away from nature is indefinitely long.

For Jefferson, we really have no knowledge of even nature's God, because we have no knowledge of nature at all. Jefferson argues in the *Notes* the philosophic view that "There is no 'nature-in-itself,' for the truth about nature varies with perspective." Human beings have no way of telling whether a "natural theology" or an "atheistic or materialistic cosmology" is true. Because the available evidence is insufficient, our picture of nature varies with our moods. "The thoughtful person stands undecided" concerning the truth about nature or the cosmos.[11]

The truth is that "The security of these rights—the really valuable thing—is not supplied by God or nature but by human beings themselves when they institute government." What is really valuable human beings make for themselves. Christians say that human action was the cause of the Fall, and salvation comes from the supernatural grace of God. But for Jefferson, "Human action is more nearly the foundation for human salvation than the basis for a fall. The Declaration's history reverses the Bible's history."[12] The Declaration's history is a tale of human self-liberation in the absence of a living God. The Declaration's true significance has nothing to do with rebelling against the

British. It is the first political application of the Lockean theology of liberation, a theology usually and wrongly thought to have Marxian roots.

So the natural rights orientation of Jefferson is really around human liberty, as opposed to nature or God. Zuckert rejects, for that reason, any version of the continuity thesis, the view that the Declaration or the founding are rooted in the nation's Christian, natural-law inheritance. For him, the real alternative to the Declaration's politics is "the politics of the Puritans." Calvinist legislation, rooted in a distrust of "natural liberty," has "earned the censure of mankind as Puritanical."[13] So Zuckert takes a side in the modern culture war that he sees as characterizing American history between the liberals and the Puritans. The liberals have won and have deserved to win most of the victories. For both philosophic and moral reasons Jefferson contests the view "that reform Christianity provides the key to the American political tradition"[14]

Zuckert contends that the leading American founders adjusted themselves rhetorically to a citizenry that was largely Christian. But they aimed to transform the meaning of Christian language to make it compatible with "liberal rationalism." They did not aim to do justice to both reason and revelation. The example of Jefferson shows they were not open at all to the possible truth of revelation. They used religion as little as possible in service to reason and liberty.

The Declaration's reference to the Creator, and its appearance of an appeal to natural theology, follows Locke's rhetorical example. Locke seems to ground his teaching on nature and rights in the human being's "relationship to the 'creator,' whose workmanship all human beings are." But his argument is also, more deeply, grounded "in a *simply* nontheistic manner . . . in the self-grounding character of human selfhood." The origin of rights is in self-assertion, not in the authority of nature or God. So Locke's rhetorical theism "is an intermediate term between Christian theism and more strictly philosophic, but nontheistic reasoning."[15] Authentic or strictly philosophic liberal rationalists know that all theistic reasoning is merely rhetorical. So Locke's theistic reasoning seduced Protestant American thinkers away from their distinctively Christian premises, while allowing them, if need be, to remain theists. America has worked best when Christians have allowed themselves to be seduced, when religion and rights have seemed perfectly compatible.[16] Experience has shown that in a natural rights republic religion does not and should not completely wither away. But it has also shown that the "religious sensibilities" of Christianity could be employed to support the natural rights republic. These religious sensibilties have been transformed into "the American civil religion."[17] But the fact remains that Jefferson himself was a strictly philosophic thinker. He was not an atheist only in the sense that he held open the possibility that nature might have been ordered by some purposeful intelligence.[18]

RELIGION AND LIBERAL RATIONALISM

The Lockean/Jeffersonian natural rights republic allows a personal or private place for religion. The abstract individual consents to government for the limited purpose of enhanced security. Otherwise, he is free from government to pursue happiness. The latter pursuit is actually a truer manifestation of human liberty.

The Lockean Zuckert says that "The idea of happiness, originating in the unique capacity of the human mind to form general ideas, supplies human beings with freedom, or *the nearest thing* to free will that is attainable."[19] The Christian teaching concerning free will is untrue. But the pursuit of happiness is less a product of natural determination than the pursuit of security. While pursuing security human beings are free to choose the means, such as the construction of government, but not the end. But human beings desire to exist for more than mere survival, and so they imagine ideas or ends which they believe will make them happy. These various transcendent pursuits are what form lives into different shapes. Based on how they perceive God, humans pursue different conceptions of happiness.

But Locke and Jefferson hold that the pursuit of happiness, and not happiness itself, is distinctively human. Human happiness is, at best, unstable or transient. Every satisfaction is soon replaced by uneasiness, and the uneasiness renews the pursuit. Restless discontent, not happiness, is the characteristic human condition. Human beings are "doomed to frustration in their pursuit of ever-elusive happiness," but they cannot help but pursue it nonetheless. Every human being's pursuit is inevitably futile, and so none of us really knows what happiness is.[20] Given the absence of solid evidence, how to pursue happiness properly must remain a matter of personal choice. So nature directs human beings away "from a clear evil, death and suffering, to nothing in particular."[21] The positive or religious dimension of human longing is hopeless.

It might seem that Locke and Jefferson should praise the nobility of spiritual striving, the highest form of the futile human effort at transcendence.[22] But their tendency, instead, is to divert human attention away from religion, from metaphysics, and from philosophy. Their view is that the quest to know God and the good is more productive of misery than anything else, and it gets in the way of what human beings can accomplish in the pursuit of security. The pursuit of happiness is subordinate to the pursuit of security, because while the former is distinctively human, the latter is capable of being achieved.

Thomas Pangle is right to say that Jefferson's privatization of theological controversy is an attempt to trivialize it. For Jefferson there is no metaphysical or theological truth accessible to human beings. Rational progress culminates in skepticism; the rational republic fosters religious indifference. Jefferson hoped that all Americans would comfortably accept the vague theology of Unitarianism.[23] That uniformity would free rational discourse from metaphysical and theological whimsy.

The tendency of the leading founders was to turn human longing away from transcendent happiness and toward comfortable security. They tried to identify the pursuit of happiness with the pursuit of security. And their intention, as Zuckert contends, was clearly anti-Christian. But we have to wonder to what extent their effort really depended upon, or was consonant with, Christian premises. The liberal rationalist and the Christian Augustinian or Pascalian or Calvinist agree, against Aristotle and Socrates, that human beings cannot achieve this-worldly happiness through their own efforts. They also agree that human beings are unhappy because they experience themselves as insecure; and they cannot acquire security, or the freedom from contingency for which they long, through their own efforts. The Christian shouts, while the liberal rationalist whispers, this truth about ineradicable insecurity.

But Jefferson's deepest experience of his "unique individuality" was insecurity; Jefferson was painfully dizzy in the face of the "abyss" represented by his "exposed situation" in nature. His personal experience was the same as that of the Christian Blaise Pascal, who is famous for expressing so eloquently how frightened he was by his unsupported existence. Jefferson's most personal experience was of "the limits of human domination and use of nature." He was aware that the scientific and political attempts to dominate nature are futile diversions from the miserable experience of individuality or contingency and vulnerability. Locke's abstract individual is not enough of a real individual to really encounter "the terrors of nature," but Jefferson was.[24]

So Jefferson agrees with the Christian Pascal that the liberal rationalist pursuit of this-worldly security is not so rational after all, but a diversion from the truth about the limits of all human effort. The main reason science and philosophy become active and utilitarian is to give human beings as little time as possible to reflect on the fact that the natural rights republic is rooted in the Lockean revelation of man's misery in God's absence. Philosophy and science become more an escape from the truth. The Declaration's progressivism, its theology of liberation, is most unreasonable; it is less plausible than the Christian account of the Fall.

TOCQUEVILLE ON AMERICAN UNREASONABLENESS

The best criticism of the American's unreasonable pursuit of diversion is Alexis de Tocqueville, who means in his *Democracy in America* to be a friendly critic of the leading founders. Tocqueville describes the Americans as pursuing happiness, skeptically defined as material enjoyment, but never taking time to enjoy it. They are, as Locke says, restless or uneasy in the midst of their abundance. But Tocqueville adds that they seem to be perversely proud of their misery. Their constant calculation on behalf of their pursuit is a sign of their human liberty. Actual happiness or enjoyment would be the result of their "enslavement" to nature or other men. The Americans' morality of self-interest in this respect is an assertion of individual human freedom against nature or instinct. They have affirmed the Lockean-Jefferson doctrine, quite consciously: human freedom requires the pursuit of what rational man cannot have.[25]

Preferring the pursuit of enjoyment to enjoyment or happiness may be free but it is surely not rational. Tocqueville takes this perversity as a convincing sign that Americans are beings with ineradicable spiritual needs. They feel the misery of God's absence intensely. They believe that reason leads to the conclusion that spiritual longings are insatiable, and so they must divert their efforts in a material direction. But that diversion of course fails, to some extent from the beginning. The Americans seem to know that material success cannot give them what they need, and their attempt to divert themselves from what they know becomes progressively less successful. For Tocqueville, the example of the Americans, a whole people restless in the midst of abundance, contradicts the hope of liberal rationalism that spiritual needs can somehow be transformed or attenuated.[26]

Tocqueville accepts Jean-Jacques Rousseau's criticism of Locke's individualistic extremism. In his *Discourse on Inequality*, Rousseau explains that Locke's psychology is flawed in its premise that the human construction of good government will actually make human beings feel more secure. They will be, objectively, more secure: they will live longer, less risky lives. But they will tend to experience themselves as progressively less secure. The natural drive for personal security is satisfied more with feeling than with fact. The fact is that the particular human being will never really be secure. All human beings are dependent on forces beyond their control and eventually die.

The establishment of peace and prosperity through good government gives human beings more to lose, and, despite their best efforts at diversion, more time to reflect on the truth about their contingency and mortality. And Cartesian or Lockean skeptical rationalism, the foundation of liberal democracy, deprives them of illusions about the providence of God and nature. Human beings become more death-haunted, more fearful and anxious, than ever before.[27]

If being human is acting to pursue happiness and security against nature, and if that effort makes human beings more anxious and restless, then human liberty ought to be regarded as an error. True human ethics ought to negate human liberty and return to nature. The futile human pursuit of happiness ought to be replaced by the security and contentment enjoyed by every other animal. Human uniqueness is an aberration to be eradicated in accord with nature's general intention.[28] If Locke and Jefferson are right about human freedom, then it is no good.

Locke and Jefferson might well say that to work for this eradication is unreasonable. The human pursuit of security and happiness is natural or unalterable. But Rousseau responds that those pursuits are not natural, but historical. They are human creations or constructions that might well be deconstructed. Rousseau's correction of Locke, surely, is in accord with the basic Lockean premise that nature is inhuman and worthless, and so all human value is created in opposition to nature. According to Zuckert, the Declaration's theology is a tale of salvation through human ingenuity, without which Jefferson doesn't believe human beings can make themselves happy or secure. According to Rousseau, human beings can achieve what the Christian God promised, by bringing history to an end.[29]

Tocqueville agrees with Zuckert's Jefferson that the experience of unsupported individuality is of unlimited restlessness, painful disorientation, and practical paralysis, or irrationality.[30] So the abstract individual freed from nature, family, community, and God does not experience himself as reasonable, happy, or secure. Tocqueville calls the Rousseauean judgment against this extreme experience of individuality "individualism." Individualism is an apathetic, asocial, and passionless existence: one without all distinctively human qualities. It is the judgment for the Rousseauean, or wholly inhuman nature, against the deracinated or unnatural individuality of the Lockean state of nature. That judgment is perfectly reasonable if human distinctiveness is defined in terms of futile, personal pursuits, which is the culmination of the liberal, democratic movement. For Tocqueville, human liberty must be experienced as lovable if it is to sustain itself, and so it must be moderated or shaped by genuine experiences of familial, political, and religious love. Human beings are communal and political by nature.

Tocqueville differs from Locke and Jefferson by recognizing and affirming natural limits to human liberty. He does the same for the human longing for God. Affirming the Socratic-Platonic-Christian view, he argues human beings must believe they are immortal if they are to act well.[31] The most reasonable understanding of freedom of religion must be as freedom for religious belief. Most of the leading founders, surely, would agree with Tocqueville here. But the case of Jefferson is unclear.

Tocqueville goes even further. He understands the Americans as rightly believing that religious belief is indispensable for political liberty. Human beings cannot think or act freely without some "salutary" submission to intellectual and moral authority. The effort to achieve unlimited liberty produces the conclusion that liberty is no good, and leads to the willing acceptance of political bondage. The American choice is for political freedom and religious dogma, for a common moral and spiritual authority as a guide for human action.[32] So American religion cannot be completely privatized. It is the basis of our political institutions and personal well-being.[33] Tocqueville's judgment concerning the Puritans is subtle and mixed, but he is clear that American liberty cannot be understood without them.

Tocqueville shows us that the abstract individual of Jefferson's Declaration is no rationalist and, in the long run, no liberal. But having denied that Lockeanism is a reasonable account of human experience, I must add that I disagree with Zuckert's identification of Jefferson with Locke. That identification depends on making the *Notes on Virginia* the authoritative text for understanding Jefferson, and slighting his letters.[34] Zuckert minimizes the letters' importance by arguing Jefferson sought agreement with his correspondents, not truth. But there is just too much evidence in the letters that the mature Jefferson thought of himself not as a Lockean but as an Epicurean. He claimed not to be in pursuit but in possession of happiness.[35]

Jefferson thought the Epicurean Jefferson was the most philosophical Jefferson. And if it is true that Jefferson expresses most completely the philosophic intention of the founding, we cannot avert our eyes from this form of ancient rationalism. Morevoer, Jefferson's affirmation of Epicureanism is connected with his affirmation of the moral teaching of Jesus and Christianity.

JEFFERSON, EPICURUS, AND JESUS

Jefferson was indebted to modern writers such as Locke for his understanding of political and natural science. But in his most private and theoretical reflections, he says his ethical teachers were the ancient philosophers and

Jesus. Some of these reflections are found in one of his letters to Doctor Benjamin Rush, his friend and partner in theoretical discussion. To Rush, Jefferson had the best reasons for speaking his mind. Gone, for the moment, were political and rhetorical considerations.

This letter fulfilled a promise Jefferson made to Rush in the midst of some "delightful conversations," which were a respite from the political crisis of 1798–99. Jefferson gives his views on "the Christian religion," which are "the result of a lifetime of reflections." These thoughts had occupied his mind whenever he could "justifiably abstract" it "from public affairs." Jefferson actually compares Christian with ancient philosophical ethics. He begins by denying that he accepts some "anti-Christian system." He asserts, in this private and theoretical moment, "I am a Christian," meaning that he accepts "the genuine principles of Jesus himself." Jefferson holds that Jesus' "system of morals" is "the most perfect and sublime that has ever been taught by man."[36]

But Jefferson did not regard Christian ethics as complete. He wrote in a later letter that "I . . . am an Epicurian [sic]." And he explained how he could be simultaneously a Christian and an Epicurean: "Epictetus and Epicurus give laws for governing ourselves, Jesus [provides] a supplement of the duties and charities we owe to others."[37] The greatness of the ancient philosophers, Jefferson told Rush, "related chiefly to ourselves," is how we may achieve "tranquility of mind" through the "government of passions." Because self-government is primary, Christianity is only a "supplement."[38] Personal tranquility does not induce us to do our duties to others, and so Christianity is both secondary, while morally superior, to Epicureanism.

Jefferson's acceptance of the atheistic materialism of Epicureanism is actually, of course, strong evidence for Zuckert's dismissal of the authority of nature's or any other God. Atheism, Jefferson wrote, is the basis for "the consolation of a sound philosophy, equally indifferent to hope and fear."[39] To be beyond hope and fear, of course, is to be beyond being determined either by the drive for security or the pursuit of happiness. The tranquility of indifference *is* distinctively human happiness. For the Epicurean, happiness, understood as the pleasure associated with the overcoming of mental anxiety through truthful thought, is the achievable goal of life.[40] The Epicurean Jefferson employed reason to combat the experience of "unique individuality" of the Pascalian Jefferson. He also used it to recognize the futility of the materialistic utilitarianism of the abstract individual portrayed by the Lockean Jefferson.

Happiness, Jefferson emphasized, was achieved neither through hedonism nor indolence, but by the practice of a certain kind of virtue.[41] And the test of virtue is its utility in achieving mental tranquility.[42] For the Epicurean Jefferson, what is useful in achieving tranquility is virtue. So the Epicurean will be just, because injustice brings on mental anxiety. But he will not exert himself on behalf of others in the name of justice or charity, because those exertions are not useful in gaining tranquility.

The Epicurean Jefferson reconciled liberty with happiness; he was free from the chains of common opinion for his own self-government, and knew that self-government is a way of life never lived by more than a very few.[43] Freedom from hope and fear is understood as self-sufficiency; the individual no longer desires what would make him dependent on others, and others dependent on him. For this personal cultivation only, Jefferson recommended the study of the ancient philosophers. Jefferson's love of classical learning was not, as Eva Brann claims, a "noble and baseless preference."[44] The preference was personal, tranquil, delightful, and philosophically grounded. But it was worse than useless in directing Jefferson toward his duties to others; it revealed political leadership to be mere drudgery.[45]

The ancient philosophers recommended a way of life that points away from benevolence toward human beings in general. They taught, Jefferson reports, friendship toward their own kind, and the moral duties of patriotism and justice to those not of their kind. Epicurean philosophers know that patriotism and justice are qualities necessary for political community. And they also know that political order is useful for tranquility. So the ancient philosophers "taught" or "inculcated" in nonphilosophers those political virtues, without really including them "within the circle of their benevolence."[46]

The ancient philosophers' teaching concerning nonphilosophic virtue was part of their enlightened selfishness. And they did not teach "peace, charity, and love to our fellow men" as virtues, because they did not regard them as useful; these are the virtues Jefferson regarded as particularly democratic. The ancient philosophers saw no reason to embrace "with benevolence the whole family of mankind."[47]

The ancients spoke candidly when they opposed benevolence and moral duty, because their conceptions of moral duty are always self-interested. So Jefferson ranked for his friend Rush the ancient philosophers according to their candor. Plato is the least truthful, the least openly selfish and elitist, of the philosophers. Cicero's Platonism was clear in his hypocritical attacks on Epicurus, in which the Stoics in general shared. Jefferson praised Seneca for being less Stoic than most of the Stoics. Ranking still higher is Epictetus, the last true Stoic. But in "the genuine . . . doctrine of Epicurus" is found "everything rational in moral philosophy which Greece and Rome left us."[48] Epicureanism, not Lockeanism, is rationalism for Jefferson.

Jefferson knew that the Epicurean way of life is not for most people. His application of Epicurean precepts to his own life is a key point of distinction between his own and common opinion. His deepest rational opinions are selfish and undemocratic. To explain and justify the individual's responsibility to others, he turned from philosophy to Christianity. That turn is not merely rhetorical, because Jefferson held that the Epicurean account of human nature is incomplete. Jefferson was actually more certain than most Christians that there is a natural foundation for the duties that social beings must have to each other. And so he does not agree with Augustine that there can be no justice without the loving subordination of the creature to the Creator. Jefferson's affirmation of Christian morality is wholly natural and has nothing to do with man's duties to God.

His acceptance of the moral system of Jesus has nothing to do with divine revelation. Jefferson goes as far as to call "immaterialism" a Christian heresy that can be traced to those who wrote about Jesus, but not to Jesus himself.[49] Jefferson merely affirms Jesus' and his moral doctrine's "human excellence," which he says is all that Jesus ever claimed for himself.[50] Jesus gives a better account than the ancient philosophers of our duties to others, which Jefferson holds we are inclined to perform by our nature.

Jefferson held that "moral sense" or "conscience" or "moral instinct" describe what nature gives beings "destined for society." This instinct, by giving human beings pleasure when they do their duties to others, is the source of moral action.[51] We have a natural sensitivity to the suffering of others that "prompts us irresistibly to feel and succor their distresses." The feeling of this pleasure, a source of happiness, is less distinctively human than the more free, futile, and selfish pursuit of happiness.[52] The moral instinct is given to social, not necessarily rational, beings. The Jefferson who describes the moral sense has a more positive view of nature for human beings than does Zuckert's Lockean Jefferson. Nature does, after all, provide us with what we need to live well or happily as social beings. For Jefferson, there are two forms of distinctively human happiness, one rational and selfish, the other subrational, instinctual, and social.

Action in response to moral sense or instinct is not a manifestation of human liberty. Nonetheless, Jefferson uses it to root his view that human beings equally possess natural rights. He explains that blacks may be intellectually inferior to whites, and implicitly that it is almost impossible to conceive of a black Epicurean. But blacks and whites are morally equal in their capacity to do their duties to others.[53] The possession of the moral sense, and so the capacity to distinguish between right and wrong, makes an animal human.[54]

Jefferson contends that the instinct of moral sense has nothing to do with "science," or the rational perception of the truth. It also has nothing to do, contrary to Plato, with some perception of the beautiful. Because this natural goodness is so easily distorted by the "artificial rules" imposed by reason, "the ploughman" is more likely to act morally than "the professor": the rational conquest of nature produces moral decline.[55] But it is far from clear how this subrational naturalization of Christianity can really be the foundation of natural rights. Perhaps the Jeffersonian/American acceptance of the equal freedom and dignity of all human beings must be understood as a direct result of Christian faith.

Jefferson's radical separation of the foundation of self-government in reason, and moral duty in instinct, makes Epicureanism morally salutary. The philosopher should just leave morality alone because it is unreasonable. The "learned," or modern Platonists, act unphilosophically when they serve their "own interests" by "perverting" true Christian doctrine.[56] The learned cleverly turn "primitive" into "Platonizing" Christianity, a perverse mixture which distorts beyond recognition each of its parts.[57]

Christian or true morality is most powerfully threatened by the Socratic dictum that knowledge is virtue. Jefferson wrote that the study of "moral philosophy" is "lost time," or worse than useless.[58] There is, strictly speaking, no such thing. Morality must be democratic or common, because all human beings, both the "professor" and the "ploughman," must live in society. Because most human beings are not philosophers or scientists, or even primarily rational beings, the moral sense must be rooted not in the "head" but the "heart." Jefferson says this distinction is between "science" and "sentiment."[59] Nature intends people who are pre-reasonable to act socially and morally. In fact, it is easier for them to do so.

This understanding of moral sense or instinct is Jefferson's great debt to the Scottish Enlightenment. The term "moral sense" was first used the way Jefferson does by Francis Hutcheson, a professor of moral philosophy at the University of Glasgow. Hutcheson radically separated self-love from morality or benevolence. Because moral sense is an instinct, it owes nothing to reason. So it cannot be reduced by Lockean skepticism to mere self-interest.[60]

THE UNREASONABLENESS OF CHRISTIAN EPICUREANISM

Jefferson had good reason to separate philosophy from morality in opposition to the Declaration's Lockeanism. That does not mean that Christian Epicureanism is more reasonable than Lockeanism, or Thomas Aquinas's natural law. The Thomistic account of natural law is an attempt to integrate reason and revelation by informing one by the other. Revelation completes reason, and humans beings can rationally understand nature's moral ends. Jefferson agrees with Thomas, and calls himself a Christian because human beings have a natural inclination to do their moral duty to others. The ancient philosophers knew of no such inclination. But for Thomas Aquinas, unlike Jefferson, nature intends these inclinations to be ordered and informed by reason. True human morality depends on the integration, not separation, of natural goods.

Aquinas and Jefferson also agree that charity is not a clear dictate of reason. Thomas Aquinas holds that the distinctively Christian virtues, the theological virtues, are "infused." They depend upon God's grace, upon the human being's friendship with a God who cares about his or her well-being and promises satisfaction of his or her deepest longings.[61] Thomas Aquinas reasonably denies what Jefferson seems to believe, that there is a purely natural foundation for charity. In this respect, Thomas is closer to the ancient philosophers than is Jefferson. Both Epicurus and Thomas agree that Jefferson's secularized or naturalized Christian faith in the goodness of human nature is really ungrounded.

Jefferson's partly Christian and partly Epicurean ethics seems, at first, to reflect the tension between reason and revelation that, according to Leo Strauss, is the secret to the West's vitality.[62] But that appearance is deceiving. Jefferson dissolves that tension by ignoring the moral claims of reason and revelation. Neither is the source of our duty to others. Remarkably, Jefferson reduced to such "feelings" his devotion to democracy, as well as the equality of all human beings.

EPICUREAN CHRISTIANITY, LIBERAL DEMOCRACY, AND NATURAL RIGHTS

Charles Griswold contends that Jefferson did not do justice to either Epicurean personal selfishness or Christian moral duty. In the crucial case of slavery, Jefferson's pursuit of Epicurean tranquility usually prevailed over his moral sense. While he wrote eloquently against its injustice, after 1777 he never spoke out publicly against slavery, freed his own slaves, or tried, even as president, to improve the miserable situation of blacks as slaves or freemen. Jefferson's inaction and prevarications were, Griswold explains, "directly traceable to the underlying incoherence of his philosophical position." And, Griswold adds, his inaction and incoherence are especially troubling because of Jefferson's undeniable devotion to moral integrity and the pursuit of justice. Jefferson was a great and admirable thinker and political actor who admitted he was less than perfect on both counts.[63] Jefferson often had to choose between doing his duty to others, protecting their rights, as his moral sense inclined, or maintaining his tranquil freedom from anxiety by convincing himself he was doing all that he could, which was not much. The Epicurean could even calm himself with the thought that at least he was not contributing to the worsening of the injustice of slavery. Epicureanism's most powerful effect was moral rationalizations. The truth is that Jefferson's deeds did not correspond to the eloquent and extreme condemnation of race-based slavery of his words.

Demystified Christianity was not a strong impetus to moral action. His inaction concerning slavery calls into question the natural strength of the moral sense, maybe especially in the case of philosophers. The Abolitionists, more genuinely Christian, opposed slavery more resolutely because they believed that owning slaves was sinful. The enlightened Jefferson, finding Christian doctrines such as revelation, sin, guilt, judgment, and salvation not only incredible but repulsive, took no risks on behalf of racial justice. Jefferson hated Calvinism perhaps more than any other leading founder.[64] But perhaps that passion made him too "reasonable," too cautious. Could original sin better account for man's nature than some combination of reason and generalized benevolence?

According to Zuckert, the protection of rights and especially the white denial of black rights caused Jefferson to find a very limited place for public belief and even God. The Declaration's "We hold these truths to be self-evident," properly understood, means that most Americans must accept the self-evidence of natural rights by conviction.[65]

Zuckert quotes, surely over-quotes, Jefferson's most uncharacteristic assertion about God. Found in Query XVIII in *Notes on Virginia,* it is part of an attack on the injustice and antidemocratic moral corruption caused by the presence of slavery in Virginia: "And can the liberties of a nation be thought secure when we have removed their only firm basis, a conviction in the minds of the people that these liberties are the gift of God. That they are not to be violated but with his wrath."[66] For Zuckert, Jefferson's point is that the effective security of rights depends on the belief of most Americans that rights are God-given and their violation will be God-punished. This untrue belief is the core of the American civil religion, which, as Lincoln emphasized far more insistently later, is an unphilosophical but indispensable support for the natural rights republic.

But why would this quote not apply to the philosophical Jefferson himself? Disbelief in the God-givenness of rights, and in a wrathful God, caused him to do less than he might have to secure the rights of others. And this moral deficiency was shared with many or most of the leading founders.

According to Harry Jaffa, "the widespread lack of concern over the moral challenge of Negro slavery to the doctrine of universal rights in the revolutionary generation can be traced to the egoistic quality of those rights in their Lockean foundation."[67] And, of course, Lockean and Epicurean selfishness are not really that far apart; in both cases virtue is what is useful in securing one's own happiness.

It also seems to me that Lockean-Epicurean calculation even dominates Jefferson's assertion about the violation of rights and God's wrath. Jefferson continues his jeremiad against the evils of slavery: "Indeed I tremble for my country when I reflect that God is just; that his justice cannot sleep forever; that considering numbers, nature, *and natural means only,* a revolution in the wheel of fortune, an exchange in situations is among possible events: that it may become probable through supernatural interference." Human fortunes change; those on top eventually lose power. God's justice, "an eye for an eye," dictates the destruction of the rights of the oppressors by the oppressed. Acting in fear of God means acting in fear of what will happen when blacks—increasing in numbers—eventually take power. The whites should respect their rights now in expectation that the blacks will respect theirs later.

RATIONAL CONTINUITY?

Whatever Jefferson and the other leading founders thought privately, the public presentation of the Creator usually has the intention of making clear that human beings are creatures, that is, beings not only with rights but with duties to God. The best example here, of course, is Madison's "Memorial and Remonstrance," where he says that "Before any man can be considered as a member of Civil Society, he must be considered as a subject of the Governor of the Universe."[68] The God who governs subjects is a personal God.

For Madison, the duty of the creature is part of the "property" that government protects, not controls. He even claimed that "Conscience is the most sacred of all property; other property depending in part on positive law, the exercise of that being a natural and inalienable right."[69] Acting according to conscience is the most perfect manifestation of one's freedom, of one's real ownership of one's self, of self-determination. The performance of such duty is evidence that one is not simply determined by one's political order, by the drive for security, or by the futile pursuit of happiness. Both Jefferson and Madison agree that that freedom is the one which is most natural, because it is the one least dependent on political support. But Jefferson, in Madison's view, is wrong to reduce conscience to some subrational instinct or moral sense.

The idea of inner moral freedom, not clearly present in Jefferson, is not wholly defensible without some biblical-Christian support. While the founding conception of "a created nature" can be the basis for affirming the truth of ancient or classical, or even Epicurean, thought, Christianity offers a clearer basis for arguing all human beings are equally persons because they are created in the image of a personal, free, and rational God. To experience oneself as created is to view democratically the accessibility of the true understanding of human duty through conscience. That experience is available both to the fortunate few, the followers of Socrates or Epicurus, and to all other human beings. The democratization of the transpolitical search for truth and conscience, and of the conviction that this search can be the foundation of human duty and human society, appears decisively biblical and Christian.

Madison's and Jefferson's rather extreme opposition to public promulgation of civil theology and political religion can be understood in terms of their understanding of the limits of politics for free and social beings. Political life, it seems, mainly consists of cooperative and coercive efforts to provide for bodily needs and does not extend to the formation of conscience. It does not participate in human fulfillment in the fullest extent. On that point, the Epicurean Jefferson and the Christian agree. American religion should not be reduced to a civil theology.

Pierre Manent explains that the Lockean/Jeffersonian American solution presented by Zuckert is a characteristically modern rebellion against the confusion characteristic of medieval Europe in practice and Thomism in theory. The human being, for most medieval thinkers, had two ends, one natural, the other supernatural. The human or political world—constituted by the empire and the emperor—aimed to understand itself as naturally self-sufficient. But the spiritual or supernatural world—represented by the church—claimed to be superior to the natural or political world, and so free from merely temporal power and control. And the perfection of the supernatural world made the natural one seem unjust and unfulfilling by comparison. The result were persons burdened by two seemingly incompatible forms of domination. Both the government and the church were oppressive and ineffective.[70]

One version—arguably the dominant version—of the modern solution was to free the human being from both natural and supernatural domination. Human beings had to be freed from all dependence connected with sociability, from being a political animal or a social being under God. In the name of human freedom and good government, the modern philosophers invented the abstract individual, who consents to government he invents to satisfy his fundamentally asocial needs. But this allegedly self-constituting individual lacks the resources to constitute himself. His liberated will is insufficiently directed and limited to be effective, because modern liberation is achieved through the denial of the social and spiritual longings characteristic of actual human beings. As Tocqueville predicts, and the history of the past century confirms, self-assertion culminates in self-surrender and even the sense the self was never there at all.

So, this audacious attempt to free human beings from nature and God has clearly fallen short of complete success. While the Declaration presents human beings as free and rational, it is incoherent on the foundation of those distinctively human qualities. The various assertions concerning inalienable rights, nature's God, and the Creator (who is both Supreme Judge and the source of Divine Providence) cannot really be harmonized. We do well, in our time, to highlight those aspects of the American founding that dissent from the more extreme and discredited claims of liberalism, and to reconstitute liberalism on a less secular and individualistic foundation.

NOTES

1. Michael P. Zuckert, *The Natural Rights Republic: Studies in the Foundation of the American Political Tradition* (Notre Dame, Ind.: University of Notre Dame Press, 1996).
2. Ibid., 122.
3. Barry Alan Shain, *The Myth of American Individualism: The Protestant Origins of American Political Thought* (Princeton: Princeton University Press, 1994).
4. Zuckert, *Natural Rights Republic*, 6.
5. Ibid., 21.
6. Ibid., 126.
7. Ibid., 102.
8. Ibid., 80.
9. Ibid., 103.
10. Ibid.
11. Ibid., 64–65.
12. Ibid., 129.
13. Ibid., 145.
14. Ibid., 123–26.
15. Ibid., 182, emphasis added.
16. Ibid., 200–201.
17. Ibid., 200.
18. Ibid., 253, n. 16.

19. Ibid., 84, emphasis added.

20. Ibid., 84–85.

21. Thomas Pangle, *The Spirit of Modern Republicanism* (Chicago: University of Chicago Press, 1988), 208.

22. Zuckert, *Natural Rights Republic,* 85.

23. Pangle, *Spirit of Modern Republicanism,* 83.

24. Zuckert, *Natural Rights Republic,* 63–64.

25. Alexis de Tocqueville, *Democracy in America,* vol. 2, pt. 2, chaps. 8–13.

26. Ibid., 2.2.12–13.

27. Ibid., 2.1.1, 3–5, 7, 10, 16, 20.

28. Ibid., 2.2.2, on individualism.

29. The text of Rousseau summarized here is, of course, the *Discourse on Inequality.* See my *Postmodernism Rightly Understood* (Lanham, Md.: Rowman and Littlefield, 1999), chapter 1, for the connection between Rousseau and the famous argument for the end of history of the Hegelian Alexandre Kojève.

30. Tocqueville, *Democracy in America,* vol. 2, pt. 1, chap. 5; vol. 2, pt. 2, chap. 3.

31. Ibid., 2.2.15.

32. Ibid., 2.2, 5.

33. Ibid., 1.2.9, "Religion, Considered as a Political Institution" with 2.2.15.

34. Zuckert, *Natural Rights Republic,* 87–89. Robert K. Faulkner, who also confidently presents Jefferson as simply a modern and largely Lockean liberal rationalist, says what Zuckert suggests: "the philosophic hedonism of Epicurus is not very important to Jefferson" ("Jefferson and the Enlightened Science of Liberty," in *Reason and Republicanism: Thomas Jefferson's Legacy of Liberty,* ed. Gary L. McDowell and Sharon L. Noble [Lanham, Md.: Rowman and Littlefield, 1997], 43). But he really gives no argument for this position, and he asserts, quite implausibly, that Jefferson's Epicureanism is simply a rhetorical weapon against apolitical Christianity.

35. See Charles L. Griswold, Jr., "Rights and Wrongs: Jefferson, Slavery, and Philosophical Quandaries," in *A Culture of Rights,* ed. Michael J. Lacey and Knud Haakenssen (New York, 1988), chap. 4.

36. The letters of Jefferson can be found in *The Life and Selected Writings of Thomas Jefferson,* ed. A. Koch and W. Peden (New York: The Modern Library, 1946). They can be also found in *Thomas Jefferson: Writings,* ed. M. Peterson (New York: Library of America, 1984). My earlier and unfocused account of Jefferson's mixture of Christianity and Epicureanism is "Classical Ethics, Jefferson's Christian Epicureanism, and American Morality," *Perspectives on Political Science* 20 (Winter 1991): 17–22.

37. Jefferson, *Selected Writings,* To William Short, 31 October 1819.

38. Ibid., To Benjamin Rush, 21 April 1803.

39. Ibid., To Short, 31 October 1819.

40. My remarks on Epicurus and Epicureanism are indebted throughout to Griswold, "Rights and Wrongs," 154–69.

41. Jefferson, *Selected Writings,* To Thomas Law, 13 June 1814.

42. See Griswold, "Rights and Wrongs," 156, note 33 for references to the many times Jefferson identified happiness with tranquility in his letters.

43. Jefferson, *Selected Writings,* To Mrs. Cosway, 12 October 1786.

44. Eva Brann, *Paradoxes of Education in a Republic* (Chicago: University of Chicago Press, 1979), 86.

45. Griswold, "Rights and Wrongs," 161. On the basis of his Epicurean theory, Griswold remarks, "Jefferson's participation in public life becomes difficult to explain" (161, note 47). But the same can be said for his Lockean theory, which also holds that political life is not intrinsically fulfilling for human beings, that they are not political animals. Epicureanism, the theory of many Roman political leaders, seems a better way of articulating the tension between political ambition and personal tranquility. It gives a less abstract and more complete account of human hopes and fears.

46. Jefferson, *Selected Writings,* To Rush, 21 April 1803.

47. Ibid.

48. Ibid., To Short, 31 October, 1819.

49. See Griswold, "Rights and Wrongs," 167–68. Jefferson, *Selected Writings,* To John Adams, 15 August 1820.

50. Jefferson, *Selected Writings,* To Rush 21 April 1803.

51. The best account of Jefferson's view of the moral sense is Jean M. Yarbrough, *Thomas Jefferson and the Formation of the American Character* (Lawrence: University Press of Kansas, 1998), chap. 2.

52. Jefferson, *Selected Writings,* To Peter Carr, 10 August 1787; To Law, 13 June 1814.

53. See Thomas Jefferson, *Notes on the State of Virginia,* Query XIV, on the reconciliation of black intellectual and physical inferiority with their moral equality to whites.

54. See Griswold, "Rights and Wrongs," 176.

55. Jefferson, *Selected Writings,* To Carr, 10 August 1787.

56. Ibid., To Rush, 21 April 1803.

57. Ibid., To Adams, 13 October 1813.

58. Ibid., To Carr, 10 August 1787.

59. Ibid., To Cosway, 12 October 1786.

60. See Frank Balog, "The Scottish Enlightenment and the Liberal Political Tradition," *Confronting the Constitution,* ed. A. Bloom (Washington, D.C.: AEI Press, 1990), 196–98.

61. See especially Thomas Aquinas, *Summa Theologiae,* II-II, question 56 with question 65.

62. See Leo Strauss, "Progress or Return?" in *The Rebirth of Classical Political Rationalism* (Chicago: University of Chicago Press, 1989), 270.

63. Griswold, "Rights and Wrongs," 150–52.

64. For abundant evidence of Jefferson's hatred of Calvinism, see Griswold, "Rights and Wrongs," 187, note 106.

65. Zuckert, *Natural Rights Republic,* 46–49.

66. Jefferson, *Notes on Virginia,* Query XVIII, quoted by Zuckert, *Natural Rights Republic,* 201.

67. Harry Jaffa, *The Crisis of the House Divided* (Chicago: University of Chicago Press, 1982), 324.

68. Marvin Meyers, ed., *The Mind of the Founder: Sources of the Political Thought of James Madison,* rev. ed. (Hanover, N.H.: University Press of New England, 1981), 7.

69. Ibid., 187.

70. Pierre Manent, *Modern Liberty and Its Discontents* (Lanham, Md.: Rowman and Littlefield, 1998), 102–3.

CHAPTER SEVEN

The Transformation of Protestant Theology as a Condition of the American Revolution

Thomas G. West

The Early Puritan Understanding of Politics

I begin with my conclusion. One original feature of American Puritanism, along with four modifications of the original Puritan self-understanding, brought Protestant theology to the point where it became unambiguously supportive of the principles of the American Revolution. The original feature was the fierce Puritan spirit of independence from all human authority while being totally devoted to Christ. This made them radical democrats, but with a deep personal sense of moral and religious responsibility. Four changes in Puritan theology followed. First, reason was restored as a legitimate Christian supplement to the authority of scripture. Second, man's imperfect or fallen nature was acknowledged to be unchanged by divine grace. Therefore, limited government and the rule of law were indispensable. Third, the Puritans embraced warlike manliness and wily prudence on behalf of liberty as fundamental Christian virtues. Finally, the Puritans adopted, *as part of their theology,* European social compact theory as taught by Locke and others—the theory that became the principled ground of the American Revolution.

Over the last century religion's place in the founding has been a subject of intense controversy. Michael Zuckert argues in chapter 1, "Natural Rights and Protestant Politics," that the founding is an amalgam or blend of two disparate traditions, Enlightenment reason and Protestant revelation. He implies that the two are not altogether compatible. When Zuckert says bluntly, in his book *The Natural Rights Republic,* that the principles of the American founding lead necessarily to "the essentially secular character of the society," he suggests that those principles are not only not religious but are at bottom indifferent or hostile to religion.[1]

In fact, however, the founders expected "the society" to be mostly religious, and that meant mostly Christian. The purpose of religious liberty, according to the 1776 Virginia Declaration of Rights, is not to free men from the shackles of religious concern so that they can go out and turn to materialistic concerns like moneymaking with a free conscience. It is for the sake of "religion, or the duty which we owe to our Creator." It is certainly not for "freedom *from* religion," as our current textbooks on civil liberties sometimes suggest. Locke's argument for toleration was similar to Virginia's: "For obedience is owed first to God, then to the laws." Precisely because the care of the soul and obedience to God are the most important things, Locke argues, we should never entrust them to the arbitrary will of another: "no one can so far abandon the care of his own eternal salvation as to embrace under necessity a worship or faith that someone else prescribes."[2]

The founding was so far from being based on a break with Christianity that it was supported by the Catholic and Protestant clergy in all thirteen colonies. It is true that the founding principles were taught by Enlightenment writers like Locke. But it is also true, although it is often forgotten, that Locke was a major theologian whose interpretation of Christianity was tremendously influential in Britain and America. Consequently, Christian theology, as it was understood at the time of the founding, fully supported the idea of the equal natural rights of all men and women. One can only be godly when one respects the God-given rights of others, including the right of the ungodly to religious toleration.

Moreover, even apart from specifically Christian doctrine, the founding was based on a theological teaching, as the Declaration of Independence indicates: the laws of nature are also the laws of "nature's God"; men are "endowed by their Creator" with inalienable rights; America has "a firm reliance on the protection of divine providence"; and Americans appeal "to the Supreme Judge of the world for the rectitude of our intentions." The language of the Declaration of Independence alone, to say nothing of many other official documents of the founding, proves that the traditionalists are right to say that the founding was religious, in the sense that it was based on a distinct understanding of God, his laws, his providence, and his judgment in the affairs of men.

But it is also wrong to say that the principles of the founding are *exclusively* Christian. For the idea of *self-evident* truth, and of the laws of *nature's* God, implies that any reasonable human being, whether Christian or not, can discover the principles of moral and political truth. The founding was not intended, as were the Puritan settlements of the early 1600s, "to advance the kingdom of our Lord Jesus Christ" (quoted from the New England Confederation of 1643).[3] It was intended to secure the inalienable rights of all mankind.

Theological Transformation, Not Secularization

There is a widespread tendency, shared by many scholars, to see eighteenth-century New England as undergoing a secularization, a turn away from God and religion to merely worldly concerns. Perry Miller's influential books on the New England mind hammer this point home. Alan Heimert sees the mid to late eighteenth century as an ongoing battle between "rationalist" liberals and faith-based Calvinists. Zuckert's account, which rightly emphasizes that American Protestants strongly supported the principles of the American Revolution, is a helpful corrective to the "secularization" thesis. (A number of historians also oppose that thesis, for example Nathan Hatch in *The Sacred Cause of Liberty*.)[4] But Zuckert wavers on the crucial question: Was the change a secularization, or was it a different understanding of what God expects of man? When Samuel Langdon, Puritan preacher and president of Harvard, spoke to the assembled political leaders of Massachusetts in his 1774 sermon on the occasion of their election, he used the natural rights language of Locke and the Declaration of Independence. Zuckert comments: "This is no longer political theology." But then he backtracks: "or if it is, it is political theology of the sort that Locke himself in his *Second Treatise* and Jefferson in his various writings patronized—natural political theology." But natural theology, as is well known, is unable to establish by reason the existence of God as judge or particular divine providence—two of the divine attributes mentioned in the Declaration of Independence. My question is: why does Zuckert assume, or tend to assume, that the political theology of the Declaration of Independence "is no longer political theology"?

Zuckert's wavering is an expression of a deeper problem with his analysis. He does not tell the whole story of the transformation of Puritanism. First, he does not bring out the important changes that Puritan theology had already undergone long before the Puritan encounter with Locke and European social compact theory after 1700. Second, he does not show the logic of these and later changes as they were understood from within the Puritan experience itself. The Puritans did not think of themselves as turning away from Christian political theology, but as approaching more closely the truth of that theology, as they continually wrestled with its meaning in light of the political and philosophical challenges of a century and a half. Third, Zuckert does not acknowledge sufficiently that supposedly secular Enlightenment writers like Locke, many of whose views certainly were adopted by Puritan divines, were also theological writers in their own right. Locke's political theology was not merely natural but also Christian. In other words, no Zuckertian "convergence between Locke and Protestantism" was necessary, because Locke already was a Protestant theologian.

Puritan theology remained the dominant theology in New England from the time of the first settlement in 1620 to American independence in 1776 and beyond. But the moral and political content of that theology shifted dramatically during that time. This essay will tell the story of how this happened. The gist of it is this: There was an initial faith in the possibility of a perfect community of Puritan saints, animated by Christ's grace and communal love. The trust in the transforming power of divine grace led, logically and inevitably, to Anne Hutchinson's fanatical attack on the Puritan leaders in the name of her own personal experience of God and Christ. Likewise, the trust in a community bound together by no other limits than brotherly affection led to lawless government. Hutchinson was exiled, limits were set on government, and a definite legal code was instituted. The early Puritan hope for a community of love gradually gave way to an awareness that selfish human nature was still alive in New England, no less than in old Europe.

Besides suffering these internal stresses, the Puritans were also squeezed from the outside. The pressure came first from the Indians, who devastated New England in the 1670s. The Puritans had to ask themselves whether a political theology could be true if it focused on prayer and outward acts of piety at the expense of guns and military skill. The manly virtues therefore came to be celebrated as equal to such pietistic virtues as humility, prayer, churchgoing, repentance, and self-denial.

But this Indian attack was followed by another, ultimately more dangerous, attack from Europe. New England had enjoyed de facto autonomy since 1620. During most of this early period England was either distracted by civil wars and other domestic turmoils or actively approved of the Puritans. The Americans were therefore mostly left free to govern themselves as independent political communities. But after the monarchy was restored in 1660, England tightened the screws. In the 1680s, representative government was abolished, a royal governor was appointed, and private property was threatened and sometimes seized. Exasperated, Massachusetts rebelled in 1689, jailed the governor, and restored democracy. This revolution was partially rolled back by the new British king. All this led to a rethinking of the proper relationship between man and God.

Into this ferment, books containing the new European social compact theory arrived on the scene, apparently about 1715. Over the next fifty years, this theory was gradually adopted by preachers and by educated Americans in general, not just in New England but throughout the thirteen colonies.

These changes in the Puritans' self-understanding, which began almost at the moment of their arrival in America, developed with a stringent theological-political logic that culminated in the Lockean political theology of mid-eighteenth-century Congregationalism—a theology that most American Christians believed in, more or less, during the struggle with Britain that culminated in independence and the founding.

The Puritan Spirit of Independence

However old-fashioned the Puritans were in their deep Christian devotion, they were radicals in their hostility to all traditional forms of authority, religious and political. They asserted in the Mayflower Compact: "we all came into these parts of America with one and the same end and aim, namely, to advance the kingdom of our Lord Jesus Christ and to enjoy the liberties of the Gospel in purity with peace." Far from being "extraordinarily deferential" to unelected rulers, as Thomas Pangle has claimed, the Puritans strived to look beyond human authority, directly to God and his revealed word. The only human rulers to whom they were deferential were those freely elected by the people.[5]

The Puritans' refusal to rely on anyone but God—their denial of any human authority not approved by themselves—habituated them to an orderly self-reliance and self-assertiveness. Their conviction that most men are sinners, and that God is relentless in his punishment of sin, made them tough-minded within themselves and equally tough-minded as they confronted the outside world. The novelist Harriet Beecher Stowe observed that the Puritans' God had something in common with the physical terrain of New England:

> Working on a hard soil, battling with a harsh, ungenial climate, everywhere being treated by Nature with the most rigorous severity, they asked no indulgence, they got none, and they gave none. They shut out from their religious worship every poetic feature, every physical accessory which they feared would interfere with the abstract contemplation of hard, naked truth. . . . Their investigations were made with the courage of the man who hopes little, but determines to know the worst of his affairs. They wanted no smoke of incense to blind them, and no soft opiates of pictures and music to lull them; for what they were after was *truth*, and not happiness, and they valued *duty* far higher than *enjoyment*.[6]

Thus the Puritans turned their backs on what they regarded as the softer traditions and illusions of traditional Christianity. The Catholic and Anglican churches provided beautiful images of heaven to enchant the soul, as well as comforting priestly hierarchies that seemed to guarantee salvation if followed faithfully. The Puritans' single-minded longing for God without such trappings made them individually tenacious in their pursuits, whether moral, theological, political, or commercial. Their sense of infinite responsibility in fulfilling the duties that God demanded of them developed strong, independent characters. These qualities eventually contributed mightily toward the success of democracy in America.

The Puritans of the eighteenth century, such as Rev. Thomas Prince, still spoke of these Puritan practices and convictions with pride:

> Purity in churches is opposed to human mixtures, and the freer they are from these, the purer they are; which is the great and professed design of ours who in religious matters make the revelations of God their only rule and admit of nothing but what they apprehend these revelations require, both in discipline and worship as well as doctrines and manners. And freedom in churches is a liberty to judge of the meaning of these revelations, and of professing and acting according to our judgment of the meaning of them; and in particular the free choice of our own pastors and ways of discipline and worship, and our consciences in these things not subjected to any power on earth.[7]

Winthrop's Vision of a Community of Love

To understand better the Puritan point of departure, let us consider the extravagant teaching of John Winthrop's *A Modell of Christian Charity* (1630). Winthrop, more than anyone else, deserves the title of Founder of Massachusetts Bay, the most important of the early Puritan colonies.

Their aim, Winthrop wrote, was nothing less than the building of a perfect community, bound together neither by fear, by law, by interest, or by opinion, but pure love. Winthrop believed that this was the deepest promise of the Reformation turn to purity of faith and the rejection of all artificial human authority:

> [I]n this duty of love we must love brotherly without dissimulation, we must love one another with a pure heart fervently, we must bear one another's burdens, we must not look only on our own things, but also

on the things of our brethren. . . . [F]or this end, we must be knit together in this work as one man. . . .[8]

Their lofty goal, if it succeeded, would make New England a model for all
Christendom: "[M]en shall say of succeeding plantations: the Lord make it
like that of New England: for we must consider that we shall be as a city upon
a hill, the eyes of all people are upon us."[9]

Winthrop called his account *A Modell of Christian Charity* because the religious community they were about to found was to be a model or form for the
world to admire and imitate, and its principle was to be *Christian charity*. This
charity is the love of God and of man that arises when Christ comes into
the soul, causes a "new birth," and transforms a man into a "new creature."
"[E]very man is born with this principle in him, to love and seek himself only;
and thus a man continueth till Christ comes and takes possession of the soul,
and infuseth another principle, love to God and our brother."[10] The first
American Puritans were a band of men and women convinced that they had
been reborn and re-created through the power of divine grace.

For Winthrop, the "community of pleasure and pain" is thought to be
fully attainable. Through Christ, the body of his true church can be made as
much one as the body of each individual is one by nature: "First, all true
Christians are of one body in Christ. . . . [T]hey must needs partake of each
others' strength and infirmity, joy and sorrow, weal and woe, 1 Cor. 12:26. If
one member suffers all suffer with it, if one be in honor, all rejoice with it."[11]

The religious community described here was to be governed by laymen,
not ministers. The Puritans regarded politics as something lower than the
church. Winthrop called it "mere civil polity."[12] A polity should support the
church, but it should be governed by men who understand worldly affairs,
not by ministers of God's word. So it is not right to call the Puritan government a theocracy, as is often done. Churches were supported by the government, but churches were forbidden from controlling government. A 1648
Massachusetts law said: "Nor shall any church censure, degrade, or depose
any man from any civil dignity, office, or authority he shall have in the commonwealth."[13] In the end, a civil polity is not the same as a religious community because of the limits of political rule: it cannot touch the soul and
salvation, for it can only regulate external conduct. Still, the political community was emphatically a religious community, for only members of Puritan
churches were admitted as citizens.

In Winthrop's original plan, there was no religious liberty and, at the beginning, not even the rule of law. Regulation of public morals was so intrusive

that, as Tocqueville remarks, it became "bizarre or tyrannical."[14] Nathaniel Hawthorne's novel *The Scarlet Letter* made famous the "A" which adulteresses were required to wear. (This public shaming of adulterous women continued as late as 1788, when the wearing of the "A" was required under the laws of the state of Vermont.)[15] Besides obvious physical injuries like rape, theft, and murder, punishable offenses included fornication, lying, smoking, long hair, blasphemy, sorcery, and witchcraft.

Because of the equality among those who were truly born again in Christ's law of grace, the Puritans held that government could justly arise only from the consent of the governed. This consent was expressed in the famous Mayflower Compact (1620) made by the Plymouth Puritans, in the Fundamental Orders of Connecticut of 1638, and in the democratic procedures adopted in Massachusetts.[16]

Governor Winthrop affirmed the consent principle in his "Defense of an Order of Court": "no man hath lawful power over another, but by birth [referring to parental rule of children] or consent. . . . No commonweal can be founded but by free consent."[17] Winthrop was no egalitarian. He held that "in all times some must be rich, some poor; some high and eminent in power and dignity, others mean and in subjection."[18] But the Puritans did not believe political authority should be hereditary as in England, where the king and aristocracy ruled by right of inheritance. Public election of government officials elevates those who deserve to rule and rightly excludes those who do not. Those whom Jefferson called the "natural aristoi," those naturally best, would be chosen:

> Where God blesseth any branch of any noble or generous family, with a spirit and gifts for government, it would be . . . a sin against the honor of magistracy to neglect such in our public elections. But if God should not delight to furnish some of their posterity with gifts fit for magistracy, we should expose them rather to reproach and prejudice, and the commonwealth with them, than exalt them to honor, if we should call them forth, when God does not, to public authority.[19]

As in the Declaration of Independence, consent was required not only in the founding but also in the operation of government. Connecticut's Fundamental Orders required elections of representatives twice annually in every town; these in turn elected the governor and other officials once a year. Massachusetts had annual elections. Every freeman (church member) was eligible to vote.

A remarkable 1637 document of the Massachusetts town of Newtown shows how democratic the freemen's conception of government was from the start. First comes a definition of the people's liberty: "That the people may not be subjected to any law or power among themselves without their consent." This "power of a popular state" is "unlimited in its own nature," being "bounded in order only, not in power." This means that no external human authority can put limits on popular government. Further, such government must operate by majority rule: "there is an inseparable incident to all bodies politic, which are composed of voluntary members, that every one (in his admission) gives an implicit consent to whatever the major part shall establish, not being against religion or the weal public."[20]

These instances show that in Puritan New England—for the first time in the modern Western world—democratic principles were being officially advanced and adopted by the governing bodies of actual political societies.

The First Crisis of Puritanism: Anne Hutchinson and the Return to Reason

In theology, early American Puritans emphasized the immediate experience of divine grace as the best access of men to the interpretation of God's word. The "law of nature," or the "moral law," exists. It is discovered by reason. But among true Christians, writes Winthrop, it is replaced by "the law of grace," or "the law of the gospel."[21] The consequence of this view was an early tendency, which we have already remarked, to disparage reason and learning and to elevate the dangerous passions connected with fanaticism and persecution.

This rejection of learning did not outlast the remarkable Anne Hutchinson, whose passionate eloquence nearly overturned the infant Puritan commonwealth. (Nathaniel Hawthorne wrote a sensible short story on this crisis.)[22] Hutchinson appealed over the heads of dignitaries like Winthrop to God himself, claiming that they were not fit men to lead the Puritan exodus. She herself claimed to be the privileged recipient of the divine presence. She had the experience and feeling of grace in herself. Was that not the main Puritan criterion of salvation? She claimed that the male leaders were distorting the pure Reformation doctrine by their teaching that one must perform correct works. She took the *sola fidei* slogan literally, and therefore disparaged the authority of the respectable men of learning. She even attracted John Cotton, perhaps the leading minister of the village of Boston, to her teaching sessions. Historian Perry Miller explains what happened: "Cotton, to whom Mrs. Hutchinson had first looked as the sole spokesman of the spiritual interpretation, seeing at last the terrible consequences for social morality of her theories, and incidentally the possible loss of his social position in Massachusetts Bay, turned upon her with the rest." She was exiled to Rhode Island in 1637.[23]

The Hutchinson episode compelled the Puritans to back away from the embrace of irrational spirituality, as their "by faith alone" principle initially led them to do. From now on, Puritan theology was always respectful toward outward signs of Christian righteousness. Not only or primarily one's internal feeling, but external standards of conduct, would be the measure.

Connected with this change was a gradual Puritan readmission of the fruits of human reason to the education of scholars and ministers. Throughout the 1600s, Harvard used products of the philosophical tradition, including the pagan authors, in its curriculum. Aristotle's *Ethics* was particularly admired, usually in the form of later paraphrases. In addition to scripture and grace, the Puritans respected reason as a legitimate path to God's order and law.

In this respect Puritanism returned to the moderate Protestantism that had prevailed in England after the Reformation. Perhaps surprisingly, Puritans also returned to the Catholic tradition of respect for philosophy and science. This led to the paradox, described by historian Norman Fiering, that "In the area of moral philosophy, at least, there is almost no better reference work to which one can turn for enlightenment on seventeenth-century Puritan thinking than the *Summa Theologica* of [Catholic Scholastic] Thomas Aquinas." Fiering reports that many of the standard Catholic commentaries are mentioned and discussed in student notebooks of the period. Thomas Shepard, a first-generation Puritan theologian, quoted Aquinas with approval in his discussion of the moral and natural law. Shepard also made use of Aquinas's division of the law of the Old Testament into moral, ceremonial, and judicial precepts.[24]

This Puritan return to reason was the first important change in their theology. At first it opened their learning to the tradition of classical moral philosophy. In the eighteenth century, it led to openness to modern authors like Pufendorf and Locke.

The Second Crisis of Puritanism: Limits on Government

At the beginning, the Puritan government in Massachusetts was elected by the body of the church members, called freemen. Once the officials were elected, they expected to be left alone to rule as they saw fit until the next election a year later. They ruled without standing laws. They thought the prudential judgment of government officials was superior to fixed laws that treat everyone the same regardless of circumstances. Here was the classic argument against the rule of law.[25] Winthrop deplored the notion that everyone, ordinary and extraordinary, should have to be judged by the same inflexible rule. He and the other officials were confident that they, as regenerate Christians living under the law of grace, could be trusted to judge each case in accordance with true standards of righteousness. They maintained that a sensible man's prudence on the spot is better than inflexible rules, as long as magistrates are trustworthy, which they would be in a community of believers whose fallen nature had been transformed by grace.

But if love is tainted by private passions and interests, and ordinary human error, then men acting in accord with their private judgment may become arbitrary. That is just what the freemen said of Winthrop and his colleagues. Checks on government were needed. Winthrop and other elected officials dragged their feet, but the freemen demanded and eventually got a written legal code.[26] The code of 1641 was called the "body of liberties," and the right of the people to send their representatives to participate in the government was called their "liberty."[27] While Winthrop spoke of love, trust in the rulers' wisdom, and Christian charity, the people spoke of liberty and law.

Winthrop said he "could not help but bewail the great differences and jarrings" that divided early Massachusetts. But he had to admit that the people thought themselves "very unsafe, while so much power rested in the discretion of magistrates." That is, Winthrop had to admit what was after all an item of faith with the Puritans: that most of human nature was corrupt. He was reluctant to admit that selfishness was present in his own "city on a hill," which he had hoped would be a perfect community of love. But the incessant quarrels proved that even New England was flawed. "So hard a matter it is, to draw men (even wise and godly) from the love of the first fruit of their own inventions."[28]

Plymouth, the earliest Puritan colony, actually began as a communist community, under their original charter; all property was owned by the people in common. William Bradford, governor of Plymouth almost from the beginning, described what happened. With no one in particular responsible for producing the needed goods and services, colonists evaded work in the fields whenever they could. Famine resulted. Men stole from each other "by night and day." Over half of the original settlers had died of starvation and disease when in desperation they "assigned to every family a parcel of land." Bradford wrote of this reform:

> This had very good success, for it made all hands very industrious. . . . The women now went willingly into the field, and took their little ones with them to plant corn, which before would allege weakness and inability. . . .

The experience that was had in this common course and condition, tried sundry years, and that amongst godly and sober men, may well evince the vanity of that conceit of Plato's and other ancients, applauded by some of later times: that the taking away of property, and bringing in community into a commonwealth, would make them happy and flourishing; as if they were wiser than God. For this community (so far as it was) was found to breed much confusion and discontent and retard much employment that would have been to their benefit and comfort. . . .

Let none object this is men's corruption, and nothing to the course itself. I answer, seeing all men have this corruption in them, God in his wisdom saw another course fitter for them.[29]

In this light, the Plymouth men's turn to private property, and the Massachusetts freemen's demand for liberty, are nothing more than an acknowledgment that the demands and pretensions of perfect love are inappropriate for imperfect, selfish human nature. Winthrop and the other early Puritan leaders believed that "a family is a little commonwealth, and a commonwealth is a great family." But they soon came to agree with Aristotle: a political community cannot be a large family because the family is the natural limit of a community based on love.[30]

In this way the logic of Puritan experience led the Puritans to this second change in their political theology. No longer expecting the imperfections of this world to be cleansed by divine grace, they adopted governments limited in their powers by the rule of law, thereby anticipating some of the main features of post-1776 governments in America.

PURITAN THEOLOGY ENDORSES MARTIAL VIRTUE

The Third Crisis of Puritanism: King Philip's War and the Puritan Embrace of Self-Defense

Early New England Puritanism stressed the virtues of humility, prayer, orthodoxy in belief, correct modes of worship, fasting, and self-denial. As we have seen, the Puritans came to respect the discoveries of human reason, for they regarded reason as a gift of God. But they had not fully thought through what this meant.

In 1675 a great war began in New England, known as King Philip's War after the chief who led it. The Indians, seeing the wilderness relentlessly taken by English settlers, decided to drive them away once and for all. They staged a massive attack in which families were slaughtered and towns destroyed. In casualties per capita, it was the most destructive war in American history.[31] This terrible war caused a crisis in Puritan theology. Two rival interpretations of the war agreed New Englanders had sinned and that the war was a divine punishment. But what was the sin?

Increase Mather, speaking for the Puritan traditionalists, argued that their sins were "great unthankfulness for, and manifold abuses of, our wonderful peace . . . ; ill entertainment of the ministry . . . ; the apostasy of many from the truth unto heresies and pernicious errors; inordinate affection and sinful conformity to this present evil vain world." His remedy was for the government to "appoint . . . a day of public humiliation, with fasting and prayer, throughout this whole colony; that we may set ourselves sincerely to seek the Lord, rending our hearts, . . . and pursue the same with a thorough reformation."

The government accordingly undertook measures for "suppression of those proud excesses in apparel, hair, etc. . . . ; against such as are false worshippers, especially idolatrous Quakers." Laws were passed to imprison Quakers ("and there to have the discipline of the house applied to them"), to punish long hair and luxurious clothing, excessive drinking, swearing, abuse of the Sabbath, disrespect for parents, and more.[32]

Samuel Nowell presented the alternative view to this conventional Puritanism in his sermon *Abraham in Arms*. Nowell says little about the virtues of contrition, humility, and self-denial praised by Mather. Nor does he complain about the decline in orthodoxy or the rise of idolatry. Instead, he speaks of the need to cultivate the art of war. Nowell builds his argument on a story from the book of Genesis. A group of armed men had kidnapped Abraham's nephew Lot. Abraham organized and trained an informal militia, a sort of rival gang, to rescue Lot and defeat his enemies. For this exploit, Nowell notes, Abraham received a blessing from Melchizedech, a priest of God, a priest who was "eminently a type of Jesus Christ." Nowell concludes, "Frequent trainings for the instructing of men in military discipline that they may be ready and expert for war, is a commendable practice, yea a duty which God expecteth of all God's Abrahams in their respective places."[33]

Nowell supports his argument with both scripture and reason. He mentions the law of nature, "which teacheth man self-preservation," and among other passages he quotes Luke 22:36, where Jesus says, "he that hath not a sword, let him sell his garment and buy one." For Nowell, "God helps those who help themselves." As Nowell matter-of-factly remarked, "God can work miracles, but when ordinary means may be had, he will not work miracles."[34]

Nowell's sermon is full of the "don't tread on me" prickliness that characterized the American Revolution. Let us "learn to defend ourselves, or resolve to be vassals," he writes. He expresses contempt for the biblical Issachar, who prefers base slavery to hard-fought freedom: "It is a base spirit that of Issachar, a strong ass between two burdens, he saw that rest was good, and the land was pleasant, and bowed his shoulders to bear, and became a servant to tribute. . . . Low spirited men, let them have Issachar's lot, that make his choice."[35] Issachar as an image of slavish submission to unjust authority was used on more than one occasion in the sermons of the eighteenth century leading up to the American Revolution.[36]

Nowell also hinted at another, more controversial, use of military skill:

> There are our rights, both as men, and as Christians, our civil rights and liberties as men and our religious liberties and rights as Christians; both which we are to defend with the sword, as far as we are able, or to commit ourselves to God in the way of duty in doing of it. There is such a thing as liberty and property given to us, both by the laws of God and men; when they are invaded, we may defend ourselves. God hath not given great ones in the world that absolute power over men, to devour them at pleasure, as great fishes do the little ones; he hath set rulers their bounds. . . . He that rules over men must be just, that is, should be so, ruling in the fear of God: therefore kings are commanded to read the book of the law, because it is a boundary of their authority, as well as of the people's liberty.[37]

Nowell is carefully but firmly indicating the possible need to rise up and oppose the encroachments of England on the liberties and properties of New Englanders. That is, he is speaking of the right of revolution. He does so in the name of "our rights both as men and as Christians." Here, for the first time that I know of, we see in a Puritan sermon an appeal to the rights of men, that is, natural or human rights. We see here, stated with manly clarity, the link between the natural and divine right to liberty and property, and the right to revolution, that became the faith of most Americans by 1776. I do not know whether Nowell had read any of the European authors who had written on the subject. He may have picked up this language from the many Whig pamphlets that were published in England in these years, some of which must have circulated in America.[38] In Nowell's sermon, it seems, we hear the opening salvo of the century-long struggle between England and America over who should rule.

The theological difference between Mather and Nowell had its counterpart in the practical reaction of two exemplary New Englanders. Mary Rowlandson, captured by the Indians in King Philip's War, later published a widely read narrative of her sufferings. She sees in her trials divine punishment for her sins, such as being careless of the Sabbath. She prays for relief, which eventually comes. She is passive, humble, remorseful, repentant.[39]

Her contrast with Benjamin Church could not be more striking. Captain Church had hunted down and killed King Philip, the leader of the Indian forces. Church's son published an account of his father's exploits some years later. Unlike Mary Rowlandson, Church was not a man of passive piety trusting in God to save him, but rather "a person of uncommon activity and industry," an enterprising, courageous, wily, and tough Indian fighter. He was the embodied spirit of Nowell's *Abraham in Arms*. Church studied Indian methods of fighting and used them effectively against the enemy.[40] Benjamin Church was a Christian, but he did not rely on prayer or divine intervention to get things done. He said that "calling to mind that God is strong, I endeavored to put all my confidence in him." What that meant in practice was that he made good use of his God-given talents to defeat the enemy and put a stop to the wanton murder of the colonists.[41]

It was Nowell's view, not Mather's, that won out among New England Puritans in the succeeding years. It was not Mary Rowlandson but Benjamin Church who became the model American Christian in wartime. Because Nowell, Church, and their fellow Puritans trusted in reason and experience, and in a God who wanted men to make full use of reason and experience, they were able to learn the lesson of King Philip's War. From then on, Protestant Christian piety was no longer a merely private relation between the individual and God. It became inseparable from patriotism and military valor.

One historian of New England sermons writes that Nowell's sermon "would lay down the main lines of martial preaching in time of war for the century to follow."[42] Nowell taught that God requires men to train and to kill in defense of their lives and liberties. His was a fighting Christianity that was quick to repel evil and stood firm in defense of civil liberty. [43]

The Fourth Crisis of Puritanism: Despotism, Rebellion, and the End of the Puritan Commonwealth

Meanwhile, a threat to American liberties was brewing in England more dangerous than the Indians. King Charles II and his successor, James II, attempted to convert England into a monarchy on the model of Louis XIV's

France. Parliament, which had given the monarchy such trouble, would be dispensed with.[44] The colonial side of this policy was unveiled with full explicitness in the 1680s. After many lesser encroachments after the restoration of the monarchy in 1660, Britain finally abolished the New England democracies outright and appointed a royal governor, Sir Edmund Andros. He ruled the newly formed "Dominion of New England" without the consent of the governed. This hated government proved to be short lived. Historian Jack Greene writes:

> Embittered over the loss of their charter, alarmed at the loss of representative government, and resentful of the efforts of Andros to levy taxes without the consent of a legislature, to alter the system of land tenure so that property titles would be held by a grant from the Crown, to encourage the growth of Anglicanism in the colony, and to enforce the Navigation Acts strictly, the Puritans were ripe for revolt.[45]

The Glorious Revolution in England overthrew James II in 1688. In 1689, the Bostonians, encouraged by this news, overthrew and imprisoned Governor Andros in a rehearsal for the American Revolution eighty-five years later. This first American revolution produced justificatory tracts as in the 1770s, but there was as yet no talk of the equal rights of mankind. The natural rights argument was beginning to be widely known in Britain at this time—Locke's *Two Treatises of Government* was published in 1690—but, other than Nowell's brief mention, it had not yet penetrated into America. As in the 1770s, the cry was, "no taxes shall be levied on the subjects without consent of an assembly chosen by the freeholders for assessing the same."[46] But the Puritan writers generally did not go beyond an appeal to the rights of Englishmen in defense of their cause. The two pamphlets justifying the overthrow of Andros were *The Revolution in New England Justified* and *The Humble Address of the Publicans*.[47]

By 1700 the Puritan commonwealth had lost much of its sectarian religious character, for Britain required citizenship and toleration to be extended to most residents. The democratic and religious spirit remained strong in Massachusetts, but the political community gained an identity of its own apart from the Puritan convictions that continued to pervade, if less intensely than before, the lives of the people.[48] A new vocabulary of liberty had begun to be heard, as we already saw in Nowell. Earlier, Robert Child, a non-Puritan, had petitioned the government to secure for all colonists—whether church members or not—"civil liberty and freedom."[49] Could this growing concern for liberty and property rights be consistent with or intended by God's will?

The Puritan commonwealth had failed. Winthrop's original vision of a brotherhood of loving fellow Puritans had faded away long ago. But the appeal to the rights of Englishmen had done New Englanders little good. Locked in Britain's embrace they had neither communal piety or political liberty. What was God's will for New England under these new conditions?

Some Puritan preachers bewailed the increasing turn to liberty understood as rights against government rather than as the freedom gained through faith in Christ. In 1673 Uriah Oakes affirmed that a religious people are likely to be as stout asserters of their liberties as any. Nevertheless,

> I would dissuade from an extreme and undue affection of liberty. Here is a great cry in the country at this day about civil liberties: these and those (in the frightful imaginations of some men) are about to rob us of our liberties. . . .
>
> Again, the loud outcry of some is for liberty of conscience: that they may hold and think and practice what they will in religion. This is the Diana of some men, and great is the Diana of the libertines of this age.[50]

But Oakes was wrong. The "frightful imaginations of some men" correctly anticipated the British attack on New England liberties. And "liberty of conscience," the right to free exercise of religion (at least for Protestants), was required by British law.

In 1700, Samuel Sewall of Boston published a condemnation of the enslavement of blacks. He wrote, "It is most certain that all men, as they are the sons of Adam, and coheirs; and have equal right unto liberty, and all other outward comforts of life. . . . So that originally, and naturally, there is no such thing as slavery." Sewall used the word *naturally,* but his argument was based on scripture: God "hath made of one blood, all nations of men, for to dwell upon the face of the earth" (Acts 17:26).[51] Sewall was speaking of the natural right to liberty, but he did not yet have a full understanding of that notion.

A new spirit was alive in Protestant Christendom, in Europe as well as America. That spirit was not yet modern in the sense of the political philosophy of Locke and the Enlightenment, of which little was heard in New England's first century. But New England was resolutely democratic and promoted individual self-reliance to a higher degree than Christendom had yet seen. Massachusetts and Connecticut were unable to be Puritan commonwealths. Nor did they wish to be. They were ripe for a theology that could make sense of the confusing new situation, in which Britain ruled America partly without its consent. That theology was provided by John Locke and other European writers who taught the doctrine of the social compact. Its ultimate implication was the necessity for independence of Britain.

THE EIGHTEENTH-CENTURY PURITAN DISCOVERY
OF NATURAL RIGHTS

The "New Learning" Comes to America

At some point around 1715, Puritans began to discover what some called the "new learning." It seems that the leading seventeenth-century European writings penetrated Connecticut earlier than Massachusetts. This may be due to Jeremiah Dummer, Connecticut's agent in England. In 1714, Dummer sent Yale a gift of a collection of modern books. Prior to that time, according to Samuel Johnson, the students had heard "of a new philosophy that of late was all the vogue, and of such names as Descartes, Boyle, Locke, and Newton, but they were warned against thinking anything of them, because the new philosophy, it was said, would soon bring in a new divinity and corrupt the pure religion of the country."

But after Dummer's gift, Johnson said, he "had all at once the vast pleasure of reading the works of our best English poets, philosophers, and divines, Shakespeare and Milton, etc., Locke and Norris, etc., Boyle and Newton, etc. . . . All this was like a flood of day to his low state of mind. . . . And by the next Thanksgiving, 1715, I was wholly changed to the New Learning."[52] Locke and Newton began to be taught at Yale (by Johnson and a fellow tutor) the following year.

One of the first sermons, perhaps the earliest, to mention a "new learning" philosopher as an authority was John Bulkley's *The Necessity of Religion in Societies* (1713). Bulkley too was from Connecticut. This sermon defends the Christian religion as both true and useful. It contains such traditional Puritan themes as the "depraved . . . nature of man in his fallen state" and the need for government to fund "an establishment for the support of the gospel."[53] But we are surprised to find Machiavelli called a "great politician." He is quoted with approval three times, as someone who supports religion as "tending to the prosperity and welfare of civil societies."

John Wise was the first American to publish a full account of the social compact theory that would eventually become the theory of the American founding. He did so in his 1717 book, *A Vindication of the Government of New-England Churches*. This book is one of the most remarkable published in America in the entire eighteenth century. Other than Nowell, hardly any other

Puritan had spoken of our individual rights "as men." No one had discussed in print the equality and liberty of human beings in a state of nature, or had argued that the purpose of government should be limited to protecting people against injury. Suddenly, in Wise's book, the social compact theory of the founding appears entire.

In *The Necessity of Religion in Societies* (1713), quoted above, the Connecticut minister John Bulkley asserted that

> Rulers are designed by God to be a shield and defense to those under them in their just rights and liberties; such as by the laws of GOD and their own (consonant thereto) are settled upon them. . . . As for men's civil rights, as life, liberty, estate, etc., God has not subjected them to the will and pleasure of rulers; nor may they . . . invade or disturb their free enjoyment of them. . . . [T]he divine law (natural or positive) . . . [determines] that the enjoyment of them be free and undisturbed.[54]

No philosopher is cited in support of this claim. We do not know whether Bulkley had read Locke yet. At any rate, twelve years later, in 1725, Bulkley published an account of Locke's basic doctrine in an article defending the colonists' right to occupy the territory of America in spite of the Indians' being there first. As far as I have been able to tell, this article, Bulkley's preface to *Poetical Meditations*, is the first American publication that explains Locke's argument. It may be the first to mention his name. (Perhaps the first mention of Locke by an American governmental body was Daniel Dulaney's 1728 *Right of the Inhabitants of Maryland to the Benefit of English Laws,*[55] published at the request of the Maryland House of Representatives.)

The Adoption of the New Political Theology

Wise's was the only New England publication that discussed the social compact theory of the founding before 1720. After that date, several writers besides Bulkley picked up the typical lines of argument. Outside of clerical circles, James Franklin, Benjamin's older brother, began publishing excerpts of *Cato's Letters* in his newspaper. ("Cato" was John Trenchard and Thomas Gordon, English writers who popularized the social compact theory of Locke, Algernon Sidney, and others in a series of essays that were widely reprinted in America.) The following year, Benjamin Franklin printed passages from *Cato's Letters,* number 15 and 31, in his Silence Dogood papers in Boston.[56] In 1722, John Mather published a defense of the English colonists' right to acquire land in America without the permission of the Indians. His argument was like Bulkley's already mentioned, but without reference to Locke and without as clear an understanding of the argument as Bulkley.[57] These, along with Wise's book, were the earliest appearance in New England of what became the theory of the American Revolution.

By the 1730s and 1740s, a few other preachers began to pick up these Lockean themes. Jared Eliot of Connecticut cites Locke on government in a 1738 sermon:

> We are in the first place to consider man as in a state of nature. Some have thought that none of mankind were ever in that state, because history furnisheth us with no instances. But as a great writer well observes, that affords no argument; because government is before history and records.[58]

Elisha Williams gave the first extended presentation of John Locke's argument for religious toleration in an eloquent 1744 piece. Williams's four-page summary of Locke's account of the origin and purpose of government is one of the clearest and most complete given by any American in the eighteenth century. "[H]erein [I] have given a short sketch of what the celebrated Mr. Locke in his *Treatise of Government* has largely demonstrated; and in which it is justly to be presumed all are agreed who understand the natural rights of mankind." Williams goes through the arguments for equality, liberty, and consent (arbitrary government being "where the people don't make their own laws"). [59]

Williams's statement gives the first full-scale argument for the free exercise of religion, not only as a natural right discovered by reason, but also as a requirement of scripture. One of Williams's main arguments is this:

> That the sacred scriptures are the alone rule of faith and practice to a Christian, all Protestants are agreed in; and must therefore inviolably maintain, that every Christian has *a right of judging for himself* what he is to believe and practice in religion according to that rule: Which I think on a full examination you will find perfectly inconsistent with any power in the civil magistrate to make any penal laws in matters of religion.[60]

Zuckert sees in Williams's simultaneous appeal to both faith and reason a blending of Protestantism and Lockeanism. It is more accurate to say that Protestant theology had become more sensitive to those passages in Scripture, and those themes in the Christian theological tradition, that support the conclusions of reason. Christianity itself had come to be seen as reasonable, as a religion that teaches the law of nature discovered by reason.

The view of Christianity that many American ministers adopted had been presented in John Locke's *Letter on Toleration* (1689) and *Reasonableness of Christianity* (1695). Many political scientists today know Locke mainly through the *Two Treatises of Government*, which do not speak much about Christianity. But Locke was a major theologian, and he was respected as such throughout the eighteenth century. In the *Letter on Toleration*, Locke argued that the core of Christianity is its moral teaching: "he who wishes to be a soldier in Christ's church ought to declare war on his own pride and lust; otherwise, without holiness of life, purity of morals, kindness and mildness of mind, he vainly seeks for himself the name of Christian. . . . For in the Gospel, if the Apostles are to be believed, no one can be a Christian without charity, without faith that works through love, not force."[61] Locke gave a full exposition of the argument behind this conclusion in the *Reasonableness*. In that book, there are three main duties of every Christian. The first is faith that Jesus is the Christ, the savior, and the king whose laws must be obeyed. Second is repentance. "These two, faith and repentance, i.e. believing Jesus to be the Messiah, and a good life, are the indispensable conditions of the new covenant, to be performed by all those who would obtain eternal life" (para. 172). But third, genuine repentance requires obedience to the law of Christ (or at least a sincere effort), which is stated in the Sermon on the Mount, and includes the law of nature (181).

Locke's theological argument was based on the Protestant view, affirmed by Elisha Williams, that scripture alone is the authority for Christians. Locke also accepted the Luther-Calvin notion of the two kingdoms, of this world and the next. Far from denying the authority of Christianity, Locke insisted that man's duty to God is higher than to man: "For obedience is owed first to God, then to the laws" (*Toleration,* 127). The goal of a Christian is life eternal—a goal not attainable in this world.

The Great Awakening

Puritan theology had always insisted on the primacy of faith as the basis of true Christianity. However, we have seen that during the 1600s it became increasingly open to the insights of reason. By the third decade of the 1700s, however, Puritan "New Lights" like Jonathan Edwards, who emphasized faith and "the heart, rather than the head," had grown increasingly critical of theologians who seemed to rely so much on reason that they neglected faith. As Edwards said, "Some make philosophy, instead of the Holy Scriptures, their rule. . . ."[62] Edwards, George Whitefield, and other like-minded preachers began an influential movement called the Great Awakening, lasting from about 1739 to 1742.

Those "Old Lights" on the other side like Charles Chauncy, who emphasized the importance of reason in Christianity, accused their opponents of
"enthusiasm." Chauncy wrote, "While the passions are uppermost, and bear
the chief sway over a man, he is in an unsafe state."[63]

By the end of the Great Awakening, important differences remained, but
both sides came to see that their common ground was greater than the opinions that divided them. After all, few Old Light "rationalists" rejected the
authority of scripture and the primacy of faith. Few New Light "enthusiasts"
rejected the importance of reason.[64] Historian Harry Stout writes,

> Even as New Lights admitted that true religion required, in Tennent's
> words, a "right Reason" that governed "our own fickle and often partial
> and byass'd *Fancies* and *Humours,*" so Old Lights conceded that reason
> alone, "without Revelation, and the Assistances of God's Spirit" was "not
> sufficient" to transform the soul.[65]

For our purposes, however, what deserves to be noted is that the two sides
did not disagree in any important respects on the questions of political theology that we have discussed. By the mid-eighteenth century, the "Calvinists"
were no less devoted to the new understanding of politics than the "rationalists." "Calvinist" Levi Hart and "rationalist" Samuel West both spoke of the
social compact origin of civil society, the state of nature, the laws of nature,
and the need for government by elected representatives. Both found support
for their political theory in reason and philosophy as well as in Scripture.
(Hart cited the Lockean poet Alexander Pope, and West cited Locke himself.)[66]

The Consensus after 1760 on Reason

By around 1760, what had been a radical and unusual position when John
Wise proclaimed it in 1717 had become the consensus of New England preachers. They manfully rejected that effeminate Christianity which Machiavelli
denounced, according to which the splendor of eternity makes political life
unworthy of serious attention. Consider this ringing affirmation of liberty by
the Reverend Jonathan Mayhew in 1750, from what has been called "the most
famous sermon preached in pre-Revolutionary America":

> Tyranny brings ignorance and brutality along with it. It degrades men
> from their just rank into the class of brutes. It damps their spirits. It sup-
> presses arts. It extinguishes every spark of noble ardor and generosity in
> the breasts of those who are enslaved by it. It makes naturally strong and

great minds feeble and little, and triumphs over the ruins of virtue and humanity. This is true of tyranny in every shape. There can be nothing great or good where its influence reaches. For which reason it becomes every friend to truth and humankind, every lover of God and the Christian religion, to bear a part in opposing this hateful monster.[67]

Abraham Williams's 1762 Massachusetts election sermon rehearses the following arguments: the need to "surrender to the society the right they before had of judging in their own case, and of executing those righteous judgments," a right which one has in the state of nature; the limited purpose of civil society (namely, the regulation of "men's outward behavior," "that they may be secure in the enjoyment of all their rights and properties righteously acquired"); the difficulty of knowing the law of nature due to carelessness, prejudice, and vice; and the "rights of conscience." These are arguments stressed by Locke in his *Two Treatises* and *Letter on Toleration*.[68]

In a 1766 Thanksgiving sermon William Patten speaks of sentiments entertained by the great Mr. Locke, which he has very clearly expressed, in his essay on government. . . . After consulting the doctrine of passive obedience, he proceeds thus:

> "Here, 'tis like, the common question will be made, who shall be judge whether the prince or legislature act contrary to their trust? This, perhaps, ill-affected and factious men may spread among the people, when the prince only makes use of his just prerogative. To this I reply, the people shall be judge; [for] who shall be judge whether his trustee or deputy acts well, and according to the trust reposed in him, but he who deputes him, and must, by having deputed him, have still a power to discard him, when he fails in his trust? If this be reasonable in particular cases of private men, why should it be otherwise in that of the greatest moment, where the welfare of millions is concerned; and also, where the evil, if not prevented, is greater, and the redress very difficult, dear, and dangerous."[69]

Jason Haven touches the same theme in his election day sermon in 1769, which made its way into "the hands of so many people in this province."[70]

The doctrine of passive obedience and non-resistance, which had so many advocates in our nation a century ago, is at this day generally given up as indefensible, and voted unreasonable and absurd. The unreasonableness and absurdity of it, hath indeed been proved by some of the greatest reasoners of our age.

"Wheresoever law ends," says the great Mr. Locke, "tyranny begins, if the law be transgressed to another's harm. And whoever in authority exceeds the power given him by law, and makes use of the force he hath under his command, to compass that upon the subject which the law allows not, ceases in that to be a magistrate; and, acting without authority, may be opposed as any other man, who invades the right of another."— "Here, 'tis likely, (continues he) the common question will be made, who shall be judge, whether the prince or legislature act contrary to their trust? [The rest of section 240 of Locke's *Second Treatise* is transcribed here, as in the Patten sermon just quoted.][71]

Peter Whitney's Fast Day sermon quoted the same passage in 1774:

But when [rulers] . . . encroach on the natural and constitutional rights of the people; when they trample on those laws, which were made, at once to limit their power, and defend their subjects: in such cases the people are bound not to obey them, but resist them as public robbers and the destroyers of mankind and of human happiness. Says the great Mr. Locke in his treatise upon government: "Wheresoever law ends, tyranny begins . . . who invades the right of another." And in these cases the people must be judge of the good or ill conduct of their rulers; to the people they are accountable.[72]

John Lathrop reaches the same conclusion on the basis of a different Lockean passage in a 1774 sermon. He speaks of the right of self-defense against individuals or nations who would deprive a man of what he has a right to, citing Locke's *Second Treatise,* chapter 3 (on the state of war) in support.[73]

Simeon Howard, in his 1773 Artillery Sermon, cites Locke on the state of nature:

In a state of nature, or where men are under no civil government, God has given to everyone liberty to pursue his own happiness in whatever way, and by whatever means he pleases, without asking the consent or consulting the inclination of any other man, provided he keeps within the bounds of the law of nature. Within these bounds, he may govern his actions, and dispose of his property and person, as he thinks proper. Nor has any man, or any number of men, a right to restrain him in the exercise of his liberty, or punish, or call him to account for using it. This however is not a state of licentiousness, for the law of nature which bounds this liberty, forbids all injustice and wickedness, allows no man to injure another in his person or property, or to destroy his own life.[74]

I have quoted Howard's entire paragraph in order to answer historian Bernard Bailyn, who is among the most influential of a group of scholars who deny Locke's primacy as an authority for the founders and for New England theology. Stephen Dworetz has provided the most comprehensive list to date of the many references to Locke in the New England sermons of this period.[75]

During the 1770s, Samuel West, Judah Champion, Nathaniel Whitaker, and Samuel Stillman—a Massachusetts Puritan, a Connecticut Puritan, a Presbyterian, and a Baptist—also cite Locke as their authority on the equal liberty of human beings in a state of nature. Champion paraphrases the *Second Treatise,* sections 77 (origins of society) and 123 (defects of the state of nature), and transcribes section 23 (no one can voluntarily enslave himself).[76]

John Tucker's 1771 Election Sermon gives an unusually full account of the origin of legitimate political power. He is attempting to prove that government and taxation without representation are slavery:

> All men are naturally in a state of freedom, and have an equal claim to liberty. No one, by nature, nor by any special grant from the great Lord of all, has any authority over another. All right therefore in any to rule over others, must originate from those they rule over and be granted by them. . . . To suppose otherwise, and that without a delegated power and constitutional right, rulers may make laws, and appoint officers for their execution, and force them to effect, i.e., according to their own arbitrary will and pleasure, is to defeat the great design of civil government, and utterly to abolish it. It is to make rulers absolutely despotic, and to subject the people to a state of *slavery.* . . .
>
> It is essential to a free state, for without this it cannot be free, that no man shall have his property taken from him, but by his own consent, given by himself or by others deputed to act for him. Let it be supposed then, that rulers assume a power to act contrary to this fundamental principle, what must be the consequence? If by such usurped authority, they can demand and take a penny, by the same authority they may take a pound, and even the whole substance of the subject, so as to make him wholly dependent on their pleasure, having nothing that he can call his own; and what is he then but a perfect *slave?*[77]

In support, Tucker transcribes several sentences from "Locke on Civil Government," including these, which were quoted again and again during the revolutionary period: "[N]obody hath a right to take their [men's] substance, or any part of it from them, without their own consent. For I truly have no property in that which another can by right take from me when he pleases, against my consent."[78]

Locke, to be sure, was not the only political writer respected by the revolutionary divines. Other writers, both modern and classical, are also quoted. But Locke's name appears more often by far than anyone else's in the period leading up to the revolution.[79]

The Consensus after 1760 on Revelation

The purpose of this essay is to demonstrate that the political theology of the American Revolution was grounded on both revelation *and* reason. No "blending" or "amalgam" of Protestant theology with secular rationalism was needed, because scripture was understood to teach the same political principles as philosophy. The preachers quoted in the last section relied as much on their interpretation of scripture as on the writings of Locke, Sidney, Hoadly, Trenchard and Gordon, and other European "Whig" thinkers. Besides, the first three of these writers were far from presenting themselves as mere "rationalists" in their writings. Locke was a theologian in his own right, as we have already noted; Sidney relied heavily on scripture in his book; and Hoadly was a bishop of the Anglican church.

In support of the righteousness of the use of violence in defense of the rights of life, liberty, and estate, two passages from the Old Testament were frequently quoted. One was Jeremiah 48:10, "Cursed be he that keepeth back his sword from blood." Another was Judges 5:23, "Curse ye Meroz, said the angel of the Lord, curse ye bitterly the inhabitants thereof; because they came not to the help of the Lord, to the help of the Lord against the mighty." Nathaniel Whitaker chose the Meroz passage as the theme of his 1777 sermon, *An Antidote against Toryism.*[80]

By far the favorite New Testament passage quoted in support of the right to revolution was Romans 13:1: "Let every soul be subject to the powers that be. . . ." Other frequently cited passages included 1 Peter 2:13–14, "Submit yourselves to every ordinance of man for the Lord's sake"; Titus 3:1, "Put them in mind to be subject to principalities and powers, to obey magistrates, to be ready to every good work"; and Galatians 5:1, "Stand fast therefore in the liberty with which Christ hath made us free."[81] Philips Payson's 1778 Election Sermon was devoted to Galatians 4:26, 31: "But Jerusalem, which is above, is free, which is the mother of us all. So then, brethren, we are not children of the bond woman, but of the free."[82]

In his powerful 1776 Massachusetts Election Sermon, delivered on the eve of independence, Samuel West rightly notes that Romans 13 "has been made use of by the favorers of arbitrary government as their great sheet-anchor and main support." West then observes, "A very little attention, I apprehend, will be sufficient to show that this text is so far from favoring arbitrary government, that, on the contrary, it strongly holds forth the principles of true liberty." In the passage in question, the apostle Paul writes, "The powers that be are ordained of God; and they that resist shall receive to themselves damnation; for rulers are not a terror to good works, but to the evil. . . . [I]f thou do that which is evil, be afraid; for he beareth not the sword in vain: for he is the minister of God, a revenger to execute wrath upon him that doth evil." Samuel West comments:

> If the apostle, then, asserts that rulers are ordained of God only because they are a terror to evil works and a praise to them that do well; . . . if the sole reason why they have a right to tribute is because they devote themselves wholly to the business of securing to men their just rights, and to the punishing of evil-doers,—it follows, by undeniable consequence, that when they become the pests of human society, when they promote and encourage evil-doers, and become a terror to good works, they then cease being the ordinance of God; they are no longer rulers nor ministers of God; they are so far from being the powers that are ordained of God that they become the ministers of the powers of darkness, and it is so far from being a crime to resist them, that in many cases it may be highly criminal in the sight of Heaven to refuse resisting and opposing them to the utmost of our power. . . . Hence we see that the apostle Paul, instead of being a friend to tyranny and arbitrary government, turns out to be a strong advocate for the just rights of mankind. . . . [This passage] ought, perhaps, rather to be viewed as a severe satire upon Nero, than as enjoining any submission to him.[83]

West's explanation of Romans 13, the classic biblical text that had been cited in favor of passive obedience to all governments, was not unique to the American founding era. The same argument had been presented at length in Jonathan Mayhew's 1750 sermon. It had been made in John Milton's *Defence of the People of England* (1651), Algernon Sidney's *Discourses Concerning Government* (1698), and Locke's *Two Treatises*.[84] Other European theological writers had developed a similar argument, at least as early as "Junius Brutus's" *Defense of Liberty against Tyrants* (1579).[85]

For the idea of religious liberty, a favorite passage was "Render to Caesar the things that are Caesar's, and to God the things that are God's."[86] Another was John 18:36, Christ's kingdom is "not of this world."[87]

In sum, the constant theme among New England preachers during the founding era was that God gives us two ways to learn his laws: reason, or the exercise of our own observation and thought to figure out what the rules are that promote human well-being; and revelation, or scripture (sometimes called "the sacred oracles"), which teach us our rights and duties by divine authority. On the occasion of the ratification of the Massachusetts Constitution of 1780, Samuel Cooper gave a sermon to the assembled dignitaries in which he made this characteristic observation:

> We want not, indeed, a special revelation from heaven to teach us that men are born equal and free; that no man has a natural claim of dominion over his neighbours, nor one nation any such claim upon another; and that as government is only the administration of the affairs of a number of men combined for their own security and happiness, such a society have a right freely to determine by whom and in what manner their own affairs shall be administered. These are the plain dictates of that reason and common sense with which the common parent of men has informed the human bosom. It is, however, a satisfaction to observe such everlasting maxims of equity confirmed, and impressed upon the consciences of men, by the instructions, precepts, and examples given us in the sacred oracles; one internal mark of their divine original, and that they come from him "who hath made of one blood all nations to dwell upon the face of the earth," whose authority sanctifies only those governments that instead of oppressing any part of his family, vindicate the oppressed, and restrain and punish the oppressor.[88]

Secularization?

It is commonly said by historians that eighteenth-century Puritanism underwent a secularization, a lowering of the standards from the high spiritual goals of the early Puritan "errand into the wilderness." Perry Miller is the most famous of the many who have made this argument. Zuckert more or less follows it in chapter 1 of this volume. He writes, "In the Mayflower Compact the secular is for the sake of the sacred," while, in contrast, the Declaration of Independence "affirms a wholly this-worldly end for political life."

I am suggesting something quite different. If I am right, the secular continues to be for the sake of the sacred. What happened was not a *secularization* but the opposite: a *sacralization* of what had previously been held worldly and low. For the eighteenth-century Christians whom we are discussing, the earlier Puritans had mistakenly limited the sacred to the realm of human life that is focused on the next world, or that presupposed the transformation of the human soul by divine grace: the church, worship, prayer, and the virtues of love, self-denial, and humility. The Congregational preachers of the 1760s and 1770s were convinced that the realm of the sacred includes what some (but by no means all) earlier Christians would have considered merely secular. Thus Elisha Williams speaks of "the sacred rights of conscience," which of course includes the natural right not to be a Christian. (One should be clear, however, that this is a natural right against the coercion of other men, not a right against God.) Samuel West's 1776 sermon says, "this ought to be looked upon as a sacred and inalienable right, . . . viz., that no one be obliged to submit to any law except such as are made either by himself or by his representative." These rights, in their view, had been neglected, in part because of deliberate misinterpretations of Christian doctrine by power-seeking priests in alliance with oppressive kings and aristocrats.[89]

"Secular" writers like Jefferson shared this understanding. Jefferson used the word *sacred* three times in his "rough draft" of the Declaration of Independence.[90] Just as in early Puritanism, the secular is for the sake of the sacred. But the sacred now includes respect for the God-given liberty of all.

By 1776, Puritanism was not dead. But it had changed. God was still in his heaven, but the law of God most emphasized in discussions of politics was the law of nature.[91] The sacred cause of Winthrop's city on a hill had been rejected, for divine grace does not change the earthly nature of entire political communities. But the "sacred cause of liberty," as Samuel West called it, had taken its place. From now on, Christianity in America would include devotion to the principles of the Declaration of Independence. Catholics too would agree on this, as John Carroll, the first Catholic bishop of the United States, appealed to the natural rights of all men—"the luminous principles on which the rights of conscience and liberty of religion depend"—in his pleas for full citizen rights for Catholics. Jews also endorsed the doctrine of the revolution. The Jewish congregation in Newport, Rhode Island, addressing President Washington during his visit in 1790, said that the government of America, protecting "liberty of conscience" and securing "the blessings of civil and religious liberty," is "the work of the great God."[92]

Many scholars today find this view of things unbelievable. Like the early Puritans, they cannot easily conceive of Christianity as a religion that commands toleration, or promotes the killing of wartime enemies. Many Christians today seem to pride themselves on the irrationality of their faith and its irrelevancy to the realistic cares of political life. They feel that what they call the spiritual dimension of Christianity is somehow compromised when Christians take the moral commandments of Christ to be largely identical to the law of nature, as the Christians of 1776 did.

If it is claimed that those who thought of themselves as Christians in the founding era were not really Christian, then one must confront the paradox of a nation that sincerely professes a religion whose leading tenets they have grossly misunderstood. I believe it is more in keeping with the historical facts to say that the Christians of the founding era held a different understanding of Christianity, perhaps erroneous, but perhaps superior to the one that prevails today.

Alexis de Tocqueville visited the United States during the 1830s. He reported that all religious denominations here shared the republican consensus that is evident from the sermons I have quoted from. That of course included the "liberal" Christians found in the vicinity of Boston, who by then had openly embraced Unitarianism, as well as the Baptists, Presbyterians, and Methodists, who were of the more Calvinist and Evangelical variety.

The Catholic prayer with which I will conclude could easily have been a Protestant prayer, or (omitting the reference to Christ at the end) even a Jewish prayer. Tocqueville says he heard this prayer at a "political gathering [in "one of the largest towns in the Union"] whose purpose was to come to the assistance of the Poles to get arms and money to them."

> God Almighty! God of Hosts! thou who didst maintain the hearts and guide the arms of our fathers when they sustained the sacred rights of their national independence; thou who made them triumph over an odious oppression and granted our people the benefits of peace and freedom, O Lord! turn a favorable eye toward the other hemisphere; regard with pity an heroic people who today struggles as we did formerly for the defense of the same rights! Lord, who have created all men on the same model, do not permit despotism to come to deform thy work and to maintain inequality on earth. God Almighty! watch over the destiny of the Poles, render them worthy of being free; that thy wisdom reign in their councils, that thy strength be in their arms; spread terror over their enemies. . . . God Almighty, answer our prayer today; save the Poles. We ask this of thee in the name of thy much loved son, our Lord Jesus Christ, who died on the cross for the salvation of all men. Amen.[93]

This prayer sums up the transformed political theology of Puritanism, which became the predominant political theology shared by the majority of Americans at the time of the revolution.

NOTES

1. Michael Zuckert, *The Natural Rights Republic* (Notre Dame, Ind.: University of Notre Dame Press, 1996), 26.

2. Virginia Declaration of Rights (1776), in Kurland and Lerner, *Founders' Constitution* (Chicago: University of Chicago Press, 1987), 1:7. David M. O'Brien, *Constitutional Law and Politics,* vol. 2: *Civil Rights and Civil Liberties,* 4th ed. (New York: W. W. Norton, 2000), 655 (chapter title, "Freedom from and of Religion"). John Locke, *Epistola de Tolerantia: A Letter on Toleration,* ed. Raymond Klibansky, trans. J. W. Gough (Oxford: Clarendon Press, 1968), 127, 67 (I have modified the translation slightly).

3. The New England Confederation, May 19, 1643, in Henry Steele Commager, ed., *Documents of American History,* 9th ed. (Englewood Cliffs, N.J.: Prentice Hall, 1973), 26.

4. Perry Miller, *The New England Mind: The Seventeenth Century* (Cambridge, Mass.: Harvard University Press, 1939). Perry Miller, *The New England Mind: From Colony to Province* (Cambridge, Mass.: Harvard University Press, 1953). Alan Heimert, *Religion and the American Mind: From the Great Awakening to the Revolution* (Cambridge, Mass.: Harvard University Press, 1966). Nathan O. Hatch, *The Sacred Cause of Liberty* (New Haven: Yale University Press, 1977).

5. Thomas L. Pangle, "The Constitution's Human Vision," *The Public Interest* 86 (Winter 1987), 78. The New England Confederation, in Commager, *Documents of American History,* 26.

6. Harriet Beecher Stowe, *Oldtown Folks* (orig. pub. 1869; Cambridge, Mass.: Harvard University Press, 1966), ch. 29, 392, 402.

7. Thomas Prince, *Election Sermon* (1730), in A. W. Plumstead, ed., *The Wall and the Garden: Selected Massachusetts Election Sermons, 1670–1775* (Minneapolis: University of Minnesota Press, 1968), 208.

8. John Winthrop, *A Modell of Christian Charity* (1630), Collections of the Massachusetts Historical Society (Boston: Little and Brown, 1838), 3rd series, 7:45, 46.

9. Ibid., 47.

10. Ibid., 41.

11. Ibid., 40.

12. Ibid., 45.

13. Massachusetts General Court, *The Laws and Liberties of Massachusetts* (repr. of 1648 ed.; Birmingham: Legal Classics Library, 1982), under the heading "Ecclesiastical."

14. Alexis de Tocqueville, *Democracy in America,* ed. and trans. Harvey C. Mansfield and Delba Winthrop (Chicago: University of Chicago Press, 2000), I.1.2, p. 39.

15. *Laws of Vermont,* ed. Allen Soule, *State Papers of Vermont* (Montpelier: Secretary of State, 1964), 72:38–39.

16. Mayflower Compact, in Kurland and Lerner, *Founders' Constitution,* 1:610. Fundamental Orders of Connecticut, in Commager, *Documents of American History,* 22–24.

17. John Winthrop, "Declaration in Defense of an Order of Court" (May 1637), in *Winthrop Papers* (Boston: Massachusetts Historical Society, 1929–), 3:423. Also Thomas Hooker: "There can be no necessary tie of mutual accord and fellowship come, but by free engagement." Hooker, *A Survey of the Summe of Church-Discipline* (1648), pt. 1, 47, quoted by John Witte, "How to Govern a City on a Hill: The Early Puritan Contribution to American Constitutionalism," *Emory Law Journal* 39 (1990): 47.

18. Winthrop, *Modell of Christian Charity,* 33.

19. John Cotton, *Certain Proposals Made by Lord Say . . . with the Answers Thereto,* in Edmund S. Morgan, ed., *Puritan Political Ideas* (Indianapolis: Bobbs-Merrill, 1965), 165.

20. "Libertye and the Weale Publick reconciled" (1637), in Thomas Hutchinson, ed., *The Hutchinson Papers* (New York: Burt Franklin, 1967), 1:74–76.

21. Winthrop, *Modell of Christian Charity,* 34.

22. "Mrs. Hutchinson" (1830), in Hawthorne, *Selected Tales and Sketches* (New York: Penguin, 1987), 14–21.

23. Miller, *New England Mind: Seventeenth Century,* 390–91.

24. Norman Fiering, *Moral Philosophy at Seventeenth-Century Harvard: A Discipline in Transition* (Chapel Hill: University of North Carolina Press, 1981), 66. This book is also the source for the previous paragraph. Thomas Shepard, *Theses Sabbaticae, or The Doctrine of the Sabbath* (London, 1649), in *The Works of Thomas Shepard* (orig. pub. 1853; repr. New York: AMS Press, 1967), 3:44–47, 51–53.

25. Plato, *Statesman,* 294a–c.

26. John Winthrop, Journal, May 22, 1639, September 4, 1639, and November 12, 1641, in James K. Hosmer, *Winthrop's Journal: "History of New England," 1630–1649* (1908; repr. New York: Barnes & Noble, 1946), 1:302–5, 1:323–24, 2:49–52.

27. *Winthrop's Journal,* May 22, 1639, 302. Massachusetts Body of Liberties, in Morgan, *Puritan Political Ideas,* 178.

28. *Winthrop's Journal,* September 4, 1639; June 5, 1644; May 3, 1644; and October 30, 1644; 1:323, 2:170–72, 2:189, 2:211–17.

29. William Bradford, *Of Plymouth Plantation, 1620–1647* (ca. 1650; New York: Modern Library, 1981), 132–34.

30. Winthrop, "Defense of an Order of Court," in *Winthrop Papers,* 3:424. Aristotle, *Politics,* book 2, 1260b–1264b. Founder James Wilson discusses early American communism in Plymouth and Virginia in "History of Property," *Works of James Wilson,* ed. Robert McCloskey (Cambridge, Mass.: Harvard University Press, 1967), 2:718.

31. Richard Slotkin and James K. Folsom, *So Dreadfull a Judgment: Puritan Responses to King Philip's War, 1676–1677* (Middletown, Conn.: Wesleyan University Press, 1978), 3.

32. Increase Mather, *A Brief History of the War* (1676), in Slotkin and Folsom, *So Dreadfull a Judgment,* 102–5; the government's response is in Morgan, *Puritan Political Ideas,* 226–33.

33. Samuel Nowell, *Abraham in Arms* (1678), in Slotkin and Folsom, *So Dreadfull a Judgment*, 274–77.

34. Nowell, *Abraham in Arms*, 282–84. Algernon Sidney, *Discourses Concerning Government*, ed. Thomas G. West (1698; repr. Indianapolis: Liberty Classics, 1990), ch. 2, sec. 23, p. 210. Benjamin Franklin, *Writings* (New York: Library of America, 1987), 1201 (from *Poor Richard*, 1736).

35. Nowell, *Abraham in Arms*, 288.

36. Samuel Cooke, *A Sermon* (Election Sermon, Boston, 1770), in Plumstead, *The Wall and the Garden*, 331. Samuel Sherwood, *A Sermon, Containing, Scriptural Instructions to Civil Rulers, and all Free-Born Subjects* (New Haven, 1774), in Ellis Sandoz, ed., *Political Sermons of the America Founding Era: 1730–1805* (Indianapolis: Liberty Fund, 1990), 378. Simeon Howard, *A Sermon Preached to the Ancient and Honorable Artillery Company in Boston* (1773), in Charles S. Hyneman and Donald S. Lutz, ed., *American Political Writing during the Founding Era, 1760–1805* (Indianapolis: Liberty Press, 1983), 1:197. Thomas Bradbury, *The Ass: or, the Serpent, A Comparison between the Tribes of Issachar and Dan, in their Regard for Civil Liberty* (orig. pub. London, 1712; repr. Newburyport, Mass., 1774), in Hyneman and Lutz, *American Political Writing*, 1:240–56. A pre-Nowell use of Issachar is John Oxenbridge, *New England Freemen Warned and Warmed, to be Free Indeed* (Boston, 1673), 27.

37. Nowell, *Abraham in Arms*, 282–83. In the next sentence, Nowell mentions the example of Ahab's theft of Naboth's vineyard.

38. See Anonymous, *Touching the Fundamentall Lawes* (London, 1643), in Joyce Lee Malcolm, ed., *The Struggle for Sovereignty: Seventeenth-Century English Political Tracts* (Indianapolis: Liberty Fund, 1999), 274–75 ("God and nature hath ordained government for the preservation of the governed." The people delegated power to the king "for the people's preservation, yet it was never intended that by it he might compass their destruction, contrary to the law of nature; whereby every man, yea everything is bound to preserve itself"). William Ball, *Constitutio Liberi Populi, Or, The Rule of a Free-born People* (London, 1646), in Malcolm, *Struggle*, 287, 292–93 (men have "original freedom"; according to the law of nature, "All power and authority is given for preservation, and edification, nothing for destruction and desolation"). John Goodwin, *Right and Might Well Met* (London, 1649), in Malcolm, *Struggle*, 319, 326, 330 (the "law of nature and necessity" justifies overthrow of a king who attempts to deprive subjects of "lives and estates" and "the kingdom's liberties"). William Allen, *Killing Noe Murder* (1657), in David Wootton, ed., *Divine Right and Democracy: An Anthology of Political Writing in Stuart England* (New York: Penguin, 1986), 373 (the laws of God and nature permit men to defend themselves by force against those who threaten their lives and properties; that includes the tyrant, "the common robber of mankind").

39. Mary Rowlandson, *The Sovereignty and Goodness of God, . . . Being a Narrative of the Captivity and Restauration of Mrs. Mary Rowlandson* (1682), in Slotkin and Folsom, *So Dreadfull a Judgment*, 316–69.

40. I do not mean that Church imitated the Indians' willingness to kill innocent women and children. I mean that he, as Rev. Oliver Peabody recommended in a 1732

sermon, believed that Christian soldiers should "study their enemies" and "be exercised and skilled in the . . . manner of fighting used by savages in the wilderness," including the ability to "fight in the woods." Oliver Peabody, *An Essay to Revive and Encourage Military Exercises, Skill, and Valour among the Sons of God's People in New-England: A Sermon Preached before the Honourable Artillery-Company* (Boston, 1732), in James A. Levernier, ed., *Souldiery Spiritualized: Seven Sermons Preached before the Artillery Companies of New England, 1674–1774* (Delmar, N.Y.: Scholars' Facsimiles, 1979), 27, 34.

41. T.C., *Entertaining Passages Relating to Philip's War . . . with Some Account of the Divine Providence towards Benj. Church Esqr* (1716), in Slotkin and Folsom, *So Dreadfull a Judgment*, 370–470. The quotations are on 395 and 397.

42. Harry S. Stout, *The New England Soul: Preaching and Religious Culture in Colonial New England* (New York: Oxford University Press, 1986), 83.

43. Here are some sermon titles from the years that followed: *The Man of War* (1699). *Good Soldiers Described and Animated* (1720). *An Essay to Revive and Encourage Military Exercises, Skill, and Valour among the Sons of God's People in New England* (1732). *Martial Wisdom Recommended* (1737). *The Expediency and Utility of War, in the Present State of Things, Considered* (1759). *The Importance of Military Skill.* These titles are listed in Levernier, *Souldiery Spiritualized,* appendix B.

44. Richard Ashcraft makes a persuasive case against Charles II in *Revolutionary Politics and John Locke's Two Treatises of Government* (Princeton: Princeton University Press, 1986), ch. 1.

45. Jack Greene, ed., *Settlements to Society, 1607–1763* (New York: Norton, 1975), 184.

46. Town of Ipswich, statement of August 23, 1687, quoted by T. H. Breen, *The Character of the Good Ruler: Puritan Political Ideas in New England, 1630–1730* (New Haven: Yale University Press, 1970), 144. John Wise may have written it.

47. Anonymous, *The Revolution in New England Justified* (Boston, 1691), and Anonymous, *The Humble Address of the Publicans of New-England* (London, 1691).

48. David S. Lovejoy, *The Glorious Revolution in America* (New York: Harper Torchbooks, 1972), chaps. 7, 8, 10, 13, has a fuller account of the events summarized here.

49. George L. Haskins, *Law and Authority in Early Massachusetts* (New York: Macmillan, 1960), 55.

50. Uriah Oakes, *New England Pleaded With* (Cambridge, Mass., 1673), 51–52.

51. Samuel Sewall, *The Selling of Joseph: A Memorial* (Boston, 1700), in M. Halsey Thomas, *The Diary of Samuel Sewall, 1674–1729* (New York: Farrar, Straus, and Giroux, 1973), 2:1117.

52. Samuel Johnson, *His Career and Writings* (New York, 1929), 1:6–7, 2:186, quoted in Claude M. Newlin, *Philosophy and Religion in Colonial America* (New York: Philosophical Library, 1962), 23–24.

53. John Bulkley, *The Necessity of Religion in Societies* (Boston, 1713), Evans 1598, 4, 63.

54. Ibid., 19, 38, 46.

55. Daniel Dulaney, *The Right of the Inhabitants of Maryland to the Benefit of English Laws* (Annapolis, Md., 1728), Evans 39881, 2, 9–10, 30.

56. Bernard Bailyn, *Ideological Origins of the American Revolution* (enlarged ed.; Cambridge, Mass.: Harvard University Press, 1992), 43. John Trenchard and Thomas Gordon, *Cato's Letters: Or, Essays on Liberty, Civil and Religious, and Other Important Subjects,* 2 vols. (Indianapolis: Liberty Fund, 1995).

57. J. M. [John Mather], *The Original Rights of Mankind Freely to Subdue and Improve the Earth, Asserted and Maintained* (Boston, 1722), Evans 2346.

58. Jared Eliot, *Give Cesar His Due, Or, The Obligation that Subjects are under to their Civil Rulers,* Election Sermon (New London, Conn.: T. Green, 1738), 27.

59. Elisha Williams, *The Essential Rights and Liberties of Protestants* (1744), in Sandoz, ed., *Political Sermons,* 51–118. The quotations are on 59.

60. Ibid., 55.

61. Locke, *Letter on Toleration,* 59.

62. Johnathan Edwards, "Thoughts on the Revival of Religion" (1742), in Alan Heimert and Perry Miller, ed., *The Great Awakening: Documents Illustrating the Crisis and Its Consequences* (Indianapolis: Bobbs-Merrill, 1967), 264–65.

63. Charles Chauncy, *Enthusiasm Described and Caution'd against* (1742), in Heimert and Miller, 249.

64. Ibid., 246; "The increase of learning in itself is a thing to be rejoiced in, because it is a good, and, if duly applied, an excellent handmaid to divinity." Johnathan Edwards, *A History of the Work of Redemption* (1739), in Heimert and Miller, 23.

65. Stout, *New England Soul,* 215, quoting Gilbert Tennent, *Irenicum Eccliasticum* (Philadelphia, 1749), 369, 371. Similarly from the "Old Light" side is Samuel West, *A Sermon Preached at the Ordination* (Boston, 1764), Evans 9869, 20: "Can any imagine that he faithfully preaches Christ, who very seldom in his discourses mentions his name; and who never insists on the doctrine of atonement, with which the New Testament so much abounds? . . . Where the doctrines of mere natural religion are insisted on to the neglect of the peculiar doctrines of revelation, we can at most expect to find only a few fashionable, civil gentlemen, but destitute of real piety. As on the other hand, where the distinguishing doctrines of Christianity alone are insisted upon, we shall find that men are very apt to run into enthusiasm. A true Gospel minister should seek to avoid both these extremes. When he insists on moral virtues, he should enforce them with Christian motives. He should preach up the perfections of God, to regulate our devotion; the doctrine of atonement and regeneration, to bring us to Christ, and social virtues as the effects of a Christian temper."

66. Levi Hart, *Liberty Described and Recommended* (Hartford, Conn., 1775), in Hyneman and Lutz, *American Political Writing,* 306–11; Samuel West, *On the Right to Rebel against Governors* (Boston, 1776), 410–37. Donald Weber, *Rhetoric and History in Revolutionary New England* (New York: Oxford University Press, 1988), 1 (criticizing the view promoted by "many secular academics themselves partisans of the Enlightenment" who portray "the Revolution as a secular, rational, political movement").

67. Jonathan Mayhew, *Discourse Concerning Unlimited Submission and Nonresistance to the Higher Powers*, Boston, 1765, in *Pamphlets of the American Revolution*, ed. Bernard Bailyn (Cambridge, Mass.: Harvard University Press, 1965), 1:214. The "most famous sermon" statement is made by the editor on 204.

68. Hyneman and Lutz, *American Political Writing*, 1:3–18.

69. William Patten, *A Discourse Delivered at Halifax* (Boston: Kneeland, 1766), 17–18, quoting Locke, *Second Treatise*, sec. 240.

70. *Boston Weekly Newspaper*, November 23, 1769, quoted in Steven Dworetz, *The Unvarnished Doctrine: Locke, Liberalism, and the American Revolution* (Durham, N.C.: Duke University Press, 1990), 181.

71. Jason Haven, *A Sermon* (Boston: R. Draper, 1769), 41–42. The first quotation is from sec. 202 of Locke's *Second Treatise*.

72. Peter Whitney, *Transgression of a Land*, Fast Day Sermon (Boston: John Boyle, 1774), 16–17, quoting Locke's *Second Treatise*, sec. 202. The full quotation from Locke is in the Haven passage just quoted.

73. John Lathrop, *A Sermon*, Artillery-Election Sermon (Boston, 1774), repr. in Levernier, *Souldiery Spiritualized*, 8.

74. Simeon Howard, *A Sermon* (Boston, 1773), in Hyneman and Lutz, *American Political Writing*, 1:187.

75. Bailyn, *Ideological Origins of the American Revolution*, 28. Dworetz, *Unvarnished Doctrine*, exposes Bailyn's error on 111–12.

76. West (Boston, 1776), in Hyneman and Lutz, *American Political Writing*, 1:413. Judah Champion, *Christian and Civil Liberty*, Election Sermon, printed at the request of the Assembly (Hartford, Conn.: E. Watson, 1776), 7–8. Whitaker (1777) and Stillman (1779) in Frank Moore, ed., *Patriot Preachers of the American Revolution* (New York: Charles T. Evans, 1862), 198, 264.

77. John Tucker, *Election Sermon* (1771), in Hyneman and Lutz, *American Political Writing*, 1:162–63, emphasis added.

78. Hyneman and Lutz, *American Political Writing*, 1:163, from Locke, *Second Treatise*, sec. 138.

79. Donald S. Lutz, *Origins of American Constitutionalism* (Baton Rouge: Louisiana State University Press, 1988), 143.

80. Nathaniel Whitaker, *An Antidote against Toryism* (1777), in Frank Moore, ed., *Patriot Preachers of the American Revolution* (New York: Charles T. Evans, 1862), 186–231. Both passages are quoted by Samuel West, *On the Right to Rebel*, 439. In Virginia, Presbyterian Samuel Davies quotes the Jeremiah passage in *The Curse of Cowardice* (1758), in Daniel C. Palm, ed., *On Faith and Free Government* (Lanham, Md.: Rowman & Littlefield, 1997), 94.

81. The first three of these passages are cited in Abraham Williams, *An Election Sermon* (Boston, 1762), in Hyneman and Lutz, *American Political Writing*, 7. Also Samuel West, *On the Right to Rebel*, in Hyneman and Lutz, 410, 423, 424. Daniel Shute quotes Romans 13 in his 1768 Election Sermon, in Hyneman and Lutz, 112. John Tucker preached an election sermon (1771) on 1 Peter 2 in which he discusses Romans 13; see

Hyneman and Lutz, 158, 161, 165. Simeon Howard, *A Sermon Preached to the Ancient and Honorable Artillery Company in Boston* (1773), Hyneman and Lutz, 186, preached on Galatians 5:1. Gad Hitchcock, 1774 Election Sermon, quotes and discusses Romans 13, in Hyneman and Lutz, 285. Peter Whitney, *The Transgression of a Land Punished by a Multitude of Rulers* (Boston, 1774), 15–19 (on Romans 13). Zabdiel Adams's 1782 Election Sermon discusses Romans 13, in Hyneman and Lutz, 541–43.

82. Philips Payson, *Election Sermon,* in Hyneman and Lutz, 523. Elisha Williams quotes the same passage to the same effect in *Essential Rights and Liberties of Protestants,* in Sandoz, *Political Sermons,* 86.

83. West, *On the Right to Rebel,* 423–25.

84. Mayhew's *Discourse Concerning Unlimited Submission,* 1765, was entirely devoted to Romans 13, in Bailyn, *Pamphlets of the American Revolution,* 215–47. Milton, *Defence of the People of England,* ch. 3, in John Alvis, ed., *Areopagitica and Other Political Writings of John Milton* (Indianapolis: Liberty Fund, 1999), 166–67. Sidney, *Discourses Concerning Government,* ch. 3, sec. 10, pp. 370–73. Locke quotes Romans 13 in *Two Treatises,* I.92 (contrary to Zuckert's assertion that Locke does not quote Romans 13 in the *Treatises*).

85. Junius Brutus, *A Defence of Liberty against Tyrants: A Translation of Vindiciae contra Tyrannos* (orig. pub. 1579; English trans. pub. 1689; London: G. Bell, 1924) (Romans 13 discussed at the end of the First Question). Benjamin Hoadly's interpretation of Romans 13 was in effect plagiarized by Mayhew in his interpretation of Romans 13: Bailyn, *Pamphlets,* 208.

86. Zabdiel Adams, *Election Sermon* (1782), in Hyneman and Lutz, 556.

87. Abraham Williams, *Election Sermon* (1762), in Hyneman and Lutz, 7.

88. Samuel Cooper, *A Sermon Preached before his Excellency John Hancock* (1780), in Sandoz, *Political Sermons,* 637.

89. John Adams, *Dissertation on the Canon and Feudal Law,* in *Works of John Adams,* ed. Charles Francis Adams, 10 vols. (Boston: Little, Brown, 1865), 3:463.

90. "We hold these truths to be *sacred* and undeniable"; the "most *sacred* rights of life and liberty" of slaves; and "we pledge to each other our . . . *sacred* honor." Samuel West, *On the Right to Rebel,* in Hyneman and Lutz, 1:438. *The Papers of Thomas Jefferson,* ed. Julian P. Boyd (Princeton: Princeton University Press, 1950), 423, 426–27 (my emphasis).

91. "The Constitution of the God of nature." Williams, *Election Sermon* (1762), in Hyneman and Lutz, 15.

92. John Carroll, "To John Fenno of the Gazette of the United States," June 10, 1789, in Thomas O. Hanley, ed., *The John Carroll Papers* (Notre Dame, Ind.: University of Notre Dame Press, 1976), 1:365. Anson P. Stokes, *Church and State in the United States* (New York: Harper, 1950), 862.

93. Tocqueville, *Democracy in America,* I.2.9, p. 277.

CHAPTER EIGHT

The Contingencies of Christian Republicanism

An Alternative Account of Protestantism and the American Founding

Mark A. Noll

Most historians do not do as well with essential states of affairs as do experts in political theory. Historians are usually, in the phrases of J. H. Hexter, "splitters" who attend to contingency, rather than "lumpers" who limn the Big Picture.[1] Even from the angle of a splitter, however, there is much to admire in Michael Zuckert's lumping account of natural rights and Protestant politics, especially his effort to trace the genealogy of the ideological mixture that undergirded the American Revolution, the American Constitution, and the American founding more generally. Zuckert's picture of "the Lockeanization of Protestant politics" is particularly apt for describing an ideological world dominated by secular political values yet also shaped at almost every point by religious convictions, religious language, religious instincts, and deeply entrenched religious traditions. His account of the importance for the founding generation of natural and individual rights does, of course, challenge the exalted place that many historians over the last generation have given to republican categories of virtue, corruption, and disinterested public service in their depiction of the nation's founding. Yet because it forces all interested parties back to a re-analysis of speeches, private communications, and published writings—and also the contexts in which opinions were uttered—Zuckert's challenge is particularly beneficial for historians like myself who continue to find republican reasoning not only omnipresent in the emergence of the United States, but also critical for the contingent events that brought secular and religious convictions together in resistance to Parliament, deliberation over a constitution, and the creation of a national political culture.

An assessment of "Protestantism and the American founding" keyed to religious events that took place between the Great Awakening of the 1740s and the expansion of evangelical Protestantism in the early decades of the nineteenth century—and seeking to discover when, under what conditions, and to what ends political speech became significant in religious speech—will not look the same as Zuckert's forcefully argued account. Yet such an assessment is particularly well suited to benefit from the Niagara of recent literature on the ideology of the founding era (to which Zuckert has made a significant contribution). A brief sketch of that historiography is, thus, an appropriate introduction to a splitter's outline of steps that led to the manifest, but also complex, mixture of religion and politics in the American founding era.[2]

HISTORIOGRAPHY

Recent historical writing has made it abundantly clear that simplistic summaries cannot deal with the multivalent, tumultuous, and often extraordinarily fluid ideas of America's founding era. Although the heated historical debates over the last half-century concerning the place of republican and liberal ideologies in the founding of the United States easily became counterproductive, they also produced important benefits. These benefits come particularly from failed attempts at defining a single, dominant ideology for America's early political life. In the years after World War II, the process began with assertions by a Lockean school of political scientists concerning the centrality of a timeless set of liberal principles for the American founding. "The Perspectives of 1776," as described in an influential book by Louis Hartz, came from John Locke's "basic social norm, the concept of free individuals in a state of nature." According to Hartz, "the master assumption of American political thought" was "the reality of atomistic social freedom."[3]

The republican "nay" to this liberal "yea" represented a first-order historical challenge, but also eventually became the subject of massive historiographical attention itself.[4] Ancient commitments to public justice and historically conditioned standards of public virtue were the new keys unlocking the meaning of the American founding, not modern principles of individual liberty or abstract rights applied in an American setting. In the influential view of Bernard Bailyn, a number of historic influences had come to bear on the founding generation, but the writers who "dominated the colonists' miscellaneous learning and shaped it into a coherent whole" reflected "the radical social and political thought of the English Civil War and of the Commonwealth period." That writing, in turn, was given "permanent form . . . at the turn of the seventeenth century and in the early eighteenth century, in the writings of a group of prolific opposition theorists, 'country' politicians and publicists."[5] What these commonwealth or country theorists advocated was a stance that Gordon Wood identified as distinctly republican: "The sacrifice of individual interests to the greater good of the whole formed the essence of republicanism and comprehended for Americans the idealistic goal of their Revolution."[6]

It was the special contribution of J. G. A. Pocock to trace a pedigree for these republican values deep into early modern Europe. Pocock would later summarize his own understanding of this tradition, first excavated in *The Machiavellian Moment* (1975) and then refined in a series of learned rejoinders to critics, as preoccupation with a single word: "To be 'republican' . . . was not merely to take up a posture on the left wing of mixed-government doctrine; it was also to commit oneself to engaging, one way or another, in a discourse about 'virtue'." Pocock, though, also repeatedly insisted on the complexity of that engagement: "The reflective discourse of the eighteenth century was deeply concerned with the problematic nature of virtue; with the difficulty of maintaining it and the difficulty of moving away from it; with the gains to human culture that came from specialization, politeness, and enlightenment; with the losses to human culture that came from abandoning the belief that the moral personality expressed itself directly in political activity."[7] To Pocock, grasping the dense complexity of republican (but also liberal) wrestling with "virtue" was critical for understanding the American founding.

The thesis that the new American nation rested on a civic humanist, Real Whig, and republican foundation soon generated a sharply argued antithesis reasserting the central place of a more sophisticated, more democratic, and more historically conditioned liberalism. In revisions proposed especially by Joyce Appleby and Isaac Kramnick, the liberalism of the revolutionary era was viewed as incorporating some of the republican emphases stressed by Bailyn, Wood, and Pocock, but it was defined primarily by concern for personal interests in the new commercial, proto-capitalist contingencies of the late eighteenth century.[8] According to Kramnick, "The radicals of the later eighteenth century, both English and American, were much more likely to base their arguments on natural rights than on historical rights; they were preoccupied less with nostalgic country concerns than with very modern socioeconomic grievances." Again, "the interests of the talented and hard-working middle class" were critical for understanding protests against British imperial authority.[9]

Joyce Appleby's criticism of the republican interpretation has stressed developments in the constitutional period and following years. As Appleby studied the second half of the eighteenth century, she concluded that new possibilities in commerce, science, and psychological self-understanding were defining a propitious moment for the exaltation of personal liberty. An alteration of material conditions was critical for American ideology: "The importance of the free market to this development cannot be reduced to economics. . . . It was the economy's ordering of society with minimal compulsion that stirred the Jeffersonian imagination."[10] In her picture, "This changing balance between the demands of the community and the individual helps explain . . . why liberalism with its core affirmation of the individual's claim upon society to protect his natural rights could so easily have displaced the devotion to order which animated colonial life a half-century earlier."[11] To these critics of a universal republican interpretation, principles of disinterested justice, balanced liberty, and classical virtue may explain some aspects of early American thought, but not nearly as many as individual and individualistic responses to rapidly changing social and economic conditions.

The most important benefit for recent students of the American founding is a realization that this particular historiographical battle is unwinnable. In particular, the clash of interpretations has pushed understanding of the really existing historical situation toward greater flexibility, multivocality, and nuance. Elements that historians once attempted to describe as discrete and competing principles, constructs, or conceptual languages are now much easier to see as overlapping, intermingled, and combining in ways not conforming to modern categories. Gordon Wood, who still defends the importance of discriminating between republican and liberal perspectives, nonetheless states clearly what many others have also concluded: "Classical republicanism in the eighteenth century was not a clearly discernible body of thought to which people self-consciously adhered. And what we call Lockean liberalism was even less manifest and less palpable." If, in Wood's account, "None of the historical participants, including the Founders, ever had any sense that he had to choose between republicanism and liberalism, between Machiavelli and Locke," then neither should modern historians. "These boxlike categories of 'republicanism' and 'liberalism' are . . . necessarily dangerous distortions of past reality."[12]

An important contribution of those who in debates over the American founding still contend for a more principal Lockeanism has been to show that intellectual commitments, once treated as distinct, actually existed together in the integrated thought of important individuals or groups. Thus, Alan Houston described principles that later historians pictured as competitive streams labeled "liberal" and "republican" as actually working together for Algernon Sidney in the late seventeenth century, as well as for many of those who harkened back to Sidney over the course of the next century. Michael Zuckert proposed the same conclusion for the Real Whig arguments of "Cato" (John Trenchard and Thomas Gordon) from the early 1720s. And John Dunn showed some time ago that Locke was read with appreciation by many colonists who described themselves self-consciously as republicans.[13] These demonstrations highlight the danger of letting modern categories tyrannize over the thought of historical actors, but they also encourage efforts to probe more deeply into other intellectual alliances, including the alliance of political thought and religious conviction.

For this essay, the most direct benefit from the republican-liberal debates has been a broader reconceptualization of intellectual history in the periods of the revolution and early republic. Recognizing that neither an airtight republicanism nor an equally hegemonic liberalism dominated public intellectual life has led at least some historians to reevaluate the place of religion. Richard B. Morris nicely captured this broader ideological purview by noting that "the Founding Fathers were a product of covenant theology, common-law teaching, of a belief in the supremacy of the parliament over the king, mixed with radical commonwealth thought, plus a heavy dose of Enlightenment thinking, leavened with Hume and Scottish Enlightenment thought, and some unique constitutional ideas of their own."[14] Coming directly from the debate over republican versus liberal paradigms, Isaac Kramnick has contended that a bipolar depiction of early American ideology is simply too simple. Rather, at least four "distinguishable idioms" existed: the republicanism and liberalism familiar from a thousand discussions, but also what Kramnick calls "work-ethic Protestantism" and "state-centered theories of power and sovereignty."[15] John Murrin has gone even further in contending that at least six "discernible value systems" were being put to use by those who formed the American nation: besides civic humanism and liberalism, Murrin cites "Calvinist orthodoxy," "Anglican moralism," "Tom Paine radicalism," and "Scottish moral sense . . . philosophy."[16] Other historians have added still other intellectual streams, like natural law reasoning and political economy.[17] The important point here is that these more comprehensive accounts of American ideology understand religious thought as fully active in the ideological clearinghouse that was the early United States. Rather than assuming that religious belief functioned merely as private opinion, or as passively held intellectual convictions reacting to supposedly more basic commitments strewn along the republican-liberal axis, historians now have new arenas for research.

The general opening up of early American ideological history to the possibility that religious belief played an active role is supported by two other historiographical trends. First, a number of researchers have criticized the paradigm-setting discussions precisely for neglecting the ideological force of religion in the early republic.[18] Second, a number of impressive studies have begun to make the case for how that religious influence actually worked.[19] If some of the writing emphasizing the foundational role of religious conviction in the era's most important political conclusions repeats the all-or-nothing tendency of earlier republican-liberal standoffs, most does not. It argues not for the singular domination of religious conviction but its relative importance in relation to other value systems. By making such claims, religious thought is not only restored to its proper place in America's history, but it is also opened up for study in relationship to the era's other ideological forces.

This opening looms largest when the confluence of political and religious thought is observed historically. There never was in the eighteenth century a body of "religious" or "Protestant" or "Puritan" thought that existed outside time and space and that then simply came to bear on the ideas of the American founding. Rather, there were multitudes of historical actors who at different times from the 1740s to the 1820s, in different places (including many beyond New England), and in widely differing ways carried their religious convictions with them into the political sphere. The results were multivalent. Sometimes those convictions bent political views, sometimes the political views bent the religious convictions, sometimes small pragmatic decisions yielded large effects of principle, sometimes intellectual consequences went awry. In order best to observe how politics and religion, especially republican politics and Protestant religion, became so commingled during the founding era, it is necessary to follow the unfolding of events.

THE ORIGINS OF A NEW IDEOLOGICAL ALLIANCE

Whatever the long-term, tectonic forces preparing for the dominant thought of the founding era, the beginnings of the concrete ideological interchange that led directly to the political religion of that era first appeared during the colonial wars of the 1740s. Before that time, religious leaders had made vague use of both Lockean and "country" concepts, but now a shift in intellectual terrain was marked by the introduction of distinctly republican notions into traditional Protestant conceptions of divine providence and traditional Protestant denunciations of Roman Catholicism. Before the 1740s, Protestant ideology in the colonies featured an almost exclusive concentration on God's direct providential control over events and opinions. That ideology was particularly disinclined to view supposed republican realities as compatible with the exercise of divine providence. The great change of the 1740s was to align historic Protestant doctrines of providence with heretofore suspect notions of republican political action.

To be sure, the main Christian traditions in the colonies had not been entirely unfamiliar with either liberal or republican political discourse. By their nature, the Protestant nonconformists who peopled the colonies were wary of any authority preferentially linked to the Anglican establishment.[20] Edmund Burke featured this sensitivity in his famous appeal before Parliament for conciliation with the colonists on March 22, 1775: they were, Burke argued, "protestants; and of that kind, which is the most adverse to all implicit submission of mind and opinion." Moreover, "this averseness in the dissenting churches from all that looks like absolute government" was a fundamental reality of "their history."[21]

In that history, however, dissenting wariness about British power only occasionally drew on specifically civic humanist, republican, Real Whig—or Lockean—thinking. Among all colonial religious traditions, and especially among the New England Puritans, attention to divine revelation, concern for eternal life, and a belief in God's direct control of quotidian existence insured that secular political analysis enjoyed, at most, a secondary place. After Massachusetts lost its original charter in the mid-1680s, Puritan leaders like Cotton Mather did display an awareness of commonwealth ideology. When Mather's Massachusetts Election Sermon for 1692, as an example, described how ancient Israelites had turned from God, he used a political vocabulary from contemporary British politics: "they were punished with a *Slavery* to *men*; a cruel *Shishak* had got them under the Yokes of his Arbitrary Government." By contrast, when things were going well in Israel, "there was no *Law,* and no *Tax,* imposed upon them, except what their own Acts concurred unto." Mather's conclusion was to pose rhetorical questions of the sort that many others would also ask over the course of the next century: "Is it not *Well,* that all *Christian Liberties,* and all *English Liberties,* are by the Royal Charter effectually Secured unto us? . . . [and that] no *Judges,* or *Counsellors,* or *Justices* can ever hereafter be Arbitrarily Imposed upon us?"[22]

A similar familiarity with "country" rhetoric informed the writing of John Wise (1652–1725), the minister of Ipswich, Massachusetts, who otherwise shared almost nothing with Cotton Mather.[23] Wise's protests against the Mathers and others whom he regarded as elite oppressors of the people, like *A Vindication of the Government of New England Churches* (1717), drew on many thinkers, they paralleled Locke on questions like the rights of taxpayers, yet they were also infused with traditionally Protestant fears of a Roman Catholic despotism, and they mostly repeated themes of English commonwealth and country writing. But Wise was a maverick; his writings have meant much more for modern students excavating the origins of American democracy than for his contemporaries. His opinions did not represent a groundswell of support for the use of secular political convictions.

The ideological transformation of the 1740s is underscored by the fact that, despite earlier indications of overlapping Protestant-republican perception, colonists until the middle of the eighteenth century were more likely to view radical Whig principles as opposed to religion than supporting it. The record of the *New-England Courant* is instructive. This newspaper was owned by James Franklin and was the first outlet for the published writings of his younger brother, Benjamin. The *Courant* was famed, or notorious, as a forum for radical ideas in both politics and religion. It reprinted *Cato's Letters* by John Trenchard and Thomas Gordon, the clearest articulation in its day of Real Whig sentiments. It also ran Benjamin Franklin's "Silence Do-Good Papers" with their biting satire on the traditions of New England Puritanism. For its combination of radical politics and heterodox religion, the paper was attacked as a licentious opponent of good order in church and state. As the *Boston News-Letter* charged in August 1721, the *Courant* was "full freighted with Nonesense, Unmannerliness, Railery, Prophaneness, Immorality, Arrogancy, Calumnies, Lyes, Contradictions, and what not, all tending to Quarrels and Divisions, and to Debauch and Corrupt the Minds and Manners of New England."[24] The general situation, even in New England where radical political views were best known, has been well summarized by Richard Bushman: "For fifty years after the issuance of the second charter [in 1691], Massachusetts Bay politicians kept the English radicals at a distance."[25]

Well into the 1740s, religious commentary in the colonies on public events maintained the traditional Protestant emphases. King George's War (1744–1748), which for the colonies featured New England's attack in 1745 upon the French fortress at·Louisbourg on Cape Breton Island, prompted the first hints of what would become the standard religious politics of the revolutionary era. But even at the time of the Louisbourg campaign, most New Englanders (who were always the most articulate colonists on public questions) were still describing events as they had long described them, especially with a focus on the spiritual character of colonial response to worldly events and on the prerogatives of God's providence. Jonathan Edwards, for example, preached several times on current events to his Northampton, Massachusetts, congregation before and after the Cape Breton expedition. His themes were resolutely traditional: the need for repentance in response to the war as a sign of God's displeasure, the special danger of sin during the upsets of warfare, and the adoration of God for his sheer mercy in bringing about the defeat of the French.[26] These responses were standard for the Puritans of New England, but also typical for Protestants elsewhere in the colonies.[27]

From the mid-1740s and onward, a different pattern would prevail, in which Protestant leaders added secular political concepts, terms, and modes of reasoning—taken especially from republican intellectual resources—to their traditional spiritual reasoning. In light of how important the newer amalgamation of religion and secular reasoning became, it is important to understand how much antagonism had existed historically between the main strands of republican reasoning and the most important representatives of British and colonial Protestantism.

Puritans and republicans had joined forces during the English Civil Wars, but their intellectual instincts remained quite different. Puritans built their lives around trust in providence, they relied on scripture and prayer, and they exalted the divine grace that chose the elect for salvation.[28] In their forthright supernaturalism, Puritans were more medieval than modern. While Puritans did promote reason, learning, and careful attention to the world, their main concern was suprarational fellowship with God.[29] By contrast, Marchamont Needham, James Harrington, John Milton, and others who in the 1650s created the English republican tradition trusted preeminently in human reason, relied upon a study of history, Aristotle, and other classical authorities, and relativized religion by treating it primarily as a prop for the virtue required in republican commonwealths. Republicans were modern in their this-worldly rationality. While some did not despise piety, all of them sought classically defined *virtù* above all.

In a careful analysis of the religion of James Harrington, whose *Oceana* of 1656 was the era's fullest statement of republican principle, Mark Goldie has spelled out the conditions under which republican and Puritan views could move beyond simple cooperation against a common foe. The key, according to Goldie, was the softening of Puritan theological orthodoxy: when Puritans remained committed to traditional Christian ideas of human depravity, the sovereignty of divine grace, and the need for a revelation from God, they also remained antagonistic to republican ideas. But, in Goldie's phrase, "wherever puritan thought leaned towards acceptance of the possibility of universal salvation and hence of universal priesthood, or to the Socinian idea that Christ was God-in-humanity, then Puritanism became as intensely secular and naturalistic as it was Biblical and Apocalyptic."[30] Most observers in the seventeenth and eighteenth centuries would have agreed. It was only when Christian orthodoxy gave way that republicanism could flourish.

A long line of distinguished modern historians—including Caroline Robbins on the English commonwealthmen, J. G. A. Pocock on Machiavelli, Paul Rahe on the republican traditions more generally, J. C. D. Clark on eighteenth-century English society, and J. B. Schneewind on the rise of moral philosophy—has documented the persistent link during the centuries before 1750 between political republicanism and such heterodox religious views as Socinianism, Arianism, Unitarianism, and atheism.[31] Of special note was the tie between republican views of human nature that transferred responsibility for the health of society from God to humanity and unorthodox views (whether Socinian or Arian) concerning the person of Christ. For the latter, Jesus was a good man and valuable for his example of personal morality, but he was not the son of God whose saving work opened the only door to human salvation.

An expressly religious suspicion of republican ideas continued widely in the new world. The American Samuel Johnson was outraged when Trenchard and Gordon's *Independent Whig* was reprinted in New York City at midcentury. To Johnson, as a traditional Anglican, the Real Whig arguments were "pernicious" outbursts from "famous infidel authors."[32] He was not alone in these opinions. Other New Yorkers accused the sponsors of the *Independent Reflector,* where Trenchard and Gordon were reprinted, of being atheists and noted that its publisher, James Parker, had been indicted for "blasphemous libel" against Christianity only shortly before reprinting these English Real Whig opinions.[33]

The long history of antagonism between republicanism and traditional Christianity therefore poses a major interpretive problem for students of American history, since, in the carefully chosen words of philosopher Charles Taylor, "for all the well-documented tensions between Christianity and the republican tradition, the United States starts its career by linking the two closely together."[34]

Suspicion of republican ideas as intrinsically antireligious did not fade easily. But when war with papist France broke out once again in the mid-1740s, the ideological situation underwent a dramatic change. In particular, republican convictions marched into the fortresses of Protestant thought under the familiar banner of anti-Catholicism.

In the crucible of imperial struggle a number of colonial ministers from across the theological spectrum began to link the fate of genuine Christianity to hopes for the future of liberty. Most of these ministers were from New England, but significant voices came also from other colonies. The Presbyterian Gilbert Tennent in New Jersey, for instance, hailed the reduction of Louisbourg as the rescue "of our civil and religious Liberties" from an enemy "who unweariedly labours to rob us of our civil and religious Liberties, and bring us into the most wretched vassalage to arbitrary Power and Church Tyranny."[35] In Virginia, it was probably William Stith, the Anglican chaplain of the Virginia House of Burgesses, who published two articles showing how biblical precedents helped explain the struggle of freedom and tyranny being played out in conflict between Britain and France.[36]

Yet as with most other areas of colonial thought, Puritan New England led here also in bringing together what had previously stood apart. The liberal Charles Chauncy of Boston was starting to mix once-separated categories by referring to the "Salvation" that God had secured for the colonies in the defeat of the French.[37] The theological moderate Nathaniel Walter of Roxbury went even further by finding biblical prototypes for the "good Commonwealth's Man" of New England who had fought so valiantly at Louisbourg. As Walter saw it, Moses was "the brave Soldier, expiring in the Cause of Liberty and Virtue." Even more strikingly, Jesus was one who had carried "every Virtue to the highest Pitch," including "that Devotedness to the publick Service, and those other Virtues which render Antiquity venerable."[38] An evangelical promoter of revivals, Thomas Prince, chimed in with Chauncy and Walter to employ a full "country" vocabulary in describing the conflict with France. Prince preached a memorable sermon at Boston's South Church on August 14, 1746, as part of a dual celebration. While continuing to rejoice over the colonists' triumph at Louisbourg, he was also responding joyously to news of the destruction of Bonnie Prince Charles's Highland, Roman Catholic army at the Battle of Culloden in the far north of Scotland earlier that same year. The printed version of Prince's sermon contained a sharply contrasting pair of definitions that came right out of the republican bible: Tories, according to Prince, were "for the absolute, hereditary, and unalienable Right of Kings . . . tho' they are *Papists* and rule *arbitrarily,* illegally, tyrannically and cruelly; and they are also for the *Persecution* of Protestant Dissenters." Whigs, by contrast, "are only for the hereditary Right of Kings . . . as long as they are *Protestants* and rule according to the *Laws*; but when they are *Papists* or *Tyrants,* then to set up the next *Protestant* of the *Royal Line,* who is like to govern legally and preserve the Constitution; they are also against *persecuting* any Protestant."[39]

Real Whig ideology had obviously arrived in America. Yet an older ideology was still more prominent in these sermons from the mid-1740s—hereditary, if now inflamed, anti-Catholicism. Phrases used by Massachusetts ministers Charles Chauncy and Joseph Sewall revived that spirit by referring to the pope as "Antichrist" and "the Man of Sin" as they rejoiced over the defeat of the French.[40] Several of their colleagues were only slightly less aggressively anti-Catholic.[41] Such anti-Catholic convictions were of great significance.[42] If the American colonists, especially orthodox and evangelical Protestants, were now innovating in beginning to rely on a republican picture of the world that their spiritual predecessors (as well as religious contemporaries outside the colonies) associated with heresy, the colonists' vigorous anti-Catholicism both maintained an older tradition and may have obscured innovations taking place in the use of a new political vocabulary.

It is important to stress again that the timing of these innovations was critical. Besides war with France, the other great circumstance of the 1740s throughout the colonies was rampant revival.[43] The affective preaching of George Whitefield and his many imitators produced spectacular results—from crowds of unprecedented size gathering to hear traveling preachers to unusually large additions to church membership rolls and a new sense of shared religious commitment linking partisans of the revival from Savannah, Georgia, to Portland, Maine. Yet for political history, one of the most significant consequences of this colonial Great Awakening was the collapse of New England's Puritan churches as the all-encompassing guardians of public ideology. In the wake of the revivals, New England's church-state establishments were drastically weakened. Substantial ecclesiastical parties—differentiated by degrees of enthusiasm for the Awakening—were now competing vigorously against each other. Despite holding on for nearly a century more in Massachusetts and almost that long in Connecticut and New Hampshire, the Puritan establishments would never recover their once nearly complete—and once welcomed—control of public life and thought. Republican discourse, in other words, became a significant influence in colonial religious discourse only when the grand experiment of the Puritans' godly commonwealths had suffered its most serious setback. The major revivalists had only the most marginal interest in grand political questions. Nonetheless, their work greatly altered the ideological, as well as the religious, landscape of the colonies, especially in New England. That work disabled the Puritans' vision of a unitive godly society. One of the resources immediately to hand for putting their world back together again was the republican promise of social order through virtuous public service. That resource was only the more useful when it also could explain the dynamics of warfare with France. Alasdair MacIntrye was not thinking of colonial American politics when he wrote about the function of radical political thought in the age of Enlightenment, but his words nevertheless apply directly to the American setting *in* war and *after* revival: "Republicanism in the eighteenth century *is* the project of restoring a community of virtue."[44]

The ideological transformation of colonial religious usage in 1745 and 1746 provides the necessary context for understanding why Jonathan Mayhew's sermon of January 30, 1749/50, *A Discourse Concerning Unlimited Submission and Non-Resistance to the Higher Powers*—with its potent blend of liberal religion, commonwealth politics, and fervent rhetoric—was such a sensation when first preached and has always been such a landmark for historians.[45] The way in which Mayhew's religious republicanism was typical became apparent once orthodox and evangelical clergymen began to weigh in with religious commentary after the renewal of hostilities against France in 1754.[46] During this new imperial crisis, the Real Whig vocabulary spread everywhere. It was, for example, already integral to the Connecticut Election Sermon of 1753—"Without Vice supprest, Vertue encouraged, and Learning promoted, a civil Government can't subsist long, the Foundations will sap, and the whole Frame of Government must fall."[47] In 1755 the Presbyterian Samuel Davies of Virginia preached the first of several stirring war sermons that dressed orthodox theology in the garments of Whig liberty. The ostensible purpose of the sermon was to exploit the calamities of war as an appeal for repentance and the new birth, but Davies's analysis of the war was thoroughly republican: "our religion, our liberty, our property, our lives, and everything sacred to us are in danger," especially of being "enslaved" by "an arbitrary, absolute monarch" enforcing conformity to "the superstition and idolatries of the church of Rome."[48] Although historians have focused mostly on New England as a center of religious republicanism in this period, the same conjunction was present elsewhere in the colonies as well.[49]

Several circumstances explain why evangelical and orthodox clergymen throughout the colonies deviated so readily from earlier Protestant patterns in embracing a republican analysis of the imperial wars with France. The sense of apocalyptic struggle between the forces of godly liberty and satanic slavery, which was a major theme in the revivalistic preaching of the 1740s, certainly played a role.[50] Almost as certainly, the unfolding of the French wars stoked hereditary Protestant fear of Catholicism and also linked that fear with a rising spirit of nationalism.[51] In addition, republicanism itself may have been losing its tinge of radicalism by the 1750s. Blair Worden has speculated that the influence of Montesquieu was moving some influential Englishmen to regard monarchy as compatible with republican government.[52] Students of the New Englanders' Louisbourg campaign of 1745 have also described its course as promoting secularization in a situation where increasing concern for the wider worlds of commerce, diplomacy, and war was edging out concerns for providence.[53] And because notions of virtue in the colonies had always been defined by religious standards, as opposed to the secular norms of English radicals, it was less of a step for colonists to unite secular and religious meanings of the term than was the case in Great Britain.[54]

Whatever the exact cause, by the end of active fighting against the French in 1760, an unusually strong bond had emerged in the American colonies between republican political ideology and traditional religious convictions. The crisis over the Stamp Act that followed immediately—and then the spiraling process of alienation from Britain—deepened, expanded, and sharpened American Christian republicanism. In particular, that process turned a rhetoric with British origins into a powerful protest against the British king and Parliament. But in ideological terms, the turn against Britain as villain represented only an extrapolation of what was already in place by 1760. The importance of the religious-republican synthesis was its usefulness for explaining so much of how the world seemed to be working for so many Americans—whether Protestant, deist, or nonreligious—over the last third of the eighteenth century. Specifically religious events, like protests over plans for a colonial Anglican bishop, which increased throughout the 1760s, or over the Quebec Act of 1774, reinforced the plausibility of the republican categories. It was not, however, conflict with Britain over specifically religious matters that encouraged colonial Protestants to accept Real Whig republicanism; rather, the mingling of what had been previously antagonistic concepts took place in the traumas of war with France well before overt hostility flamed against the mother country.

BROADENING THE NEW ALLIANCE IN THE REVOLUTIONARY PERIOD AND BEYOND

When viewed "from below," from the perspective of contingent religious events, the course of American ideology from approximately 1765 to 1835 features the following developments:

- The merger of Protestant convictions about providence, covenant, and virtue with secular convictions about liberty, rights, and virtue, which had once been only occasional and adventitious, became ubiquitous and systemic.
- That merger proved exceedingly useful for many projects, both religious and political.
- The content of the political convictions taken up by Protestants remained strongly republican, but always included healthy components of Lockean

principle; that content also shifted over the course of these decades from a more classical republicanism toward a more liberal republicanism.

• When the new nation's religious makeup changed dramatically from the 1780s with the rise of populist evangelical movements (especially Methodists, Baptists, and Restorationists), the merger of secular politics and Protestant beliefs was strengthened in ways that followed the trajectory of religious-political confluence in the revolutionary era.

Brief exposition of these developments cannot hope to take the measure of a complex period of rapid change in United States history, but they can prepare the way for concluding reflections on how Michael Zuckert's "Natural Rights and Protestant Politics" has advanced consideration of ideological commitments in the founding era.[55]

During and after the war for independence, a wide range of Americans joined together Protestant Christian beliefs and secular political convictions as they were joined nowhere else in the world. Presbyterian Elias Boudinot of New Jersey was Washington's commissary of prisoners during the war, a president of the Continental Congress, director of the mint, and the first president of the American Bible Society. In an address for the Fourth of July, 1793, Boudinot propounded what had become a standard interpretation: the war for independence, "our miraculous deliverance from a second Egypt," had made "freedom and independence . . . the most invaluable gem of our earthly crown" and established "the rational equality and rights of men, as men and citizens." Boudinot's hope for the future was expressed as an injunction to his audience that compounded religious and republican imperatives: "On your virtue, patriotism, integrity, and submission to the laws of your own making, and the government of your own choice, do the hopes of men rest with prayers and supplications for a happy issue."[56]

Benjamin Rush (1745–1813), a leading Philadelphia physician, a signer of the Declaration of Independence, and a tireless reformer, maintained close connections to Presbyterian interests throughout a long life of spiritual searching. As a young adult Rush was trained in revivalistic New Side Presbyterianism; at the age of 20 he also rejoiced in the efforts by Philadelphians to repudiate the Stamp Tax and so "to put a stop to arbitrary power."[57] Rush journeyed to Europe (first Edinburgh, then London and Paris) for medical training, where he also undertook a parallel education in dissenting politics. Through systematic reading of Algernon Sidney, hero of resistance to the Catholic James II in the 1680s, and conversation with several of the major republican figures of his era—Tom Paine, John Wilkes, Catherine Macaulay, James Burgh, Joseph Priestley, Adam Ferguson, and the Frenchman Jacques

Barbeu Dubourg—Rush's republican leanings expanded into settled convictions.[58] In the crucible of revolutionary America, Rush's political and religious faiths became one. From the mid-1770s into the early nineteenth century, no one in North America was more eloquent in advocating a Christian republican synthesis. Rush wrote to John Adams in July 1789, "The precepts of the Gospel and the maxims of republics in many instances agree with each other." Two years later he expressed the same to the Baptist minister Elhanan Winchester: "Republican forms of government are the best repositories of the Gospel." To Thomas Jefferson in 1800, Rush was even more emphatic: "I have always considered Christianity as the *strong ground* of republicanism. The spirit is opposed, not only to the splendor, but even to the very forms of monarchy, and many of its precepts have for their objects republican liberty and equality as well as simplicity, integrity, and economy in government. It is only necessary for republicanism to ally itself to the Christian religion to overturn all the corrupted political and religious institutions in the world." In 1775 Rush had supplied Tom Paine with the title for his tract, *Common Sense,* and arranged for its publication. Never once did Rush doubt that his promotion of Paine's radical republicanism was a specifically Christian deed. As he wrote to Granville Sharp in England in 1783: the "language" of American independence "has for many years appeared to me to be the same as that of the heavenly host that announced the birth of the Saviour of mankind. It proclaims 'glory to God in the highest—on earth peace—good will to man.'"[59] Rush put matters as clearly as they could be put, but he was joined in such sentiments by a very wide range of influential leaders among Americans of many different denominational persuasions.[60]

In such expressions, republican themes of liberty as the fruit of virtue, tyranny as the product of vice, and social well-being as incompatible with arbitrary power were more prominent than the Lockean themes of natural rights, social contract, and civic individualism, but the former by no means excluded the latter.

The Protestant politics of the revolutionary era was never an abstract project, but always attuned to the demands of circumstance. Tom Paine's *Common Sense* from 1776 is probably the most famous instance where a radical politician self-consciously enlisted scriptural themes familiar to Bible-reading Protestants in order to make his case against the British Parliament. Paine's skill at marshaling biblical narratives for republican ends was masterful, as in the following précis of ancient Jewish history:

Near three thousand years passed away from the Mosaic account of the creation, till the Jews under a national delusion requested a king. Till then their form of government (except in extraordinary cases, where the Almighty interposed) was a kind of republic administered by a judge and the elders of the tribes. . . . And when a man seriously reflects on the idolatrous homage which is paid to the persons of kings, he need not wonder that the Almighty, ever jealous of his honor, should disapprove of a form of government which so impiously invades the prerogative of heaven.[61]

Even if Paine's religious convictions strayed far from historic Protestant orthodoxy, he gauged exactly the power that deploying standard Protestant resources would add to his political appeal.

The interchange could also work in the other direction. When in the early 1770s the Baptist Isaac Backus published appeals for religious liberty aimed at Massachusetts and its monopolistic Congregational establishment, he enlisted "the dearest of all liberties, LIBERTY OF CONSCIENCE," to bolster that appeal.[62] Similarly, during and after the war itself, a number of revivalistic Protestants, including several disciples of Jonathan Edwards like Levi Hart of Connecticut and Samuel Hopkins of Rhode Island, self-consciously deployed the secular language of tyranny, natural rights, slavery, and liberty to mount an attack on slavery that arose in the first instance from their theological convictions.[63]

The Presbyterian Jacob Green of New Jersey, another student of Jonathan Edwards, who had also traveled with George Whitefield, perfected this way of attacking slavery. To Green, republican discourse was ideal for promoting what was at root a Christian reform: "it is demonstrable that . . . slave holders are friends to slavery, ergo are enemies to liberty, ergo are enemies to our present struggle for liberty, ergo are enemies to these United States. . . . These slavish slave holders will watch for an opportunity to establish slavery and bondage in the United States: ergo they will, as they have the opportunity, join with our enemies who are attempting this same thing. . . . [Slave holders are] tories of the worst sort."[64]

By merging the spheres of sacred and secular thinking, both political actors and religious reformers gained broader purchase for their arguments. In the process they also solidified the bond between those spheres.

Testimony to the solidity of the merger of republican and Christian thinking abounded on every side in the early decades of the republic. The classic expression was George Washington's Farewell Address of 1796. This address was a primer in classical republicanism, with warnings about the dangerous public effects of passion, praise for the Constitution as "sacredly maintained," and cautions against standing armies and political factions. Reminding his fellow Americans of the way religion supported republics was central to

Washington's purpose: "Can it be, that Providence has not connected the permanent felicity of a Nation with its virtue?" For maintaining that virtue, Washington evoked religion:

> Of all the dispositions and habits which lead to political prosperity, Religion and morality are indispensable supports. . . . A volume could not trace all their connections with private and public felicity. . . . And let us with caution indulge the supposition, that morality can be maintained without religion. . . . 'Tis substantially true, that virtue or morality is a necessary spring of popular government.[65]

Religious leaders remained just as eager as Washington to use the mingled categories of secular political analysis and traditional Protestant belief. By the early decades of the nineteenth century, it had become a matter of routine for American believers of many types to speak of such values with a single voice. In 1816, the radical populist Elias Smith, whose movement, the "Christian Connection," existed to protest the corruption of traditional denominations, published a manifesto. The Connection, Smith averred, stood for "One God—one Mediator—one lawgiver—one perfect law of Liberty—one name for the children of God, to the exclusion of all sectarian names—A Republican government, free from religious establishments and state clergy—free enquiry—life and immortality brought to light through the gospel."[66] In 1822, James Smith, a former Methodist minister who on seeing the light of Unitarian faith had abandoned the ministry, wrote on religious matters to Thomas Jefferson. Smith reported that he had given up on "priestly" religion but had found "shelter under the mild and peaceable Gospel of Jesus Christ, the most perfect model of Republicanism in the Universe."[67] Only a few years later, a well-educated, conservative Presbyterian clergyman, John Breckinridge, who regarded Elias Smith's ecclesiastical democracy and James Smith's Unitarianism with equal disdain, nonetheless joined them in linking Christian truth and republican liberty. Breckinridge noted the way in which similar words hid contrasting realities: "What do the *rights of man* mean, at Vienna, or St. Petersburg? What does *sovereign* mean in America? . . . What does freedom, or liberty of the press, or Christianity mean at Rome, at this day? Our freedom is our peculiarity, as it is our glory."[68] In sum, the strength of a Protestantized politics in the early United States arose from its utility for both political and religious leaders.

The specifically political contribution to the regnant American ideology was always a melange of themes. That melange is nowhere better illustrated than by the proclamation issued on November 1, 1777, by the Continental

Congress to fix a day of public thanks for the recent victory at Saratoga. Samuel Adams, who composed the resolution, expertly wove together Lockean, republican, and Christian themes into a single powerful statement. The resolution began by reminding the colonists that it was "the indispensable duty of all men to adore the superintending providence of Almighty God; to acknowledge with gratitude their obligation to him for benefits received, and to implore such farther blessings as they stand in need of." But it went on to say that similar adoration was due to God for his providential aid "in the prosecution of a just and necessary war, for the defense and establishment of our unalienable rights and liberties." Congress was calling the people to prayer on the eighteenth of December, so that they might "consecrate themselves to the service of their divine benefactor; and . . . join the penitent confession of their manifold sins, whereby they had forfeited every favour, and their humble and earnest supplication that it may please God, through the merits of Jesus Christ, mercifully to forgive and blot them out of remembrance." Congress also asked the people to pray for material prosperity, but ended by stressing the need to cultivate "the principles of true liberty, virtue and piety, under his nurturing hand, and to prosper the means of religion for the promotion and enlargement of that kingdom which consisteth 'in righteousness, peace and joy in the Holy Ghost'."[69] Whatever the degree of religious sincerity among the congressmen who passed this resolution, they successfully reassured most traditional Protestants that in the new United States republican allegiance did not subvert true religion.

That same mixing of intellectual traditions became even stronger as the decades wore on. In 1789 Alexander Hamilton could quip that there was no reference to God in the Constitution simply because the framers forgot to put one in.[70] Fifty years later political parties, like the Whigs, who embodied a general Protestant ethos, and the Anti-Masonic, Liberty, and American parties which were founded on specific planks from an evangelical Protestant creed, were winning elections throughout New England and the mid-Atlantic states.[71] After only a few more years, Abraham Lincoln, though himself not a church member, was quoting the scriptures—in a way unimaginable from the nation's earliest presidents—in order to draw the nation back together after the Civil War.[72]

My own sense after thirty years of reading religious and political publications from the revolutionary, early national, and antebellum period is that while the ingredients of American political religion remained constant, a shift took place in the proportion of ingredients. The religious-political discourse of the revolution had joined classical republican themes of disinterested public service to late-Puritan themes of God-oriented public duty.[73] After the first years of the war, however, an overwhelming preponderance of carefully sifted historical evidence points to the fact that American ideology was shifting toward ways of thought that accommodated commercial expansion, economic and political rights, and the fulfillment of the individual self. That is, classical republican views gradually yielded more place to Lockean principle and the practices of democratic individualism. When and how rapidly that shift took place does remain a historically contested question. A few historians date the transition as early as the 1760s, a few during the Revolutionary War itself, more in the years immediately following that conflict, and still more in the early years of the nineteenth century.[74] John Murrin's discussion of the historiographical situation summarizes clearly the points of consensus, as well as the lingering disagreements: Virtually all students "have insisted . . . that there was a transition, a before and after. We do not believe that America was born modern [i.e., liberal]. . . . We probably do agree that the shift to modernity was virtually complete by the 1820s, but no doubt we can still quarrel about how it happened, among whom, and why."[75] Yet this shift was one of emphasis. Lockean accounts of natural rights were present all along; the classical republican account of disinterested public virtue never passed away.

Once it is understood that America's increasing liberalism did not necessarily obliterate a broad commitment to republican values—in other words, that a simple antithesis between republicanism and liberalism is a modern construct rather than a historical reality—much else becomes clear about the early national period. Americans of almost all political convictions did embrace stronger notions of individual rights, and most of them also wanted to see the powers of government limited to at least some degree. But these commitments did not represent a repudiation of the republican heritage of the revolutionary era. Rather, as Daniel Walker Howe has put it, "Liberalism, far from being a threatening rival to republicanism, became in fact its welcome ally in the task of making free government work."[76] John Murrin skillfully subverts the convention that republicanism and liberalism had to be opposing forces as he makes the same historical point. In an analysis of why concern for corruption was so great in the early United States, Murrin concedes that "we surely ought to see republicanism as the recessive and liberalism as the dominant configuration by 1815." Yet he also insists that "we cannot even begin to make sense of the content of public life unless we see the two as a continuing dichotomy." Murrin argues that "Without continuing acceptance of republican values, corruption would not have become a serious issue, much less an obsession, in an environment that was rapidly becoming more participatory and democratic." The result was a situation where actions did not square easily with ideology, but where both were inextricably woven together: "As Jefferson should have said, 'We are all republicans; we are all liberals.' Republicanism remains the political conscience of a liberal society."[77]

Finally, it is important to understand that the great evangelical resurgence that began in the 1780s and lasted until after the Civil War replaced the prevailing Puritan and Enlightenment Protestantism of the 1760s and 1770s with a much more activistic, pietistic, biblicistic, entrepreneurial (though still Enlightenment) form of Protestantism.[78] Yet this new brand of religion reconfirmed in strongest terms the political religion that less evangelical minds had first promoted in the years before and during the revolution. In fact, it was probably the later evangelicals who made the founders' earlier vision of a virtuous republic actually work.

The major founding fathers, though they differed among themselves on many questions of religion as well as politics, did come to a basic agreement on the place of religion in society. A fine recent book by John G. West, for example, documents a wide range of agreement on such questions among John Jay and John Witherspoon, who were evangelicals in something like the modern sense of the term; James Wilson and Alexander Hamilton, whose attachment to Christian orthodoxy fluctuated; George Washington and James Madison, who shared devotion to the republic and an extreme reticence about disclosing their personal religious beliefs; and Benjamin Franklin, John Adams, and Thomas Jefferson, deists or Unitarians who, if only for pragmatic reasons, did not rule out public activities by more traditional believers.[79] All of these major founders wanted the new United States to promote religious liberty and none wanted the national government to dictate religious beliefs or practices. They were thoroughly committed to the radical innovation of separating church and state. Yet the founders also agreed among themselves that disestablished religion had an important part to play in the new republic.

The surprising degree of agreement among those whose own religious convictions differed so considerably rested on two shared assumptions: first, that the moral goods promoted by the churches largely coincided with the moral goods promoted by the government, and, second, that the churches had a role to play in making the moral calculus of republicanism actually work.

This moral calculus of republicanism was an extraordinarily significant assumption for many Americans, religious and nonreligious alike. As the calculus was expressed in the first century of the United States, it held that religion could and should contribute to the morality that was necessary for the virtuous citizens without which a republic could not survive. The practical challenge inherited from the founding era was how a new kind of church, which had given up the rights of establishment, might insert itself as a promoter of morality into a public sphere from which the old form of establishments had been excluded by the founders' commitment to religious freedom.

A magisterial interpretation of the relationship appeared in Supreme Court Justice Joseph Story's *Commentaries on the Constitution* of 1833. Story fully supported the separation of church and state as defined by the First Amendment, but he also took for granted that "The promulgation of the great doctrines of religion," which included cultivation of "all the personal, social, and benevolent virtues," could "never be a matter of indifference in any well ordered community." So fundamental did Story consider the relationship between religion and the health of American society that he was prepared to make a further assertion: "Indeed, in a republic, there would seem to be a peculiar property in viewing the Christian religion, as the great basis, on which it must rest for its support and permanence, if it be, what it has ever been deemed by its truest friends to be, the religion of liberty."[80] This judgment was representative of the vast sweep of American public opinion of this era.

As the evangelical sects expanded in the early years after the Constitution, so also did they rise to the challenge of promoting republican morality. Although evangelicalism in a recognizably modern form contributed only slightly to fashioning the basic guidelines for church-state and religious-social interaction in the founding generation, Methodists, Baptists, Presbyterians, Congregationalists, and many members of other churches nonetheless committed themselves wholeheartedly to the republican calculus as defined by the founders. In fact, evangelical eagerness to baptize the founders' framework for religious-political interaction became part of the more general process by which they embraced the comprehensive logic of republican politics.

The ideological bartering that evangelicals accepted, though it may have been entered into unconsciously, had a very important consequence. By taking on a version of republicanism, evangelicals put themselves in position to offer their religion to the new nation as a competitor to the rational, moralistic faith of the founders. As it turned out, that struggle was almost no competition at all. The new wineskin of a republic without an established church was a secular creation, but the new wine that filled it was evangelical.

The success of evangelicals in shaping public morality for a disestablishmentarian republic was widely perceived at the time. Alexis de Tocqueville's comments are best known. As he perceived the American clergy, they "separate themselves carefully from all parties, and avoid contact with them with all the ardor of personal interest." As a result, "one cannot say that in the United

States religion exerts an influence on the laws or the details of public opinions, but it directs mores, and it is in regulating the family that it works to regulate the state."[81] De Tocqueville's conclusion on the matter followed exactly the prescriptions of the founders. What had intervened in the generation between Washington's death in 1799 and de Tocqueville's visit to the United States in the early 1830s was the dramatic expansion of the evangelical churches.

Domestic observers said the same thing. A writer in the *Christian Spectator* from 1829 posed a question about connections between religion and the American state. The response: "In the form of ecclesiastical alliances, nothing; but in its operation as a controlling, purifying power in the consciences of the people, we answer, it has every thing to do, it is the last hope of republics; and let it be remembered, if ever our ruin shall come that the questions which agitate, the factions which distract, the convulsions which dissolve, will be but secondary causes: The true evil will lie back of these, in the moral debasement of the people."[82]

By the early nineteenth century evangelical Protestantism had become the unofficially established religion in a nation that had forsworn religious establishments. More ministers were agreeing with Ezra Stiles's assertion of 1783 that the blessings promised to Israel were "allusively prophetic of the future prosperity and splendor of the United States." When early in his presidential tenure Abraham Lincoln, even though he was not a church member, spoke of American citizens as God's "almost chosen people" and of United States freedom as "the last, best hope of the earth," he reflected not simply an extension of Stiles's opinions but their reconstitution in specifically evangelical terms.[83]

CONCLUSION

The account in this paper of Protestantism and the American founding is intended as an alternative rather than a contradiction of Michael Zuckert's "Natural Rights and Protestant Politics." My reading does see more place for a strong Christian republicanism in the founding era and thereafter, but not to the exclusion of Lockean emphases. It remains well attested that, as Zuckert puts it, "both Locke and the ministers 'tended to treat natural and revealed law as two consistent, complementary, and interdependent expressions of a single divine will.'" Yet as my essay suggests, it is also well attested that a secular language of republican virtue was also easily, swiftly, and massively infused with a language of Christian virtue.

Historical work by splitters, rather than overturning the work of systematizing lumpers, asks only for caution in treating the past and care in attempting to exploit the past for present purposes. The founding era of the United States was intellectually messy. No essentialist reading of its history—whether Lockean, republican, Enlightenment rationalist, or Protestant evangelical—can ever be faithful to the reality that actually took place. In addition, because they are preoccupied with the results of actions both foreseen and haphazard, historians insist upon full attention to the unpredictability of what actually happened. The Great Awakening, by altering the practice of religion, led to surprising changes in how religion and politics could be blended together. After colonial anti-Catholicism was inflamed by warfare with France, a new republican ideology was adopted in ways that could not have been predicted before war broke out. The events of the Revolution often outran the intentions of responsible agents and led to results that fit no one's preconceived principles. The American Constitution solved some obvious problems of the confederation era yet led to new ones that no one at Philadelphia in 1787 envisioned. Evangelical religion did not have to flourish in the wake of the Constitution's passage, but once it began to expand, an evangelical tone became all-important for the religious-political interchange. Attention to such events does not negate the value of attending to enduring principles, but it shows how important context has always been for the understanding, articulation, reception, and transmission of principles.

Similarly, a historian's insistence upon the messiness and the contingencies of the American founding era does not mean that the history of that era is irrelevant to current concerns. It means, rather, that every bit of the nuance necessary for understanding the past is equally necessary for putting the past to use in the present.

NOTES

1. J. H. Hexter, *On Historians: Reappraisals of Some of the Makers of Modern History* (Cambridge, Mass.: Harvard University Press, 1979), 241–43 (as part of an assessment of Christopher Hill as a "compulsive lumper").

2. This essay attempts a synthesis of material I have published in various forms, e.g., "The American Revolution and Protestant Evangelicalism," *Journal of Interdisciplinary History* 23. (Winter 1993): 615–38; "Presbyterians and the American Revolution,"

in *Dictionary of the Presbyterian and Reformed Tradition in America,* ed. D. G. Hart (Downers Grove, Ill.: InterVarsity Press, 1999), 18–20; and "Evangelicals in the American Founding and the Evangelical Political Mobilization Today," in *Religion and the New Republic: Faith in the Founding of America,* ed. James H. Hutson (New York: Rowman and Littlefield, 2000), 137–58. The essay's arguments abridge a presentation that is fully documented in *America's God, from Jonathan Edwards to Abraham Lincoln* (New York: Oxford University Press, 2002).

3. Louis Hartz, *The Liberal Tradition in America* (New York: Harcourt, Brace, 1955), 60, 62. Hartz and like-minded thinkers promoted this Lockean vision as a self-conscious alternative to a picture of the founders as motivated primarily by material self-interest. For Hartz's criticism of Charles A. Beard, the leading proponent of such a "progressive" interpretation, see ibid., 28–29.

4. Outstanding accounts of this historiography include the forum on Gordon Wood's *The Creation of the American Republic, 1776–1787* (Chapel Hill: University of North Carolina Press, 1969), in *William and Mary Quarterly* 44 (July 1987): 549–640; Daniel T. Rodgers, "Republicanism: The Career of a Concept," *Journal of American History* 79 (June 1992): 11–38; Joyce Appleby's essays collected in *Liberalism and Republicanism in the Historical Imagination* (Cambridge, Mass.: Harvard University Press, 1992); Paul A. Rahe, *Republics Ancient and Modern: Classical Republicanism and the American Revolution* (Chapel Hill: University of North Carolina Press, 1992); and several of the essays in *The Republican Synthesis Revisited,* ed. Milton M. Klein, Richard D. Brown, and John B. Hench (Worcester, Mass.: American Antiquarian Society, 1992), esp. the "Afterword" by Gordon Wood. For clear reports in media res, see Robert Shalhope, "Toward a Republican Synthesis: The Emergence of an Understanding of Republicanism in American Historiography," *William and Mary Quarterly* 29 (1972): 49–80; and Shalhope, "Republicanism and Early American Historiography," *William and Mary Quarterly* 39 (1982): 334–56.

5. Bernard Bailyn, *The Ideological Origins of the American Revolution* (Cambridge, Mass.: Harvard University Press, 1967), 34.

6. Wood, *Creation of the American Republic,* 53.

7. J. G. A. Pocock, "States, Republics, and Empires: The American Founding in Early Modern Perspective," in *Conceptual Change and the Constitution,* eds., Terence Ball and J. G. A. Pocock (Lawrence: University Press of Kansas, 1988), 64, 65.

8. An important work that sided with Appleby and Kramnick in reasserting the dominance of liberalism in the founding, but which did so in order to attack the self-destructive immorality of that liberalism, was John Patrick Diggens, *The Lost Soul of American Politics: Virtue, Self-Interest, and the Foundations of Liberalism* (Chicago: University of Chicago Press, 1984). A different kind of reassertion of Lockeanism in the founding era was presented by political theorists, sometimes influenced by Leo Strauss, who have attacked the way in which historians relativized political principles in specific historical contexts—e.g., Thomas Pangle, *The Spirit of Modern Republicanism: The Moral Vision of the American Founders and the Philosophy of Lock* (Chicago: University of Chicago Press, 1988).

9. Isaac Kramnick, "Republican Revisionism Revisited," in *Republicanism and Bourgeois Radicalism: Political Ideology in Late Eighteenth-Century England and America* (Ithaca, N.Y.: Cornell University Press 1990), 170.

10. Joyce Appleby, "Republicanism in Old and New Contexts," in *Liberalism and Republicanism*, 337.

11. Appleby, "Liberalism and the American Revolution," in *Liberalism and Republicanism*, 144.

12. Wood, "Afterword," in *Republican Synthesis Revisited*, 145. Other statements of roughly the same conclusion include Pocock, communication to the editor, *William and Mary Quarterly* 45 (Oct. 1988): 815; Pocock, "States, Republics, and Empires," 65; and Pocock, *Virtue, Commerce, and History* (Cambridge, Eng.: Cambridge University Press, 1985), 266–72. For an early statement about this ideological complexity for the 1780s and 1790s, see Bernard Bailyn, "The Central Themes of the American Revolution: An Interpretation," in *Essays on the American Revolution*, eds. Stephen G. Kurtz and James H. Hutson (Chapel Hill: University of North Carolina Press, 1973), 19. For the same judgment from a perspective outside the United States, see Denis Lacorne, "Les infortunes de la vertu," in *L'Amérique et la France: deux révolutions*, ed. Élise Marienstras (Paris: Orbonne, 1990), 115.

13. Alan Craig Houston, *Algernon Sidney and the Republican Heritage in England and America* (Princeton: Princeton University Press, 1991); Michael P. Zuckert, *Natural Rights and the New Republicanism* (Princeton: Princeton University Press, 1994); John Dunn, "The Politics of Locke in England and America in the Eighteenth Century," in *John Locke: Problems and Perspectives*, ed. John W. Yolton (Cambridge, Eng.: Cambridge University Press, 1969), 45–80, esp. 78–80.

14. Richard B. Morris, "The Judeo-Christian Foundation of the American Political System," in *James Madison on Religious Liberty*, ed. Robert S. Alley (Buffalo, N.Y.: Prometheus, 1985), 112.

15. Kramnick, "'The Great National Discussion,'" in *Republicanism and Bourgeois Radicalism*, 261.

16. John M. Murrin, "Religion and Ideological Change in the American Revolution," in *Religion and American Politics From the Colonial Period to the 1980s*, ed. Mark A. Noll (New York: Oxford University Press, 1990), 27.

17. For example, Forrest McDonald, *Novus Ordo Seclorum: The Intellectual Origins of the Constitution* (Lawrence: University Press of Kansas, 1985).

18. See, as examples, Ruth Bloch, *Visionary Republic: Millenial Themes in American Thought, 1756–1800* (New York: Cambridge University Press, 1985), 3–4; James T. Kloppenberg, "The Virtues of Liberalism: Christianity, Republicanism, and Ethics in Early American Political Discourse," *Journal of American History* 74 (June 1987): 12–14; Rodgers, "Republicanism," 17–27; J. C. D. Clark, *The Language of Liberty, 1660–1832: Political Discourse and Social Dynamics in the Anglo-American World* (Cambridge, Eng.: Cambridge University Press, 1994), 21–22; Barry Shain, *The Myth of American Individualism: The Protestant Origins of American Political Thought* (Princeton: Princeton Univer-

sity Press, 1994), xv–xvi; and several of the essays in the *William and Mary Quarterly* forum (vol. 44, July 1987) on Gordon Wood's *Creation of the American Republic,* including Ruth Bloch, "The Constitution and Culture," 554; John Howe, "Gordon S. Wood and the Analysis of Political Culture in the American Revolutionary Era," 571–72; J. T. Main, "An Agenda for Research on the Origins and Nature of the Constitution of 1787–1788," 594–95; and Wood, "Ideology and the Origins of Liberal America," 637.

19. For example, Bloch, *Visionary Republic*; Patricia U. Bonomi, *Under the Cope of Heaven: Religion, Society, and Politics in Colonial America* (New York: Oxford University Press, 1986); Shain, *Myth of American Individualism*; Clark, *Language of Liberty*; John G. West, Jr., *The Politics of Revelation and Reason: Religion and Civic Life in the New Nation* (Lawrence: University Press of Kansas, 1996); James H. Hutson, *Religion and the Founding of the American Republic* (Washington, D.C.: Library of Congress, 1998); Christopher Grasso, *A Speaking Aristocracy: Transforming Public Discourse in Eighteenth-Century Connecticut* (Chapel Hill: University of North Carolina Press, 1999); Derek H. Davis, *Religion and the Continental Congress, 1774–1789: Contributions to Original Intent* (New York: Oxford University Press, 2000); and Hutson, ed., *Religion and the New Republic.*

20. See especially Patricia U. Bonomi, "Religious Dissent and the Case for American Exceptionalism," in *Religion in a Revolutionary Age,* eds. Ronald Hoffman and Peter J. Albert (Charlottesville: University Press of Virginia, 1994), 31–51; T. H. Breen, *The Character of the Good Ruler: Puritan Political Ideas in New England, 1630–1730* (New Haven: Yale University Press, 1970), chap. 7, "The Country Persuasion"; and Carl Bridenbaugh, *Mitre and Sceptre: Transatlantic Faiths, Ideas, Personalities, and Politics, 1689–1775* (New York: Oxford University Press, 1962).

21. Edmund Burke, "Speech on Conciliation with America," in *The Debate on the American Revolution, 1761–1783,* ed. Max Beloff (2nd ed., London: A. & C. Black, 1960), 208.

22. Cotton Mather, *Optanda: Good Men Described and Good Things Propounded* (Boston: Benjamin Harris, 1692), 32, 33, 86. For outstanding discussion of the political circumstances of this sermon, see Harry S. Stout, *The New England Soul: Preaching and Religious Culture in Colonial New England* (New York: Oxford University Press, 1986), 120–21.

23. For a thorough discussion, see Breen, *Character of the Good Ruler,* 251–61.

24. *Boston News-Letter,* Aug. 21, 1721, as quoted in Breen, *Character of the Good Ruler,* 263.

25. Richard L. Bushman, *King and People in Provincial Massachusetts* (Chapel Hill: University of North Carolina Press, 1985), 255, with Bushman's entire "Appendix: Country Party Rhetoric in Massachusetts," 253–67, an insightful discussion.

26. See Gerald R. McDermott, *One Holy and Happy Society: The Public Theology of Jonathan Edwards* (University Park: Penn State University Press, 1992), 31–32 (with citations from Edwards's unpublished sermons).

27. For other examples from New England, see Samuel Checkley, *Prayer a Duty, when God's People Go Forth to War* (Boston: B. Green, 1745); Thomas Prentice, *A Sermon*

Preached at Charlestown, on a General Thanksgiving, July 18 1745 (Boston: Rogers and Fowle, 1745); Thomas Prince, *Extraordinary Events the Doings of God* (Boston: D. Henchman, 1745); Samuel Niles, *A Brief and Plain Essay on God's Wonder-working Providence for New-England, In the Reduction of Louisbourg* (New London, Conn.: T. Green, 1747); Jared Eliot, *God's Marvellous Kindness Illustrated* (New London, Conn.: T. Green, 1745); and Joseph Sewall, *The Lamb Slain, Worthy to be Praised* (Boston: D. Henchman, 1745).

28. See especially Blair Worden, "Providence and Politics in Cromwellian England," *Past and Present* 109 (November 1985): 55–99.

29. An outstanding accounting of the Puritans' restrained enthusiasm is found in John Morgan, *Godly Learning: Puritan Attitudes towards Reason, Learning and Education, 1560–1640* (New York: Cambridge University Press, 1986).

30. Mark Goldie, "The civil religion of James Harrington," in Anthony Pagden, *Languages of Political Theory in Early Modern Europe* (Cambridge: Cambridge University Press, 1990), 203. After the American Revolution, Ezra Stiles, president of Yale College and an esteemed Congregationalist minister, had lost all sense that Harrington's ideas posed a threat to religious orthodoxy. In his view, the new United States had "realized the capital ideas of Harrington's *Oceana*." Stiles, *The United States Elevated to Glory and Honor* (New Haven: T. & S. Green, 1783), 8.

31. Caroline Robbins, *The Eighteenth-Century Commonwealthman: Studies in the Transmission, Development and Circumstance of English Liberal Thought from the Restoration of Charles II until the War with the Thirteen Colonies* (Cambridge, Mass.: Harvard University Press, 1959), 6, 222; J. G. A. Pocock, *The Machiavellian Moment: Florentine Political Thought and the Atlantic Republican Tradition* (Princeton: Princeton University Press, 1975), 133, 202, 213, 399, 462, 550; Rahe, *Republics,* 220–29, 264, 302–3, 485; J. B. Schneewind, *The Invention of Autonomy: A History of Modern Moral Philosophy* (New York: Cambridge University Press, 1998), 308–9; J. C. D. Clark, *English Society, 1688–1832* (Cambridge, Eng.: Cambridge University Press, 1985); Clark, *The Language of Liberty: Political Discourse and Social Dynamics in the Anglo-American World* (New York: Cambridge University Press, 1994), with 38–40, a succinct summary of the major argument of Clark's two books.

32. David L. Jacobson, "Introduction" to selections from *The Independent Whig,* in *The English Libertarian Heritage* (Indianapolis: Liberty, 1965), liv.

33. Milton M. Klein, "Introduction," *The Independent Reflector . . . By William Livingston and Others* (Cambridge, Mass.: Harvard University Press, 1963), 18 (quotation from Klein), 19 (unattributed quotation from period).

34. Charles Taylor, "Religion in a Free Society," in *Articles of Faith, Articles of Peace: The Religious Liberty Clauses and the American Public Philosophy,* eds. James Davison Hunter and Os Guinness (Washington, D.C.: Brookings Institution, 1990), 101.

35. Gilbert Tennent, *The Necessity of Praising God for Mercies Receiv'd: A Sermon Occasion'd, By the Success of the Late Expedition* (Philadelphia: William Bradford, 1745), 7, 37.

36. Edmund S. Morgan, *American Slavery, American Freedom: The Ordeal of Colonial Virginia* (New York: W. W. Norton, 1975), 371–72.

37. Charles Chauncy, *Marvellous Things Done by the Right Hand and Holy Arm of God in Getting Him the Victory* (Boston: M. Cooper, 1745), 11.

38. Nathaniel Walter, *The Character of a True Patriot* (Boston: D. Henchman, 1745), 17, 10, 18.

39. Thomas Prince, *A Sermon Delivered at the South Church . . . Being the Day of General Thanksgiving for the Deliverance of the British Nations by the glorious and happy victory near Culloden* (Boston: S. Kneeland and T. Green, 1746), 20–21n.

40. Chauncy, *Marvellous Things,* 22; Sewall, *The Lamb Slain,* 32–33.

41. Tennent, *The Necessity of Praising God,* 37; Prince, *Extraordinary Events,* 34; Niles, *A Brief and Plain Essay,* 15–16.

42. For background, see especially Mary Augustina (Ray), B.V.M., *American Opinion of Roman Catholicism in the Eighteenth Century* (New York: Columbia University Press, 1936); and Charles P. Hanson, *Necessary Virtue: The Pragmatic Origins of Religious Liberty in New England* (Charlottesville: University Press of Virginia, 1998), 6–14.

43. The next paragraph summarizes material presented in my chapter, "The Long Life and Final Collapse of the Puritan Canopy," in *America's God.*

44. Alasdair MacIntyre, *After Virtue,* 2nd ed. (Notre Dame, Ind.: University of Notre Dame Press, 1984), 236.

45. An outstanding general treatment is Charles W. Akers, *Called Unto Liberty: A Life of Jonathan Mayhew, 1720–1766* (Cambridge, Mass.: Harvard University Press, 1964).

46. See especially Nathan O. Hatch, *The Sacred Cause of Liberty: Republican Thought and the Millennium in Revolutionary New England* (New Haven: Yale University Press, 1977), 21–54.

47. Ebenezer Devotion, *The Civil Ruler, a Dignify'd Servant of the LORD, but a Dying Man* (New London, Conn.: T. Green, 1753), 35.

48. Samuel Davies, "God the Sovereign of all Kingdoms" (March 5, 1755), in *Sermons on Important Subjects,* 3 vols. (4th American ed.; New York, 1828), 3:173.

49. For only a few of many more possible examples, see William Hobby, *The Happiness of a People, Having God for their Ally* (Boston: S. Kneeland, 1758); Ebenezer Devotion, *Fortitude, Love and a Sound Judgment, very needful Qualifications for the Christian Minister* (New Haven: James Parker, 1762); Aaron Burr, *A Discourse delivered at New-Ark, in New-Jersey. January 1, 1755. Being a Day set apart for solemn Fasting and Prayer, on Account of the late Encroachments of the French, and their Designs against the British Colonies in America* (New York: Hugh Gaine, 1755); and Samuel Finley, *The Curse of Meroz; or, The Danger of Neutrality; in the Cause of God, and our Country* (Philadelphia: James Chattin, 1757).

50. Bloch, *Visionary Republic,* 10–21.

51. Linda Colley, *Britons: Forging the Nation, 1707–1837* (New Haven: Yale University Press, 1992), 18–30, 328–32.

52. Blair Worden, "The Revolution of 1688–89 and the English Republican Tradition," in *The Anglo-Dutch Moment: Essays on the Glorious Revolution and its World Impact,* ed. Jonathan I. Israel (Cambridge, Eng.: Cambridge University Press, 1991), 268–69.

254 | *Mark A. Noll*

53. George A. Rawlyk, *Nova Scotia's Massachusetts, 1680–1784* (Kingston-Montreal: McGill-Queen's University Press, 1973), 174–75; and Douglas Edward Leach, *Roots of Conflict: British Armed Forces and Colonial Americans, 1677–1763* (Chapel Hill: University of North Carolina Press, 1986), 64–75.

54. This suggestion is advanced by Jack P. Greene, "The Concept of Virtue in Late Colonial British America," in *Virtue, Corruption, and Self-Interest: Political Values in the Eighteenth Century,* ed. Richard K. Matthews (Bethlehem, Pa.: Lehigh University Press, 1994), 35–42.

55. Works that have been especially important for shaping my sense of religious-political connections in this era include Daniel Walker Howe, *The Political Culture of the American Whigs* (Chicago: University of Chicago Press, 1979); Robert H. Wiebe, *The Opening of American Society* (New York: Knopf, 1984); Nathan O. Hatch, *The Democratization of American Christianity* (New Haven: Yale University Press, 1989); Gordon S. Wood, *The Radicalism of the American Revolution* (New York: Knopf, 1992); and Daniel Walker Howe, *Making the American Self: Jonathan Edwards to Abraham Lincoln* (Cambridge, Mass.: Harvard University Press, 1997).

56. Elias Boudinot, *The Life, Public Services, Addresses, and Letters of Elias Boudinot,* ed. J. J. Boudinot, 2 vols. (Boston: Houghton, Mifflin, 1896), 2:358, 341, 365.

57. *Letters of Benjamin Rush,* 2 vols., ed. L. H. Butterfield (Princeton: Princeton University Press, 1951), 1:18.

58. See the superb monograph by Donald J. D'Elia, *Benjamin Rush: Philosopher of the American Revolution,* Transactions of the American Philosophical Society, vol. 64, part 5 (Philadelphia, 1974), 20–51.

59. Rush to Adams, 21 July 1789; Rush to Winchester, 12 Nov. 1791; Rush to Jefferson, 22 Aug. 1800, in *Letters of Rush,* 1:523, 1:611, 2:820–21; and Rush to Sharp, 7 Apr. 1783, in "The Correspondence of Benjamin Rush and Granville Sharp, 1773–1809," *Journal of American Studies* 1 (April 1967): 17, as quoted in D'Elia, *Benjamin Rush,* 52.

60. For further examples of such views, see K. Alan Snyder, "Foundations of Liberty: The Christian Republicanism of Timothy Dwight and Jedidiah Morse," *New England Quarterly* 56 (1983): 382–97; Thomas F. Taylor, "Samuel E. McCorkle and a Christian Republic, 1792–1802," *American Presbyterians* 63 (Winter 1985): 375–85; Robert M. Calhoon, *Evangelicals and Conservatives in the Early South, 1740–1861* (Columbia: University of South Carolina Press, 1988), part II, "Revolution and Republic"; Fred J. Hood, *Reformed America, The Middle and Southern States, 1783–1837* (Tuscaloosa: University of Alabama Press, 1980); and Mark A. Noll, *Princeton and the Republic, 1768–1822* (Princeton: Princeton University Press, 1989), 8–9, 79–80, 200–205, 220–21.

61. Tom Paine, *Common Sense* (Garden City, N.Y.: Doubleday, 1960), 20.

62. Isaac Backus, *A Seasonable Plea for Liberty of Conscience Against Some Late Violent Proceedings* (1770), as quoted in William G. McLoughlin, *Isaac Backus and the American Pietistic Tradition* (Boston: Little, Brown, 1967), 122.

63. See Levi Hart, *Liberty Described and Recommended* (Hartford, Conn.: Ebenezer Watson, 1775; Samuel Hopkins, *A Dialogue concerning the Slavery of the Africans* (Nor-

wich, Conn.: Judah P. Spooner, 1776); and Hopkins, *A Discourse Upon the Slave-Trade, and the Slavery of the Africans* (Providence, R.I.: J. Carter, 1793).

64. Jacob Green, [Letter on Slavery], *New Jersey Journal,* Jan. 10, 1781.

65. "Farewell Address" (Sept. 19, 1796), George Washington, *Writings,* ed. John Rhodehamel (New York: Library of America, 1997), 972, 971.

66. Elias Smith, *Herald of Gospel Liberty,* 7, no. 181 (Dec. 22, 1815), 721, as quoted in Michael G. Kenny, *The Perfect Law of Liberty: Elias Smith and the Providential History of America* (Washington, D.C.: Smithsonian Institution Press, 1994), 232.

67. James Smith to Jefferson, 4 Nov. 1822, in *Jefferson's Extracts from the Gospels,* ed. Dickinson W. Adams, *The Papers of Thomas Jefferson, Second Series* (Princeton: Princeton University Press, 1983), 410.

68. John Breckinridge, *An Address, Delivered July 15, 1835, Before the Eucleian and Philomethean Society of the University of the City of New York* (New York, 1836), 34, as quoted in Hood, *Reformed America,* 48.

69. *Journal of the Continental Congress, 1774–1789,* vol. 9 (Oct. 3–Dec. 31, 1777) (Washington, D.C.: Government Printing Office, 1907), 854–55. For expert analysis of the Congress' religious proclamations, see Davis, *Religion and the Continental Congress.*

70. See Douglass Adair, "Was Alexander Hamilton a Christian Statesman?" in Adair, *Fame and the Founding Fathers,* ed. Trevor Colbourn (New York: W. W. Norton, 1974), 147–48 n8.

71. See particularly Howe, *Political Culture of the American Whigs*; and Allen C. Guelzo, *Abraham Lincoln: Redeemer President* (Grand Rapids: Eerdmans, 1999).

72. Gordon Wood's judgment is pertinent on the state of religion in the nation by this time, *Radicalism of the American Revolution,* 333: "Nowhere in Christendom had religion become so fragmented and so separated from society. Yet nowhere was it so vital. By the second quarter of the nineteenth century, the evangelical Protestantism of ordinary people had come to dominate American culture to an extent the founding fathers had never anticipated."

73. An older set of essays, which have been neglected but not refuted in recent scholarship, elaborates this conviction. See Charles W. Akers, "Calvinism and the American Revolution," in *The Heritage of John Calvin,* ed. John H. Bratt (Grand Rapids: Eerdmans, 1973), 158–176; Sacvan Bercovitch, "How the Puritans Won the American Revolution," *Massachusetts Review* 17 (1976): 597–630; Emory Elliott, "The Puritan Roots of American Whig Rhetoric," in *Puritan Influences in American Literature,* ed. Elliott (Urbana: University of Illinois Press, 1979), 107–27; and especially Edmund S. Morgan, "The Puritan Ethic and the American Revolution," *William and Mary Quarterly* 24 (Jan. 1967): 3–43.

74. The 1760s—Kramnick, "Republican Revisionism Revised," in *Republicanism and Bourgeois Radicalism,* 171. During the Revolutionary War—Drew R. McCoy, *The Elusive Republic: Political Economy in Jeffersonian America* (Chapel Hill: University of North Carolina Press, 1980), 66–72. Immediately after the Revolutionary War—Wood, *Radicalism of the American Revolution*; and Eve Kornfeld, "From Republicanism to Liberalism: The Intellectual Journey of David Ramsay," *Journal of the Early Republic* 9 (Fall 1989):

289–313. Late eighteenth century—Richard R. Beeman, "Deference, Republicanism, and the Emergence of Popular Politics in Eighteenth-Century America," *William and Mary Quarterly* 49 (July 1992): 401–30; and Michael Lienesch, *New Order of the Ages: Time, the Constitution, and the Making of Modern Political Thought* (Princeton: Princeton University Press, 1988). Early nineteenth century—Wiebe, *Opening of American Society,* 146; and Steven J. Ross, "The Transformation of Republican Ideology," *Journal of the Early Republic* 10 (Fall 1990): 323–30. In and because of the War of 1812—Steven Watts, *The Republic Reborn: War and the Making of Liberal America, 1790–1820* (Baltimore: Johns Hopkins University Press, 1987).

75. John M. Murrin, "Self-Interest Conquers Patriotism: Republicans, Liberals, and Indians Reshape the Nation," in *The American Revolution: Its Character and Limits,* ed. Jack P. Greene (New York: New York University Press, 1987), 226.

76. Howe, *Making the American Self,* 13; and for an excellent general argument along the same lines, ibid., 10–17.

77. John M. Murrin, "Escaping Perfidious Albion: Federalism, Fear of Aristocracy, and the Democratization of Corruption in Postrevolutionary America," in *Virtue, Corruption, and Self-Interest,* 138–39.

78. On that surge of evangelical religion, see Hatch, *Democratization of American Christianity*; Donald G. Mathews, *Religion in the Old South* (Chicago: University of Chicago Press, 1977); and Roger Finke and Rodney Start, "How the Upstart Sects Won America, 1776–1850," *Journal for the Scientific Study of Religion* 28 (March 1989): 27–44.

79. West, *The Politics of Revelation and Reason,* with 11–78 on the founding era, and the rest of the book a learned interpretation of evangelical politics in the period 1800–1835, with concentration on Sunday mails and Cherokee removal.

80. Joseph Story, *Commentaries on the Constitution of the United States* (1833; New York: Da Capo Press, 1970), vol. 3, sec. 1865, pp. 722–23, and sec. 1866, pp. 724–26.

81. Alexis de Tocqueville, *Democracy in America,* trans. and ed. Harvey C. Mansfield and Delba Winthrop (Chicago: University of Chicago Press, 2000), 278. See also, 280: "Religion, which among Americans, never mixes directly in the government of society, should therefore be considered as the first of their political institutions; for, if it does not give them the taste for freedom, it singularly facilitates their use of it."

82. Undocumented quotation in Perry Miller, *The Life of the Mind in America from the Revolution to the Civil War* (New York: Harcourt, Brace & World, 1965), 71.

83. Stiles, *United States Elevated to Glory and Honor,* 7. Lincoln, "Address to the New Jersey Senate" (Feb. 21, 1861), and "Annual Message to Congress" (Dec. 1, 1862), in *The Collected Works of Abraham Lincoln,* 9 vols., ed. Roy T. Basler (New Brunswick, N. J.: Rutgers University Press, 1953), 4:236, 5:537.

CHAPTER NINE

Natural Rights and Protestant Politics

A Restatement

Michael P. Zuckert

Attentive and open-minded readers might well come away from this collection of essays convinced that Mark Noll is correct when he says of the eighteenth century that it was "intellectually messy"; they might be tempted to apply that same judgment to the debate contained in the essays as well. The authors disagree with each other across a wide range of issues, including the central or thematic issue of the collection: What is the relationship between Protestant thought and the thought of the American founding? Although there are many tempting byways running off in one direction or the other, for the most part I will attempt to keep to this main highway in my restatement.

I particularly welcome the opportunity to attempt a restatement, for the assembled essayists have made clear that the menu of alternative answers I proposed in my original statement on the subject in chapter 1 stands in need of expansion in order to encompass the various positions taken in the essays. A restatement, moreover, gives me an occasion to reformulate and clarify my position, which was misunderstood to a degree by several of the essayists.

CONTINUITIES AND DISCONTINUITIES

In the book from which my essay in this volume was adapted I identified four positions in the literature on the nature of the relationship between the political thought of the first American founding era, the era of Pilgrims and

Puritans, and the political thought of the second founding era, the era of the Declaration of Independence and the Constitution.[1] At one extreme is the position I called strong continuity, the view that the Americans of 1776–1787 were drawing off and restating the political principles of the Americans of 1620–1630. At the other extreme is the minimal continuity thesis, described in its most uncompromising form by Tom West in chapter 7 of this volume as the position that holds that the principles of the founding, deriving from Enlightenment thinkers like John Locke, are not only independent from Christian theology, but are at root hostile to it. Let me rename this end of the continuum "strong discontinuity." Between those who straightforwardly affirm continuity and those who more or less entirely reject it lie two other important positions. One of these affirms continuity but sees the second American founding as a secularized version of the first. A fourth and sometimes overlapping thesis is the doctrine of eclectic continuity. This last position finds "the political and social theories of New England Puritanism" to be one among "several main sources of the ideas and attitudes of the Revolutionary generation."[2]

In the first chapter I concluded that the case for strong continuity was weak; although something can be said for each of the other positions, none of them seemed to capture the situation as well as a position I called the American amalgam, a complex pattern of thought according to which Protestant thinkers of the eighteenth century combined the essentials of Lockean political philosophy (as expressed in relatively pure form in the Declaration of Independence and other more secular statements) and more traditional Protestant positions.[3] My notion of an amalgam obviously has something in common with the fourth of the alternatives I identified in my survey of the chief positions taken in the literature. Like "eclectic continuity," the amalgam thesis affirms a mixing of disparate elements, but the mixture I have in mind has a good deal more structure to it than "eclectic continuity" posits. The Lockean element was not merely added on as miscellaneous bric-a-brac to a set of other views but filled a particular niche within a much more structured system of thought. In order to explain that particular niche I presented at some length Luther's doctrine of the Two Kingdoms. Luther's reformation of Christian doctrine extended to laying down the true principles of politics as he understood them from within the version of Christianity he accepted. Luther's politics were thus pure political theology, for they stemmed from his broader theological doctrine and depended on his grasp of the meaning of the Christian revelation. His politics did not follow from universal principles potentially available to all human beings regardless of their theological commitments. They were, he believed, the true political principles, following from the true principles of reformed Christianity.

Luther's view of Protestant politics did not sweep all before it, just as his broader version of reform theology did not. Others were perhaps even more apt to deviate from his politics than from other aspects of his thought. However, in one respect Luther set a stamp on Protestant political thought that did pretty well stick. I refer to the form of the doctrine of the Two Kingdoms itself, that is, to the notion that there are separate and different spheres of existence and sets of institutions to which different principles of operation belong. This distinction of spheres was meant to give the political sphere a certain independence from the religious sphere, and thus to elevate the dignity of the political at the same time that it kept the church out of the tempting, nay corrupting, business of secular governance. For Luther, the principles governing the two kingdoms were different from each other, but they were both firmly rooted in biblical teachings—he claimed no authority for his principles other than biblical texts. As he frequently said, it was a position dependent on "scripture alone"—*sola scriptura.*

Although succeeding generations and sects of Protestants, notably including Calvin and the offshoot movements of international Calvinism, significantly modified Luther's substantive political doctrine (and ecclesiology, and much else), nonetheless they retained for the most part the form of the doctrine of the Two Kingdoms. Even the Puritans, who, as I explain in my essay in chapter 1, were constantly tempted and more than occasionally succumbed to the temptation to move back toward the kind of theocratic positions Luther was especially eager to render illegitimate, even they formally adhered to the formal separation of state and ecclesiastical institutions.

The amalgam I describe is well understood as a modification of the Protestant two kingdoms idea. What is different about it, however, is that in place of a doctrine for the kingdom of this world drawn from biblical or specifically sectarian sources and premises is "liberal" social contract/natural rights philosophy. In a sense, then, the amalgam theory is like "eclectic continuity," but it has a quite specific structure to it that eclectic continuity normally does not have. The chief point of my essay was nothing other than to show that the amalgam I have just described came, over the course of a century and a half, to replace the original Puritan/Pilgrim political thought as expressed in places like the Mayflower Compact and John Winthrop's sermon on Christian Charity. My secondary goal was to seek some insight into how this amalgam came to be, a theme to which I shall return below.

Of the essays in the present volume, none takes the strong continuity position. Tom West takes a position that might be confused with it, but on the whole, however, his is different from any of my four original alternatives. I will call his position "evolutionary continuity": West insists that the political principles characteristic of the second founding are quite different from the principles of the first founding, but he maintains that the changes represent a natural evolution within Protestant thought, so that in the most important sense we do see continuity, but not of the sort affirmed in the strong continuity thesis.

The other essays fit rather well within the set of categories I initially extracted from the literature and thus do not require any further addition to the original typology. Mark Noll holds to eclectic continuity, for he finds eighteenth-century Protestant political thought to be a mixture of traditional Protestant and republican themes. He is more interested in tracing out the "contingencies," that is, the historical events, that led to the emergence of the mixture of Protestant and republican themes than with clearly articulating the character of the mixture itself. His relative inattention to the latter task makes it difficult to judge whether he is best understood as adhering to "eclectic continuity" or to a variant of the amalgam thesis. As it stands, his construal of the thought of the second founding era differs from my amalgam in two ways. Where I find Lockean political theory to be the politically significant element in the amalgam, he finds republicanism; where I attempt to provide a structured account of how the amalgam relates to traditional Protestant political thought, he leaves matters much looser. This last difference probably reflects, to a degree at least, the difference between us to which he forcefully calls attention near the beginning of his essay: he is a historian interested in contingency and fully at peace with the "messiness" of history. I am a political theorist, interested in (as he has it) "essentialisms," and apparently driven to find (or, he might say, impose) order on the world, no doubt more order than he thinks warranted.

Despite their provocative title, "The Godless Constitution," which suggests strong discontinuity, Isaac Kramnick and R. Laurence Moore are also best seen as adherents of the "eclectic continuity" thesis. They are eager to disprove strong continuity and the more extreme claims one hears from time to time about America being a "Christian nation," but their manner of doing so on the whole coheres better with eclectic continuity, or even with some form of the amalgam thesis, than with strong discontinuity. Consider their parting caveat: "The political convictions of the men who struggled to ratify a godless Constitution were not products of personal godlessness." That is, the makers and ratifiers of the Constitution combined an essentially secular or "godless" plan for the political order with other, more religious views.

Carey McWilliams finds that I understate "the peculiar harmonics of the American tradition," by which, I take it, he means that my account is on the whole correct but that I underestimate the continuing independence of and tension between the elements of the amalgam. The "biblical voice" or "the spirit of religion," while submerged or secondary to the secular, Lockean "spirit of liberty," nonetheless remains a distinct and oppositionist voice within the American political tradition. McWilliams, I conclude, therefore, hovers between minimal continuity (or strong discontinuity) and eclectic continuity.

Peter Lawler's essay is in certain respects the most difficult to classify of all, for he claims to argue in favor of the continuity thesis, but he does so by emphasizing that the most characteristic thought of the second founding is in fact completely distinct from the much sounder thought of the first founding, and behind that, of the Christian tradition of political thought all the way back to Aquinas or Augustine. He takes the view that our philosophic commitments (i.e., our views of what should happen) do and should shape our views of what did happen. His is a plea, therefore, that we *should* interpret the second founding so as to emphasize elements of continuity. He wishes to highlight "the philosophic necessity for taking the continuity seriously. . . . The American founding, at its best, *should be regarded* as a modification, not a rejection, of the nation's Christian natural-law inheritance" (emphasis added). That is how it should be regarded, but the actual thought Lawler finds there, for example, the thought of Thomas Jefferson, reveals far more discontinuity. I do not think it matters too much where we place Lawler, so long as we recognize that one aspect of his argument points to the continuity end of the continuum, while the other aspects point to the discontinuity end. I believe that the truly interesting things he has to say are those that relate to discontinuity claims, so that is the context in which I shall discuss him.

We might thus visualize the array of positions defended in this volume along the following continuum:

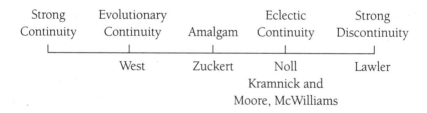

Strong Continuity	Evolutionary Continuity	Amalgam	Eclectic Continuity	Strong Discontinuity
	West	Zuckert	Noll	Lawler
			Kramnick and Moore, McWilliams	

In *The Natural Rights Republic* I identify many other scholars who may be located at the various positions on the continuum, but for present purposes it suffices to limit attention to those present here.

THE AMALGAM AND STRONG DISCONTINUITY

The partisans of strong discontinuity make an interesting and in some cases very far-reaching argument, but on reflection I do not find it persuasive. Before I can respond to it, however, I must attempt to correct a misunderstanding present in several of the essays: Lawler and West mistakenly attribute to me the strong discontinuity thesis. Lawler identifies the position I attribute to the second founders as a "clearly anti-Christian" view.[4] West claims my position is more subtle than that of some contemporary conservatives who deviated from the notion of the religious founding; he does notice that I explain the founding as "an amalgam or blend of two disparate traditions, Enlightenment reason and Protestant revelation," but he insists that at the end of the day my version of the second founding affirms "principles [that] are not only not religious but are at bottom indifferent or hostile to religion."

I trust I have already made clear what the difference is between the amalgam thesis to which I adhere and the strong discontinuity doctrine West and Lawler attribute to me. Lawler understands my position as he does because he believes Locke is hostile to Christianity and thus incompatible with it. West places me as he does because he believes I read Locke in that way, even though read properly (in his way) Locke is not only not hostile to Protestant Christianity but is himself a Protestant theologian. Although there is much to take issue with in West's account, nonetheless we are in agreement on the fact that the empirics of the situation in eighteenth-century America do not on their face come anywhere close to corroborating the view that Locke or Lockeans were hostile to Christianity or to religion in general. *The* striking fact is just what I attempted to capture in my notion of an amalgam—the Protestant clergy spoke "Lockean" when they talked politics (sometimes with attribution, sometimes not). In *The Natural Rights Republic,* moreover, I cite many other scholars of the period who emphasize just this same phenomenon. Locke was there, he was absorbed by the clergy, and he was not seen by them as hostile to their Christian commitments.

West claims I read Locke as hostile to religion on the basis of a sentence he quotes from *The Natural Rights Republic:* "When Zuckert says bluntly . . . that the principles of the American founding lead necessarily to 'the essentially secular character of the society,' he suggests that those principles are not only not religious but are at bottom indifferent or hostile to religion." West has mistaken the "suggestion" in my sentence, which might perhaps have better read, "the essentially secular character of the polity," a point I thought tolerably clear from the immediate sequel in *The Natural Rights Republic:* "the rights doctrine" implies "the embrace of the idea that liberty . . . not salvation forms the legitimate *end of the liberal state*" (emphasis added). That is, I was speaking of political society or the state, and not of society as such. I had made it clear in many places that neither Locke nor Jefferson nor I expected or sought the "withering away of religion" in the modern liberal political order.[5] More than that, I had insisted that "America has worked best when the convergence between liberal modern (Lockean) politics and religion has held most tensionlessly. American politics seems beset by its gravest moments of self-doubt and sense of crisis when the two fall into disharmony and tension."[6]

Although I take issue with West's characterization of Lockean theory as a version of Protestantism per se, I do argue that Lockean theory has a strongly theistic dimension, and, as opposed to some other philosophies of the age of Enlightenment, coheres comfortably with religion, especially the kind of tolerant Protestantism Locke helped bring into existence. It is certainly correct that Locke, Jefferson, and many other thinkers of the era saw tensions between certain forms of Christianity and the rational moral and political order, but Locke did not infer from that that religion was altogether pernicious and should be rooted out. His theory of toleration was meant to be a solution to the tension. As Locke came to see, the old policy of state imposition of religious uniformity on its subjects, whether for civil or religious purposes, was counterproductive and improper. It was counterproductive because in the conditions of post-Reformation Europe it was not religious diversity per se that led to civil disorder, but rather the conflicts set off by the effort of one party or the other to impose religious uniformity. Civil order is better served by leaving people free to follow their own consciences, and by seeking other means of producing social unity. Locke's discovery that economic interdependence knits society together was one of the main pillars of his alternative view of the sources of social unity. Since the imposition of religious unity could do no good from a civil point of view, and since from a religious view it could not secure salvation—salvation depending on one's own beliefs and/or deeds (depending on the sect to which one adhered)—it was altogether improper for the civil authorities to attempt to control the religious lives of their subjects.

Lawler quotes some authorities who maintain that the Lockean policy of toleration and separation of church and state was meant to breed indifference to religion, but Lawler himself brings out the most effective counterargument to that claim. He appeals to Tocqueville as his champion against what he believes to be the teachings and pernicious influence of the ilk of Locke, but it was Tocqueville who gave the most potent defense of the Lockean toleration principle. Tocqueville took America to prove that religion thrived best when it was free, for Americans were both the most religious of peoples and

the most free, especially in their political arrangements for religion. He tried
to show that this confluence of the spirit of liberty and the spirit of religion
(pace McWilliams) was not mere fortuity, but a set of connected facts. Tocqueville is not a counterargument to Locke but, in a different context, is a
champion of the Lockean dispensation.

Lawler turns Tocqueville into an anti-Locke only via some very question-
able interpretations of both thinkers. He claims, for example, that according
to the Frenchman, "American religion, cannot be completely privatized." It
is hard to say exactly what Lawler means by "completely privatized," or, therefore, by the negation of that, but whatever he has in mind, Tocqueville and
Locke seem to intend just the same regime of religious freedom and separation of church and state. It is true that Tocqueville sees the need for some convergence between religion and politics, as opposed to church and state; it is
also true that Locke sees the need for that same convergence. Indeed, if anything, it is Locke who brings religious themes more centrally into his writing
and it is Tocqueville, never Locke, who claims that he is concerned only with
the political effects of religion, not with its truth.[7] Where Tocqueville emphasizes the positive contributions of religion more loudly than Locke, the cause
is not a fundamentally different understanding of the phenomena but the very
different context in which the two men were writing. Tocqueville in the 1830s
was addressing a post-French Revolution world in which the party of liberty
had waged open war on religion. That had not been the case in Locke's world,
so he had no need to emphasize the foolishness of that position as Tocqueville
did. One of Tocqueville's chief aims was to use America to teach the French
that the spirit of religion could be friendly to, perhaps even indispensable for,
the spirit of liberty. And, one should remind Lawler, vice versa.

Locke was so far from seeking to root religion out that he had a deep
analysis showing why religion was natural, inevitable, and (when in its proper
sphere, i.e., not imposed on people and not following extravagant projects
suggested by the imagination) salutary. He lent his considerable argumentative powers to supplying a proof for the existence of God. The picture of
Locke as French Enlightenment atheist, making open war on religion, just
does not hold water.[8]

In a word, the facts of American history do not support strong discontinuity. The eighteenth-century clergy embraced Locke in droves; they may
have understood there to be some tensions between Lockean liberal political
philosophy and religion, or Christianity, as McWilliams insists there are, but
they perceived nothing like the opposition posited by adherents to the strong
discontinuity thesis. Locke himself does not correspond to the image of him
drawn by some of the strong discontinuity partisans. If he did, it is difficult

to imagine Locke coming to be embraced so warmly by a people so religious as eighteenth-century Americans were. A convergence between liberal rationalism and Protestantism was the true state of the relationship, not hostility and open warfare.

Rejecting strong discontinuity does not, however, entail losing sight of two important facts that its adherents rightly cling to. The Lockean liberal political doctrine that becomes part of the amalgam was indeed *very* different from the original and authentic versions of Protestant political theology. In my essay in this volume, and in parts of *The Natural Rights Republic,* I have attempted to specify some of those differences, and I will not restate them here. To reject strong discontinuity by no means warrants a revival of the strong continuity thesis, nor even, I shall argue below, of evolutionary continuity.

The adherents of strong discontinuity also rightly insist that there are tensions between the elements of the amalgam. The political Lockean liberal element does not merely differ from, but in some cases opposes, abiding elements of Protestantism. Those differences do not amount to the repellant polarities posited by the strong discontinuity school, but the presence of such tensions is undeniable.

The two true and important facts that are part of the strong discontinuity thesis in turn pose two large questions: Wherein lie and how intense are the tensions, and, given the differences between the amalgam's constituent parts, how did it ever come to be? Among other reasons, the essayists who affirm eclectic continuity are valuable precisely because they raise those two questions.

Eclectic Continuity

Professor McWilliams is concerned with the first of the two questions. He agrees that the blending of Locke and Protestantism I described did take place, and he thinks there were many reasons why both secular and sacred thinkers might welcome, or even require, such a blending. But he believes there were limits to the merging that occurred. He charmingly reverses the standard argument for "esoteric" expression, according to which secular and antireligious thinkers accommodate themselves in the expression of their views to socially dominant religious opinion. McWilliams argues for the obverse of this phenomenon as well: more orthodox religious thinkers (perhaps himself?) accommodate themselves to more secular and rationalist opinion when it is very powerful, as he believes it was at the time of the second founding. But this accommodation is only on the surface; the more religiously orthodox writers, under cover of philosophical or secular orthodoxy, attempt to move the discussion back toward the more religiously orthodox views, views like, say, those Winthrop propounded in his famous sermon. McWilliams gives the example of Nathaniel Niles, concealing just beneath the surface of his text some sharp criticism of liberal theorizing in politics and religion.

McWilliams's picture surely coheres better with the historical evidence than those at either end of the "continuity continuum." His picture is also in a deep sense compatible with, if not identical to, the amalgam thesis. He emphasizes more explicitly than I did a point we share—although the Protestant and Lockean liberal strands blend together, they derive from different sources, in many ways tend in different directions, and potentially stand in tension with each other. We differ in that McWilliams believes that the moments of tension, or the moments of assertion of the subdued (religious) voice, are the best moments in American political history, while I argue that the best moments occur when the amalgam works best. As McWilliams puts it, "religion has won its victories, sometimes great ones, in those early battles and in the republic's succeeding moments of decision—slavery and the 'crisis of the house divided,' for example, or the grand combats of the Age of Reform, or in the Civil Rights Movement—providing a critical voice, a vocabulary of protest, and, especially, an egalitarianism warmed into a conviction of fraternity." I would classify the moments and movements McWilliams cites, however, as instances where the amalgam has held and been particularly energized rather than come apart. Take the pre–Civil War agitation over slavery. Here was a case where the amalgam was central; the abolitionists and free-soilers and others who spoke out against slavery spoke in the language of liberal rights, liberal freedom, liberal equality, *and* of biblical justice and religious duty. The "spirit of religion" by itself was disappointingly slow and ambiguous in its stance toward the "peculiar institution"—some of the most powerful defenses of slavery came fully armed with biblical authority, from the sons of Ham to Paul's Epistle to Philemon. If one looks at the substance of abolitionist writing, or to Lincoln's speeches, or to Martin Luther King, one finds that the goals sought come from the language of liberal discourse; the biblical side of the amalgam lends energy, urgency, and authority to substantive appeals largely deriving from elsewhere. McWilliams, for example, seems to see the tensions between the "spirit of religion" and the "spirit of liberty" to reside centrally in the advocacy of community or fraternity on the one side versus advocacy of individualism on the other. But the appeal of a Garrison or a Lincoln is precisely to justice understood as liberal rights; Martin Luther King, one may recall, "had a dream" that every individual would be judged as an individual.

However that may be, McWilliams sees in Niles, and no doubt sees Niles as merely illustrative of a much larger phenomenon, the persistence of the original Puritan political vision, the vision of Winthrop, et al., well beyond the moment of the forging of the amalgam. Niles attempts, in a subtle and sometimes indirect manner, "to remind his shrewdest readers of the fundamental antagonism that divided them from secular liberals and partisans of natural religion." In place of liberal individualism and natural rights, Niles affirms "the old Puritan utopia"; like Winthrop, he finds "our freedom" in "our capacity to love" and our "civil liberty" in our "dedication to the common good." Niles, like Winthrop, combines these Christian themes of the transformative or utopian power of love with an Aristotelian conception of the primacy of the *polis* or community. Thus Niles, like his Puritan predecessors, has no truck with a pre-political state of nature or with natural rights traced to such a state or, ultimately, to the privacy and self-possession of individuals. Our rights are not natural possessions of individuals but are socially assigned, "distributed among . . . individuals according as they appear in the eyes of the body politic, to be qualified to use them for the good of the whole." Rights are "the public interest deposited in the hands of individuals." "Even our *persons*," McWilliams points out, "naturally belong to the whole." This is surely different from the doctrine of the Declaration of Independence and all the clergy who endorsed the principles so elegantly stated in the Declaration. As McWilliams indicates, this is a view very akin to Aristotle's pre-liberal conceptions.[9]

McWilliams and Niles thus do an excellent job of reminding us what the original Puritan political vision was, and how different the political theory incorporated in the second founding's amalgam. He also reminds us of an important point: the transformation of Protestant thought of which I spoke was not complete or universal. Individuals remained who clung to the old version and refused to accept as a "module" in their overall system of thought the Lockean-liberal component so widespread in the latter part of the eighteenth century. McWilliams is surely correct about the eighteenth century, just as his point still holds in the early twenty-first-century. One need think only of the work, say, of Stanley Hauerwas, whose recent book, *With the Grain of the Universe,* dissents mightily from Reinhold Niebuhr's mid-twentieth-century restatement of the American amalgam.[10]

Mark Noll also affirms a version of eclectic continuity, this version emphasizing the combination of Protestant and classical republican themes. The latter include the "republican categories of virtue, corruption, and disinterested public service." Noll finds "republican reasoning . . . omnipresent" and also "critical for the contingent events that brought secular and religious convictions together . . . in the creation of a national political culture." Noll's essay is particularly valuable for reinforcing the point that original Protestant political thought, indeed the thought prevailing up into the 1740s, was both different from and hostile to the secular kind of political thinking that Noll denominates "republicanism." "In light of how important the . . . amalgamation of religion and secular reasoning became, it is important to understand," he tells us, "how much antagonism had existed historically between the main strands of republican reasoning and the most important representatives of British and colonial Protestantism." This is a point relevant to West's argument that the natural rights republicanism of the second founding was a natural evolution out of the original Puritanism of the first founding. Noll implies that this could hardly be so, the differences in orientation being as great as they are. The Puritans explained political events in terms of Providence and commanded repentance as the appropriate action. The republicans "transferred responsibility for the health of society from God to humanity." The Lockean liberal tradition of which West speaks, of course, does the same.

For Noll the identification of republicanism as the political dimension in his version of the amalgam is particularly important, not just because he finds "republican reasoning . . . omnipresent in the emergence of the United States, but also critical for the contingent events that brought secular and religious convictions together in resistance to Parliament, deliberation over a constitution, and the creation of a national political culture." By the latter point, I take it he means that republicanism and only republicanism was capable of forging that link, otherwise so problematical, given the initial opposition between Protestant modes of political thought and essentially secular and humanist approaches like republicanism.

Noll places great emphasis on the moment when the Protestant-republican amalgam began to emerge—in the 1740s, in the wake of two great events that shook colonial society. The first was the colonial wars of the 1740s, pitting the Anglo-American Protestants against the French. The second was the Great Awakening. The latter prompted "the collapse of New England's Puritan churches as the all-encompassing guardians of public ideology." The New England "church-state establishments were drastically weakened." They thus lost their "once nearly complete . . . control of public life and thought." The Awakening and subsequent weakening of Puritan control provided an opening for republicanism, for this was "one of the resources immediately to hand for putting their world back together again" through "the republican promise of social order through virtuous public service."

Noll is less clear in articulating how the wars served to promote his amalgam. The best I can piece out is that the wars energized and actuated the colonists' long-standing and deep-rooted anti-Catholicism, and linked the cause of anti-Catholicism with preservation of political liberty and effective political action, concerns spoken to by republicanism. He seems to be of the view that nothing short of war against Catholics could overcome the Puritan providentialist approach to politics. In effect, he disagrees with West, who saw a somewhat similar shift occurring decades earlier, inspired by wars against the Indians.

Lurking beneath the "contingencies" that Noll emphasizes so much are features of the republican tradition possessing great affinities with Puritanism, and which, although he does not emphasize them, seem to have been the deeper link, the facilitating connection that allowed his contingencies to operate as they did. He emphasizes republicanism as a moral orientation that calls for, in the words of Gordon Wood, "the sacrifice of individual interests to the greater good of the whole." Or, as Noll puts it more precisely, "a secular language of republican virtue was . . . easily, swiftly, and massively infused with a language of Christian virtue." The link is the emphasis on the common good and on virtue in both, in some cases different virtues to be sure, but there is also a deep congruity between Christian and republican self-denial. This, I believe, is why Noll sees republicanism as so important; the Lockean, liberal, Enlightenment tradition does not have such a "hook" as republicanism does; it cannot form the deep and pervasive link that republicanism does.

As Noll emphasizes in his essay, there is no necessary contradiction between his account of the formation of the amalgam and mine. He is more interested in pinning down the specific moments when Puritan thinkers opened themselves to secular political principles, while I was more interested in laying out the precondition for this in the loss of confidence and the hope which initially marked the Puritan experiment.[11] The decisive thing, I think, was the realization that scriptural politics would not in itself suffice. That opened the Puritans to secular modes of political thought to take the place of the kingdom of this world as developed in the Protestant two kingdoms political theology. I have suggested in my essay elements of Lockeanism, well brought out and exploited by Elisha Williams, that made Locke's political philosophy especially well suited to playing that role.[12]

My other disagreement with Noll concerns the role he gives to republicanism. Although Noll is much more eclectic than the earlier proponents of the republican synthesis, he nonetheless tends to see republicanism as communal, public-spirited, and centered on virtue; liberalism as individualistic, privatistic, and centered on self-interest. As he indicates, the debate about liberal versus republican roots has gone on for a long time now, and it would be fruitless to review here the weaponry and order of battle on both sides. I very much agree with his conclusion that the war, as defined, is unwinnable by either party. He and I differ somewhat on the reasons for thinking so, however. He thinks it unwinnable because both traditions coexisted, often in the same persons. Thus, he finds the eighteenth-century world to be "messy"— messier than partisans of either side like to believe. I argue, on the other hand, that the war is unwinnable as defined because of the way it is currently defined. Republicanism and liberalism are not parallel and competing theories of politics, but discourse at different levels: Lockean liberalism is an instance of what Thomas Jefferson called "theory," which promulgates "the general principles of liberty and the rights of man, in nature and in society." Complementing theory is what he calls "practice," the best example of which that he knew of was *The Federalist,* a work that lays out how political institutions operate and how men act in the political world. Although it would not be quite accurate to say one can just mix and match different versions of political philosophy with different versions of political science, that is nearer to the truth than the either/or opposition that the partisans of the republican synthesis tend to affirm. In any case, I have argued that a highly integrated and very influential—especially in America—combination of Lockean political philosophy (natural rights/social contract theory) and the style of political science, tracing back to Machiavelli, to which the republican synthesizers look, was worked out early in the eighteenth century by John Trenchard and Thomas Gordon writing as "Cato." Cato is always one of the figures the synthesizers look to as an exemplar of their kind of republicanism; be that as it may, the simple fact is that on the issues of political philosophy Cato is a Lockean, complete with all the typical Lockean doctrines—natural rights, natural freedom and equality, social contract, limited government, the importance of property and commerce, religious toleration, the right of revolution.[13] In other words, the Lockean and republican traditions are not different and opposed as the republican argument affirms.

   In my essay in this volume I cite Charles Chauncy as an exemplar of the Lockean-Protestant amalgam; Noll cites him as an exemplar of republicanism, presumably for his commitment to the common good and public virtue. Yet if we look at Chauncy's 1747 election sermon we find frequent and massive appeals to Lockean doctrine. He reiterates the standard Christian view (traceable to Paul at least) about the divine ordination of government: government originates in the nature of things, which makes it the will of God, "for the voice of reason is the voice of God." Chauncy thus does not follow Luther or Calvin or Winthrop or innumerable other Protestant thinkers before him who insist that the principles for the political sphere must be gleaned from scriptures. However, like Elisha Williams, writing at about the same time, he finds the political sphere to have its own rationally discernable principles.[14] Those principles are grasped in a very Lockean way: political power exists "for the general good of mankind," which he specifies as: "to keep confusion and disorder out of the world; to guard men's lives; to secure their rights; to defend their properties and liberties."[15]

Chauncy does recommend dedication to the public interest over private interest as the proper means to achieve those Lockean goals, the basis on which, presumably, Noll sees Chauncy as a voice in the republican tradition. Moreover, he sees Christian morality, for example, "ruling in the fear of God," as a very desirable and perhaps even necessary means to achieving rule in the public interest, which in turn is in service to the Lockean political ends. At this point, Noll's argument does pick out something significant. Nonetheless, two caveats are in order: first, the appeal to the public good is not an exclusive possession of the republican tradition. Locke gives it a prominent role in his very definition of political power.[16] He places less emphasis than Chauncy on the sufficiency of "fear of God" in keeping rulers on course, but then it is not clear how much weight Chauncy himself gives it. He is preaching to the governor and his council, and an appeal of this sort is a suitable one for a preacher in these circumstances to make. It is clear that he would not commend sole reliance on the goodwill or "God fearingness" of the rulers to keep them aligned with the common good.

Chief among the tasks of good rulership to which Chauncy is exhorting his audience is the maintenance of the value of the currency circulating in society.[17] Fluctuations in the value of currency lead to uncertainty in commerce and hardship in the lives of individuals. He is especially concerned with the problem that inflation eats away at the value of contracts whose monetary terms were set in the past. The very center and chief point of his sermon, in fact, is to urge the rulers to take note of the dire plight of many of the clergy in Massachusetts, men whose pay was set in terms of a currency no longer worth what it was when those terms were set.[18] His main goal is to urge the rulers to adjust the pay of the clergy. Now this was no doubt an admirable and even desirable goal, for Chauncy draws such an effective picture of the plight of the clergy that 250 years later we still must sympathize with them. But this is not a theme of the classical republican tradition. It is surely not a call for self-denying virtue in submersion of self in the public.

EVOLUTIONARY CONTINUITY

Tom West's essay stands apart in this collection and is most striking for its many paradoxes. The uniqueness of the essay and its paradoxes lie in the same place: on the one hand, West admits, as all the other authors do, that there are important differences between the political theory of the first founders and that of the second founders, but he disagrees that any part of the impulse for the second founding comes from a source different from or foreign to the original Protestantism. Locke is a source for the second founders, but he is best understood as a Protestant theologian. The political principles of Winthrop constitute "an extravagant teaching" according to West; he sees the thought of the second founders as the more mature and true form of Protestant political theology. Thus West differs from the point of view taken by the other authors here as well as from some of the most eminent students of the American political tradition, such as Harry V. Jaffa, who endorsed a position much closer to the amalgam thesis. According to Jaffa: "American civilization was, in a high degree, formed by the conjunction of two main currents of thought and conviction. One was the Puritan religious tradition, the other the secular tradition known in the eighteenth century, and since, as the Enlightenment."[19] All the authors in this volume except West agree with Jaffa that there was a difference between the Puritan and Enlightenment traditions. West's position also is paradoxical, in that he maintains that the thought of the two foundings is both very different and much the same.

The decisive issue as West sees it seems to be whether the thought of the second founding can properly be called political theology or not. He believes that it can. Since in his view the original Puritans accepted a form of political theology and the Americans of 1776–1787 did so also, then, apparently applying an old mathematical axiom (two things equal to a third are equal to each other), he concludes that the thought of the second founders is a form of the thought characteristic of the first founders.

West finds that in my essay I "waver" on this key issue; on the one hand, I say that the political thought of the generation that made the revolution is not political theology, or if it is, it is natural political theology. West, to the contrary, sees no reason to waver or hesitate: the theory of the Declaration and related documents is political theology. When I said it was not political theology I had in mind the definition given by Leo Strauss: "By political theology we understand political teachings which are based on divine revelation." On the contrary, "political philosophy," says Strauss "is limited to what is accessible to the unassisted human mind."[20] By that standard I considered the political thought of the Protestants from Luther through Calvin and on to the American Puritans to be self-consciously political theology. Scripture is the basis for understanding the fundamentals of political life, as expressed by Luther, Calvin, and Winthrop, too. They all were hostile to efforts to discover principles of moral and political life on the basis of reason, whether that reason be exercised by pre-modern thinkers like Aristotle or more recent Enlightenment thinkers.

I conceded that one could call the thought of the Americans in, for instance, the Declaration of Independence "natural political theology," if one applied a laxer definition than Strauss's, that is, if one considered political theology to be any thinking about politics that had reference to the divine. I left it as I did (what West calls a "wavering") because I did not see the need to settle definitively the question of how we ought to define political theology (I lean to Strauss's way myself), and to indicate that whichever definition one uses, there is an important difference between the kind of thought we find in Luther, Calvin, and Winthrop and the thought we find about politics in Locke, Williams, and Jefferson. Nothing is gained by blurring the distinction, as West does, because the differences are so great between these two styles of political thinking. The first founders and their teachers look to revelation and base their political reasoning on principles taken from sacred texts. The second founders and their teachers look to reason; although reason may teach them of nature's God and his laws, they do not confuse this God with God as known through revelation. As Harry Jaffa said, "the preamble to the Declaration of Independence invokes not the God of Israel or the persons of the Trinity, but the God of nature and is wholly a document of the rationalist tradition."[21] Thus one can accept Locke's political philosophy without being a Calvinist or any sort of Protestant, or even a Christian. Surely that cannot be said for any version of Puritan political thought per se.

West proclaims Locke a Protestant political theologian. However, he never explains what he means by the claim nor provides any argumentation in its favor. In my opinion the connections between Locke and Protestant Christianity are not nearly so straightforward as West seems to take them to be. Locke's political philosophy breaks with all the elements most characteristic of Protestant political thought: it is not based on *sola scriptura;* Locke insisted instead that "reason is our only star and compass."[22] He does not proceed via parsing out the implication of biblical texts; he does not set the furtherance of the Christian religion or Calvinism or any such thing as among the ends of political life. His political principles do not apply to Christians of some specific sort, but to "all men." He does not look to specifically Christian or Protestant means to achieve the ends of political life.

In insisting that the Lockean dimension of the political thought of the second founding is different from the political thought of the Puritans I am not arguing thereby that Locke's political philosophy is hostile to Christianity or religion. My point is that the Protestant preachers of the eighteenth century came to a position whereby they slotted Locke's rationalist, universalistic, secular political philosophy into a niche which, in original Protestant political thought, had been filled with a political theology of a very different sort. How they came to do that is a good question, to which West, Noll, and I have all attempted answers. I suspect our answers are partial at best. For the Protestant ministers to have turned to Locke does not claim or imply that they turned against their religion, but only that they came to see that there were better resources for orienting themselves to the kingdom of this world than sectarian interpretations of scripture. It is not all that different from the decision, also made by most Protestant clergy of the eighteenth century, to take their astronomy from modern science rather than the Bible. On third and fourth thought they realized that Newtonianism was compatible with the truths of Christianity, but for all that not among those truths as delivered in the Christian sacred texts.

NOTES

1. Michael P. Zuckert, *The Natural Rights Republic* (Notre Dame, Ind.: University of Notre Dame Press, 1996), 118–23.

2. Bernard Bailyn, *The Ideological Origins of the American Revolution* (Cambridge, Mass.: Harvard University Press, 1967), 32.

3. Zuckert, *Natural Rights Republic,* 92–96, 146–48, 183.

4. Lawler also misapprehends my broader purpose in *The Natural Rights Republic.* He seems to think I sought to present a comprehensive account of the political philosophy of Thomas Jefferson. My aim instead was to explore the natural rights themes within the context of the American founding. I was interested in Jefferson so far as he sheds light on this theme, which indeed he does. But I was not attempting an account of Jefferson's thought per se, and that is why I did not attempt to follow out every thread one finds in Jefferson. That is also why I am not going to follow Lawler in his explorations of Jefferson's Epicureanism in the last half of his essay, other than to make a brief comment: Lawler finds Jefferson more deeply Epicurean than Lockean in his intellectual orientation. According to Lawler, for Jefferson, Epicurus is the most rational of the philosophers: "Epicureanism, not Lockeanism, *is* rationalism for Jefferson." This is indeed an interesting claim, but it does not comport well with Jefferson's well-known identification of the "trinity of the three greatest men that have ever lived, without any exceptions, Bacon, Locke, and Newton" (Jefferson to John Trumbull, Feb. 5, 1789, in Peterson, ed., *Jefferson,* 939). Lawler's Jefferson would at least add Epicurus to this trinity, one would think, but the real Jefferson emphatically failed to do so, and so one cannot help but think Lawler has not got Jefferson quite right. Admittedly Jefferson's identification of his "trinity" occurs relatively early in his life and his expression of admi-

ration for Epicurus occurs some years later, opening the possibility that Jefferson changed his views on Locke and Epicurus after 1789. In fact, however, his preoccupations, especially with politics, and his opinions, especially about rights and republicanism, show his continuing orientation toward Lockean politics. Recall that in his epitaph Jefferson wished to be remembered as draftsman of the Declaration of Independence, author of the Virginia Statute for Religious Freedom, and Founder of the University of Virginia, all related, in his mind, to Lockean rights theory. (See Zuckert, *Natural Rights Republic,* 211–12.)

5. Zuckert, *Natural Rights Republic,* 76.

6. Ibid.

7. Alexis de Tocqueville, *Democracy in America,* ed. J. P. Mayer (Garden City, N.Y.: Doubleday, 1975), 291.

8. It would take me too far afield to draw out the complexities of Locke (and Jefferson) on religion, but I have attempted the beginning of such an effort in my *Launching Liberalism* (University Press of Kansas, 2002), especially in the introduction to that volume.

9. Aristotle, *Politics,* 1262b30–1264b25.

10. Stanley Hauerwas, *With the Grain of the Universe: The Church's Witness and Natural Theology* (Grand Rapids: Brazus Press, 2001).

11. See Zuckert, *Natural Rights Republic,* 196–201.

12. Ibid., 183–93.

13. See Zuckert, *Natural Rights and the New Republicanism,* 297–312.

14. Charles Chauncy, "Civil Magistrates Must Be Just, Ruling in the Fear of God" (1747), in Ellis Sandoz, ed., *Political Sermons of the Founding Era* (Indianapolis: Liberty Press, 1991), 143.

15. Ibid., 145, 158–59.

16. John Locke, *Two Treatises of Government,* Peter Laslett, ed. (Cambridge: Cambridge University Press, 1988), II, 3.

17. Chauncy, "Civil Magistrates," 150–51.

18. Ibid., 159–62.

19. Harry V. Jaffa, *Crisis of the House Divided* (Seattle: University of Washington Press, 1973), 228.

20. Leo Strauss, *What Is Political Philosophy?* (Glencoe, Ill.: Free Press, 1959), 13.

21. Jaffa, *Crisis,* 229.

22. Locke, *Two Treatises,* I, 58.

Contributors

*

Thomas S. Engeman teaches in the political science department at Loyola University Chicago. Recent works include, with Raymond Tatalovich, *The Presidency and Political Science: Two Hundred Years of Constitutional Debate* (Johns Hopkins, 2003), and, as editor, *Thomas Jefferson and the Politics of Nature* (Notre Dame, 2000).

Issac Kramnick teaches in the government department at Cornell University. His books include, with R. Laurence Moore, *The Godless Constitution: The Case against Religious Correctness* (W. W. Norton, 1997), and *Bolingbroke and His Circle: The Politics of Nostalgia in the Age of Walpole* (Cornell, 1992).

Peter Augustine Lawler teaches in the government department at Berry College. Recent books are *Postmodernism Rightly Understood: The Return to Realism in American Political Thought* (Rowman and Littlefield, 1999) and *The Restless Mind: Alexis de Tocqueville on Origins and Perpetuation of Human Liberty* (Rowman and Littlefield, 1993).

Seymour Martin Lipset is on the faculty at George Mason University. He is the author of *It Didn't Happen Here: Why Socialism Failed in the United States* (W. W. Norton, 2000) and *American Exceptionalism: A Double-Edged Sword* (W. W. Norton, 1997), in addition to twenty-one other books.

Wilson Carey McWilliams teaches in the political science department at Rutgers University. He edited *The Federalists, the Antifederalists, and the American Political Tradition* (Greenwood, 1992) and wrote *The Idea of Fraternity in America* (California, 1973).

R. Laurence Moore teaches in the history department at Cornell University. His writings include *Touchdown Jesus: The Mixing of Sacred and Secular in American History* (John Knox, 2003) and *Religious Outsiders and the Making of Americans* (Oxford, 1996).

Mark A. Noll teaches in the history department at Wheaton College. He is the recent author of *America's God, from Jonathan Edwards to Abraham Lincoln* (Oxford, 2002) and *The Rise of Evangelicalism: The Age of Edwards, Whitefield, and the Wesleys* (InterVarsity Press, 2004).

Thomas G. West teaches in the politics department at the University of Dallas. Prominent works include *Vindicating the Founders: Race, Sex, Class, and Justice in the Origins of America* (Rowman and Littlefield, 1997) and *Plato's Apology of Socrates: An Interpretation* (Cornell, 1979).

Michael P. Zuckert teaches in the department of government at the University of Notre Dame. Recent books are *Launching Liberalism: On Lockean Political Philosophy* (Kansas, 2002) and *The Natural Rights Republic: Studies in the Foundation of the American Political Tradition* (Notre Dame, 1999 [1997]).

Index